The Black Watch
and
The Great War

REDISCOVERED HISTORIES
FROM THE REGIMENTAL FAMILY

Edited by

Fraser Brown & Derek J.

To my loving Auntie Jean in memory
of your Father and Uncles who
served the King and in particular
Robert Gellatly who made the ultimate
sacrifice in High Wood at the
Somme on the 27 July 1916.
       Love and affection
              Billy

TIPPERMUIR
· BOOKS LIMITED ·

The Black Watch and the Great War:
Rediscovered Histories from the Regimental Family
edited by Fraser Brown & Derek J Patrick.
Copyright © 2020. All rights reserved.

The right of the contributors to the book (as listed therein) to be
identified as the authors of the Work has been asserted in accordance
with the Copyright, Designs & Patents Act 1988.

This first edition published and copyright 2020 by
Tippermuir Books Ltd, Perth, Scotland.
mail@tippermuirbooks.co.uk — www.tippermuirbooks.co.uk

No part of this publication may be reproduced or used in
any form or by any means without written permission from
the Publisher except for review purposes.
All rights whatsoever in this book are reserved.

ISBN 978-1-913836-01-6 (paperback)

A CIP catalogue record for this book is available from the British Library.

Editorial and Project coordination by Dr Paul S Philippou.
Cover design by Matthew Mackie.
Editorial support: Stuart McAdam, and Steve Zajda.
Text design, layout, and artwork by Bernard Chandler [graffik].
Text set in Bulmer MT Std 11.5/15pt with Bulmer titling.

Printed and bound by CPI Group (UK), Croydon, CR0 4YY.

———

To the memory of the 8,000 men of the Regular, Territorial and Service Battalions of The Black Watch who gave their lives in the Great War this book is dedicated.

———

"NEMO ME IMPUNE LACESSIT"

.

FREIMDUN DHU: THE BLACK WATCH

Dark is thy tartan, Freimdun Dhu;
Black and green, and green and blue:
Now in it I see a thread of red -
The blood our Highland host has shed.

Joe Lee, *Ballads of Battle* (1916)

ACKNOWLEDGEMENTS

The editors wish to record their thanks to the extended Black Watch Regimental Family, that is those who have served and worn the Red Hackle, their descendants, close associates of The Black Watch (Royal Highland Regiment) and The Black Watch Regimental Association. Without their ever-generous support this book could not have been produced. Members of the Regimental Family willingly gave their time and talent; and submitted to often rigorous interviews and even more rigorous research criteria, shared family stories, and freely gave sight of precious family mementos for further research, or to be used as illustrations. The book would have been impossible without these contributions which highlight the enduring nature of relationships which span generations and many hundreds of miles. To quote Field Marshal Archibald Wavell, 1st Earl Wavell, 'the Regiment is the foundation of everything'.

Lieutenant-Colonel (Retired) Roddy Riddell, OBE, and Major (Retired) Ronnie Proctor, MBE, O St J, FSA Scot, gave generously of their time. Their advice on regimental and other matters was invaluable, as was the assistance of Heather Edment and Anne Amos on word processing, illustrations and other related areas.

The editors are also deeply grateful to Lieutenant-General Sir Alistair Irwin, KCB, CBE, and Tom Smythe MA, former archivist of The Black Watch Regimental Museum at Balhousie Castle for their unfailing encouragement, wise counsel and support for this venture, and above all for constructive and helpful comments on the content of the book. Their presence as external readers or 'extra eyes' was both invigorating and reassuring. They are also grateful to the Reverend Professor Norman Drummond, CBE, FRSE who contributed the postscript at very short notice.

The editors also wish to acknowledge the assistance they have received from the local studies sections of different libraries and local authority archives in the old 42nd Regimental Area. Special thanks are also due to the DC Thomson Archive in Dundee for their support and permission to reproduce several images from various publications. The editors also thank The Black Watch Castle and Museum for permission to access the regimental archives and photograph several artefacts in the collections for use as illustrations in this volume.

They would also like to thank Dr Paul S Philippou of Tippermuir Books whose patience, encouragement, advice and support helped bring the project to a successful conclusion. Thanks go also to Stuart McAdam and Steve Zajda for proof-reading and offering editorial suggestions, Bernard Chandler for his skills in producing a great-looking book and Matthew Mackie for the cover design.

An earlier version of 'And Man, You're a Damn Fine Type': Private Charles Craig, One of 'Dundee's Own' appeared in William Kenefick and Derek J Patrick (eds), *Tayside at War* (Dundee: Abertay Historical Society, 2018). The author would like to thank the Abertay Historical Society for permission to reproduce the chapter in the current volume.

Versions of 'I am Proud to belong to the 8th Black Watch': Loos, 25-27 September 1915; 'Through a Deluge of Fire': The Black Watch at High Wood, 30 July 1916; The 9th Black Watch at Arras – 'The Crushing Defeat of the Enemy on April 9th [1917] was due to the Discipline, Hard Work, Untiring Energy and Magnificent Gallantry of all Ranks'; The 9th Black Watch at Frezenberg, 31 July 1917; 'A Sea of Mud and Shell-Holes' – The 8th Black Watch at Passchendaele, 12 October 1917; and 'Fife Soldiers Escape from Captivity' were published in *The Courier*, 2014-18. The author would like to thank Caroline Lindsay and DCT Media for permission to reproduce the articles in this collection.

An early version of 'The Award of the Croix de Guerre to the 6th (Perthshire) Battalion, The Black Watch,' written by Roddy Riddell is posted on the official 51st Highland Division website and online museum (https://51hd.co.uk).

Hostilities Will Cease...and Troops Will Stand Fast...': Mons, Belgium, 11 November 1918 by Earl John Chapman was originally published in *Canada's Red Hackle* (30 August 2018).

———————————

CONTENTS

FOREWORD

Sir Alistair Irwin

THERE IS NO SHORTAGE of books specifically dedicated to telling the story of The Black Watch. Furthermore, very few general histories of the major conflicts since 1739 fail to mention the regiment. The story of the senior Highland regiment in peace and war is therefore well covered: the training, the battles, the acts of conspicuous gallantry, the notable occasions, all are recorded for posterity. So it might be thought that there would be no room for yet another volume on crowded bookshelves. There is, however, room for this one because its pages shine a well-deserved light on those parts of the regiment's history for which the other books, however reluctantly, have had no space.

The editors have assembled a fascinating collection of pieces written by a wide range of authors focussing on that most important part of any regiment's success, its people. Most of the names that inhabit the pages that follow will not be immediately familiar, but they are all the more important for that, because they represent the bedrock of the regiment's story. Without them the triumphs and the collective steadfastness in adversity would not have been possible. Indeed, the very character of the regiment would have been quite different. Accordingly, it is absolutely appropriate that a book of this kind should open the door on these hitherto unsung comrades and, through them, all the many thousands of others who over the years were proud to say that they were in The Black Watch.

The many vignettes and longer chapters in this book mainly but not exclusively concern the First World War. A combination of personal recollection and contemporary research based on family documents, newspaper archives and other sources offers a fascinating and, in many cases, moving insight into the lives and sacrifices not only of the regiment's officers and men but also of their families and the local communities from which they were recruited. It is particularly good that this aspect should

1

be given space because regiments do not exist in a vacuum and they could not do their business properly if they did not have support from home. For example, it is just as important for us to read of the schoolgirls in Blairgowrie who set about raising funds for comforts for the troops at the front, as it is to read of the enterprising escape from German captivity of men of the 7th (Fife) Battalion. And again, it is just as important to the regimental story to recognise the devotion to duty of ministers of the Kirk who set aside their non-combatant status and took up arms as it is to learn about the gallant underage men, boys in fact, who somehow managed to slip through the net and face the enemy at the tip of the bayonet. They and all the rest of the cast of characters who populate these pages more than deserve their place in this remarkable collection.

When Her Majesty Queen Elizabeth The Queen Mother took the salute at a parade in West Berlin to mark the 50th anniversary of her appointment as Colonel-in-Chief of The Black Watch, she remarked to the then Colonel of the Regiment, Major-General Andy Watson, as the immaculate ranks of the battalion marched past, that they were just the same men as those she had first inspected in 1937. She meant of course that in character these were exactly the men whose forebears had done so much to forge the great history of The Black Watch: a Black Watch man was a Black Watch man whether at Fontenoy, Waterloo, on the Western Front, at El Alamein or embroiled in the Cold War in Germany or the dismal business of the Troubles in Northern Ireland. There is no doubt that Her Majesty's sentiments expressed in 1987 would have applied to the later generations who went to war in the Balkans, Iraq and Afghanistan. It is an inspirational thought which this splendid book will do much to reinforce.

August
2020

Survivors of Nonne Bosschen

Last Battle of the First Battle of Ypres, 8-12 November 1914

Anne McCluskey

INTRODUCTION

IN MAY 2014, a bronze statue of a Black Watch soldier dressed in fighting order with rifle and fixed bayonet at the 'on guard' position was unveiled at a place known on Great War maps – and ever thereafter – as 'Black Watch Corner' (Zonnebeke, south western corner of Polygon Wood, near Ypres, Belgium).[1] This area, and the countryside around it, was the scene of bitter fighting in 1914 as the British Expeditionary Force (BEF) fought to hold the line after the protracted retreat from Mons which saw the men of the BEF continually on the move, marching and fighting, but seldom resting. Once in Flanders they faced three more battles fought in quick succession: Langemarck, Gheluvelt and Nonne Bosschen. Taken together these became known as the First Battle of Ypres.

Field Marshal French, commander of the BEF, wrote home of Ypres in his 'Despatch' published on 30 November 1914 in the Scottish press including *The Courier and Argus* praising Sir Douglas Haig and his divisional and brigade commanders, 'who held the line with marvellous tenacity and undaunted courage'. However, his description of the situation at Nonne Bosschen was less lyrical but much more concise:

> Whilst the whole line has continued to be heavily pressed, the enemy's principal efforts since 1st November had been concentrated upon breaking through the line held by the 1st British Division and 9th French Corps, and thus gaining possession of the town of Ypres. About 10th November, after several units of these Corps had been completely shattered in futile attacks, a division of the Prussian Guard which had been

operating in the neighbourhood of Arras was moved up to this area with great speed and secrecy. Documents found on dead officers prove that the Guard had received the Emperor's special commands to break through and succeed where their comrades of the line had failed. They took a leading part in the vigorous attacks made against the centre on the 11th and 12th, but, like their comrades, were repulsed with enormous loss.[2]

BLACK WATCH MEMORIAL BY ALAN HERRIOT
AT BLACK WATCH CORNER
(South western corner of Polygon Wood, near Ypres) Zonnebeke, Belgium
(Anne McCluskey)

The Field Marshal – for very good reason – did not mention that by 8 November the British forces holding the Ypres area, depleted after three months of constant warfare, amounted to just some 7,850 soldiers of all arms. On 11 November, the 1st Guards Brigade, deployed along the Menin Road and corner of Polygon Wood during the final battle for

Nonne Bosschen, consisted of the 1st Black Watch, 1st Scots Guards and 1st Queen's Own Cameron Highlanders – all badly in need of reinforcements. At that point, the 1st Black Watch consisted of only nine officers and 228 soldiers, while the whole of the 1st Guards Brigade numbered around 800 men, approximately the strength of a single battalion. Here, the BEF faced 25 fresh battalions of the German Army, six of which were from Guards regiments. At the end of the following day (12 November 1914) and after another hard fight, the strength of the 1st Battalion, The Black Watch, had been depleted to two officers and 109 soldiers. The Scots Guards' remnant comprised a single officer and 69 soldiers; and the Queen's Own Cameron Highlanders were left with two officers and 140 soldiers.[3] Amazingly, this small band of war-weary soldiers had fought off the elite Prussian Guard, halting their entry into Ypres and thus a breakthrough to capture the Channel Ports.

These battles of First Ypres were most demanding of the men of the 'old contemptibles'. Nevertheless, these troops steadfastly and determinedly endured as they took on the elite Guards infantry of the Kaiser's pre-war German Army. But just as field marshals send home their despatches, the ordinary soldiers who marched and fought so hard sent home their versions of events. This chapter concentrates on the experiences of some of the wounded in the days leading up to and during the Battle of Nonne Bosschen as these appeared in letters, or as related to the local press in interviews while on home leave. Although these men seldom spoke of the great sweep of grand strategy, and rather more of the detail of wounds and hard times, their voices have much to contribute to our understanding of this phase of the war. Of course, only the survivors could talk, so that with the fit men still in the trenches and the dead silent, it was the wounded who had most to say, and here they speak for themselves, often in extended form. More than a century after the battle, it is also important to bear in mind that in Scotland where every little town had at least one newspaper, and the public were desperate for news, no editor or reporter worthy of the name failed either to publish soldiers' letters home or interview returned soldiers – either the wounded or local men on leave.

A 'COUTHY' TALE AND HARD REALITY

In 1914, the 42nd Regimental area was home to at least 41 local newspapers. Some were published weekly and others twice weekly or daily, but all were very widely read in the areas they covered. They varied in style, but all were highly patriotic and though newsprint shortages and lack of skilled men shrunk the print acreage as the war progressed, all but one remained in print during the war years. The widely read *People's Journal* appeared across Scotland in several regional editions and in the early part of the war did adopt something of a 'couthy' tone, particularly in articles about wounded soldiers which did much to soften the reality of wounds on the Western Front for the families involved. The reality was invariably something different, but many of these letters show how rapidly news could travel in a pre-digital age. One example appears in this report. It began:

> On the outskirts of Dundee, at Baldragon, a mother stood at her doorstep watching and waiting. Presently her eyes lit up as the stalwart figure of a young soldier approached. He covered the last few yards in bounds, and was locked in her arms.[4]

Lance Corporal Alexander Dewar, of the 1st Black Watch, wounded at Ypres, had returned on a brief visit after a stay in hospital at Boulogne. His mother had another two sons serving, one in the Scots Guards and the other in the Territorials of the 4th Black Watch. She also knew of his award of 'Mentioned in Despatches' from a lady from Farnham whose husband had written home about Lance Corporal Dewar's bravery. The letter, shown to the reporter, explained how Dewar was forced to mount his machine gun outside a quarry in the open to fire, and continued firing steadily with great effect, despite the shell and rifle fire directed at him, so his name was sent to the General:

> 'This, I know, will please you, and make you feel proud of him, so I hasten to tell you' [added the lady. The article continued:] 'Oh, that's a stale story!' was the modest soldier's remark. 'Don't put anything in about me!' he added. However,

he did think his number was up that time when a bit of shell struck his heel. Corporal Dewar went on to display his little collection of war souvenirs. Firstly, a neatly patched tear on the right sleeve of his jacket near the shoulder. 'That's where this went in,' he remarked, holding up a nasty little piece of shell, which had glanced off his machine gun and torn into his flesh. Another grim souvenir was a shrapnel bullet and a fourth, an ugly chunk of metal —part, of a 'Jack Johnson'— which struck Dewar's heel, without injury.[5] He was not so lucky one night when on picket duty. A bullet 'whizzed' out of the darkness and scraped his neck. Though effectively only scratching the flesh, 'the weight of the blow,' said Dewar, 'was just as if I had been struck by something the size of that!'— clenching his brawny fist. 'For three or four days I was going about with my head drooping sideways on my shoulder. When I was struck, chums thought I was done for. I was knocked right among their sleeping forms. They woke up, and thought it was a lifeless corpse tumbling on top of them'.[6]

The reality of Corporal Dewar's story was more deadly. The regimental history explained how on the night of 8 November, the situation of the Loyal North Lancashire Regiment was so dire that 90 Black Watch men under Captain Fortune, as well as a Black Watch machine-gun section, were sent to their aid. [7] The machine-gun section consisted of Captain Fortune assisted by Corporal Alexander Dewar, Lance Corporal Charles Roy and Private Alexander Mitchell, who moved both of their section's Vickers machine guns undetected into a position to enfilade a trench previously held by the Loyals, but now held by the enemy. This was a real feat of endurance for men who had been constantly fighting for the previous three weeks considering the fact that the total weight of the gun, tripod and water to cool the barrel was almost 70 pounds and that one box of 250 rounds of .303 ammunition once packed, weighed another 22 pounds. In the morning, 23 of the enemy lay dead in the bottom of their trench. The *1st Black Watch War Diary* recorded the event in three terse sentences concluding with the remark that the enemy rifles had been collected and sent to the Quartermaster.[8] Corporal Dewar was deservedly 'Mentioned Dispatches' for this action. Fortunately, the machine-gun section survived the war and interestingly, both Dewar and Roy ended the war as sergeant majors in the newly formed Machine Gun Corps.[9] Dewar was awarded the Military Medal whilst serving with them.

BULLY BEEF, WHEELBARROWS, WOUNDS AND GOOD AND BAD LUCK: INDIVIDUAL EXPERIENCES AS REPORTED

At the earlier Langemarck battle (21-24 October 1914), the same Private Alexander Mitchell mentioned earlier won the Distinguished Conduct Medal for evacuating his wounded pal, James Mackie, to safety on a wheelbarrow then returning to continue the fight, but on this occasion Private Mitchell was part of the machine-gun team.[10] Once home in Dundee recovering from his wounds, Mitchell informed relatives that he had taken part in a remarkable adventure at Ypres on 11 November 1914. At that point, the Prussian Guards were mounting an attack when he discovered that the machine-gun ammunition had run out. At that juncture, a six-foot Prussian Guardsman rushed up intent on bayonetting him. Mitchell picked up a bully beef tin and threw it at the Prussian. The tin struck the Prussian in the face and bowled him over, then another British soldier finished him off. Amazingly, Mitchell's luck also held later in an incident which should have disabled him. On that occasion, a German bullet had exploded nine cartridges in his bandolier, but because he was kneeling, the bullets hit the ground, and only one bullet scratched him slightly on the knee. (The tenth cartridge in the bandolier, lacerated and with the bullet still in place was brought home as a souvenir.) On another occasion, Mitchell had carried a wounded soldier through shrapnel fire to a place of safety.[11] Mitchell later became a sergeant in the King's African Rifles.

Without any elaboration on the detail of his wounds, Private Archibald Anderson of the 1st Black Watch wrote home to his brother in Kirkcaldy from hospital in Norfolk. He suffered from three wounds in his back. Part of his kilt had been blown into his body, and three operations later,

'SURVIVORS OF NONNE BOSSCHEN'
A cartoon by the late Rab Simpson depicting Private Alexander Mitchell evacuating
his friend James Mackie in a wheelbarrow during the Battle of Langemarck.
(Family of Tom McCluskey)

portions of the cloth still remained in the wound. He related that he had been 'through it all' and had been in the retreat from Mons, marching 320 miles in 11 days. Anderson then experienced some rough fighting in Flanders where he was wounded.[12]

At this point, lying in the Second Western General Hospital, Manchester, was 20-year-old Private David Niven of 'D' Company, 1st Black Watch, from Dundee. Niven's right leg had been amputated, but he bore his suffering with uncomplaining fortitude. Niven, whose parents resided at Hospital Wynd, Dundee, joined The Black Watch Reserve in 1911, aged 17. In August 1914, he was called out, and camped at Nigg until mid-September, then moved out to France. Hard fighting and equally hard work were his lot. On 8 November at Ypres, he was wounded in the right leg. The trench he lay in was captured by Germans, but he managed to creep into a little side trench and escaped notice. For three days he lay there without water. His leg tortured him almost to madness, for it had only been roughly dressed by himself. On discovery, he was taken to hospital at Boulogne, where his leg was amputated at the knee. Once fit he was sent to Manchester to recuperate, but his leg was in such a condition that a second amputation was necessary; this time near the thigh. Despite this, he was in the best of spirits, and looked forward eagerly to his return to Dundee.[13]

Word reached Lochgelly, Fife, at this point that a young sergeant, George Sands, had been killed in action on 9 November. He was a reservist just returned from Barry Camp when war was declared. His army record shows that Sands was born in Sunderland and enlisted at Lochgelly. When promoted to sergeant, aged 18, Sands was apparently the youngest sergeant in the British Army. Prior to the war in civil life, Sands had been a lieutenant in the Dysart Boys' Brigade. The 9th of November was a day of heavy shelling, but unfortunately, Sands fell, shot through the head by a sniper after only two days in the trenches.[14] At this time, the trench lines were very basic in form, hastily dug with neither sufficient depth or revetting, unlike the more sophisticated multiple parallel lines of trenches connected by communication trenches that would develop later and offer more protection. Described as a smart and keen soldier, Sands, aged 23 at his death, left a widow and three little children at Charlotte Street, Kirkcaldy – he never saw his youngest child.[15]

Private William Murray arrived home at Kirk Street, Lochee, to recover from five shrapnel wounds sustained on 10 November at the First Battle of Ypres. He commented to the local press on the tragic death of his friend, Private Charles Reekie of Brown Constable Street, Dundee, who was killed aged 31:

> At Ypres we were sent to the trenches directly and we were there for a number of weeks. It beats me to know how the Kaiser's guns got the range of our trenches. It seems as if some of their officers had come up and measured the distance with a surveyor's chain. My company, 'D' Coy was just about wiped out. There were 7 of us in one trench, 2 of us were killed and 3 wounded.
>
> The two others escaped death by going for assistance. I was the first to be wounded that day, a piece of shrapnel made a hole in my hip. One companion, Reekie, asked if I had been seriously wounded and I crawled up to where he was. He had a peculiar habit of sitting up while all the others lay and slept,

and when I got up to him he asked me to wait a minute and he would endeavour to get me away from the trench and fix my wound. I was so done up that I laid my head on his knees and waited. Then there was a tremendous crash just over our heads. A shrapnel shell rained its leaden death on top of us. I was struck several times about the hips and the small of the back. Reekie didn't move. I looked up into his face. His eyes were closed, and a thin stream of blood trickled down from a wound in his forehead. He was dead. Somehow--I can't remember anything of it...I managed to drag myself from that death trap, to a dressing station, where I had my wounds dressed. I was hit in five places.[16]

Private David Rough, 1st Black Watch, was home in Cambuslang suffering from a severe wound. From a military family, Rough's father had been a soldier and two of his brothers and two brothers-in-law were serving. Private Rough told the *Daily Record*:

I have been through all the horrors, Mons, the Aisne, and Ypres, and taken part in at least eight important engagements. In my experience the Germans will do almost anything rather than face the British bayonets. On one occasion a few of us, faced by enormous odds of Germans in the dark, clattered our bayonets together and induced the belief that it was superior to the enemy in numbers. The ruse succeeded, and to our great delight, the Germans, dreading the cold steel, turned and fled. I was wounded in the left foot at Ypres. Twenty-three of us went into a trench, and within half-an-hour fifteen were rendered hors de combat. The remaining eight removed the dead and wounded, and then returned to the trench. Five minutes later another five were wounded, and only three of us were left to carry our comrades to a safe place. On my way back to the trench I was laid low by a German bullet, which penetrated my left foot. I toppled into the trench thus out of the range of the enemy snipers. After 3 weeks in Leeds Infirmary, I was sent home to Cambuslang, and delighted to be able to spend Christmas and New Year with wife and family.[17]

Lance Corporal William Trueland from Edinburgh represented a fine type of British soldier — apparently fearless, intelligent and indomitable. Trueland recalled the opening days of November as being 'very trying for us'. Trueland was promoted to lance corporal on 3 November 1914:

> On 10th November my chum Sergeant Lawson was killed outright by the bursting of a shell. We were then at the left front, about five miles in advance of Ypres. The Germans were entrenched about 150 yards off, and the section of which I was in charge got orders to fire a volley which we did several times. The Germans replied with heavy automatic gun fire which created great havoc in our trenches. It was at this time I was wounded, and the wonder is I was not killed. The fighting around Ypres was in open country and in cold, wet weather. The strain was dreadful and it was impossible to see a dozen yards in front owing to the mist, and one had to depend a great deal on one's hearing which made the strain all the more severe. The food was pretty good. To begin with there was a lack of matches, making the want of a smoke harder to bear; we were allowed to smoke only during the day. In the trenches a bottle of water had to serve a man three days. This was due to the Germans destroying the water mains at Vendresse with a coal box.[18]

Trueland had participated in some very heavy fighting. He received at least eight distinct injuries to the head and one to his left side, due to the heavy German automatic fire. He crossed the Channel to Southampton, then by ambulance train to the military hospital at Camberwell. On recovery, he returned to his home at Miller Pit, Bo'ness, West Lothian, in December 1914 on ten days furlough.[19]

THE GUYAN BROTHERS

PRIVATE WILLIAM GUYAN, 1ST BLACK WATCH
Kirkcaldy War Albums, 1899-1914
(Kirkcaldy Public Library)

The Black Watch, like many pre-war Regular infantry formations, frequently had sets of brothers serving together, often in the same battalion. Two 1st Battalion brothers, Privates William and David Guyan, natives of Footdee, Aberdeen, were only one example.[20] The two brothers left Aberdeen two years previously with their father Edward, who was employed in shipbuilding in Toronto, to reside at Mill Street, Kirkcaldy. Both brothers were wounded on 11 November 1914. William was wounded first in the shoulder then in the back, while David suffered more severely, having been shot in the mouth. Despite losing his speech and being fed through a tube, David continued to communicate with home, albeit by letter. William returned home, having greatly improved, but had still to undergo a further operation for the removal of shrapnel. Their story was published in full detail in a report of a lengthy conversation with William in the *Fifeshire Advertiser*, which was quick to point out that William was a 'most modest and intelligent young soldier' who was happy to return to fight once recovered, and therefore presumably a man to be believed. The article concentrated on what might be described as the 'thrilling aspect' of their experiences and is of local significance because of the unusual level of detail given of a Kirkcaldy man's experiences.[21] In effect, William said that while in the trenches at Ypres in November he found himself so crowded for room that he determined to make a break for the trench in which his brother David was placed some 50 yards away. At no little risk he reached his brother's side and found him busy. Shortly afterwards William was put on sentry duty, and while on duty a German shrapnel shell burst above him and some of the fragments went through his tunic into his left shoulder. William tried to hide his condition from his 19-year-old brother David, but when it became unbearable, he casually began to move away with the remark that he thought he would go back to his own trench. David's suspicions were awakened, however, and he saw the hole in the coat and the blood oozing through, so he bandaged his brother's shoulder as well as he could, and urged him to get away to a wood some distance off where the wounded were being taken. The trench they were in was only 18 inches wide, so William crawled as best he could over the bodies of the men as they knelt and fired. While doing so he was shot in the back but clambered out of the trench making for the wood where the wounded were being taken without further mishap.

When he reached the wood, William was stripped of his boots, tunic and equipment, and was being attended to by the men of the Medical Corps when the Germans broke through the lines held by 200 of The Black Watch; and the Highlanders had to retire. Even with the handicap of German shrapnel in his shoulder and a bullet in his back, William, with nothing on but his shirt and his kilt, sprinted four/five miles to a place of safety, leaving behind his kitbag containing a much-prized German helmet and one of the notorious saw-edged German bayonets. He arrived at a hedge manned by the British and a friendly hand came through and pulled him to safety when the Germans were little more than 200 yards behind, the British fire bringing them to an abrupt stop.

This report is also of interest for other reasons, one of which is it contains a categorical denial of a current rumour – or wishful thinking – about The Black Watch and Scots Greys charging together as the Gordons had done at Waterloo. However, it also repeats another rumour heard then, that German troops had to be forced into the attack and in a paragraph headed '2,000 German Striplings', William claimed The Black Watch had taken that number of boys (aged between 14 and 17) prisoner in one action. Likewise, German looting and atrocious behaviour was maintained in a paragraph about how the first British shell he saw fired blew up a German looter and the pig he was carrying-off. He also related how on another occasion The Black Watch were ordered to make a night attack on the opposing German trenches. Being very dark, they took about three hours to creep the 200 or 300 yards that separated them from the enemy. They had no difficulty in steering a true course as they were guided by the sounds of a gramophone, a concertina and the Germans singing. At last, they reached the trenches, taking the Germans completely by surprise, 'bayoneted the lot, and covered them up in their trenches'.[22]

On another occasion reported in *The Evening Telegraph and Post*, William was responsible for saving the life of another soldier of the 1st Black Watch from Kirkcaldy – Private George Bell.[23] According to the account, a large force of Germans had forced Bell and Guyan's company to retire for about five miles, when the Highlanders counter-attacked, and drove the enemy back again and recovered their trenches. At that point, Bell, no doubt thoroughly exhausted, tried to take a short nap in the trench when a 'coal box' landed nearby. Bell's comrade had his head blown off, while Bell was buried in the debris. William Guyan missed Bell, and asked permission to be allowed to dig him out. Spades were found, and two hours later Bell was dug out in an unconscious condition suffering from concussion. Bell survived and in late December 1914, he reported home to Kirkcaldy recuperating from the shock and associated illnesses.

On his recovery, William Guyan returned to the 1st Battalion in France. Sadly, he was killed in action at the Battle of Aubers Ridge, 9 May 1915. He was in the first wave of his battalion's attack, when 'A' and 'B' Companies were piped into battle during the assault made by the 1st Battalion on German positions on the Cinder Track at Richebourg

St-Vaast, France. William has no known grave and is remembered on the nearby Le Touret Memorial.

ENCOUNTERS WITH THE PRUSSIAN GUARD

A number of accounts of the fighting at Nonne Bosschen included detailed descriptions of the attacks made by the Prussian Guard. A number also described the experience of being wounded in a trench overrun by the enemy as well as the effectiveness of the German bombardment. Others like Private D Douglas from Selkirk described how he feigned death for self-preservation. He described the preliminary bombardment and assault in graphic terms:

> Anyway, the Germans concentrated all their artillery fire on us and nothing on earth could live under it. We had to retire to reserve trenches. Unfortunately, about twenty men, the last to leave the trench, got trapped in it, owing to part of the trench being blown in. Well, we had to lie flat as we could, and when the Prussian Guards came up in hundreds they didn't give us a dog's chance—fired point blank into the trenches, and the way I am here to-day was that a chap fell on top of me with his brains blown out. They shot him through the back, and the bullet came out of his stomach and went into my thigh. It is in my thigh yet. I had to lie very quiet, because I heard the Germans prodding the bodies with their bayonets to see if anyone was alive. They stayed for about three hours, and then went away to another trench about 30 yards away. I got wounded at 8 o'clock in the morning, and lay till one o'clock the following morning. It seems hard luck to be wounded in a trench after doing a good few attacks in the open and never being hit, although I was lucky, seeing I was the sole survivor.[24]

When he wrote to a relative in Selkirk from a London hospital, Douglas also observed that removal of shrapnel and bullets as standard procedure may not have been universal as is often assumed today:

I may say I am getting on alright and walking about though very slowly. I've still got a German bullet in the leg, and if it never bothers me any more than it is doing at present it can stay in for the rest of my life. They don't believe in taking out bullets or shrapnel here unless they are in dangerous places; nine out of ten chaps have bullets in the arms and legs. We had it pretty rough out there, and I consider myself one the luckiest blokes in the world. I think if I had one hairbreadth escape I had a hundred.[25]

An exhilarating account of experiences of Black Watch men was furnished in a letter to a friend in Perth by Lance Corporal Robert Rushford, one of three inseparable former Black Watch companions, who once time-served, had emigrated to Vancouver. On the outbreak of war, all three were called up and travelled back together, then onwards to the front.[26] From Ascot Military Hospital, Rushford wrote:

You will be surprised to hear from me at this place, Lord Robert's Convalescing Home. I am getting on splendidly. I was wounded on 11th November at Ypres. I have come through a hell of a hard time since I last saw you, and I hope to God I don't come through the same again. We were 16 days in the trenches and it was cold out there especially with the kilt on, but that was nothing. On the 11th, the Germans started to shell us at the break of day and kept it up for four hours, shelling the trenches, and our artillery pumped it back to them. But they broke through on our right and then it was a fight to the finish. But the old Black Watch stuck it. We were going down like rabbits, and I just got beside our old Colonel.[27] He was in the open, brave old fellah, rallying his men, and the Germans not more than 40 yards from us coming on with fixed bayonets, when I got banged right through my right shoulder.

I mind of the bloody Germans tramping over me, but the old Black Watch—what was left of them—charged again and again and again, and drove them back over the trenches, leaving seven hundred dead. It was an awful sight and we captured

1600 prisoners that day. I wakened up in hospital, so I am as good as fifty dead men yet. I will get to Perth in a few days. I am sorry to say that poor Donald Currie was killed two days before I was wounded. I am sure the Black Watch gave a good account of themselves. I hope that Britain will win this war and crush the bloody Germans.[28]

By late January 1915, Rushford was home in Perth, still unfit from his wound. He related that when the Prussian Guards attacked, he was wounded by a bullet fired at a range of 40 yards, and it was the doctor's opinion that it was the velocity of the bullet that saved his life. It entered his chest, glanced downward and passed out at his back.

Private James Baird, of 'D' Company, 1st Black Watch, wrote home to family at Rattray, Blairgowrie, from a Boulogne Hospital, where he was being treated for a contusion of the ankle. He was hopeful the war would soon be over as he wrote:

I am to spend my Christmas in the trenches along the French frontier. We have given the Germans the biggest fright of their lives. The Prussian Guards flew for all they were worth when we fixed bayonets and made a charge. They lost heavily, and if we keep going on, there will soon be no Germans left to fight.[29]

He also appears to have confirmed Guyan's claim about German underage soldiers:

They are sending a few schoolboys, about thirteen years old, to the firing line, and they are no good against the gallant, for we have been in three bayonet charges and laid them out. I think the war will be finished in about a month or so. We have had a great struggle to keep the enemy from getting to Calais, which they will never reach.[30]

Piper Neil McLeod, of the 1st Black Watch, invalided home to Renton, West Dunbartonshire, told of his experiences at the front. He had served for ten years with the 3rd Black Watch but enlisted in the 1st Battalion after the war broke out. At that time, he was employed with Messrs John Brown & Co, Shipbuilders, and had worked on the 'Tiger'.[31] Piper McLeod stated that the worst thing he experienced was when the regiment were in action against the Prussian Guard on 11 November 1914:

> It was a terrible slaughter that the flower of the German army received that day. The Prussian Guards came on them with the bayonet, and he considered they were about fifteen to one. They had received orders that at all costs they must break through the British lines that day. They did break through, but only to be ripped up by the British artillery, who were placed at the back ready to mow them down. Few of the Prussian Guards, the pride of Germany, escaped.[32]

Only three of Piper McLeod's comrades of the 18 strong Pipes and Drums were fit for duty by the time he was interviewed – the remaining 15 were either killed or wounded. McLeod also praised Pipe Major Clark who had distinguished himself in one of the fights at this time:

> He led them on, and what he did not get with his revolver he accounted for with his fists. He was a powerful man, and had since been invalided home.[33]

It was also the case that The Black Watch were not the only soldiers of their brigade to meet the Prussian Guard. Corporal Frank Spence of the Cameron Highlanders of Link Street, Kirkcaldy, a reservist with seven-and-a-half years' service, told of his experience at Ypres:

> I was at Ypres when the much talked of Prussian Guards broke through, and they are a fine body of men hardly any being under 6 feet. On 11th November, as soon as daylight broke in, the Germans started shelling our trenches for three solid hours. Their artillery pelted for all they were worth, and this enabled the Guards to break through. We got the order to retire—had either to

do that or be captured—but the worst of it was that we had to proceed right in the midst of the German fire for 400 yards. Our men were shot down right and left, and we were all exhausted by the time we got shelter in a wood. It was a terrible ordeal.[34]

Another soldier of the same brigade, 1st Scots Guard Reservist, Private James Rutherford, aged 27 from Milngavie, was wounded on 8 November. He gave his account to the local newspaper, stating that it was once they were firmly entrenched round Ypres that the fiercest fighting of the whole war had taken place. In that account, he explained how the incidents were more vivid in his memory, and the details more harrowing, as it was there that they fought the Prussian Guard. Here, for a considerable time, the opposing armies were entrenched within 25 or 30 yards of one another. Bullets were flying over the top like rain he wrote, and one day so hot did the attack become and so accurately did the German artillery find the range, that the trench the Scotsmen were in was blown on the top of them, many being buried alive. 'If hell is any worse than yon', he said, 'I hope I will never see it. When you are out there you don't know whether it is yourself that is shaking or the ground'.[35]

'THE SURVIVORS OF THE FIRST BATTLE OF YPRES'
Red Hackle, Pictorial Supplement, July 1921
(The Black Watch (Royal Highland Regiment) Association)

The final encounter for Private Rutherford came on 8 November. The Scots Guards attacked the Prussians with the bayonet. He stated he had bayoneted a German so badly in the head that he had not sufficient nerve to extract the steel, so he ran to the road to get another rifle. In doing so he was hit with falling shrapnel on the right leg above the knee, on the left ankle, and in the back. He lay on the battlefield from eight o'clock in the morning until 6 o'clock at night before he was discovered and taken to the hospital at Ypres. By good luck, the next day he was moved to Boulogne because that same evening the hospital at Ypres was bombarded by the Germans and reduced to ruins. Rutherford was transferred to hospital at Rouen and subsequently to a hospital in Leeds, then to Grove House Auxiliary Hospital, Harrogate. For a fortnight after being lifted from the battlefield, Rutherford was absolutely deaf, and his hair, previously a true black colour, was turned almost grey as a result of the severe nervous strain he had experienced in the trenches where the men were sometimes up to their knees in water.[36]

POSTSCRIPT

On 13 November 1914, the 1st Black Watch was withdrawn from the line and on the 16 November moved to Borre remaining in reserve until 20 December while it reorganised and re-equipped and absorbed a first draft of 280 reinforcements as part of the process of rebuilding the battalion. A visit from the King took place on 3 December followed by another by Field Marshal French on 28 December 1914.

As for the Prussian Guard, a few months later in February 1915, in an interview with General Joffre published as part of an article 'The Spirit of Our Army' by W J Fitzgerald in *The Windsor Magazine* picked up by *The Evening Telegraph and Post*, Joffre described them as 'no more than the collection of uniforms'.[37] The accuracy of that statement was a matter of debate, but a far more measured comment came in the same article: 'The shattering of the Prussian Guard opened German eyes as nothing else could do, for their grand attack was the supreme effort of the war machine'. Berlin newspapers were quick to reflect the shock and there were angry protests from the front against the picture postcards in which Tommy was ridiculed, and they were soon 'the elect of the Allied Armies'.

The Scottish press were in the habit of publishing news from enemy sources in translation throughout the war, mostly from their newspapers and magazines. One German source frequently quoted at some point in the larger local newspapers of the 42nd Regimental Area was retired *Kapitän zur See* Persius who wrote mostly on naval matters for the *Berliner Tageblatt*. Given the level of exposure of his work in translation both before and during the war in the British press, his comments would have been read with interest in official quarters. This officer's writings were not always entirely favourable to the regime as can be seen from this undated remark which was part of the article from *The Windsor Magazine*:

> One of our chief mistakes was to underestimate our opponents. The British, have been wrongly appraised. They are soldiers by profession, and put into their work all the sure and resolute qualities of their race—their direct worth as offensive and defensive warriors, as well as the indirect or moral worth which the French praise so highly in their Ally.[38]

Unfortunately for the Prussian Guard, payment for that error of judgement by the German High Command was made by them, but *Kapitän zur See* Persius did make one further prophecy in an article in the *Berliner Tageblatt* one week after the US entered the war: 'The military strength of the United States is not to be met with a shrug of the shoulder or we shall make the same mistake as with the strength of Britain'.[39]

---

1 *Red Hackle,* November 2014, pp22-31.

2 *The Courier and Argus,* 30 November 1914.

3 Tom McCluskey (senior researcher),
   Memorial Brochure, Black Watch Corner Flanders (May 2014), p3.

4 *Dundee People's Journal,* 28 November 1914.

5 A 'Jack Johnson' was a large artillery shell; big shell explosions gave off large amounts
   of dark smoke. The shell's power was reminiscent of Jack Johnson, the first
   African American heavyweight boxing champion (1908-15).

6 *Dundee People's Journal,* 28 November 1914.

7 A G Wauchope, *A History of the Black Watch in the Great War,* 1914-18, Volume 1
   (London: Medici Society, 1925), pp20-21.

8 *1st Black Watch War Diary,* 9 November 1914. The National Archives, WO95/1263/3.

9 McCluskey, *Black Watch Corner,* p80.

10 Citation in the *London Gazette,* 16 January 1915.

11 *The Scotsman,* 2 January 1915.

12 *Fife Free Press & Kirkcaldy Guardian,* 5 December 1914.

13 *Dundee People's Journal,* 26 December 1914.

14 *1st Black Watch War Diary,* 9 November 1914.

15 *Edinburgh Evening News,* 8 December 1914; *Fifeshire Advertiser,* 12 December 1914.

16 *The Courier and Argus,* 24 December 1914.

17 *Daily Record,* 8 December 1914.

18 'Coal Box' was the nickname for a high explosive German shell fired from a
   5.9-inch howitzer which emitted a heavy black smoke.

19 *Linlithgowshire Gazette,* 11 December 1914.

20 *Aberdeen Evening Express,* 4 December 1914.

21 *Fifeshire Advertiser,* 28 November 1914.

22 *Fifeshire Advertiser,* 28 November 1914.

23 *The Evening Telegraph and Post,* 29 December 1914.

24 *The Scotsman,* 31 December 1914.

25 *The Scotsman,* 31 December 1914.

26 Private Charles McIntosh (Pitlochry), Corporal Ernest Salt (Ballinluig) and Lance
   Corporal Robert Rushford (Perth). Only Rushford survived the war: Salt was killed
   at the Battle of the Aisne (8 October 1914); McIntosh died 23 December 1914.

27 The wounding of Lieutenant-Colonel Stewart and the how it was immediately
   avenged by Sergeant D Redpath, Signal Sergeant, is described in Wauchope,
   History, Volume 1, p22.

28 *Perthshire Advertiser,* 12 December 1914.

29 *Perthshire Advertiser,* 30 December 1914.

30 *Perthshire Advertiser,* 30 December 1914.

31 HMS *Tiger*, a heavily armoured British battlecruiser launched in 1913.

32 *Daily Record*, 26 February 1915.

33 *Daily Record*, 26 February 1915. Pipe Major T Clark was a Second Anglo-Boer War (1899-1902) veteran who held the rank of sergeant.

34 *Fife Free Press*, 13 February 1915.

35 *Milngavie & Bearsden Herald*, 1 January 1915.

36 *Milngavie & Bearsden Herald*, 1 January 1915.

37 *The Evening Telegraph and Post*, 9 February 1915.

38 *The Evening Telegraph and Post*, 9 February 1915.

39 *Berliner Tageblatt*, 13 April 1917.

SERGEANT WILLIAM SWAN, DCM

Brian Smith

MY GRANDFATHER, William Swan was born in Balmuir, just outside Dundee, on 20 April 1884, and joined the 2nd Battalion of The Black Watch in 1900, where he served for seven years, seeing action in South Africa and India. He was discharged to the Reserve in 1907 with the rank of sergeant. Between 1907 and 1914, he played football for Dundee Hibernian, now Dundee United, and opened two pubs, one of them aptly called *The Black Swan.*

In August 1914, as a reservist, William was again back in uniform with The Black Watch, but this time with the 1st Battalion and was serving alongside two of his brothers, John and Richard, when the battalion marched into Belgium with the British Expeditionary Force. A fourth brother, James, also joined the Army and served with the King's Own Scottish Borderers.

SERGEANT WILLIAM SWAN, DCM
(Descendants of Sergeant William Swan)

At the end of November 1914, shortly after arrival in theatre, William, John and Richard along with the remnants of The Black Watch met the Prussian Guard at Polygon Wood. As part of the 1st Guards Division, to which the 1st Black Watch was attached, they managed to hold and defeat the Germans despite being heavily outnumbered, halting their advance to Ypres and beyond to the Channel Ports. During the battle, John and a few of his comrades had taken shelter behind a wall which took a direct hit from a German shell, burying the group. Normally that would have been the end of the war for them, but they were saved by the timely arrival of William and a few others who managed to drag them from the rubble.

In January 1915, the battalion was in action at Givenchy, tasked with retaking the village. William and John were both sergeants with 'C' Company which had been held in reserve on the outskirts of the village. William was in charge of a platoon of 50 men and led them on a successful attack to retake the village church. In an interview with a journalist from the *People's Journal* while recovering at home in Dundee from this wound William recalled:

> The main body of our regiment was making a detour for a flanking attack on the village when I saw my opportunity, and we rushed forwards to take the village church. Our blood was up and we were keen for a fight. Everything I asked the men to do they did without question. After taking the church I positioned a few men in the upstairs windows of some houses to provide covering fire and the rest of us continued with hand to hand fighting through the village. With about thirty men, we reached the last German trench. We rushed the trench and eventually killed or captured all of the remaining enemy.[1]

During the charge on that trench, William received a bullet wound to his left arm. It was for his actions that day that he was awarded the Distinguished Conduct Medal and was one of the first men from Dundee to do so. His citation read:

> For gallant conduct on 25th January 1915, at Givenchy, when he led three men into a house and captured five Germans.[2]

The Swan brothers were also famous in regimental history for another reason. When Lance Corporal Richard Swan was shot at close range, his brother Sergeant William Swan saw the German soldier who had fired the shot, and as A G Wauchope stated in *A History of the Black Watch in the Great War, 1914-1918*, 'stalked him and chased him from house to house for ten minutes until he closed with him and killed him'.[3]

After recovering from his wounds at home in Scotland, in 1916, William rejoined the regiment but was posted to the 2nd Battalion, which was in Mesopotamia fighting the Ottoman forces, and remained with that battalion until the end of the war.

All four brothers received wounds, but sadly John did not survive. He died from a head wound during the battle for Aubers Ridge on 9 May 1915. William arrived home in 1919, where he continued running his two pubs until his death on 30 December 1930.

SWAN FAMILY GRAVESTONE, BALGAY CEMETERY DUNDEE
(Descendants of Sergeant William Swan)

---

1 *People's Journal (Dundee Edition)*, 13 March 1915.

2 *London Gazette,* 1 April 1915.

3 Wauchope, *History*, Volume 1, p31.

MEN OF CHARACTER
Tom McCluskey

THIS CHAPTER looks at the Great War service of three old soldiers of The Black Watch who survived the war, returned to civilian life and maintained their contact with the regiment until their deaths. These men had all served in the regiment before the Great War: Major W Fowler was serving on the outbreak of the war, Pipe Major Albert Crowe returned to serve with the Territorials of the 5th Battalion, while Sergeant J Callary re-enlisted in the 4th Battalion on the outbreak of war. In many ways, however, the service of these three men stands for much more than many years spent in uniform in peacetime and at war.

It is generally believed today that by the end of 1914 the old pre-war army was finished, and it is hard to disagree with that opinion, but the men discussed here were only three of the old Black Watch men who passed on the ethos of the regiment to the men of the Territorial Forces, New Armies and eventually the conscripts of the last two years of the war. Of course, as old soldiers they were not alone: men like them existed in all the Service and Territorial battalions and at the Depot. One picture even appeared in the *Perthshire Advertiser* of the Depot staff in 1915 under the heading 'Black Watch Veterans' showing 18 men ranging in rank from lieutenant-colonel to private whose service aggregated to 662 years.

It is also fair to say that although there has been much written about underage soldiers, very little has been written about older men, for by the standards of the old peacetime army these men were aged. Their deaths in action would never cause a storm of protest like the deaths of the underage men, but their service and influence on recruits of all ages must have been immense. Each of the men who appear in this chapter were special in their own way, but in a time of great national danger all were involved in passing on to volunteers and conscripts a clear ethos of effective soldiering based on a strong Black Watch regimental identity, so that once they joined their battalions overseas, every soldier they had been in contact with knew exactly what was expected of them.

MAJOR WILLIAM (WULLIE) FOWLER, OBE, MC

COLOUR SERGEANT WULLIE FOWLER
Later Major Wullie Fowler, OBE, MC
The Navy & Army Illustrated, 18 March 1898

On 4 November 1918, while operating as part of the 1st Infantry Brigade, the 1st Battalion, The Black Watch, attacked across the Sambre Canal in an action which met with overwhelming success.[1] After four years of war, it was clear that The Black Watch, as part of Britain's 'contemptible little army', had not only learned from the experience of the previous four years, but even before the failure of the *Kaiserschlacht* and the 'Black Day of the German Army', it had been teaching the enemy a few lessons of its own invention. Nevertheless, at the end of that final attack, Major and Quartermaster 'Wullie' Fowler, OBE, MC and 28 other ranks who had served continuously with the 1st Battalion throughout the war, were all that were left of the pre-war 1st Battalion.[2] Against all the odds they were still alive, but their chances of survival and at times even the survival of their 1st Battalion, had been boosted by the work of Fowler, Quartermaster and the much respected 'best kent' man in the battalion.

Fowler was a native of Whitemire, Dyke, Morayshire, and was educated at Delnies Public School, Nairn.[3] He enlisted into The Black Watch aged 18 on 14 July 1884 and a year later he joined his battalion in Egypt. Thereafter promotion was gained quickly. By 1898, he was Colour Sergeant serving in India where he was featured in the *Navy & Army Illustrated*, which described him as a worthy representative of the non-commissioned ranks.[4] He was promoted to Regimental Sergeant Major (RSM) after only 14 years' service in July 1898, then after 12 years' service in that rank he was commissioned lieutenant and Quartermaster on 14 January 1911.

When war was declared, the battalion was stationed in Aldershot as part of 1st (Guards) Brigade comprising 1st Coldstream Guards, 1st Scots Guards, 1st Black Watch and 2nd Royal Munster Fusiliers, and it was then that Fowler's true worth as a wartime Quartermaster was first appreciated.[5] The 1st Battalion was extremely fortunate to have in him as a Quartermaster, who as former RSM not only knew the strengths and weaknesses of his battalion, but also former and serving soldiers particularly as no fewer than 630 reservists descended on the battalion almost immediately. The mobilisation of an infantry battalion in 1914 was a major logistical and accounting exercise, but everything from changing badly fitting boots for reservists to closing accounts and ledgers and the return of surplus stores were completed under Fowler's immediate direction. It was only by his hard work that problems involving ill-fitting horse tack and worthless tailors sent from the Board of Trade were speedily sorted out, and by 8 August – as per the *War Book* – the battalion was ready to depart Oudenarde Barracks.[6] In fact, a new embarkation order meant it did not depart until 13 August, which gave extra time for training the reservists.

On 14 August 1914, the 1st Battalion arrived at Le Havre. By 6pm on the evening of 23 August, the battalion had taken up position on the Beaumont-Mons road, north of Maubeuge about 19 kilometres from Mons.[7] The following morning, on realising the overwhelming strength of the opposing forces, Sir John French gave the order to retire, and so began the weary marches to outdistance the enemy threat. Since their arrival, 1st Battalion had been continually on the move but although the men, and particularly the reservists were hardening up and becoming fitter, the long dusty marches on the hard French *pavé* roads in scorching sun made them very weary and footsore. With the exception of those on duty, at each ten-minute halt after each hour's march everyone would fall asleep. On the 28th, after marching 25 miles to Saint-Gobain the battalion were 'well together, but much exhausted'. Not only were the men suffering: the transport section's horses were also badly in need of rest.[8] Under Fowler's command, Lieutenant Anderson, Sergeant McVey and the men of the transport section had up until now given sterling service resupplying the battalion under extreme conditions, delivering food, water and other supplies on demand. The value of this logistical service led by Lieutenant Fowler to the battalion was near incalculable, for not every British battalion fared as well as 1st Black Watch. On the 29th, progress of the withdrawal was now regarded as good, and a rest day was ordered.

Up to that point the battalion had been fortunate and casualties were light, and none fatal, but the precarious nature of the withdrawal was illustrated by the fate of the 2nd Royal Munster Fusiliers at Etreux, when a cyclist held up by enemy fire failed to deliver the order to withdraw in time.[9] The fact was that no matter how gallant their attempts to hold back the German advance were, this failure of communication meant the almost total loss of that battalion and rapid redeployment of the brigade to cover the gap in the line. Throughout this incident and many other near disasters between 1914 and the end of the war, both Fowler's talent as a military administrator and his absolute reliability was invaluable. A description of the 1st Battalion at the start of 1918 in A G Wauchope's *A History of the Black Watch in the Great War, 1914-18* sums up the administrative and logistical aspect of Fowler's career:

Captain W. Fowler still combined his many duties as Quartermaster with those of officer in charge of the First Line Transport. His unfailing care for detail and readiness to accept responsibility had added greatly to the comfort and wellbeing of all ranks. His fund of happy stories and his willingness to help all in need made his nightly visits, when he brought the daily rations to the trenches, as welcome as they had been during the first year of the war.[10]

Other incidental evidence of Fowler's expertise exists in photographs of the battalion going about their daily business, but one in particular supports the claim for Fowler's effectiveness as Quartermaster. This photograph shows the battalion on parade at the hutted camp at Noeux-les-Mines and ready to move in April 1918.[11] This informal photograph highlights the good state of the men a few short days following the battle at Givenchy Ridge and Moat Farm (18-19 April 1918). It is also worth pointing out that it was there that the battalion held a major German attack during the *Kaiserschlacht,* although at considerable cost.[12] Nevertheless, here was the battalion at what looks like a battalion muster parade a few days later, with the RSM, later Major Charlie Scott, MC, checking off the nominal roll in front of what appears to be a well set up battalion.[13]

As Quartermaster it was also Fowler's responsibility to distribute the comforts assembled by the Countess of Mansfield and Mrs Hamilton sent to the men of the battalion, paid for by fundraising efforts of people in the regimental area. It was also very often his task to write hasty letters of appreciation, which in the early days of the war were generally published in the local papers. In November 1914 he wrote:

I have been instructed to write and thank you for your great kindness in sending such a nice lot of comforts and clothing to the men. These have been distributed to men of the battalion, and each and all of them send their heartfelt thanks for such needful gifts. Colonel Stewart would have thanked you personally for these gifts, but he is on duty in the trenches, which makes it impossible at the present time. We are all bearing the strain grandly, and it helps us greatly when we know our friends at home are in sympathy with us. On behalf of the battalion I again thank you for your kindness.[14]

It was inevitable that as the war proceeded, many of his former fellow Sergeants' Mess members would be killed and wounded. Very soon after writing home to thank the battalion's supporters, Fowler almost certainly would have been appointed to sort out the personal effects of two former members of the Sergeants' Mess, the first two of 61 men of the 1st Battalion to be commissioned from the ranks on 1 October 1914.[15] The first to fall was Lieutenant Alexander Lawson, formerly the Regimental Quartermaster Sergeant, killed on 11 November 1914 at Black Watch Corner during the Battle of Nonne Bosschen. Soon afterwards, on 9 May 1915, former Company Sergeant Major, then Lieutenant Alexander Wanliss was killed at Aubers. As the war continued, Fowler supervised the retrieval and care of whatever few personal possessions of the casualties and the dead could be found, regardless of rank, and made sure these were sent to relatives as the last tangible evidence of their loved one.

By 11 November 1918, with the Armistice in place, the battalion were out of harm's way at Fresnoy-le-Grand, Aisne region. Unlike in the cities at home, there was little sign of rejoicing in the billets. The past months of constant contact with the enemy had 'dulled men's senses':

> [As had the constant] strain of marching, working, fighting and marching again. In fact, if any effect were seen it was in the reaction to the strain of the last six months, the innate fatigue, both of mind and body, of gallant soldiers determined to show no sign of weariness until their task was achieved.[16]

On 8 December, in a now long forgotten parade the battalion received its Colours from Scotland with great ceremony. Very few men of the battalion had seen the Colours before, for throughout the war they had slumbered at the Queen's Barracks in Perth. No doubt the RSM, once the Drill Sergeant, would have ensured this would have been a very, very smart parade. The newly returned Colours were paraded towards the German frontier for the next ten days, and crossed into Germany near St. Vith with the 1st Battalion, where in the care of the Colour Party and placed in the centre of the marching column, they were trooped past the divisional commander on 10 December.[17] According to onlookers, the marching men of the battalion were a fine sight to behold. Much time had been spent cleaning, painting and polishing their kit.[18] With their freshly painted steel helmets sporting a Red Hackle, and their kilts no longer hidden by the khaki apron, the 1st Battalion marched onwards at a rate of 20 miles a day through Germany – supplied as always by the ubiquitous 'Wullie' Fowler.

On 24 March 1919, Major William Fowler, MC, left the battalion after 35 years' service. He had served under no fewer than 17 commanding officers, but miraculously had served throughout the entire war without a break.[19] On the day of his departure, he was given a grand send-off by the officers and men who escorted him to the station, led by the Pipes and Drums and the Military Band. At the railway station, the Military Band played 'Auld Lang Syne'. Fowler addressed the battalion said his goodbyes, and, amid much cheering, as the train left the Pipes and Drums broke into 'Scotland the Brave'.

On leaving the 1st Battalion, 'Wullie' now Major Fowler, was appointed Adjutant and Quartermaster at the School of Musketry at Hythe, where he retired on 14 January 1921. On retirement he was appointed Regimental Recruiting Officer. An early edition of the *Red Hackle* commented:

> It was with great pleasure learned that Major W Fowler, MC had been appointed first Retired Recruiting Officer of the 42nd Area, under the new civilian recruiting scheme. He took over his duties last month, and I am sure I voice the opinion of our readers in wishing him the best of luck and success in his new and most important duties. He has devoted his whole life to the Regiment, and even now, when he deserves a well-earned rest, he is still going on working for it. Certainly, he is the right man, in the right place![20]

Fowler continued to support the regiment after he retired from recruiting. He was appointed curator of The Black Watch Regimental Museum then located in the Depot at the Queen's Barracks, Perth, in 1931. From there he took recruits around the regimental area as well instructing them on Black Watch history and traditions.

Fowler died on 21 November 1940. His name is remembered on the long list of names engraved on the broadsword carried by the RSM of the 1st Battalion. His portrait in the dining room of the Sergeants' Mess was a constant reminder and even inspiration to those of us who were mess members as to what was possible and what might be expected of us some day. Major William Fowler, OBE, MC, was laid to rest in Wellshill Cemetery, Perth, as crowds lined the streets to bid farewell. On his final journey, his coffin was borne by warrant officers of the regiment, many wearing Great War medals, all of whom would have been young soldiers in that war.

PIPE MAJOR ALBERT EDWARD CROWE

On 11 April 1919, memories of the Great War were recalled at a gathering held in the *White Hart Hotel*, Arbroath, when surviving members of the old 'E 'and 'F' (Arbroath) Companies of the 5th Battalion, The Black Watch, the first Scottish Territorial battalion to be sent to France in 1914 met together again.[21] Prominent at this gathering and singing the old songs again was their former Pipe Major, Albert Edward Crowe.

Crowe enlisted into The Black Watch on 17 January 1884, falsely declaring he was 18 on his next birthday when in fact he was only 14.[22] This type of early enlistment was relatively common for young men of his background. By the age of ten Albert was boarding on a farm owned by William Vannet at Haughmond, Carmyllie, Angus.[23] The circumstances of his boarding-out are unknown, although family tradition says that he was what would now be described as virtually 'outwith parental control' after what appears to have been the death of his father and the remarriage of his mother.[24] On enlistment he was described as a farm labourer, but it seems Albert's youth was recognised, and he was held back at the Depot for almost two years during which time he was taught the pipes. On

2 December 1885, he embarked for Egypt, although his sojourn there was brief. On 1 May 1896, the 1st Black Watch departed Cairo for Malta on the SS *Poonah*, and for the next three years he soldiered with the 1st Battalion on garrison duties.[25]

Albert was a lively young soldier and his conduct sheet makes interesting reading: he was regularly confined to barracks and fined for military crimes such as occasionally being involved in a disturbance and returning late to barracks after a night out. However, his conduct was fairly standard for the time amongst single men living in barracks and occasionally kicking back at the system. Nevertheless, his *Pipe Book* dated 1884, which is in the possession of his family, shows he wrote in a neat hand, avoided spelling mistakes and presented neat musical notation with the old-fashioned steel-nibbed pens of the time. It also contained a number of tunes of his own composition, seven of which are reproduced in *A Collection of Pipe Music of the Black Watch* published in 2012.[26] After serving in Gibraltar for over two years, he returned home on 2 February 1892 and was transferred to the Regular Reserve.

After the Boers declared war on Britain on 11 October 1899, Crowe was recalled to the Colours (January 1900) and was posted to the 2nd Black Watch in South Africa where he took part in a series of operations at Wittebergen against the Boers in the eastern Orange Free State. He was awarded the bars Wittebergen and Cape Colony on his Queen's South African medal. Albert returned home to Arbroath on 23 April 1901, his Regular Reserve commitments expired.[27]

Back in Arbroath, Crowe settled down and married, and shortly after discharge he joined the Militia as a volunteer, and in 1908, he transferred to the newly formed Territorial Force of the 5th (Angus & Dundee) Battalion, The Black Watch as their Pipe Major. When war was declared in 1914, Arbroath became a hive of activity as the Territorials mobilised for war. That afternoon in Arbroath, 'E' and 'F' Companies led by Crowe and his pipers marched to Arbroath railway station to the cheers of crowds who lined both sides of the streets between the Drill Hall and the station. As the train moved off, more loud cheers were heard from the people who had congregated on Keptie Bridge and the vicinity of the station.[28] The 5th Battalion's first journey was short: their destination was their mobilisation station billets at Broughty Castle and Hawkhill School in Dundee.[29]

Three months later and after 12 weeks more training, on 1 November 1914 the 5th Battalion embarked for France arriving the following day at Le Havre and signalled their entry to the harbour with pipes playing. Sergeant Reilly from Dundee described the scene:

> The French gave us a good reception and we had some difficultly in resisting their importune demands for souvenirs. One small boy footed it by my side for ever so far, chattering French, and wanting to carry my rifle.[30]

Over the next fortnight, the 5th's pipe band led the battalion as it route marched its way towards the headquarters of the 8th Division at Estaires. Crowe was also present, when according to Sergeant Reilly on 12 November:

> The dapper little figure of the veteran, Lord Roberts approached by car as we reached Estaires. We cheered like mad. The veteran standing at the salute as the Battalion passed. At Estaires, we were inspected by the King. Scotsmen and Englishmen alike roared themselves hoarse as the King acknowledged his reception in a soldierly fashion. There were a number of motor cars with the Prince of Wales and General French being in the first, we also gave the French President a cheery shout.[31]

This was probably the last time Lord Roberts would hear the pipes for he died of pneumonia at St Omer, France, on 14 November 1914.

The *Brechin Advertiser* provides insight into the march to their destination. The local pubs did not impress the 'Jocks' of Angus:

> I must call them by that name but they are a very watered type of 'pub', not like the thorough going places we have in Scotland; and in one we had a cup of coffee.[32]

Throughout the years, however, they were to serve in France and Flanders, the humble *estaminet* would undoubtedly provide great solace to Crowe and his comrades from the rigours of the frontline.

After arriving at the 8th Division, the Pipes and Drums along with other members of the battalion were engaged in trench digging and repairs in terrible wet and muddy conditions in weather generally described as appalling. Although a number of men became victims to enemy fire, a far greater number were hospitalised because of the extreme cold and problems caused by being constantly wet whilst in the trenches. In fact, when the right half of the battalion left the trenches on 9 December, they could only muster 150 men on account of the large numbers who were temporarily out of action due to illness.[33] In spite of the terrible conditions, Crowe demonstrated his resilience simply by being fit for duty. As reported by Captain Duncan, New Year's Day was brought in, in the trenches, when Pipe Major Crowe played in 'the New Year at Headquarters within hearing distance of the German trenches'.[34]

The first 'Battle Honour' the 5th Battalion gained was Neuve Chapelle on 10 March 1915. The battalion were in reserve tasked with carrying forward supplies while the Pipe Band provided stretcher-bearers led by Crowe as Pipe Major. One man involved was Piper Arthur Howie, a former ploughman whose actions were commended for 'coolness and daring' and when he was finally killed, he fell shot in the act of bearing a badly wounded man to the rear.[35] Also killed that day was Lance Corporal Fergus Reid, formerly an employee of East Mill, Brechin, who left a wife and two children.[36] In an incident which shows the very strong bond between the men of the battalion and particularly in the Pipes and Drums, shortly before his death Lance Corporal Reid wrote a letter of condolence to the mother of Bugler Fredrick Scott who had been killed when trench digging on 1 March.[37] Some time later, Crowe was involved in another well-documented similar incident which shows something of his personal influence and the workings of the other ranks unofficial information and family support network.

A few days before the Battle of Loos, Drummer 'Bertie' Parker was wounded by a sniper while digging trenches and died a few hours later. At that point Pipe Major Crowe wrote a letter to his wife in Arbroath telling her that 'Bertie' had been killed, gave it to a man about to go on leave to Arbroath and told him to give it to his wife in Abbot Street. Just over a day later, as soon as she had the letter Mrs Crowe, as the Pipe Major's wife and 'mother of the band', immediately visited Bertie's mother and broke the news to her of his death.[38] Mrs Crowe arranged what would now be described as emotional support and helped with some of the practical needs of the younger members of the family. The official word of Drummer Parker's death came a week later, but not before Mrs Crowe had arranged with the local Boys' Brigade Company where Bertie had been an officer, to send off a consignment of comforts for the 5th Battalion.

The 5th Battalion, like other Territorial Force battalions had fathers and sons serving together: 'Bertie' Parker and father Sergeant Parker from F (Arbroath) Company who had been invalided home wounded and was in Forfar training draftees for France were a case in point. In Crowe's case the family network went further. His eldest son, Lance Corporal James Crowe was also in the Pipes and Drums at one point before being wounded while on listening patrol duty in 1916 and medically downgraded to home defence duties. Two sons-in-law were also in the 5th Battalion, although they were in different companies, while one nephew was in the High School Section and later commissioned as Second Lieutenant C Crowe in 1915. A second nephew, Sergeant Albert Crowe arrived with the 2nd Battalion from India.

Sergeant Crowe of the 2nd Battalion was 22 when he was killed at Loos. He had been promoted to sergeant almost a year before he left India and appears to have been regarded as a very promising young soldier. The following letter, an excellent example of the type of letter Black Watch officers sent to relatives of their men killed in action, was sent by his company commander to his sister explaining how he died:[39]

Dear Miss Crowe,

I write to offer you my deepest sympathy in the loss of your brother, Sergeant Crowe. He served under me as machine gun Sergeant since March, and I had the greatest regard for his character and abilities. He was killed close beside me on the 25th at about 1 pm, a long way within the German lines. He had shown great courage and enterprise in the fighting on the 25th, and had he been spared I should have recommended him for the DCM. I must again express to you the great loss I, and the Machine Gun Company in general, have suffered in his death. I trust it may be some consolation to you that he died in the execution of his duty, and for a noble cause.

On 7 March 1916, due to manning issues which meant that neither battalion could maintain two reserve battalions, the 4th and 5th Battalions were amalgamated. It was agreed that 'A' and 'B' Companies would be made up of 4th Battalion men and 'B' and 'C' Companies from the 5th with the new battalion to be titled 4/5th Battalion.[40] Thereafter, Crowe with what was left of the Pipes and Drums, and generally acting as stretcher-bearers, would take part in many important battles such as the taking of the Schwaben Redoubt between 14 and 16 October 1916. The family tradition says that it was there that Crowe had a very strong premonition that one son-in-law, Corporal J Morrison had been killed, though that turned out not to have been the case. While that premonition proved false, sadly another proved to be all too true: family tradition also says that another member of the extended family, newly commissioned into an English regiment, but whose name has been long forgotten, found out where his 'uncle Albert' was and went to visit him. However, in spite of a warning to keep his head down, this very tall young man was shot by a sniper only yards from where Crowe was with the stretcher-bearers in the second line.

Some time early in 1918, and probably before the start of the *Kaiserschlacht*, Crowe was transferred to the Labour Corps, and although there is no entry in his records, it would appear his transfer was age related.[41] Although these men were now regarded as unfit for frontline duties, the Army recognised their long service and experience were invaluable in labour battalions: unlike the Chinese Labour Corps or the French equivalent, the Labour Corps men could be called on, and relied upon to defend themselves. Still, his stay was short with the Labour Corps and he was demobbed on 11 October 1918.

On returning to civilian life, Crowe settled back in Arbroath and was employed as a timekeeper at James Keith & Blackman Works. Throughout the rest of his life, he maintained his association with the 5th Battalion and the regimental association. Furthermore, besides breeding fancy pigeons, he continued to teach piping, turning out many notable players including his own granddaughter, regarded locally as a piper of ability. Albert Crowe died aged 63 in June 1933, four years after his wife Elizabeth and left behind three sons and four daughters.[42]

SERGEANT JAMES CALLARY

In his first book of war poetry, *Ballads of Battle*, Joe Lee included a sincere, and deeply incisive tribute to Sergeant James Callary, the man who trained the group of former journalists known as the 'Fighter Writers' to be effective soldiers, and who in turn immortalised their first sergeant in their writings. It read:

> To the humour, and the good humour, of the genial sergeant I owe it that the period of my early drilling, which might thinkably have been a time of deadly dullness, afforded me much entertainment, as well as not a little valuable instruction.

What Lee identified as valuable instruction and what Sergeant Callary brought to the 4th Battalion's training was a tried method of infantry instruction. At a stroke it cut away the lax discipline that had pervaded the Territorial Forces in peacetime and put in its place a disciplined and meaningful system of rote learning where drills and weapons handling skills were endlessly rehearsed to ensure battlefield reliability of both the men and their weapons. Like all good military instructors, Sergeant Callary would pepper his performance with apt and 'couthy' phrases and sayings, which helped recruits remember the serious lessons he taught them.

These lodged in Lee's mind, particularly those about the rifle, for Sergeant Callary was always at his best when extolling the virtues of that weapon, and the necessity for treating it with respect.[43] In this poem, Lee passes on some of Sergeant Callary's lessons to his readers:

MY RIFLE

I'm the Soldier's surest friend:
I will neither break nor bend.
Straight and sterling, tried and true;
You keep me and I'll keep you.

Bolt and barrel, butt and band;
Caress me with a careful hand.
Stock and swivel, sling and sight
Rub me down, and keep me right.

Striker, trigger, cocking piece;
Give 'em all some elbow-grease
Clean me clean, and oil me well;
I'll kill your man and never tell.

Leave me dirty, oil me ill;
You're the chap I'm going to kill
Leave me lying all awry;
You're the feller's going to die.

Daily do but pull me through;
I will do the same for you.
Only use a "two by four"—
Nothing less, and nothing more.

Pull-through rag will do the trick;
A shirt or sock is going to stick!
And keep your bottle full of ile—
Remember the Virgins' parabile!

Handle me with care, I beg,
I'm not so stout as old Mons Meg!
Do not pitch me on the ground—
To break me, a hammer can be found!

The soldier who doesn't clean his rifle
Has 'listed with intent to trifle.
The chap who doesn't clean his gun
Is sorriest soldier 'neath the sun.

I'm the Soldier's surest friend:
I will neither break nor bend.
Straight and sterling, tried and true—
You keep me and I'll keep you.

James Callary was born in Lochee in 1865. His family were part of the strong Irish community in Dundee. At the age of 16, James was serving his time as a 'sprigger' (cobbler) in Albert Street.[44] He dropped out of sight after 1881, however at the age of 27 he enlisted in The Black Watch (1892) and was first posted to the 2nd Battalion in Scotland. In July 1896, he was posted to the 1st Battalion in India. On 6 October 1901, the battalion left India for South Africa and by this time James was a corporal. The battalion's sojourn in South Africa was short. Not long after he arrived back in Edinburgh in October 1902, he married Catherine Greenan (12 November) the same year and by April 1910, Sergeant Callary had completed his Colour service.

When war was declared, Callary enlisted in the 4th (City of Dundee) Battalion, The Black Watch (TF), and a month later, he was promoted to sergeant. In fact, he was 49, but declared on his re-enlistment papers that he was 35, and because some of his original documents were missing, including his conduct sheets, his enlistment was accepted. However, when his conduct sheets did turn up some time later, they made interesting reading!

It is also important to understand that Callary in his role as a training sergeant was a product of the changes that came about after the Second Anglo-Boer War (1899–1902). These changes were essentially about absorbing the bruising lesson learned in South Africa, modernising the Army and preparing for the next war which, wrongly, was expected to be a war of movement like the last great European war of 1870 between France and Prussia. Barracks and welfare provision were improved, and more importantly, musketry and fitness were stressed. Standards of fitness and individual competence were set: platoon teams for example completed a regulation combined march and shoot test, marching 11 miles in three hours before firing a set test at service targets.[45] This training ethos, no doubt absorbed by Callary when he was serving was the basis of the words of wisdom and practical soldiering skills he passed on to the Fighter Writers and which, along with other personal qualities led them to recognise his true worth.

SERGEANT JAMES CALLARY
Drawn by Joseph Lee
Ballads of Battle (1916)

Like the good sergeant he was, Callary also acted as a mentor to his men. An excellent example of a sergeant mentoring one of his men is contained the advice he gave in a private talk with the former journalist Linton Andrews just prior to leaving for France in February 1915. Linton Andrews outlined his concerns:

> The ambition that had swayed us since August 1914, the ambition for which we had left our homes, our wives, our sweethearts, our good civilian pay, our warm beds, was to

reach its long-delayed fulfilment. What were our emotions in that hour? Who shall reveal the dazzling hopes and the wormy fears- hidden in each man's heart? At times, as I walked along, kilt swinging gaily, there came upon me a wild dread of what was to come. How could I take the life of another man, some decent, honest man, and leave him mess of torn flesh like railway smash victims I had seen in my reporting days?

Sergeant Callary set him straight in a fatherly sort of way:

A bronzed Regular sergeant, good old Callary, was a great comfort. I told him of dread. 'God bless you, laddie,' he said with great heartiness. 'You've no call to worry like that. You'll think no more of putting your bayonet through a man than of putting your finger in a pot of jam. Fighting comes as natural as eating.' It was comforting to know that. I half believed it.[46]

If Corporal Andrews had ever wondered about Callary's military background in the Regular peacetime army, he found out when the 4th Battalion were attached to the 2nd Battalion, then part of the *Bareilly* Brigade at Richebourg St Vaast, and where between the 5th and 10th of March were under instruction by them.[47] 'Dundee's Ain' was subject to rapid concentrated period instruction on all the basics: drill, even saluting, acting immediately on orders, as well as personal hygiene, shaving and the care of uniforms – all to be done properly. 'Above all we must keep our rifles in first class order, for, if not, they might jam in a moment of emergency that might mean our death' they were told. 'Old Sergeant Callary put this last point better. "Pull your rifle through", he would say, "and your rifle will pull you through".[48] All too soon Callary's training was to be put to the test for on 10 March 1915 the 4th Battalion took part in the Battle of Neuve Chapelle, fighting alongside the 2nd Battalion.

Callary survived the war and continued his trade as a shoemaker on the Lochee Road. Throughout his army career, he was a noted athlete, boxing being his main enthusiasm. He was an expert trainer, having trained the Leith Athletic football team which in 1909 won the Scottish Qualifying Cup. He also trained Dundee Hibs (Dundee United from 1923) for a time.[49] Sergeant James Callary, died at home, 16 St Mary Street, Dundee, at the age of 73 in 1940.

EPILOGUE

The old soldiers remembered in this chapter were fortunate to have lived long and fruitful lives. They all made their contribution to The Black Watch in time of war: Major 'Wullie' Fowler as the Quartermaster *par excellence,* Pipe Major Albert Crowe as the patriarch who looked after the men of the Pipes and Drums and carried the wounded off the battlefield, and Sergeant James Callary, the dispenser of military wisdom, entertaining rifle instruction and mentor to his men and much more. All three in their own ways represented a sort of the golden thread of experience which in their case ran from peace to war in South Africa to peace again, then a return to war in Europe and finally peace in a near unrecognisable landscape, in a land that was not fit for heroes. These three, and others like them were always there to help rebuild the shattered battalions that formed and reformed time and again, always absorbing new men and returning wounded. Doubtless the war years would linger on in their memories with those memories becoming most poignant each year at Armistice.

Corporal Linton Andrews, once given some fatherly advice from Sergeant Callary, wrote a haunting eulogy to his old comrades:

> Dear, great-hearted comrades of the Black Watch, no darkness of the grave can keep you from my sight; nothing can dim the light of youth in your friendly eyes. You will never be old ghosts to me, but warm-hearted friends, as when we stood in the line together and talked of our dear ones at home.
>
> The horrors of those years have often haunted my dreams, but I thank God with a humble heart that I came to know and love the spirit of my old battalion.[50]

No doubt the three men described in this chapter would have wholeheartedly agreed with that statement.

1 *1st Black Watch War Diary*, 4-5 November, 1918.

2 A G Wauchope, *A History of the Black Watch in the Great War, 1914-18*, Volume 1 (London: Medici Society, 1925), p100.

3 *Aberdeen Weekly Journal*, 28 November 1940.

4 *Navy & Army Illustrated*, Volume V, 18 March 1898, p361.

5 Wauchope, *History*, Volume 2, p1.

6 *1st Black Watch War Diary*, 1-8 August 1914.

7 Wauchope, *History*, Volume 2, p4.

8 *1st Black Watch War Diary*, 28 August 1914.

9 Brigadier-General J E Edmonds Brigadier (compiler), *History of the Great War, Military Operations*. Volume 1 (1914) (London: MacMillan & Company Ltd, 1937), p223.

10 Wauchope, *History*, Volume 2, pp74-75.

11 Wauchope, *History*, Volume 1, facing p90.

12 'Not since the 9th of May 1915, had the Battalion endured such a day.' Wauchope, *History*, Volume 1, p89.

13 Major Scott's obituary in the *Red Hackle* (December 1972) explained how, with Major Fowler, these two remarkable men carried through the war from start to finish.

14 *The Courier and Argus*, 13 November 1914.

15 *1st Battalion Cameron Highlanders War Diary*.

16 Wauchope, *History*, Volume 1, pp99-100.

17 Wauchope, *History*, Volume 1, p102.

18 Wauchope, *History*, Volume 1, p102.

19 *1st Black Watch War Diary*, 1 February 1919.

20 *Red Hackle*, July 1922, p2.

21 *Arbroath Herald,* 18 April 1919.

22 British Army WW1 Pension Records 1914-20, Albert E Crowe, accessed via https://www.ancestry.co.uk.

23 1871 Census Scotland accessed via https://www.ancestry.co.uk.

24 Consultation with descendants of P M Crowe.

25 Victoria Schofield, *The Highland Furies: The Black Watch 1739-1899* (London: Quercus Publishing plc, 2012).

26 Sandy Cram, Alistair Duthie, Alistair Irwin, and Scott Taylor, *A Collection of Pipe Music of The Black Watch (Royal Highland Regiment)* (Perth: Balhousie Publications, 2012), pp6, 50, 59, 165, 237, 251, 288.

27 *The Royal Highland Regiment. The Black Watch. 42nd–73rd. Medal Roll. 1801–1911* (Printed by T & A Constable, 1913), p211.

28 *Arbroath Herald*, 7 August 1914.

29 Wauchope, *History*, Volume 2, p39.

30 *Brechin Advertiser*, 24 November 1914.

31 *Brechin Advertiser*, 24 November 1914.

32 *Brechin Advertiser*, 24 November 1914.

33 Wauchope, *History*, Volume 2, p43. Family tradition has it that the Germans replied in song.

34 *The Courier and Argus*, 7 January 1915.

35 *Glasgow Herald*, 20 March 1915.

36 *Courier & Advertiser*, 20 March 1915.

37 *The Courier and Argus*, 18 March 1915.

38 *Arbroath Herald*, 15 September 1915.

39 *Montrose Review*, 22 October 1915.

40 Wauchope, *History*, Volume 2, p67.

41 As indicated on Crowe's Medal Index Card.

42 *Courier & Advertiser*, 17 June 1933.

43 Joseph Lee, *Ballads of Battle* (New York: E P Button & Company, 1916), p12.

44 1881 Census Scotland accessed via https://www.ancestry.co.uk.

45 G A Leask, *Sir William Robertson: The Life Story of the Chief of the Imperial Staff* (London: Cassell, 1917), p91.

46 *The Evening Telegraph and Post*, 21 April 1930.

47 *4th Black Watch War Diary*, 5-9 March 1915.

48 William Linton Andrews, *The Haunting Years: The Commentaries of a War Territorial.* (London: Naval and Military Press, ND) p95.

49 *Courier & Advertiser*, 1 April 1938.

50 Andrews, *Haunting Years*, p288.

MY GRANDFATHER'S DIARY

Sandy MacDuff

WHEN WAR broke out in 1914, my grandfather Private Alexander MacDuff was mobilised on 5 August 1914 and arrived the following day at the 1st Battalion, The Black Watch, stationed at Oudenarde Barracks, Aldershot Garrison. As a reservist who had left the Army in January 1911 after completing a seven-year engagement including six years' service in India, he and many more men like him replaced the underage men left behind when the 1st Battalion went to war in 1914.

Although his mobilisation meant that he had to leave his pregnant wife Margaret behind, unlike many of the other reservists his civilian job of postman at least meant that he was fit for the long marches of the early days of the war. But Alexander (known as Sandy) Macduff, was also the holder of an Army Certificate of Education, 2nd Class. That meant that no matter what his standard of literacy and numeracy was on enlistment, a pass at this class meant amongst other things that he was capable of writing a clear, well-organised account of what he had experienced in 'a good hand' – which was exactly what he did when he wrote up his personal diary every day. However, what Sandy MacDuff would not have been aware of was that 100 years later, his writing would be one of a tiny number of private soldier's diary accounts of the 1st Battalion in action during the crucial months of September and October 1914, immediately before the action at Black Watch Corner during the Battle of Nonne Bosschen.[1]

The diary itself survived the war and returned home with my grandfather. During my childhood, I was aware of its existence, but at that time it was of no great interest to me. In fact, it was only after I had joined The Black Watch that I read it with any real understanding. Unfortunately, at some point after I had read it, a section went missing and has never been recovered. What is left of the diary begins on Sandy MacDuff's 30th birthday on 3 September and ends on 26 October 1914.

Sadly, the dates of the period covered by the missing section are unknown. My memory of that section which I read before it vanished included words I have never forgotten. These were 'Today I killed officers and men of the German Army'. In that part of the diary which has survived, however, my grandfather was not often as direct as that in his description of the action. Instead, when he described the heavy fighting of 22 October 1914 for example, he simply wrote:

> Shells and bullets whizzing all around, attacks [German] at intervals all night...[and a few days later on 24 October]...The Germans made some very vigorous attacks but were driven back each time.

One other thing that is very noticeable in the diary is that when my grandfather was not actually in action, fighting was going on fairly close to where he was at the time, even during rest periods which seldom lasted for more than a few hours. He often describes 'the guns going at it hard' or 'heavy firing on our left', so he and his comrades must have been constantly expecting to fight every single day in a way they would not later in the war when rest periods out of the trenches were properly established. One other very noticeable thing about the diary was that my grandfather very seldom recorded rumours, or news he heard about what was happening away from the 1st Battalion. Nonetheless, on 11 September 1914, he did set out what he heard when he wrote that the British Army had captured 2,000 men, a battery each of artillery and machine guns and killed 600 Germans in an unnamed action the previous day. He also wrote that General Findlay had been killed in that action; and in this case his information was accurate, because in fact Brigadier-General N D Findlay CB of the Royal Artillery had been killed, albeit the day before on 10 September.

My grandfather's description of the ordinary soldiers' daily routine during the early part of the war is very revealing: orderly sergeants shouting for men to draw rations at 4.30am opened the day. An accidental discharge on the afternoon of 12 September 1914 by a man of 'C' Company wounded two men, but that was nothing compared with what my grandfather described as 'the guns going very heavy all morning' during a 'terrific battle fought yesterday' in which the French were engaged.[2] He also recorded many of the little incidents that would have made life a little easier for the men: on 18 September, his mess chum Lance Corporal Scott got a parcel from home with a 'lot of fags' or on 1 October, the joy of 'fresh meat for dinner today and one half a potato per man'. In fact, any good dinner – and there were very few – was described in some detail, including one on 11 September where he listed everything on the menu as well as the fact that there had been stewed apples for dessert. The issue of a blanket each on 5 October – 'so we should not feel the cold so much now' – must have been very welcome as the nights grew ever cooler. The discovery of his false teeth after he lost them one night must have been a great relief. On another occasion, he was surprised to find that what he described as 'a good few' German shells were not bursting but were duds.[3] Like so many of the men of that generation, he also seems to have been a smoker, and as well as mentioning getting 'fags' in parcels, he described how it felt to be without a smoke for 'when the craving comes it is very hard to get rid of'.[4]

The routine of 'standing to arms' at first light and last light was a hard reality for these men and was an important part of their daily routine. My grandfather's description of putting up barbed wire at night in the early days of the war was an early taste of what was to come for infantry over the course of the war. He also mentioned what modern soldiers would describe as going out on listening patrol and his account of an early trench raid by the Coldstream Guards was very precise, but now and then something unexpected would appear. One example of this was how when he was sent out with Lance Corporal Scott on observation duty on 3 October, he described the beautiful moonlit night spent in front of The Black Watch frontline, or again later that month found space to write 'The sunset this afternoon was magnificent to look at and quite out of keeping with the awful roaring of the guns'.[5]

One of the most interesting parts of the diary describes the 1st Battalion's redeployment to Hazebrouk on the way to the fight at Black Watch Corner. After the battalion was relieved by the French on 16 October, they marched to Fismes where they entrained. For the

39 men in my grandfather's truck there was sitting room only, so they could not sleep and 'passed a miserable night…like herring in a box' during a journey that lasted over 34 hours.[6] The only good thing he had to say about the train journey was that getting hot water to make tea was easy and that the engine driver helped out with that. On the other hand, after detraining he saw Indian troops for the first time and was part of a foraging party in an unnamed large town where he was able to get butter, the first he had seen for two months.

PRIVATE ALEXANDER MACDUFF, HIS WIFE AND CHILDREN
(MacDuff Family)

Two other topics crop up time and again in the diary. First, my grandfather's habit of reading a passage from the Bible almost on a daily basis, and second, his contact with my grandmother who he usually described as 'my dear little wife'. Whether he read the Bible as a routine activity or because he was a quietly, but deeply religious man, I do not know. There is no mention in the diary of either what these readings meant to him or even of the parts of the Bible he read. As far as my grandmother was concerned, in spite of everything that was going on, somehow, they maintained a level of contact difficult to imagine. How many letters my grandfather was able to send to my grandmother is not known and none have survived, but it is clear from the diary that my grandmother's letters meant a great deal to him.

In 1916, he was discharged, his reserve service completed, but within weeks, he had voluntarily re-enlisted and served for the remainder of the war escaping serious injury; and retired as a sergeant in The Black Watch. He passed away at his home at St Fillans, near Crieff, on 16 March 1935 aged only 49.

---

1 'The Battalion *War Diary* for the latter half of September and all of October is missing, having been lost in the fighting at Ypres.' A G Wauchope, *A History of the Black Watch in the Great War, 1914-18*, Volume 1 (London: Medici Society, 1925), p15 (footnote).

2 Sandy MacDuff, 'Diary', 1 October 1914.

3 'Diary', 14 October 1914.

4 'Diary', 3 October 1914.

5 'Diary', 21 October 1914.

6 'Diary', 18 October 1914.

'TIK JOHNNIE!'

THE BLACK WATCH AND THE BAREILLY BRIGADE

Fraser Brown

INTRODUCTION

ON 8 AUGUST 1914, only four days after Britain declared war on Germany, the 3rd Lahore and 7th Meerut Divisions and a cavalry brigade of the Indian Army mobilised for war. To the amazement of most British officers of the Indian Army, they were to be sent to fight Germany.[1] The old colour bar principle whereby Indian troops were not to fight Europeans was dropped by the British War Council, mobilisation plans quietly developed by Lieutenant-General Douglas Haig (and others) when he was Chief of the Indian General Staff between 1910 and 1912 were implemented, and sepoys on furlough and Indian and British reservists in India reported to their cantonments. Unlike the Canadian and other troops from the Empire who were given months of training on Salisbury Plain before going into action, and although they were not equipped up to Home Army standards, particularly in artillery and communications equipment, Kitchener considered the Indian Corps ready to fight. The need for them to be deployed immediately in the frontline was too great for any delay.

On 31 August 1914, the news broke on the troopships that the enemy was Germany, and on 26 September, the main body of the Indian Corps arrived in France at which point the Indian Army's new equipment was unloaded. Some, but not all sepoys received new khaki serge uniforms and web equipment. The troops exchanged their pre-war Mark II rifles for the new SMLE which took a new improved cartridge and practised with these on French Army ranges. On the night of 23 October, men of the 57th Wilde's Rifles (Frontier Force (FF)) went into the frontline, repulsed the first German attack on Indian soldiers in Europe, suffered the first Indian casualties of the Great War and the bravery of Sepoy Usman Khan won his regiment the first Distinguished Service Medal of 1914 to be awarded to an Indian soldier. On 26 October, elements of the Ferozepore Brigade including the 57th Wilde's Rifles, 1st Connaught Rangers and 129th Duke of Connaught's Own Baluchis along with other British troops carried out the Indian Corps' first offensive action in Europe against German positions between Gaspaard and Wambeek in the Messines area. At a purely tactical level, this assault achieved little except that it was believed to have significantly disrupted a planned German attack. What it did achieve was a 'relatively inexpensive teach-in to warfare on the Western Front' which demonstrated that Indian units were able to operate with British units and formations in an offensive role, and above all showed that their 'vaunted fighting spirit was not just legend'.[2]

Although opinion regarding the effectiveness of the Indian Corps in France has varied over the years, and a full discussion of that debate is well beyond the scope of this chapter, for Sir John French, the British Expeditionary Force (BEF) commander at First Ypres, 'every man [in the Indian Corps] was worth his weight in gold'.[3] Nonetheless, accounts of Indian terror under bombardment, lack of fighting ability and complete unsuitability for the Western Front contained in books like Frank Richards' *Old Soldiers Never Die* gradually gained credence in the 1920s and 1930s. In 1990, Jeffrey Greenhut's influential assessment of the Indian Corps on the Western Front was particularly scathing, criticising it as 'poorly organised for modern war', with sepoys only capable of performing well when led by their British officers, and therefor 'a poor choice to fight a modern war'.[4] Greenhut also claimed the Indian Corps' performance in France suffered from what he termed 'the most severe imaginable form of culture shock' when sepoys, then products of a pre-industrial village-based society, were confronted with the realities of the first fully industrialised war.[5] In 1999, John Keegan condemned the service of the Indian Corps in France as a failure and their men 'scarcely suitable' for the Western Front, although he did acknowledge their bravery at Neuve Chapelle.[6] Others, like the American historian David J Silbey, quoted by George Morton-Jack viewed the Indian Army experience of the Great War as that of 'cowed colonial subordinates' who would be recruits for the Indian National Congress in the interwar years, while conveniently forgetting Ghandi and the other Congress leaders despised them for 'taking up the sword of the hireling'.[7] More recently, the director Pankaj Batra's film 'Sajjan Singh Rangroot' (2018) pandered to the Silbey position, showing the hero not only as a precursor of independence, but also stereotypical scenes of racial and professional tensions between British and Indian soldiers.

This general view has been challenged very effectively in *Sepoys in the Trenches* by Gordon Corrigan who described the terms of these criticisms: 'Some have emerged as total fiction, from either genuine misunderstandings or from more nefarious motives'.[8] In addition, Morton-Jack's *The Indian Empire At War* has re-evaluated the part played by the Indian Corps in France. While Morton-Jack acknowledged both the failings of the Corps and identified the difficulties it faced, he nonetheless provided a timely and detailed corrective – both to the 'crazier' stories in the British press and the critical assessments of earlier historians.

This chapter sets out to contribute to the Corrigan and Morton-Jack's corrective by looking in some detail at one example of British-Indian professional co-operation at an inter-battalion level, in this case between the 2nd Battalion, The Black Watch, and the 58th Vaughan's Rifles (FF) between their joint arrival in France in 1914 and the departure of the Indian Corps from France in November 1915. In addition, it will look at relations between sepoys of the Bareilly Brigade and the soldiers of the 4th (City of Dundee) Battalion, The Black Watch (TF), as these were described in the writings of William Linton Andrews and Joseph Lee of the 4th Battalion. [For readers unfamiliar with the Indian Army, Appendix I details aspects of the Indian Army relevant to this chapter.]

THE 2ND BLACK WATCH AND 58TH RIFLES: FINAL AND FIRST CONTACTS

In December 1915, when Lieutenant-Colonel A G Wauchope, commanding the 2nd Black Watch, discovered that the 58th Rifles were not to accompany the 2nd Black Watch to Mesopotamia, he wrote to Colonel

Murray, the British officer commanding that regiment, expressing his deep regret, and that of the 2nd Black Watch, that 'we cannot go on fighting together in the new campaign as we have for so long, in good times and evil, in France'.[9] This letter was clearly of considerable significance to the 58th Rifles for it was published in its entirety in the 'Extracts from Letters and Orders' section of *A Record of the 58th Rifles F. F. in the Great War 1914-1919*.[10] In it, Wauchope acknowledged the depth of his sense of loss at the departure of the 58th Rifles, admitting that he 'wrote in haste' but that he also 'wrote with such feeling that he could not write with clarity' as he remembered those friends who had gone. Significantly too, he hoped Colonel Murray would remember him not only to British friends in the regiment but also to the Indian officers (Viceroy Commissioned Officers) 'with some of whom I have fought in attack and in reconnaissance'. In the main section of the letter, however, he identified memories of three salient events which in retrospect could be said to have been the foundation of the close relationship which developed between both battalions while in the Bareilly Brigade. These were memories of 23 November 1914 when together the 2nd Black Watch and 58th Rifles drove the Germans out of the British line, memories of joint scouting patrols, and finally memories of the intervention of the 58th Rifles to protect the exposed left flank of the 2nd Black Watch at Loos.

While Wauchope's letter mourned the demise of the matured and highly effective working relationship between the two battalions, the memories he mentions were only some of the what might be termed the professional highlights of this connection. The first contact between the 2nd Black Watch and 58th Rifles was recorded in *A Record of the 58th Rifles F. F. in the Great War 1914-1919* as occurring in India on 14 August 1914 when 'the Battalion made the acquaintance of the 2nd Battalion, The Black Watch, with which it was afterwards to be so closely associated'.[11] The first contact of the 58th Rifles with the Germans came on 30 October when the battalion moved to relieve the 2/8th Gurkha Rifles in a very insecure section of the frontline with virtually no trench system, but found the Gurkhas had been shelled out of their position and the Germans ensconced in it. At that point, instead of being the relief battalion, the 58th Rifles immediately became the reserve element of a counterattack by a half battalion each of the Bedfords and West Riding regiments. That attack failed, but a second attempt by the 58th Rifles in the early hours of the next morning led by Major Davidson-Houston succeeded at almost no cost to the 58th. Amongst the casualties of that first full day of fighting, however, were both the adjutant and the commanding officer; and one other British officer killed and one other wounded – one quarter of their British officer complement.

These heavy losses within the British officer element of all the Indian units was almost certainly a major factor in the growth of connection between the 58th Rifles and the 2nd Black Watch. As Wauchope pointed out, British officer casualties were extremely hard to replace and that it was 'no disparagement to the Indian battalions to state the obvious fact that with the loss of leaders known and trusted by them, their efficiency as units decreased'.[12] Because of that, and because the desperate manpower situation within the BEF at the end of 1914, Indian units very soon began to be set alongside British units. At first, these deployments were in company or even platoon strength, but in 1915, according to the *War Diaries*, battalion sectors were often defended by mixed battalions comprising as much as two companies of Indian troops or two of British under command of the stronger element's British or Indian Army commanding officer. In these pairings the 2nd Battalion was almost always set alongside the 58th Rifles.[13]

As 1914 drew to a close, the level of co-operation and joint working between the 2nd Black Watch and the 58th Rifles grew in frequency and complexity. The entry for 12 November of the *War Diary* of the 58th Rifles specifically mentioned the 2nd Black Watch as being next to them in the frontline for the first time.[14] It explained how the next night a German sap which had been causing both units some trouble was rushed by the 58th who bayoneted a number of Germans and chased the rest away while a party of 2nd Black Watch filled in the saps.

During November, night patrolling by both regiments continued apace. On 9 November, a night raid on a German machine gun in a sap close to the 2nd Black Watch frontline was made by a group of 20 men of the 2nd Black Watch under Captain Forrester. The machine gun had gone but the group penetrated the German lines and in the hand-to-hand fighting that followed, a number of Germans were killed, and three Black Watch men were wounded. This constant German sapping towards the 2nd Black Watch frontline from the flank was countered by aggressive 'flanking' patrolling by the 58th Rifles which culminated in an attack on 18 November by a fighting patrol from H (Afridi) Company stalking up to, then attacking the angle of the main German trench which was the start and control point of the sapping. They surprised and killed a large number of Germans, blew up that part of the German position and more importantly, collected a vast number of German papers for intelligence analysis. Two days later, German sapping began again and both battalions vigorously attacked the sap heads, but on 23 November, the Germans made a heavy attack along the entire front of the Indian Corps.

In this action, by about 10.30 that morning, the Germans penetrated the Indian Corps line on the left of the 58th Rifles which in turn was on the left of the 2nd Black Watch. As the Germans, at this point far better trained and well equipped with bombs, began bombing their way along the frontline trench, the 58th Rifles attempted and succeeded at some cost in forming stops and in establishing a flank guard on the left of The Black Watch sector. One incident at a 'stop' for which Captain Bull of the 58th Rifles was awarded the Military Cross, gave a strong indication of how effective co-operation between both regiments could be, partic-ularly considering it occurred at the point where the two battalion sectors joined. Bull 'got into a ditch with men of the 58th and Black Watch to form a 'block' and there held on with grim determination, stopping the German advance', in spite of being bombed by a party of Germans no more than 15 yards away.[15]

In the counterattack by the 58th Rifles and other Indian units that followed at 4.30 that afternoon, what Wauchope described as 'a number of Black Watch' led by Company Sergeant Major J Kennedy accompanied the 58th Rifles' attack, were according to the *Record of the 58th* actually two full platoons. The officer commanding the 58th Rifles wrote in his report that he had been greatly assisted by four men of The Black Watch who accompanied him on the final rush and 'by their example gave a fine lead to my Dogra Company, in front of whom we were'.[16] Once the objective had been taken, the four Black Watch men were placed by the commanding officer of the 58th covering an old sap and held 300 yards of frontage between the 8th Gurkhas and the 58th Rifles for some time and until reinforcements arrived. Some days later, an Indian Army Order of the Day dated 7 December 1914 specifically complimented both units on 'the steadiness of the Black Watch and the portion of the 58th Rifles next to them'.[17]

On 25 December, the decision to take the Indian Corps out of the line to be rested, to refit and to train was implemented. This respite was particularly useful for the 58th Rifles at this point because of their need to integrate new drafts from India which were of variable quality at that point. By and large, these drafts were composed of well-trained, fit men though often from other regiments, which could upset the class company balance and at times did contain reservists who were unfit for service through age or illness. Along with the rest of the Indian Corps, both the 2nd Black Watch and the 58th Rifles formed part of the Army Reserve behind the line near Lillers.

THE 2ND BLACK WATCH AND 58TH RIFLES: SCOUTING AND PATROLLING

The Indian Corps left the Army Reserve at the end of January 1915 and by mid-February, the twinning arrangements mentioned earlier, where companies of the 2nd Black Watch joined those of the 58th Rifles, began again; and entries appear in the *Record of the 58th* to that effect. It was also at this point that joint scouting and patrolling between the two battalions, which had begun in November 1914 and are mentioned specially in Wauchope's letter, developed to a new and more sophisticated level. Nevertheless, before any discussion of what gave every appearance of an excellent inter-regimental working relationship takes place, it is important that an incident involving men of the 58th Rifles is described.

The issue of promotion was very occasionally the cause of serious trouble within the Indian Army and in spite of the British officers' best efforts, did on one occasion in 1915 give cause for serious alarm at brigade level. It also involved The Black Watch in a very unwelcome disciplinary incident concerning some of the Afridi Company of the 58th Rifles.

The incident began on 3 March 1915 when a standing patrol of six Afridi sepoys and an NCO deserted to the enemy, and the relief of 12 Afridi sepoys under Jemadar (Lieutenant) Mir Mast, an Indian Army officer whose 'courage, devotion to duty and reliability had previously been unquestioned' sent to find them and man the piquet also deserted. At the time, it was thought Havildar (Sergeant) Guli Jan who had been 'passed over' for a vacant *Jemunderi* was the prime mover in the incident. Later it transpired that in fact Mir Mast who was the leader, had acted in response to German jihadist leaflets, changed sides and volunteered to take part in an ill-fated German mission to Afghanistan.

UNKNOWN NAIK (CORPORAL) OF
THE BAREILLY BRIGADE, 1914
Illustration by Joseph Lee
(University of Dundee)

Under orders of the brigade commander, the remainder of the Afridi Company were disarmed and marched to the rear by a party of Seaforths while a platoon of Black Watch took over the piquet. After certain members of the Qambar Khel tribe, all sympathisers and relatives of the deserters, were sent to a labour unit in Egypt, and after the remaining Afridis asked to be permitted to wipe out the disgrace to their company brought on by the deserters and thus regain their honour, they were rearmed and reinstated in the battalion.[18]

Nevertheless, in what must have been an act of great trust, the joint Black Watch and 58th Rifles patrols simply carried on as before. A remark in the *Record of the 58th* confirmed that, describing how Naik (Corporal) Zar Baz of the same Afridi Company and his section had held onto an exposed and valuable outpost during the action at Neuve Chapelle; and also mentioned that Baz had recently distinguished himself by a daring and important piece of scouting work in company of some men of the 2nd Black Watch. Unfortunately, no more detail appears in either regimental history or in the *War Diaries,* but that report suggests this incident took place almost immediately after the desertions on 3 March and before the action at Neuve Chapelle on the 10th of that month. Certainly, in the weeks after Neuve Chapelle when the 2nd Black Watch were in the line they continued their scouting and patrolling activities with the 58th Rifles.

In April 1915, Numbers 3 and 4 Companies of the 2nd Black Watch led by Major Wauchope were attached to the 58th Rifles under the command of Colonel Davidson-Houston of that regiment. Wauchope noted that at that time 'Battalion Scouts were reorganised and...patrolling far in advance of our lines over ground not yet consolidated by the Germans after the Neuve Chapelle battle'.[19] Wauchope was at that point in charge of the battalion scouts and was firmly of the opinion that mixed parties of Black Watch and Pathan companies were the best patrols with which he had ever worked. The *History* explained: 'The Pathans were unequalled in 'stalking' and gaining an enemy trench unseen, while the Highlanders gave the necessary steadiness and feeling of security to the whole patrol'.[20] It also appears that whenever possible, until the Indian Corps left France, this joint activity continued – including during the days before the Battles of Aubers Ridge (9 May) and Loos (25 September-8 October).

THE 2ND BLACK WATCH AND 58TH RIFLES:
THE LOOS CONTROVERSY

The third memory described by Wauchope of the advance of the 58th Rifles to protect the exposed flank of the 2nd Black Watch at Loos requires a brief explanation. The role of the Indian Corps at Loos was to execute a holding attack in order to 'hold' or even attract enemy reserves to that part of the field. According to Wauchope, the attack was given 'practically unlimited forward objective' in what was intended as a deep offensive. The attack was to be made by the Meerut Division with the Garhwal Brigade on the right and the Bareilly Brigade on the left with the Dehra Dun Brigade in Divisional Reserve. The Bareilly Brigade formed up with the 2nd Black Watch on the left, the 69th Punjabis in the centre and the 4th Black Watch on the right – the 33rd Punjabis and the 58th Rifles were in reserve. Immediately the 2nd Black Watch attacked, the 58th Rifles were to occupy their trenches; then move forward to help consolidate gains made. The 2nd Black Watch flank being on the extreme left of the assault was clearly likely to be vulnerable – and increasingly so if the attack was successful, which it was in the first instance. It was intended for that flank to be protected by the 60th Brigade of the 20th Division. As the Bareilly Brigade attack progressed and took ground, it was clear the Garhwal Brigade attack had essentially failed, which exposed the right flank of the Bareilly Brigade held by the 4th Black Watch. The left flank held by the 2nd Black Watch, which was to have been protected by the 60th Brigade also became badly exposed. It was at this point in the battle that the 58th Rifles became deeply – and controversially – involved in the battle.

At around ten o'clock, Wauchope realised the weakness of his left flank and asked for artillery support and more troops to secure it. As there were no British officers present, he ordered Subedar Tikla Khan of the 58th Rifles to take his double company out of the German second line and form what amounted to a flank guard. Davidson-Houston, the officer commanding the 58th Rifles, was informed of this and added more men to the Subedar's company. At some point – allegedly without orders, or in defiance of orders which was the point of controversy – Davidson-Houston advanced to support the withdrawal of the 2nd Black Watch.

The Colonel Davidson-Houston and the rest of his headquarters including his adjutant, Lieutenant J H Milligan, two Indian officers and an unknown number of sepoys left their position to make what the *Record of the 58th Rifles* described as a 'gallant and successful attempt to cover the withdrawal of the left of our [that of the 2nd Black Watch] line'.[21] The result was that the whole of the battalion headquarters' personnel and large numbers of men of the rifle companies were killed or missing. No officer, either British or Indian of this group survived and with them disappeared all orders and papers received or issued from the time the action started.

This advance in support of the 2nd Black Watch was roundly criticised in the First Edition (1917) of *The Indian Corps in France*.[22] This caused great offence until what Colonel Lind described in the *Record of the 58th Rifles* as the 'crude and inaccurate account' of Colonel Davidson-Houston's action in support of the 2nd Black Watch was corrected in the Second Edition (1919).[23] Nevertheless, even after that correction, judging by the tone of the language describing the incident when the *Record of the 58th Rifles* was published in 1933, the memory was still very raw. It is also worth mentioning that part of the letter of condolence written by Wauchope to the 58th Rifles which dwelt on Davidson-Houston's personal qualities appeared immediately after the account of the battle in the *Record of the 58th Rifles* and alongside his obituary in *The Times*. It was also clear from the excerpt from the Wauchope letter that although he had not passed any opinion on the incident, this tribute by Wauchope had been written by someone who had not only known Davidson-Houston, but also his work and the high quality of his professional judgement.[24]

This close professional connection between the two commanding officers of the 2nd Black Watch and the 58th Rifles appears to have included a shared view of the tactical requirements of units operating on the Western Front. At one level, given that the two men had been in relatively close contact since 31 October 1914 when Davidson-Houston assumed command of the 58th Rifles, this is not surprising. As second in command of the 2nd Black Watch at that point, Wauchope always appears to have commanded The Black Watch element of the pairings mentioned earlier, so a common understanding between both men as to joint working arrangements had time to develop. Wauchope's involvement in general training during the time the Indian Corps was in Reserve in 1915 also meant direct contact with both the Indian as well as the British officers of the 58th Rifles.

There is also a case to be made for regarding Wauchope's own personal conduct towards the Indian officers and sepoys to have been a major contributory factor to the successful association between the two battalions. This conduct was consistent and his acknowledgement of good, professional soldiering by Indian officers and men in reports of actions and in letters to the officers commanding Indian battalions continued throughout the war. These reports and letters were at least partly instrumental in gaining honours for any man mentioned by name: an honourable mention might lead to the award of a medal or the discretionary grant of a *jagir,* or post-war land grant, given to all ranks of the Indian Army for meritorious service. In any case, the extent of his ability to work effectively with the Indian officers was confirmed by the presentation of an address in November 1915 before The Black Watch left France stating that they looked on him as one of their own officers and that they regarded The Black Watch as their most trusted fiends.[25]

THE 4TH BLACK WATCH AND THE INDIAN TROOPS: COMMUNICATION AND COMRADESHIP

The question arises as to whether there was a deeper empathy between Black Watch soldiers and the sepoys that cut across rank, religion and race and in some way lessened the likelihood of long lasting and serious racial tensions which could end in violence as alleged to have been common in 'Sajjan Singh Rangroot'? The existence of anything of that sort between the Indian Corps and The Black Watch as a whole rather than between a few battalions brigaded together would have required a number of conditions to have been in place. Some level of contact between both sides and an ability to communicate at a very basic level are the two most obvious requirements. So too was the ability, and even a willingness to recognise and record the fundamental characteristics of this interracial and intercultural relationship. In fact, in the case of the 4th Black Watch, the men of that battalion also had two highly articulate spokesmen who discussed such comradely empathy publicly, but unfortunately no such voice exists to speak on behalf of the sepoys. *Indian Voices of the Great War*, a collection of translated censored mail assembled in 1999 by David Omissi, contains no letters from sepoys of the Bareilly Brigade on the subject.[26]

SOLDIERS OF THE BAREILLY BRIGADE
Illustrations by Joseph Lee
(The Black Watch Castle and Museum)

Nevertheless, perhaps Linton Andrews' description of the comradeship between the men of the 4th Battalion and the Indians explains a great deal. He wrote:

> We of the Black Watch got on with these soldiers by sheer force of comradeship, unaided by any but the most rudimentary form of exchange of ideas...We had been warned from the beginning not to fraternise with the Indians...We were told they were queer fellows. Moreover we had heard, though not officially, the old story that the only way to make an Indian respect you was to treat him roughly. We never did that.[27]

Instead, Linton Andrews described how as they passed Indian troops, they greeted them just as they did 'The Tigers of Leicester and the Devil May Cares of the Connaught Rangers', and as he wrote, 'all would smile very happily'. Andrews also described other contacts with the Indian troops such as a 4th Battalion four-hour long halt at La Couture where Indian troops, realising The Black Watch men were very hungry, gave them dates and started cooking what sounds like rough army *chapatis* for them. There were abiding memories too of The Black Watch greeting and being greeted with 'Tik Johnnie' and 'Allyman no bon' and the 'Black Watch dam good' reply. Acts of kindness such as those involving Pipe Major Low of the 4th Battalion who painted the names of dead sepoys on grave markers for the dead men's friends and who later when he was wounded was given special care by Indian medical orderlies in hospital were recorded by Linton Andrews and in the *Dundee Advertiser*.[28] (In Andrews' words, this was 'a story in which our battalion came to take great pride'.)[29] Memories of two Punjabis joining in a 2nd versus 4th Battalion boxing match when neither man had any idea what to do but took part anyway was another. Other similar stories appear, but the reality was the disposition of the different Black Watch battalions on the Western Front meant that only the 2nd and 4th Battalions had anything approaching regular contact. The report in *The Evening Telegraph and Post* that the 6th Battalion got its first inkling of the reality of war as they marched towards the frontline when they saw a busload of Indian soldiers going by, then paused in a village where a large number of Indian wounded lay, actually indicates the occasional rather than regular nature of contact between the Indian troops in general and The Black Watch as a whole.[30] Of course, it is difficult to imagine that words and attitudes – or worse – of a racist nature were never heard or witnessed, in the case of the 2nd and 4th Battalions, but on balance, Black Watch–sepoy relations appear to have been good natured, comradely and mutually respectful.

Linton Andrews' description of each parties' actual grasp of the others language was less than generous. Of the 4th Battalion, he described the average Black Watch soldier's Hindustani vocabulary as extending to around six words. His description of friendly communication was 'as a rule we just called out the few single words of Hindustani we understood'. The ability of Indian and British troops to operate jointly does suggest at least a basic but effective level of communication between them. Certainly, there were individual Black Watch men like Second Lieutenant W George who spoke at least one Indian language (recently commissioned into the

2nd Battalion) who was killed at Neuve Chapelle while posting Indian ammunition bearers under cover. As long as British Indian Army officers were present communication would not have been a problem, but communication between Indian NCOs and sepoys and Black Watch men was rather different, particularly because in times of heavy fighting Indian Army British officers were far less likely to have survived than British officers in British regiments. Indian officers did not always speak English, though many did, but they too were not invulnerable. Most importantly, on the battlefield and elsewhere, they did not have power of command and punishment over British troops, yet somehow Indian units and the 2nd and 4th Black Watch at least all operated very successfully together. Given the number of joint patrols and incidents like that of Black Watch men joining in the counterattack of the 58th in October 1915 and 'by their example giving a lead' to sepoys, effective communication of some sort clearly existed, particularly in the 2nd Battalion.

One partial explanation for this can be found in a footnote in Wauchope's *History*. Before the 2nd Battalion left India, it received 20 reservists who had taken their discharge in India and had taken up jobs there which would have required some level of fluency in an Indian language. In addition to that, just as some Black Watch Regulars from India could often speak a little pretty uncouth Hindustani ('bolo the baht a toro'), Indian troops very quickly caught on to English and French, so that for example, hand grenades were known as 'allemande ka razhun' in the 58th Rifles.

At a more serious, level the 1st Battalion magazine, *The Red Hackle* , published in a gossip section entitled 'Orderly Room Blotting Paper' the names of three different officers who had achieved passes in Lower and Higher Standard Hindustani and Lower Standard Pushto between February and September 1898 alone.[31] *The Red Hackle* also carried a further article in its May 1898 edition encouraging all its readers to learn a native language, pointing out that the language in the teaching text *Forbes Grammar* was written in Roman script, the services of a 'munshi' cost around 20 rupees for a course and stressed the commercial advantages of language knowledge if a discharge was taken in India.[32] It also claimed that knowledge of a native language 'opened the door to appointments worth obtaining'. In fact, the issue of whether a soldier should take his discharge in India was fully discussed in *The Red Hackle,* and amongst the suggestions for employment were the railways, the police, and telegraph service; but best of all was attendance at Roorkee College for engineering which offered entry to basic, but very well paid survey work. There was also another very good reason for able Regular soldiers in India to take languages seriously: the possibility of posting to a unit like the Indian Army Transport Division where linguistically inclined soldiers could progress very quickly and draw substantial additional local pay and allowances.[33]

In addition to Linton Andrews, the Indian troops had a number of other admirers including Joseph Lee, pre-war Dundee journalist, poet and illustrator, and later soldier of the 4th Battalion when it was part of the Bareilly Brigade. Lee was already an established poet before the war. (Lee's life and work are the subject of *Fighter Writers* by Bob Burrows.[34]) It is where Lee's work touches on the Indian soldiers that is of interest here. Lee had been the editor of the *People's Journal* before the war and remained in touch with his old colleagues. After his two books of poetry, *Ballads of Battle* and *Work-A-Day Warriors,* were published during the war, the *People's Journal* published individual poems from each book every week. Lee also illustrated his own work and both volumes carry a number of fine sketches of the men, including sepoys, he knew. The *People's Journal* also published a full-page compendium of his sketches including several sketches of Indian soldiers which appeared in his books in a more refined form.[35] One sepoy in particular, Allah Dad, appeared in his poem 'Tik , Johnnie' – Lee's tribute to his Indian comrades-in-arms.

This chapter does not in any way set out to provide a critique of Lee's 'Tik Johnnie', rather to engage with one aspect of the association between both the 2nd and 4th Black Watch and the Indian troops, the work of the Indian stretcher-bearers. In 'Tik Johnnie', Lee specifically comments on their work:

> And when on stretchers dripping red,
> You bore the dying and the dead
> With pity in your wistful eye,
> Your greeting seemed half sob, half sigh –
> 'Tik Johnnie![36]

TIK, JOHNNIE!

" Tik, Johnnie ! " (pronounce Teek)—the friendly and familiar salutation between the British Tommy and his Indian comrade-in-arms, heard so frequently during the first year of the war. Freely translated, it means " good," '' all right " ; and many a time it seemed to render more tolerable, desperate and well-nigh intolerable conditions.

ALLAH DAD and Hira Singh,
You and I fought for the King !
Hajal Moka, Suba Khan,
You stood with us, man to man—
    Tik, Johnnie !

When we were tottering to our knees
Beneath a barbed cheval-de-frise,
And struggling through the muddy miles,
You'd meet us with a face all smiles
    And—Tik, Johnnie !

When we were crouching in the trench,
And choking in the smoke and stench,
The bullets falling like a flail,
You'd pass us with a friendly hail—
    Tik, Johnnie !

ALLAH DAD

'ALLAH DAD'
Poem and illustration by Joseph Lee, *Work-a-Day Warriors* (1917)

Accompanying the poems in *Ballads of Battle* is a sketch of the Indian stretcher-bearers at work simply entitled 'Via Doloroso' and subtitled 'Bringing in the wounded after the 9th of May'. This sketch is a fitting tribute to the Indian Medical Service work after the Battle of Aubers Ridge fought on that date in 1915, and which caused the whole brigade large-scale casualties. The initial attack was carried out by the Dehra Dun Brigade but failed due to ineffective bombardment and the existence of a very wide deep ditch in front of the German lines. A second attempt by the Bareilly Brigade was made that afternoon by the 2nd Black Watch, 41st Dogras and 58th Rifles joined by one company of the 4th Black Watch but that too failed for the same reason – and at dreadful cost. Thereafter, the last two companies of the 58th Rifles filed into the frontline trenches with two companies of the 4th Black Watch and waited for the whistle. At that point Joseph Lee, Linton Andrews and other Dundee journalists-turned-soldiers realised that this might well be the end, shook hands and made ready when a senior officer arrived and halted the attack.

'VIA DOLOROSO' [INDIAN SOLDIERS AT AUBERS RIDGE]
'Bringing in the wounded after 9th May'
Poem and illustration by Joseph Lee, *Work-a-Day Warriors* (1917)

The reality of Lee's sketch the 'Via Doloroso' and the involvement of the Indian Medical Service and sepoys like Allah Dad with The Black Watch came after dark when Lieutenant S Gordon, the medical officer of the 58th Rifles went into no-man's-land and organised the stretcher-bearers of the regiment to bring in the wounded. Because of the layout of the support trenches in his battalion's part of the line, Gordon was able to arrange secondary bearers in relays which allowed the battlefield to be cleared of wounded very much faster than usual. The *Record of the 58th Rifles* recorded that on that night, they had been able to bring in not only their own wounded but also all those of The Black Watch and Seaforths who had attacked over the ground in front of their trenches.[37]

CONCLUSION

Without hearing Indian voices, any conclusion must be at best partial, but reading through the war diaries and regimental histories of both regiments, the association between the 2nd Black Watch and the 58th Rifles gives every appearance of a sound working relationship based on mutual respect and trust – Afridi deserters notwithstanding – and on professional competence, generously acknowledged by both parties. It all seems rather a long way from the situation described by the Indian Corps detractors or offered in 'Sajjan Singh Rangoot' and is rather more in the spirit of Corrigan and Morton-Jack. It also seems to have been more than that too in the case of the 4th Battalion and very probably the 2nd Battalion as well. Andrews description of inter-regimental comradeship within the Bareilly Brigade, Lee's illustration – 'Via Dolorosa' – and description of Allah Dad appears to confirm that. Perhaps Lee's last wish for his old comrades in the last verse of 'Tik Johnnie' sums it up:

> May Allah, when you go above,
> Grant you the Heaven you would love;
> And if our straying footsteps meet
> Then free and friendly-like we'll greet –
> Tik, Johnnie!

---

[1] By November 1915, when the Indian Corps redeployed to the Middle East, 23 Indian infantry battalions and 17 cavalry regiments had fought on the Western Front. Over 90,000 men of the Indian Corps served on the Western Front of which over 8,500 were killed and some 50,000 wounded. In addition, around 50,000 men of the Indian labour companies served in and remained in Europe until 1919.

[2] Gordon Corrigan, *Sepoys in the Trenches: The Indian Corps on the Western Front 1914-15* (Stroud: The History Press, 2006), p56.

[3] George Morton-Jack, *The Indian Empire at War: between victory and jihad, the untold story of the Indian Army in the First World War* (London: Little, Brown, 2018), p121.

[4] Jeffrey Greenhut, 'The imperial reserve: The Indian Corps on the western front, 1914–15', *The Journal of Imperial and Commonwealth History*, 12:1, 1980, pp54, 70. See also Jeffrey Greenhut, 'Sahib and Sepoy: An Enquiry into the Relationship between British Officers and Native Soldiers of the British Indian Army', *Military Affairs*, 84:1, 1984, pp15-18.

5   Greenhut. 'The imperial reserve', p69.

6   John Keegan, *The First World War* (London: Pimlico, 1990), p141.

7   Morton-Jack, *The Indian Empire at War*, p16.

8   Corrigan, *Sepoys in the Trenches*, pxi.

9   Colonel A G Lind, DSO, *A Record of the 58th Rifles F.F. in the Great War (1914-1919)* (Dera Ismael Khan: Commercial Steam Press, 1933), p2.

10 Lind, *Record of the 58th Rifles*, p145.

11 Lind, *Record of the 58th Rifles*, p150.

12 A G Wauchope, *A History of the Black Watch in the Great War, 1914-18*, Volume 1 (London: Medici Society, 1925), p168.

13 Two companies of the 58th Rifles attached to the 2nd Black Watch and two companies of the 2nd Black Watch joined the 58th Rifles in 'B Sub section from the Cinder Track to the Orchard'. Lind, *Record of the 58th Rifles*, p23.

14 *58th (Vaughan's) Rifles F. F. War Diary*, 13 November 1914.

15 Colonel H C Wylly, *History of the 5th Battalion 13th Frontier Force Rifles 1849-1926* (London: Andrews, 2011 – facsimile 1929 edition), p70. (The 58th Vaughan's Rifles was redesignated the 13th Frontier Force Rifles in 1922 as part of a reorganisation of the Indian Army.

16 Wauchope, *History*, Volume 1, p169. Privates Swan, Venters, Boyd, McIntosh and Stewart and CSM J Kennedy each received the Distinguished Conduct Medal.

17 Lind, *Record of the 58th Rifles*, pp146-147.

18 Nine were captured by Cossack troops in Iran while escorting a German and Turkish military mission to Afghanistan, court martialled and transported to the Andaman Islands for 14 years. Mir Mast died of influenza in Germany in 1919 and Guli Jan ran a tobacconist business and a group of three ladies of easy virtue in Berlin after the war. Others were allegedly assassinated in the tribal areas following the war. None returned from the Andaman Islands. Lind, *Record of the 58th Rifles*, p25.

19 Wauchope, *History*, Volume 1, p179.

20 Wauchope, *History*, Volume 1, pp179-180.

21 Lind, *Record of the 58th Rifles*, p39.

22 Lieutenant-Colonel J W B Mereweather and Sir Frederick Smith, *The Indian Corps in France* (London: Murray, 1919 – Second Edition), pp448-453.

23 Lind, *Record of the 58th Rifles*, p39.

24 Lind, *Record of the 58th Rifles*, p42.

25 Wauchope, *History*, Volume 1, p180.

26 David Omissi, *Indian Voices of the Great War: Soldiers' Letters, 1914-18* (Basingstoke: McMillan, 1999).

27 William Linton Andrews, *The Haunting Years* (East Sussex: Reprint by Naval & Military Press), p65.

28 Linton Andrews, *Haunting Years*, p65; *Dundee Advertiser*, 24 December 1917. The orderlies left Low presents of what appears to have been Indian sweets (*mithai*) and special nutritious milk drinks (*lassi*).

29 Linton Andrews, *Haunting Years*, p65.

30 *The Evening Telegraph and Post*, 11 May 1915.

31 *The Red Hackle* at that point was the 1st Battalion magazine; not the regimental journal of the same name first published in 1921.

32 A *munchi* was an Indian teacher of native languages at all levels.

33 Staff Sergeant Major George Forrest, 2nd Black Watch, from Brechin, attached to the Indian Army Transport Division had been in the Army seven years when he achieved this rank. Forrest attended an unknown service college in India where he achieved Advanced Higher Hindustani, Pushto, Farsi (Persian) and French and was briefly an instructor. He died of cholera in Mesopotamia on the eve of commissioning into the Indian Army.

34 Bob Burrows, *Fighter Writer: The Eventful Life of Sergeant Joe Lee, Scotland's Forgotten War Poet* (Derby: Breedon Books, 2004).

35 *People's Journal*, 27 November 1915.

36 Joseph Lee, *Work-A-Day Warriors* (London: John Murray, 1917).

37 Lind, *Record of the 58th Rifles*, p31.

'THE McMICKING PAPERS'

David McMicking

MAJOR-GENERAL NEIL McMICKING, CB, CBE, DSO, MC
Colonel The Black Watch, 1952 – 1960

T HE AUTHOR of the 'McMicking Papers', my father Major-General Neil McMicking, CB, CBE, DSO, MC, was born on 3 June 1894. He was educated at Eton College and attended Royal Military College, Sandhurst, before being commissioned into The Black Watch in 1913 and posted to the 2nd Battalion in India. At some point, most probably after the Second World War, the General produced a body of writing, described here as the 'McMicking Papers', which when taken as a whole gives every appearance of being the first skeleton draft of a set of memoirs covering aspects of his service during the Great War and its immediate aftermath. These writings, hereafter the 'Papers', were assembled in loose leaf binders, with entries written in a clear, confident hand and set out in in such a way as to be easily amended, and perhaps also developed further at some point in the future.

Even so, skeleton draft or not, those sections reproduced here describing the General's time as a staff officer in France and Flanders, Belgium, allow a glimpse of a wartime world one step behind the frontline and beyond the mud and bullets, all presented in well measured, lively and very readable descriptive prose. There is a sense of immediacy and confidence about this writing which suggests he possessed an innate ability to identify what was important in what he observed. It is clear from those occasional remarks he made about his own relations with senior officers, that here was a man who regarded discretion as a virtue. His comments on daily life away from headquarters were invariably astute, pithy and concise and not without a touch of irony or dark-edged humour as some of the following short selection of excerpts show.

The war began in earnest for my father on 12 October 1914 when 2nd Battalion arrived in France from India as part of the Bareilly Brigade of the 7th Indian (Meerut) Division. A few weeks later, on 23 November 1914, the then Second Lieutenant McMicking took part in a raid on a German sap with another ten men led by the company commander of Number 3 Company, then Major and later Major-General A G Wauchope.[1] On that occasion, the Germans bolted, but at Neuve Chapelle, Second Lieutenant McMicking was amongst the wounded and was recommended for the Military Cross and the Distinguished Service Order by his commanding officer, the newly promoted Lieutenant-Colonel A G Wauchope. After the battle, and having made a good recovery from his wounds, he was posted as Adjutant to the 6th Gordons.

The General described an early encounter with the Gordon Highlanders:

My time with the 1/6th Gordons only lasted from 4th May to 25th September, 1915…I always wore my Black Watch bonnet with khaki riding breeches and this was too much for the 'K' Army battalion newly out from home. They arrested me in their trenches one day as a spy and marched me between two privates with a very trigger-happy NCO to their Bn HQ. Fortunately, I had met their adjutant so the embarrassment did not last too long.[2]

[At that point, he observed:]

In the beginning of any war unseasoned troops get spy mania in exactly the same way as seasoned troops get booby trap mania when they advance into unknown enemy country.[3]

Nevertheless, he was unstinting in his praise for the quality of the 'New Army' men he met in the Gordons, describing them as 'magnificent material' though very young and often underage at around 16.

It was during his service with the Gordons that he was wounded for the third time. This was a head wound above the left eye and this time he was evacuated by horse-drawn ambulance to a clearing hospital, then by hospital train to Rouen. The doctors thought his skull was cracked and he was put on HMHS *St. Andrew*, a former cross-Channel steamer adapted to carry 180 wounded, for Southampton. He was sent to a hospital in London but was allowed to go to a Home Service Battalion at Nigg on 25 January 1916.

By then, he had survived two years in the trenches where, according to John Lewis-Stempel, the life expectancy of a British officer in the Great War was six weeks; and in March 1917 he rejoined the 1st Battalion on the Somme.[4] The commanding officer at that point was Victor Fortune who had survived two and a half years unscathed since the 1st Battle of Ypres where he was one of only two officers left standing. In another undated excerpt, a hint of the same dark humour appears when a long forgotten German artillery tactic was described:

I was returning from the line with Rowan Hamilton when the Germans suddenly started sniping at us with field guns. This was a trick they did by estimating where we would be in two minutes and then letting go a salvo at the spot! Guy was walking behind me when suddenly shells began bursting at about 50 yards from us in soft mud in a beautiful pattern at 11, 1, 5 & 7 o'clock.[5]

It goes without saying that both men left the area in some haste.

In May 1917, my father became GSO3 in 24 Division which was the start of his connection with the world of tanks. The 'Papers' indicate that he, like so many of his contemporaries, was not immune to the so-called shock of the new and could still be surprised – as he was at seeing a tank for the first time, noting the date as 10 June 1917.[6] No doubt to his delight, in January 1918, he was made Brigade Major of the newly formed 4th Tank Brigade. However, if the tank was something of a revelation, so too was what he found at the 1st Army School at Neufchâtel-Hardelot:

> One of the things that impressed me was a visit to the Camouflage School at Wimereux. One was taken round and told to notice as much as possible. Suddenly one would find oneself looking at a field gun only five yards away which one had not previously seen owing to the camouflage net and other known modern ways of disguising it. But in those days this was quite normal. The camouflage experts were quite capable of making a dummy bullet proof tree trunk and substituting it for a similar derelict tree trunk in the front line. Thus providing a very good OP.[7]

Occasionally descriptions of what being a GSO3 actually meant appear, and while my father did wear his red tabs on his tunic, he also make a point of describing how he avoided wearing the red banded staff officer's hat. Nevertheless, membership of the 'red tabbed gentry' notwithstanding, his description of making his rounds with Kay, his much admired GSO1, gives something of a flavour of his morning routine and how easily that could be disturbed:

> I was, as GSO3, round the first line trenches nearly every day. I usually started at daylight as that was a comparatively quiet time and the routine was to ride as far as possible, leave the horses with a groom mounted on my second horse and then proceed to the front...I revelled in going round the line with Kay: I admired him so much. We got lost one morning and were not sure if we were in front of our own front line. The

trenches were not continuous. I can remember him drawing his revolver and I followed suit. Eventually we located ourselves on a trench map just in line with our most forward strong point.[8]

Another point worth making which emerges from a reading of the 'Papers' is how frequently individuals were moved around, and how fluid staff and command structures were in terms of personnel:

When I could get any time off, I used to ride over and see friends, especially those in The Black Watch who were scattered throughout the Armies. It was considered nothing to ride 32 miles to see someone: but often when one went one found on arrival they had moved.[9]

One final comment should be made here. The 'Papers' are written on one side of the page only and generally in pencil, but entries in either ink or in a less 'tired' version of the same hand and written in the same prose style appear on the second side of some pages. These give the distinct impression that the General revisited what he had written at some point. Amongst what might be termed those revisits were a number of interesting sections. One in particular stands out from other observations he made about senior officers:

Whilst at Tank Corps HQ at Bermicourt, General Freyberg one day walked in having broken down nearby on his way to Boulogne on leave. He wanted to borrow a car... I could not keep my eyes off his wound stripes; they appeared to go all round his arm. Actually he was wearing nine.[10]

Other remarks, such as that concerning the inability of the French ever to start an operation on time and what that said about the quality of their staff work, as well as his opinion of the Portuguese were also confined to the reverse pages.

Of course, there is a great deal more to the 'Papers' than those shown in this short sample. The post-war sections not discussed here do deserve serious academic attention, particularly where these touch on contact with the White Russians in Silesia under Lieutenant-General Deniken. The 'Papers' are also valuable in that they give a very good indication of the weight of responsibility borne by very young officers during the Great War, particularly given it took 12 years of peacetime soldiering for my father to reach the rank he had held in 1919, and 16 years to reach GSO2 again. Nevertheless, there is more than a hint in the text that good luck and good fortune had been with the General in the trenches and South Russia and would remain with him even during the Second World War. Even so, the appearance of the 'Papers' almost a century after they were produced does beg the question – how many more similar sets of papers exist within the extended regimental family?

---

[1] A G Wauchope, *A History of the Black Watch in the Great War, 1914-18*, Volume 1 (London: Medici Society, 1925), p169.

[2] 'McMicking Papers', p15. The Black Watch Museum Archive.

[3] 'McMicking Papers', p15.

[4] John Lewis-Stempel, *Six Weeks: The Short and Gallant Life of the British Officer in the First World War* (London: Weidenfeld & Nicholson. 2010), p5.

[5] 'McMicking Papers', p30.

[6] 'McMicking Papers', p28.

[7] 'McMicking Papers', pp20-21. An OP was an 'observation post'.

[8] 'McMicking Papers', p31.

[9] 'McMicking Papers', p31.

[10] 'McMicking Papers', p51 (reverse side). General Bernard Freyberg, VC, was a New Zealander and the youngest general in the British Army during the Great War. He served in Gallipoli and on the Western Front. He won three Distinguished Service Orders.

THE WAUCHOPE MEDALLION

A HUNDRED YEARS ON

Fraser Brown

INTRODUCTION

AT THE END of the section on the 2nd Battalion Black Watch's service in Mesopotamia in Brigadier A G Wauchope's three-volume study, *A History of the Black Watch in the Great War, 1914-18,* an explanatory note appears regarding the Wauchope Medallion. This was an award, commissioned by the then Lieutenant-Colonel Wauchope, awarded only to men of 2nd Battalion over the relatively short period of time he commanded the battalion.[1]

The note begins with an acknowledgement that in a regiment such as The Black Watch, 'many gallant acts go unrewarded', but that while the rank and file understood this, nevertheless their commanding officer was 'eager' to recognise distinguished service in battle. That recognition was given practical shape by the award of a silver medallion which Wauchope awarded to individual non-commissioned officers and soldiers for acts of gallantry or leadership in battle. The obverse displayed an allegory of 'Victory' holding out a victor's crown, while the reverse was engraved with the owner's name, a designation including the name of the action involved, and the legend 'Presented by Colonel A G Wauchope'. According to the note, 60 of these medals were given to men who had been recommended for gallantry awards after Loos, the 'Battle Beyond Baghdad' (also known as Mushaidie) and to men involved in scouting in no-man's-land before Loos. However, the note does not mention the award of another four Wauchope Medallions made for gallantry following the explosion of a German mine at Givenchy. Two other Wauchope Medallions were awarded to the Regimental Sergeant Major and the Pioneer Sergeant: 'For valuable services towards the capture of enemy trenches'. The note ended with the observation that Wauchope

Medallions were highly prized by the men who won them but too often 'are treasured by the widows as a symbol of great deeds done by men of The Black Watch for their regiment and country'.

A century later, at a time when Great War memorabilia commands not only high prices at auction, but also often holds significant research interest for collectors, the appearance of a Wauchope Medallion for sale is something of an event. In 2014, research by Bill Longair and Tony Leszczuck published in Volume 2 of *Great War Medal Collectors Companion* identified a total of 95 men awarded Wauchope Medallions with three men winning a second thus making the total number of Wauchope Medallions awarded as 98.[2] This figure matches the results of a 2010 unpublished research paper, *The Wauchope Medallion*, by Tom Smyth, former Archivist of The Black Watch Regimental Museum.[3] Longair and Leszczuck claim the total number identified as surviving in collections is 28 and The Black Watch Castle and Museum confirm the existence of eight in its collection. The research notes of Tom Smyth also indicate a steady trickle of requests for information on individual winners from families throughout his time in post which in turn suggests that the award of a Wauchope Medallion to a Black Watch soldier has become part of both wider individual family and regimental historical memory of the Great War. Yet, important as collectors, museums and family collections of memorabilia are to the survival of Wauchope Medallions in general, their physical existence is only one aspect of their importance to the regimental story. As for the wider history of the 2nd Battalion, of far greater importance is what the award of these Wauchope Medallions reveals about the men who won them, the actions they fought in, the nature of the unit they belonged to, and indeed the man who awarded them.

At a superficial level, the Wauchope Medallion might be seen as the gift of a proud commanding officer to a group of men whose service he regarded as deserving of recognition, yet who had been overlooked for more formal honours. However, the deeply respectful tone of local newspaper reports of these awards, as well as the high regard in the regimental heartland and beyond in which these medallions were held by families and comrades in arms, clearly indicates the award of a Wauchope Medallion was much more than that. This chapter sets out to explore what that wider importance to the story of the 2nd Battalion actually was, not only in the celebration of episodes of individual gallantry, but also what these awards reveal as to the kind of conduct on the battle-field was deemed worthy of special mention. It will also examine the relationship between Colonel Wauchope's training regime, the action of individual soldiers on the battlefield and recognition of their behaviour by the award of Wauchope Medallions. Finally, some thoughts are offered on the importance of local press reports and the influence of the Wauchope name in assuring the contemporary status and the longevity of interest in the award.

THE CIRCUMSTANCES IN WHICH AWARDS WERE MADE

The vast majority of awards of Wauchope Medallions were made for two 2nd Battalion actions: the diversionary attack as part of the Indian Corps on the first day of Loos in September 1915 and the fight at Mushaidie in March 1917. In discussion of the action at Loos, this section draws heavily on the information contained in a handwritten list of officers and other ranks held in The Black Watch Museum Archive apparently compiled in the aftermath of the action at Loos and referred to here as the *List of Recommendations*.[4] This list, which includes all of the recommendations for the Victoria Cross (VC) and Distinguished Conduct Medal (DCM) made by the 2nd Battalion, coincides exactly with the list of men awarded a Wauchope Medallion for Loos. Included in the list, appearing at the side of each name are the individual citations for the awards recommended. Unfortunately, no such list has been located for Mushaidie.

In many ways it is difficult to imagine two battles more different in every respect than Loos and Mushaidie, yet in both cases three clearly identifiable common features were present. First, each fight began with very heavy losses amongst the subaltern ranks, and second, each battle followed on from a period of intensive training which evidence suggests was directed by Colonel Wauchope. Finally, Wauchope was present at the two major actions and appears to have either witnessed or been close to other activities for which Wauchope Medallions were awarded.[5]

According to the *2nd Black Watch War Diary* and the account of the actions at Loos and Mushaidie in the Wauchope *History,* as commanding officer, Wauchope was not only involved in running these battles at battalion level but was also invariably in the parlance of the time – 'well forward'. At Loos, he was close to the frontline in the nights before the battle. That in turn meant he was in a position to witness many of the incidents of gallantry or individual assumption of leadership roles which were acknowledged later by the award of a medallion. In addition, during the blowing up of the German mines at Givenchy on 3 October 1915, which resulted in the award to Sergeant Hutchinson and three other men, Wauchope was not present, but was in command of the battalion and therefore close to the action in the third or more likely second-line trenches. [6]

On the evidence of the *War Diaries* entries for Loos and Mushaidie, it is clear that the very early heavy loss of subalterns did create situations where the need for non-commissioned ranks to assume leadership responsibilities was urgent. At Loos, for example, '[at 6am] half the officers were casualties before the enemy front line was reached' and when officer casualties at this point are examined, they were overwhelmingly from within the subaltern ranks who were the platoon commanders. In fact, by the end of the battle that group accounted for four dead and five wounded of the 15 officer casualties, while of the four company commanders, one was killed and two were wounded. By 7am, 'twelve out of the twenty officers' who began the day were casualties with the remaining three falling later. The full impact of these losses is clear from 'Point 2' of the explanation of the withdrawal phase in the *2nd Black Watch War Diary* when the author explained in something of an understatement, 'lack of officers made reorganization difficult'. In an action such as Loos, fought out in a complex enemy trench system where the ebb and flow of battle meant immediate tactical perspectives changed rapidly, the loss of the battalion second-in-command, the adjutant and three of the four company commanders could easily have been catastrophic for the surviving men of the battalion had the next layers of the command and control structure not held firm.

The extent to which the next level of leadership was able to assume responsibility was illustrated in the account of Loos in Wauchope's

History (written by Wauchope himself) when Company Sergeant Major (CSM) Houston, Sergeants Whytock, Lees and Strachan, and Lance Corporal Martin were named as having led their platoons on the death or wounding of their officers. Lance Corporal Martin's citation states that he showed 'Great gallantry and judgement in leading his Platoon after his seniors had been killed, through three lines of German trenches' which suggests not only that the platoon officer, sergeant and the corporals had been killed, but that as lance corporal he was the most senior soldier left.[7] Interestingly too, a close reading of the *List of Recommendations* referenced earlier shows the citations of the other four men mentioned as assuming command of platoons all employ language which suggests not only gallant, but also effective leadership was highly valued. In that respect it is also noticeable that the idea that these men displayed 'good judgement' appears in all five citations in combination with either 'coolness', 'daring' or 'gallantry'. Other entries on the *List of Recommendations* for men who took leadership roles when their immediate superiors became casualties employ similar language. Included in that category was the note for Private McGregor who led his section when his corporal was killed, and Lance Corporal Wynn who not only held a 'block' but who, as the last NCO left alive, carried out a successful withdrawal when ordered.

The same idea of both effective and gallant action is also seen in the citations involving fighting round the 'blocks' set up at Loos to protect the battalion's weak left flank from vigorous German counterattacks and infiltration of their bombers along their own trench lines. The account of that battle in Wauchope's *History* indicates that German bombing parties were met by counter bombing and by dogged resistance wherever 'blocks' were set up, and though Black Watch men holding these were relieved by soldiers of the 60th Brigade on their left, nonetheless other 'blocks' were set up later in an attempt to secure the battalion's left flank. The *List of Recommendation*s indicates that at least six of the 11 men mentioned as having been noticed for their 'cool and determined fighting' were named as 'holding' or 'establishing' a 'block'. It is also noticeable that when Privates John McKinnon and A Clark held their 'blocks', they had no hesitation in using German bombs when their own supply ran out, or of picking up and using German rifles when their own failed. The reason for these weapon failures was not stated but given that resupply of ammunition was an ongoing concern at Loos and the fact that citations were written for three men sent back to bring up the reserve ammunition, lack of ammunition may have been the cause.

Private Clark was not alone in using captured or abandoned enemy firearms, an action which in itself indicates not only desperation to hold on, but also a level of personal confidence associated with very well-trained soldiers. That level of confidence must also have included a high level of trust in their officers, because a British soldier in action found without his rifle (unless they slung their SMLEs while using the G98s) could be seen as having 'shamefully cast aside his arms'- a charge which carried the death penalty. Similarly, there is also a sense in which the sergeants who took over platoons which they led to achieve their objectives could only have succeeded as they did if they were well briefed both about their objectives and the geography of the enemy position, particularly at Loos where the German trench system was fairly complex. It can also be argued that it was Wauchope's leadership and particularly his training regime put in place before both Loos and Mushaidie which was responsible for both building confidence and 'skilling up' non-commissioned men awarded medallions to first assume, then effectively execute leadership roles as officer casualties mounted. Certainly, Wauchope Medallion awards went to men who were not only gallant, but also the successful products of his training regime. In that context, it is important to look at the role of Wauchope as a trainer, particularly in the case of bombers awarded a Wauchope Medallion and nominated for the DCM.

TRAINING, PERFORMANCE AND AWARDS: LOOS

When Wauchope's *History* is read alongside the *2nd Battalion War Diaries*, it is clear that Wauchope's reputation as a trainer of troops for battle was widely known and respected, even to the extent that he was seen as 'a commanding officer who had a genius for training troops for war and who brought to the task an energy and driving power that allowed no opportunity to be wasted'.[8] In the days before Loos and later, particularly in the first days after the arrival of the 2nd Battalion in Mesopotamia, entries in the *2nd Black Watch War Diary* and Wauchope's *History* indicate Wauchope took a strong interest in the training of his battalion. The extent to which that interest either predated or was greatly developed during his short stay with the 3rd Battalion training at Nigg in 1915 is debatable, but what is clear is that along with other wounded officers and NCOs, he was heavily involved in what the *History* describes as 'the development of training for modern war'.[9] It is also fair to say that from evidence elsewhere across all three volumes of the *History* and Black Watch *War Diaries* in general, although a strong training ethos existed across the entire regiment, Wauchope's tenure as commanding officer of the 2nd Battalion was particularly noteworthy in that respect.

On 6 September 1915, Wauchope (as Major) assumed command of the 2nd Battalion on appointment to temporary command of the Dehra Dun Brigade of Colonel William James St John Harvey. A few days later he introduced what was for the time, a highly innovative training regime. At that point in the war aerial photography was in its infancy, but a set of pictures showing the German positions were received by the Battalion and immediately Wauchope ordered a full-scale model of the enemy's trench system to be reconstructed on the ground behind the lines. Later in the war this training method was near universally adopted for attacks, but at that point as Wauchope's *History* clearly states, this was a fairly novel approach and its value was not then widely understood. Nevertheless, the battalion practised over the model and in the opinion of the author of that section of Wauchope's *History* 'to Major Wauchope's foresight the Battalion owed the advantage undoubtedly obtained in the attack from the precious rehearsals'.[10]

Of course, to some extent any training regime set up by Wauchope would have been subject to constraints of training directives from higher authorities, but as officer commanding the 2nd Battalion he would have had considerable discretion which he appears to have used. This was particularly noticeable in the training of bombers, always a vital component of any attack on German trench systems during the Great War, and which was a priority across the Army as a whole. Ironically, given that Wauchope's own wounds which caused him to be sent to

Nigg early in 1914 as an instructor were caused by both rifle and hand grenades, it was he who gave the first instruction in bomb throwing at that camp. Even so, this training of bombers was given a special mention on several occasions including the *2nd Black Watch War Diary* entry for 7-11 September 1915 when the battalion was in divisional reserve at La Gorgue noted the organisation and 'training of specialists in bombing'.

Part of the reason that so much attention was paid to the training of bombers before Loos was that in the early days of the war the British Army was largely untrained in the use of grenades, and was issued with at least six different types, most of which had fuses that had to be physically lit, therefore accidents were common and results poor.[11] Moreover, the famous Mills bomb had not been adopted as the standard British Army grenade: that did not happen until a decision of the Army Council of 20 November 1915 although a few of the earliest version were used as early as July 1915. In the 2nd Battalion, however, at this time and almost certainly across the regiment as a whole, a tactical doctrine appeared to be developing which regarded bombing sections as vital to both the fighting ethos of the battalions and their operational performance. This view was best expressed by the author of the section of *History* listing the 2nd Battalion officers and NCOs – including bombing sergeants and corporals – on arrival in Mesopotamia.[12] He wrote:

> They were picked men and became a moral asset in every company...[the bombing sections were] as ready with the rifle and bayonet as the grenade formed rallying points or gave fresh impetus to the attack.[13]

The extent to which that remark was also true at Loos can be seen in the numbers of men from that group named in Wauchope's *History* and also in details of their actions in the *List of Recommendations*.

At Loos, of the four men recommended for the VC that day, all were involved in bombing. Sergeant John Mitchell, DCM, recommended unsuccessfully three times for the VC during the war won a bar to his DCM for leading his bombers and driving back the enemy over 250 yards, then continuing the fight using German bombs until relieved by another unit. Sergeant John Easton, who led his platoon and continued to re-supply them with grenades – even though his uniform and equipment had been badly burned – by crossing open ground by crossing open ground was killed and was thus ineligible for an award. Captain A Denison, after reorganising and leading his company which had been badly gassed through the German second line, then led bombing parties gaining some 300 yards of enemy trench, but he, like Sergeant Easton received no award. Finally, Piper MacDonald, who after playing his platoon through the German first and second line, continued playing at their head on top of the parapet till wounded as they bombed their way along the German third line was awarded the DCM.

Lance Corporals Pratt, Clark and Wynn and Privates Pryde, W McLaren and R McDonald were all recommended for the DCM and received medallions for their successful work as bombers. Lance Corporals Clark and Wynn were also both involved in holding 'blocks' as well as in bombing, but Lance Corporal Pratt's recommendation included mention of not only the good judgement he employed as leader of a bombing party, but also his earlier valuable work in training bombers. Private Pryde's endurance and Private McLaren's leadership were also recognised, whereas Private Ronald MacDonald was recognised for rushing ahead as bayonet man of a bombing party that gained over 300 yards of enemy trench and in his case was awarded a DCM. Private Archibald Stirton led his party over 250 yards of German trenches, captured 15 prisoners and killed others.

It is also interesting to note that a number of men who were very definitely not members of bombing sections were involved – or involved themselves in bombing at Loos. That in turn lends credence to the assertion that bombers were 'moral assets' and 'formed rallying points or gave fresh impetus' to an attack'. In fact, when the entries on the *List of Recommendations* are taken as a whole a number of examples of that trend emerge. Piper Armitt, recommended for his gallant piping, joined in the bombing while Private James Ferguson, a runner who carried messages across open ground until his captain was killed also joined a bombing party. Private John Gibb, the commanding officer's orderly joined in locating enemy bombing groups at close range – an activity completely unrelated to his usual duties which would have included carrying messages and keeping contact with the rifle company commanders who had survived.

WAUCHOPE MEDALLION
Awarded to Private James Ferguson, 2nd Black Watch

TRAINING, PERFORMANCE AND AWARDS: MUSHAIDIE – THE 'BATTLE BEYOND BAGHDAD'

While training of bombing sections was the clear priority on the Western Front, the move to Mesopotamia in 1916 brought a new set of training requirements. During the voyage every effort had been made to keep the men fit, but during a halt at Amarah on the Tigris, the 2nd Battalion were able to carry out a practice attack which 'bore fruit' when the battalion was required to 'attack in earnest with no time for preparation or orders' at Shaikh Sa'ad.[14] Nonetheless, as might be expected, that engagement was a costly failure resulting in Wauchope being wounded and the 2nd Battalion being reduced to around half of its disembarkation strength. The assault on Hanna, the formation of the Highland Battalion with the remnants of the Seaforths, the assaults on Sannaiyat and the Fall of Kut followed, but in July 1916 the Highland Battalion paraded for the last time and the 2nd Battalion reformed.

With the coming of the cooler weather the health of 2nd Battalion improved, and on 4 November 1916 it was split once more into four companies for tactical purposes. Even so, sickness and small but regular numbers of casualties meant constant change of command in companies and platoons. Nevertheless training for the next fighting season was well under way, led by Wauchope who had returned from convalescence in India in late May 1916.[15] The issue of Lewis guns to the Indian Corps for the first time in August 1916, an allocation which rapidly increased from one gun per company to four, meant skilling up Lewis gun teams was perhaps the most immediate training need, but the demand for scout, signaller, sniper and bombing training was also very high. Night exercises were a constant feature of time outwith the trenches and largely the means by which the men were made fit to endure the long marches that would come when they returned to the offensive in December 1916. In the mind of the author of Chapter V of the *History*, this had been effort well spent and that there was after that point a strong and continuous sense in which the successes in operations was 'due chiefly to the thoroughness and knowledge with which this period of training was used'.[16] The same author also observed 'what a disciplined and handy machine for open warfare it [the 2nd Batallion] had become as a result of the training in the summer' and more ominously, 'The hour was fast approaching when the value of this training, the fine quality of the unit it had produced and the worth of the men who composed it were to be proved in pitched battle'.[17] However all battles are by their nature highly unpredictable affairs, so while training and planning for heavy officer casualties could go some way to maintaining the effectiveness of any battalion, a note of realism was injected by a remark in Wauchope's *History* that on arrival in Mesopotamia 'though men were held in readiness to take the place of every leader, the greater number of these 'second strings also fell' in the first weeks in theatre.[18]

Certainly, Wauchope had no doubt as to the link between high quality training and individual and unit performance. The clearest statement of that idea appeared in the *2nd Black Watch War Diary* on 28 March when he addressed the battalion following a reading of the letter of congratulation from the corps commander, General Cobb, on their behaviour at Mushaidie on 14 March 1917. Wauchope's reaction was to drive home the message that 25 September 1915 (Loos) and 14 March, 1917 (Mushaidie) would always be Red Letter Days for they 'showed what good work could be done by constant training, discipline and a good feeling of comradeship between all ranks'.[19] That opinion of the 2nd Battalion's performance at

Mushaidie was echoed in Wauchope's *History*: 'The victory at Mushaidie stands out as the finest achievement of the Battalion during the war'.[20]

At Mushaidie – as at Loos – casualties amongst junior officers were heavy: seven of the 15 subalterns were killed or wounded quite early in the fight. Although there is no equivalent *List of Recommendation* for Mushaidie as there was for Loos, nevertheless the language used in the citations of men who were awarded the DCM for that engagement placed placed as great a value on initiative and effectiveness as on personal gallantry. The citation of CSM J M Millar when read alongside Wauchope's *History* is a very good example of that tendency.[21]

> After all his company officers had become casualties he took command and led forward his company with the greatest coolness and judgement. …he reorganised two companies and by his resource enabled an early continuance of the advance…

In addition, the *History* described how Millar had seven bullet holes in his kilt and several more in his equipment which gives some indication of the risks involved in leading his men with 'great dash' as described in his citation.[22] The final sentence read simply, 'His zeal and energy were beyond all praise'.

The wording of the award of the DCM to Sergeant J Strachan followed a similar pattern. He was one of two NCOs named in the *2nd Black Watch War Diary* as the recipient of an 'Immediate Award' of the DCM granted by the Army Commander formally announced after Wauchope read General Cobb's letter on 28 March 1917. According to the citation, Strachan took command of the left flank of the battalion – all four of the company's officers had been wounded – and 'ably directed their fire', then later led the survivors of his company across open ground in the final assault, drove the enemy out of their positions and took some prisoners.[23] The citation of Lance Corporal D McCabe, the other man granted an 'Immediate Award' of the DCM that day, described how he saw that a gap existed between the Indian Regiment (56th Rifles) and his own and that all their officers in that area were casualties. He immediately took charge of the Indian Lewis guns and closed up the gap then later in the battle took charge of the sepoys and led them across open ground in the final charge on the Turkish positions. Again, the twin themes of effectiveness and initiative are married with either a statement or an implication of attendant gallant conduct.

Nevertheless, the three men awarded the DCM at Mushaidie account for only three of 47 Wauchope Medallions awarded for that action. The awards were made in two parades: the first on 21 January 1918 and again in March 1918 at Moscar Camp in Egypt when 27 and 20 Wauchope Medallions respectively were presented. On these, according to Longair and Leszczuck, three forms of inscription exist:

> For Gallantry in the Battle Beyond Baghdad (14 known)
> For Good Service in the Battle Beyond Baghdad (3 known)
> For the Battle Beyond Baghdad (35).[24]

Yet, evocative as these inscriptions are, they do little to clarify the circumstances in which individual medallions were won. A Mushaidie equivalent of *List of Recommendations* after Loos is sorely missed here, and the *History* is of very little help in this case because unlike the description of Loos there is no section naming men worthy of special recognition.

Unfortunately, the account of the battle by Wauchope in 'With A Highland Regiment in Mesopotamia', initially published in *Blackwood's Magazine* in August 1917 names only two men: Lieutenant Gillespie, the machine-gun officer who was killed and Second Lieutenant, but wrongly described as Sergeant Major, Ben Houston. In fact, the date of Houston's commission indicated that not only had he assumed the duties of an officer a month before but had also as second lieutenant led the patrol which secured Baghdad railway station on 11 March 1917. On the other hand, the general description of the battle suggests certain groups which might have been awarded medallions. The lance corporal who after six men senior to him became casualties led on his platoon might have been one, but so too might some of the Lewis gunners who, unable to move as quickly as the riflemen, tended to suffer heavy casualties. Similarly, the signallers, one of whom left a record of his experience of Mushaidie might also have been given awards. Certainly, Sergeant Yule, named by Private George M Brown in his memoir of service in Mesopotamia as very active in advising and training signallers on arrival in theatre did receive a .[25] Wauchope showed his awareness of their service when he remarked 'nothing was carried out with greater bravery, than the maintenance of communication throughout the battle'.[26] Men involved in the resupply of ammunition were also likely recipients of Wauchope Medallions. However, without being able to cross reference the names of men awarded medallions with individuals or groups named in some as yet undiscovered Mushaidie *List of Recommendations* or in the *History* as these were in the Loos chapter, little more can be said.

PRESS REPORTS AND
PUBLIC PERCEPTIONS

At a time when any news of local men serving overseas was at a premium, the award of the Wauchope Medallion to a local man published in any of the large number of local Scottish newspapers would have been a widely discussed topic in their old work places, churches, clubs or between their old neighbours. In fact, judging by the content and tone of a number of articles in local Scottish newspapers where the award of a Wauchope Medallion was mentioned, knowledge of both the existence and the significance of the medallion was widespread well beyond the coterie of serving Black Watch recipients and their immediate families. It was clear too, from the number of times the wording of the dedication engraved on individual medals was quoted verbatim in the press, that either soldiers included that information in letters home, or perhaps was discovered if soldiers sent their medallions home for safekeeping.

These short notices also indicate that the award of the Wauchope Medallion was something worthy of public notice. That was particularly evident in the use of Sergeant James Brodie's award by the Reverend Mr Johnston of Allen Park Church in Stirling in his address on 'Gallantry' to his congregation on 14 April 1918. During the address, the minister not only showed the congregation the medal, but also commented on how it had been awarded for 'conspicuous gallantry on the field in battle against the Turks' near Baghdad on 14 March 1917.[27] Sergeant Brodie's record of service on 'three fronts' and the fact that he had been wounded three times was also stressed, as was his father's connection with that church as church officer.

At times, a significant amount of detail of how the award was won was given. Sergeant J Hutchison's award was published in the *Fife Free Press* under the heading 'Kirkcaldy Soldier's Gallantry' and subtitled 'A Givenchy Award'.[28] The article contained an account of the action and that his award had been published in 'a short account' although there is was no mention as to where that was published. However, the *Fife Free Press* account of the action did quote part of his DCM citation verbatim so the mystery 'short account' may have been taken from the London Gazette, yet the *Fife Free Press* did not mention the actual award of that decoration. Instead, it announced the presentation of a silver medal by Lieutenant-Colonel A G Wauchope and quoted from his DCM citation stressing how after the explosion of a German mine '[i]t was due to his coolness, courage, and in grasping the critical situation that the gaps [in the defences] were filled up so promptly' and that Sergeant Hutchison's platoon was ready to meet the following attack.[29] A week later, when the same newspaper published the news that Sergeant Hutchison had been wounded while serving in Mesopotamia, it identified him first as 'Givenchy Hero' and also as a Wauchope Medallion holder.[30] No mention of his DCM has been found in the *Fife Free Press*.

Private John Queen's Wauchope Medallion, which had been won at Mushaidie with Number 2 Company arrived at his parents' house in Kirkintilloch after something of an adventure. It had been sent home to his parents for safekeeping but had been in a consignment of mail bound for Britain when the ship was sunk. The mail was salvaged some time later and the medallion arrived at Kirkintilloch when, as the article in the *Kirkintilloch Herald* announcing the award mentioned, the box had been damaged by salt water and both the medallion and box 'bore evidence of their stay in the depths of the sea'.[31] Private Queen did survive the fighting but died of 'malarial fever' in Palestine on 16 November 1918.[32]

The announcement of Lance Corporal Robert Pratt's death in action in the *Fifeshire Advertiser* mentioned not only the award of the Wauchope

Medallion to him, but also gave a detailed account of how he won it.[33] The same article included the comment that he had been recommended for the DCM on three occasions but had received nothing as well as the comment by a former comrade home on leave that he was 'the most daring and fearless man in the regiment'. The tone of the report of the award of the medal to Pratt is also typical of all similar reports: these men may not have received a DCM, but this was not in any sense a second-class award. To some extent at least that attitude can be explained not only by the unique character of the medal in that it was a private regimental award, but also by the reputation of Colonel Wauchope, the man who introduced the award.

Certainly, the very name Wauchope figured large in Black Watch iconography both before, during and after the Great War and there is no doubt that Black Watch old soldiers and new recruits alike would have been very familiar with it. In part, this was due to the death of General Andrew Gilbert Wauchope at Magersfontein at the head of the Highland Brigade and the ongoing memorialisation of both his name and that of the Highland Brigade. The erection of a memorial window in St Giles' Cathedral in May 1901, unveiled in the presence of a large Black Watch contingent present as both part of the congregation and in a ceremonial role, was a part of that.[34] Similarly in Perth, the regimental depot town, a plaque and memorial window were unveiled in St Ninian's Cathedral in May, 1903 and in St John's Church another memorial was erected in 1905, perpetuating the memory of the Wauchope name. So too in a much less genteel way did a number of travelling public slide shows such as one entitled 'Kruger and Khaki' presented by Mr Frederick Villiers, war artist for the *Illustrated London News* which invariably included a section on the death of General Wauchope.[35]

The Wauchope name was further kept alive by the opening by Lord Roberts of the Wauchope and Black Watch Memorial Home in Scott Street, Perth, on 15 August 1903. This facility was intended as a place where young soldiers could gather, write their letters home and socialise away from temptations of different sorts, and as such was a happy recruiting ground for the Army Temperance Association. It was there too, that Lady Wauchope while a guest at Kilgraston, a large mansion a few miles from Perth used as a hospital during the Great War, in September

1903, visited the widows of the officers and men killed at Magersfontein.[36] Large numbers of Black Watch men were treated there from time to time by different groups or prominent local citizens like Mrs Lawrence Pullar, who entertained 85 recruits to tea at Christmas, 1908 and another 70 men of The Black Watch Special Reserve after New Year 1909.[37]

Later in 1917, an extension to the Memorial Home was opened close to the railway station for soldiers in transit or on leave. It provided men with only a few hours to spare between trains with a safe place where they could leave their kit, get an affordable meal, a wash or even a few hours' sleep. In the period between January and June 1917, over 9,000 men slept in the extension and made use of its facilities. During the war, there was no doubt about how highly this facility was regarded by the local military establishment, for when the case of Mr Lockyer, superintendent of the Memorial Home initially assessed as unfit for service was re-assessed as fit came before the Perth Tribunal, the importance of his work was explained and he was immediately granted immediate unconditional exemption. In fact, all things considered, and given the numbers of men known to have used the Memorial Home it would have been very unusual for any Black Watch soldier who served either before the outbreak of war or during it not to have known the Wauchope name before he left Perth Depot at Queen's Barracks.

In the years after the Great War, the association of the Wauchope name with The Black Watch remained as strong as ever. Field Marshal Earl Wavell wrote in Wauchope's obituary in *The Red Hackle* that two important regimental institutions were largely the result of his energies at the conclusion of the war: the introduction of the regimental journal *The Red Hackle* and the publication of the Wauchope *History* which, according to Wavell, he financed, edited and partly wrote himself.[38] This publication was also of larger significance too, in that as Wauchope described in the book's preface, it was the fulfilment of an ambition he found amongst many of his men, for they wanted to see a history of the regiment 'written and published at such a price as would render its purchase possible by all ranks and their relatives'.[39]

A CONCLUDING QUESTION
AND A THOUGHT

So why did the Wauchope Medallion first achieve then retain such eminent status within The Black Watch regimental family and beyond? The interest of medal collectors and the ever-rising monetary value of each example certainly played a role. So too did its association with the Wauchope name. But surely of far greater importance was that this was a personal award from a commanding officer who served in close physical proximity to his men at Loos and Mushaidie, who not only knew individual soldiers but also witnessed their courage, and thus the enduring status of the award was assured.

---

1 A G Wauchope, *A History of the Black Watch in the Great War, 1914-18*, Volume 1 (London: Medici Society, 1925), p269. During the period covered by this chapter Wauchope held three different ranks: Major and Second-in-command of 2nd Battalion from 26 March 1915 – 6 September 1915; Lieutenant-Colonel of 2nd Battalion from 6 September 1915 – 20 April 1917; Brigadier of 8th Brigade from 20 April 1917.

2 Howard Williamson, *The Great War Medal Collectors Companion Volume 2* (Harwich: Collectors Guide Publications, 2014), pp903-904.

3 The author is grateful to Thomas B Smyth, former archivist, for sight of his research notes and *The Wauchope Medallion*, his unpublished research paper of 2010.

4 *Loos. 2nd Battalion, The Black Watch. List of Officers and Other Ranks Recommended for Awards* (unnumbered). The Black Watch Museum Archive.

5 Wauchope's own account of the action at Loos shows how mobile he was on the battlefield and how far forward he was. Wauchope, *History,* Volume 1, pp187-192.

6 Loos: 'Much reconnaisance and intelligence survey work was undertaken by Major A G Wauchope DSO and Sergeant A MacDonald (Scout Sergeant)', which meant that he would have been aware of the work of the ten men awarded medallions for their part in that. Mushaidie: Wauchope was with the assault companies at the beginning of the action when he 'gave the final instructions'; he was later again present with the assault companies and moved his headquarters nearer to the fighting on two occasions. *2nd Black Watch War Diary*, 18 September 1915, 3 October 1915, 14 March 1917.

7 Martin's citation *List of Recommendations.* (No page numbers.)

8 Wauchope, *History,* Volume 1, p238.

9 Wauchope, *History,* Volume 1, p348.

[10] Wauchope, *History,* Volume 1, p185.

[11] Charles Messenger *Call to Arms: The British Army 1914-18* (London: Weidenfeld & Nicholson, 2005), pp191-192.

[12] Wauchope, *History,* Volume 1, p204.

[13] Wauchope, *History,* Volume 1, p206.

[14] Wauchope, *History,* Volume 1, p211.

[15] This is described in some detail in Wauchope, *History,* beginning with a full listing the company commanders and senior NCOs. Wauchope, *History,* Volume 1, pp233-242.

[16] Wauchope, *History,* Volume 1, p239.

[17] Wauchope, *History,* Volume 1, p251.

[18] Wauchope, *History,* Volume 1, p206.

[19] *2nd Black Watch War Diary*, 28 March 1917.

[20] Wauchope, *History,* Volume 1, p257.

[21] Later commissioned (20 August 1918).

[22] Wauchope, *History,* Volume 1, p255.

[23] 'With A Highland Regiment in Mesopotamia', *Blackwood's Magazine*, August 1917, p160.

[24] Williamson, *War Medal*, Volume 2, pp904-7.

[25] Brown George M. *Part 2: Army Years 1915-1919*. The Black Watch Museum Archive (Ref. 2012.405).

[26] Wauchope, *History,* Volume 1, p76.

[27] *Stirling Observer*, 20 April 1918.

[28] *Fife Free Press*, 26 February 1916.

[29] *Fife Free Press*, 26 February 1916.

[30] *Fife Free Press*, 4 March 1916.

[31] *Kirkintilloch Herald*, 3 July 1918.

[32] *Kirkintilloch Herald*, 27 November 1918.

[33] *Fife Free Press,* 18 March 1916.

[34] *Perthshire Advertiser*, 17 August 1903.

[35] *Perthshire Advertiser*, 31 August 1900.

[36] *Perthshire Advertiser*, 16 September 1916.

[37] *Perthshire Advertiser*, 13 January 1909.

[38] *Red Hackle*, January 1948.

[39] Wauchope, *History,* Volume 1, pvii.

SMOKES FOR THE SODGERS

Fraser Brown

O N THE OUTBREAK OF WAR, schoolchildren all over The Black Watch heartlands of Angus, Dundee, Fife and Perthshire involved themselves in a wide range of activities intended to support the war effort. Most of their activities were organised by adults and children took part as volunteers, but from time to time the children and young people took the lead themselves.

One very good early account of a local fund-raising effort of this type is to be found in the *Blairgowrie Advertiser* edition of 17 October 1914.[1] This particular effort was made in support of the 'Blairgowrie Advertiser Tobacco Fund' which ran for the duration of the war with the sole purpose of providing cigarettes, pipes and tobacco for the Blairgowrie men in the frontline. In fact, it supplied a good many more soldiers than Blairgowrie men over the years, but on Saturday, 14 October 1914 the proceeds were to be donated to the Territorials of the 6th (Perthshire) Battalion, The Black Watch.

BLAIRGOWRIE HIGH SCHOOL TOBACCO FUNDRAISING GROUP
For soldiers and sailors at the front 1914. *BlairgowrieAdvertiser,* 17 October 1914

The organisation of the event was straightforward enough. A group of senior girls from Blairgowrie High School persuaded a number of local residents with large gardens to donate blooms from their gardens. These were collected by other pupils on bicycles and taken to a central depot to be made into buttonholes for sale the next day, which was the Saturday of the Blairgowrie long weekend holiday. The next day, a number of girls placed themselves at strategic points in the town literally covering all possible exits and attempted to persuade gentlemen to buy a buttonhole. They did a roaring trade by all accounts, particularly with gentlemen going off by train that day, many of whom seem to have been in a particularly generous mood. As they ran out of blooms further supplies were delivered from the depot to the sellers by senior boys on bicycles, while the buttonhole production line continued to manufacture finished articles for the rest of the day. Finally, three local bank tellers were persuaded to 'see fair play' and count the vast quantities of copper and silver that made up the takings of what was described as the 'extraordinary sum' of £50/10/-.

At first sight, and from the slightly patronising tone of the report, it appears to have been little more than a 'pretty' flower day inspired by a popular teacher called Mr J D Dobson, but organised and largely staffed by his senior girl pupils with some help from senior boys. In fact, a close reading of the newspaper account reveals the project to have been rather more than that. This was about a local community's support for 'kith and kin' of 'E' Company, 6th Black Watch in the first instance, confirmed by the card inserted into each pack of cigarettes which read 'Blairgowrie High School Senior Girls'.

Of course, if the contention that this fund-raising event was essentially about the senior part of a school supporting 'kith and kin', then there should have been some indication of that in the numbers of participants and some evidence of these types of personal and family connections. In terms of pure numbers, with 23 senior girls and 13 senior boys individually named in the *Blairgowrie Advertiser* as 'involved', more than half of the senior school had volunteered their services. Equally significant was that when the addresses of the senior girls and boys named in the *Blairgowrie Advertiser* as participants were taken from the school registers still existing in the Perth & Kinross Archives, and compared to addresses of soldiers on the many lists published locally under headings like 'East Perthshire Men of Active Service', no fewer than 16 of the 36 senior pupils had fathers or brothers already serving by the first week of October 1914 and many more would serve later in the war.[2]

This was not the only fund-raising event in support of The Black Watch or of the British war effort by school pupils, but rather one of the first of many examples of this kind of child- or young person-led war support initiatives which appeared time and again all across the 42nd Regimental Area and only ceased at the Armistice in 1918.

Of course, it is easy to read too much into events like this, but one thought occurs. Although these children had never read Carl von Clausewitz's *On War,* were they not a shining example of the accuracy of his comment on war in the post French Revolutionary era, and a comment on things to come that:

> War had again become an affair of the people...By this participation of the people in the war...a whole Nation with its natural weight came into the scale.[3]

---

1   *Blairgowrie Advertiser*, 17 October 1914.

2   *Blairgowrie Advertiser*, 5 September 1914. This list is only one of many examples.

3   Carl von Clausewitz, *On War* (Book 8) (London: N Trübner, 1873) cited in **https://www.clausewitzstudies.org/readings/OnWar1873/BK8ch03.html#a** (accessed 1 July 2019).

THE REID BROTHERS

Fiona Kantzidis

IN MARCH 1915, the neighbours of Mr and Mrs Reid of Tillyloss, Kirriemuir, would have been surprised to read in *The Evening Telegraph and Post* and elsewhere that Mrs Reid had been congratulated by the King. The article in the *Evening Telegraph* was simple, straightforward and very much to the point. It read:

Kirriemuir Woman had Seven Sons with the Colours

The mother of George Reid, postman, Blair Atholl, of the 1st Black Watch who was killed in action on the 31st December, has been congratulated by the King on the fact of her having seven sons serving with the colours. Mrs Reid resides at Tillyloss, Kirriemuir. Of the other sons, one, Private James Reid, Highland Light Infantry, formerly postman at Aberfeldy, has been missing since September. The others are serving with the 5th Black Watch, 5th Dragoon Guards, the Indian Contingent, 2nd Black Watch, 15th Battalion Australian Infantry, while one is an ex-member of the South African Garrison Artillery.[1]

Sadly, by the end of the war, Mrs Reid had lost a second son, for Private James Reid mentioned in the article as missing from 20 September 1914 was declared dead and the 'Army Council were constrained to conclude that his death took place on the 20th September', the day he was posted missing.[2] Fortunately for the Reid family, no more sons were killed, and though at least one escaped serious injury by pure luck, others were wounded but survived.

It is also fair to say, that in many ways the Reid family were a very typical Angus family of that period and one which reflected the drift from the land into urbanisation as well as the increasing survival of children into adulthood. James Reid, the patriarch of the family, was originally a ploughman and worked on many of the farms in Angus prior to becoming the head gardener at Platten the home of the Wilkies, the well-known family of jute manufacturers in Kirriemuir. Like so many of the ploughmen of that time, Reid was highly mobile, often moving on and feeing with a new farmer at term time at one of the great feeing fairs like the Mucklie Fair in Kirriemuir or the Dunning Fair in Perthshire. This accounts for the fact the Reids' nine sons and one daughter were born in a number of different parishes. There was also an imperial strand, common in Scotland at the time which applied to the Reids, for one son returned to fight with the Australian Imperial Force, another returned from South Africa and a third from India with the 2nd Black Watch. In addition, some of the sons seem to have showed the same fondness for military service in the Regular Army as many others in rural Scotland at that time: four sons had been Regular soldiers and a fifth was a Territorial – and of these, three were in The Black Watch.

The three brothers who served in The Black Watch – who are the main topic of this section – were fated never to meet in wartime. Family tradition states that William, an underage soldier with the 5th Black Watch, and Stewart, who ended the war as a sergeant with the 2nd Battalion and was serving with the Indian contingent, had somehow arranged to meet their brother George who was serving with the 1st Battalion in the first days of 1915. When they arrived at the 1st Battalion where they had hoped to meet their brother, they found out they were too late. George, the reservist mentioned in the *Evening Telegraph* article was already dead.

Private George Reid was born in January 1885 in the Angus village of Tannadice, and by the time the Reid family moved to Kirriemuir, George had completed his schooling. Initially, he became a trainee tailor before joining the 1st Battalion, The Black Watch; and on completion of his engagement, he returned to civilian life and, like many other ex-soldiers of good character, he became a postman. However, like so many others, he was listed as a Regular reservist ready to be recalled to the Colours if required. When war was declared in August 1914, George and other reservists were mobilised and after a short period of refresher training at regimental depots, were sent as reinforcements to the Regular battalions.

George's arrival in France coincided with the British Expeditionary Force's relief in the line by the French so that it could move en masse to the Belgian (Ypres) Front in order to shorten the British lines of communication. He was immediately engaged in fierce and heavy fighting in the lead up to and eventually in the First Battle of Ypres, which he survived. What he did not survive however, was becoming one of the seemingly endless random casualties which characterised trench warfare.

The *1st Battalion War Diary* recorded a good deal of German use of '*Minenwerfer*' in the days before George's death on Hogmanay 1914 and the entry for that day suggests in very bald terms indeed how he may have died:

> December 31, 1914 Givenchy 3.30pm Observation Post lost by
> a Regiment south of canal. A & D Companies of the Regiment
> relieved by B & C – the former going to PONT FIXE to form
> a reserve. In the trenches. Lance Corporal McLeod played
> Garb of Old Gaul at midnight. Casualties 1 killed, 4 wounded.
> Wind SE. Weather – Some rain.[3]

His home town of Kirriemuir was not slow to remember its war dead, and very early amongst the numerous services of remembrance where George Reid was specifically mentioned, was a service held in the parish church 'in honour of those of the parish who had fallen in the war'.[4] This was a major event and although there would be many more before the end of the war, this would have been a truly memorable affair and was reported in November 1915 in a large article in *The Courier and Argus*. The service was attended by the Provost, the Magistrates, the full Town Council, the local Red Cross, School Board and Boys' Brigade, and every soldier stationed in the town. When the list of the 20 Kirriemuir men fallen at that point was read out, the first name was Second Lieutenant George S Wilkie, son of Mr Reid's employer at Platten, and first named of 11 Black Watch men from the town who had fallen at that point.

Stewart Reid, the second eldest of the three brothers was born in the Angus farming village of Kingoldrum in November 1886 and moved with his family to Kirriemuir where he completed his schooling. He found employment as a factory worker in J & D Wilkie's jute factory prior to enlisting into The Black Watch and following in the footsteps of his elder brother George. After training he was posted to the 2nd Battalion, which was serving in India and stationed at Bareilly from where the 2nd Battalion was mobilised as part of the Bareilly Brigade of the 7th Meerut Division, Indian Army Corps, of the Indian Expeditionary Force, and eventually disembarked in Marseille in Southern France. He ended the war as a sergeant and still in the 2nd Battalion.

The 2nd Battalion as part of the 7th Division were deployed to Givenchy. Due to heavy German shelling, the line there was weakened and had to be bolstered by the 1st Brigade which included the 1st Battalion, and at that point the two brothers were fighting very closely together in a relatively small area. At the same time, their younger brother William who was in the 5th Battalion, was employed in trench warfare at Port Arthur near Neuve Chapelle waiting for an impending German offensive which never took place.

Shortly afterwards, Stewart visited the 5th Battalion and managed to meet William. Much to the amusement of both, Stewart did not recognise his younger brother at first because the last time he had seen him was 11 years earlier when William was a schoolboy still in short trousers. Sadly, the amusement did not last for long, and although the brothers made a pact to visit George at the earliest opportunity, he died of his wounds on Hogmanay night 1914. He was later interred in a local cemetery at Givenchy. William and Stewart did not meet again during the Great War, for Stewart moved with the 2nd Battalion to the warmer climes of the Middle East where he saw action in Mesopotamia, Baghdad, Palestine and Suez against the Ottoman Empire while William remained in France – at least for a few weeks because he was about to be returned to Scotland as an underage soldier.

William, the youngest of the three Black Watch brothers, was born at 69 Glengate, a two-room dwelling in Kirriemuir on 28 October 1896. Prior to World War I, he worked both as a machinist at Wilkie's jute factory, Kirriemuir and then as a porter at Kirriemuir railway station. He also served with Kirriemuir (A) Company 5th (Territorial) Battalion,

The Black Watch, in his spare time, and when war broke out, he like the rest of the men of the Territorial Forces, was mobilised for war. One half of the 5th Battalion in which William served was billeted at Broughty Ferry Castle, near Dundee, whereas the other half were stationed at Hawkhill School, Dundee. During this period, the Battalion was deployed to man the Firth of Tay defences but on 29 October 1914, William along with the rest of the 1/5th Battalion entrained at Dundee for Southampton to embark for France and arrived in Le Havre on 2 November 1914.

Nevertheless, William like a number of other young men in that battalion should never have been on the ship to France. At that point, he was barely 18 and should have remained with the 2/5th Battalion which was the holding and training battalion for underage men and recruits. In fact, in the early days of 1915, The Black Watch sent home a relatively large number of underage men who had not yet reached the age of 19, at which point they could be sent overseas to fight.[5] One group was photographed at Dundee railway station on their way home to their families (on leave) before rejoining home-based Black Watch battalions, but it is not known if William was in that photograph.

When he was old enough to fight, William returned to the battlefields and was fortunate to finish the war relatively unscathed with only the loss of a toe. He was wounded twice: once as reported on 21 May 1915 in the *Montrose Review* (amongst other local papers), during an ill-fated advance by the 5th Battalion at Ypres in support of an attack by the East Lancashire Regiment and the Sherwood Foresters which cost the battalion 160 casualties.[6] He also appeared as 'wounded' in *The Courier and Argus* of 11 August 1917.[7]

On at least one occasion, William had good fortune on his side. According to his family's account of events, one evening somewhere in the area of Neuve Chappelle, whilst the battalion was in the trenches, William was part of a group in an observation post sited in a ruined building. The off-duty members sheltered in the cellar of the ruins whilst the remainder kept watch. They drew lots to decide who would sleep in the warm corner of the cellar or the coldest area nearest the door. William drew the short straw and had to sleep next to the door, but that apparent piece of bad luck saved him from suffering the effects of mustard gas which the Germans released during the night. Although no-one in the group died from the gas on that occasion, family tradition claims that one of the men, Private 'Silver' Melloy was badly affected and died prematurely after the war.

PRIVATE WILLIAM LACKIE REID
(Reid family)

Over a century later, the historic memory of the three Black Watch brothers remains within their extended family. Stewart, the battalion sergeant, ever the old soldier, is fondly remembered for his impressive bearing and smart turnout during his years as a local postman. The family naming pattern meant that this author, had she been born a boy, would have been named after William who passed away in 1974, so sadly they never met. Although George died over a century ago, he is not forgotten, and a glass is always raised to him on Hogmanay night by his family. This author's mother who is his grandniece, her husband and family visited his grave in a French cemetery in 2014 when his great, great grandnephew played 'Flowers o' the Forrest' then 'Hielan' Laddie' and the 'Atholl Highlanders' on the pipes and his great, great grandniece laid a wreath. Finally, on 31 December 2014, his grandniece, her husband and their extended family laid a cross on the memorial wall.

1   *The Evening Telegraph and Post*, 2 March 1915.

2   *The Courier and Argus,* 10 December 1915.

3   *1st Battalion War Diary*, 31 December 1914.

4   *The Courier and Argus*, 26 November 1915.

5   See *Young Soldiers and Underage Soldiers* for an explanation of the laws on enlistment.

6   *Montrose Review*, 21 May 1915.

7   *The Courier and Argus*, 11 August 1917.

THE ARBROATH HIGH SCHOOL SECTION

A RECORD OF SERVICE

Fraser Brown

INTRODUCTION

DURING THE FIRST PART of the Great War, news of the local
Territorial Force infantry battalion, 5th (Angus) Battalion, The Black
Watch (TF), as reported in both Arbroath weekly newspapers, the
Arbroath Guide and the *Arbroath Herald*, made frequent reference to a sub
unit of 'F' (Arbroath) Company identified as Number 4 (High School)
Section. The Section, best understood as a modern infantry platoon led by
a subaltern, was unique in The Black Watch inasmuch as its members were
almost all either current pupils, former pupils (FPs) or staff of Arbroath
High School, all recruited before the outbreak of hostilities or in the first
days of the war. Experienced NCOs were drafted in to fulfil particular
roles, but essentially until after the actions at Festubert and Aubers Ridge
in 1915, membership was fairly consistently confined to High School FPs.
After that point, the High School Section appears to have faded away as a
formed unit as it lost men to death, wounds and promotion, and in any case
formally ceased to exist with the amalgamation of the 4th and 5th Battalions
into the 4/5th Black Watch on 25 February 1916.

The existence of the High School Section is not acknowledged in
the *5th Battalion War Diaries*, the second volume of Victoria Schofield's
two-volume history *The Black Watch: Fighting in the Front Line,
1899-2006* or in Major-General A G Wauchope's three-volume *A History
of the Black Watch in the Great War, 1914-18*, and it has no separate record
or even mention in The Black Watch Museum Archive.[1] As part of the
5th Battalion, the men of the High School Section were involved in all
aspects of operations, but as a rifle Section rather than a specialist Section
like the Bombers, nicknamed the 'Bullet Proof Jocks' whose exploits on

detached duties were recorded in both the *5th Battalion War Diaries* and Wauchope's history of the regiment, they could have no separate operational history.[2]

Nevertheless, with or without a written regimental record of its existence, during its short lifetime the Section featured more often in the local press than its size would have suggested. The words 'High School Section' also appeared in newspaper reports as an additional identifying feature when individual men were discussed, so that reports of conversations with Section members on leave, accounts of actions in France, obituaries and even an article in the *Arbroath High School Magazine* all carried the High School Section tag where appropriate.[3] Publication in the local press of their letters as well as press acknowledgement of the large crop of junior officers which emerged from its ranks added to popular awareness of its existence in Arbroath, for long after it ceased to exist, men were still identified in life and death as former members of the 'High School Section'.

This chapter sets out to establish a brief record of the service of the High School Section through an exploration of its formation, composition, deployment, letters home and the fate of its members.

FORMATION

In spite of the fact that the High School Section did share a number of features common to Pals battalions, no claim is made here that it should be seen as any sort of small-scale Pals formation. Although members were recruited from the same town, had a common connection to Arbroath High School and came from the same social grouping, belonged to the same cricket, football and golf clubs, several key features of a Pals unit were missing. The most important of these was that unlike the classic Pals battalions, the High School Section was not raised during the Great War specifically for the purpose of fighting overseas in that war. In fact, its formation predated the outbreak of hostilities and unlike so many of the English Pals battalions, the Section was not the result of any sort of local war enthusiasm or an ambitious patriotic project of prominent local civic figures. As Peter Simkins indicated in *Kitchener's Army*, significant numbers of pre-war Territorial units and earlier Volunteer formations had whole companies of men drawn from the same community or workplace, and it is to that tradition rather than the Pals movement that the High School Section belonged.[4] In fact, the Section was raised for home defence as part of a wider, well-publicised pre-war effort to boost recruitment to the local Territorial Force battalion of The Black Watch.

In Arbroath, recruitment of men for The Black Watch Territorials at this time was taken very seriously. Newspaper accounts of the activities of 'E' and 'F' Companies of the 5th Black Watch indicate they were involved in a very active, well-publicised training programme led by a charismatic local doctor, Captain Duncan. The officer commanding the 5th Battalion before the war was Lieutenant-Colonel Scrymgeour-Wedderburn, generally regarded as a forward-thinking officer, open to new ideas and very enthusiastic about the Territorial Forces in general. Newspaper reports of Black Watch Territorial training exercises indicate that he was either present as an umpire or as an observer more often than might have been expected. Some exercises, such as one reported in the *Arbroath Guide* in July 1913 also show the Arbroath and other companies to have achieved at least a reasonably high standard of training by Territorial Force standards.[5] That particular exercise indicated the extent of the co-ordination of the different Black Watch detachments from Friockheim, and companies from Carnoustie and Monifieth as they advanced to contact then executed a flanking movement before attacking an enemy position around ten miles from their start line. Other imaginative training exercises included the use of aircraft from Montrose in reconnaissance as early as April 1913 and other tactical exercises held around Arbroath were likely to appeal to former and present High School men.[6]

The actual origins of the High School Section can be found in the *Arbroath High School Magazine* where a two-page article by the anonymous 'Infantry Captain' appeared in the edition of June 1913 entitled 'Soldiering as a Duty and a Pastime'.[7] The author described how disappointed he had been on his return to Arbroath after some time in London to find that the 'voluntary spirit has no place in the minds of our middle class youths who may all be classed as former pupils of Arbroath High School'. He noted that in the larger cities of Scotland there were whole companies of men of that class to be found in the so-called 'Varsity Companies' such as 'U' Company of the 4th Gordons based in Aberdeen. He might also have mentioned, but did not, the College Company of the 4th Royal Scots in Edinburgh which had several Arbroath men in its ranks. 'It was unlikely', he conceded that in a town like Arbroath a whole company could be raised, but he saw no reason why a strong section of infantry could not be recruited from former pupils still resident in Arbroath.

'Infantry Captain' went on to systematically recall the willingness of High School FPs of ten years before to serve in the old Volunteers of the 1st Forfar Royal Garrison Artillery and the 2nd Volunteer Battalion, Royal Highlanders, then to berate younger FPs for their apparent unwillingness to serve in the new Territorial Forces. In fact, what he was doing was to apply a touch of pressure to the social consciences of the FPs to make an overt recruiting bid along class lines. After addressing every likely excuse, 'Infantry Captain' described how the working classes had been left to fill the need for men in spite of having less time available to them, and broadly hinted that the middle-class FPs of the High School should be doing much better. He ended with an appeal for recruits and a promise – if around 25 or more FPs would join, a named High School Section would be formed where High School FPs would serve together.

This appeal was so successful that when the *Arbroath High School Magazine* appeared again in March 1914 the High School Section was a formed subunit within 'F' Company, 5th Black Watch under the command of Second Lieutenant John Murray, the Arbroath High School Champion of 1912. The article continued:

> A gratifying response has been made to the call for recruits from amongst past and present pupils of the High School to join our county battalion…There is yet more room for men of the same stamp and it is hoped that the Section can be brought up to full strength.

In that edition, the 'FP Section' of the *Arbroath High School Magazine* carried an anonymous full-column article explaining the terms of service for Territorial soldiers in detail, so that waverers might have an accurate account of what was required. A broad hint was also dropped for pupils about future developments in the 'Between Ourselves' column in the comment: 'There is not yet a Cadet Corps in the school, but interest in, not to say enthusiasm for military matters has recently reached a high point especially in the kilted Black Watch battalion...'. Whether or not this enthusiasm for The Black Watch battalion bore any relationship to the training programme mentioned earlier is a moot point.

In the June edition of the magazine, news of the High School Section was an established feature in the 'FP Section' and this time it contained two pieces of highly significant information: first, the next year would see the formation of an entire High School company and second, almost all of the recruits had undertaken the prescribed musketry course which meant their period of basic training as Territorials was virtually complete before they went off to annual camp at Monzie near Crieff in July 1914. On 2 August, with the annual training camp over, members of the 5th Battalion, The Black Watch, did not stand down but went home on leave, to be formally mobilised two days later.

COMPOSITION

Shortly after their deployment with the 5th Black Watch on 1 November 1914 but before the death in action on 5 February 1915 of Private Horatio Savege, a photograph of the whole Section was taken. This picture, which appeared later in the *Arbroath High School Magazine* of June 1915 along with the list of those present, shows the Section at full strength on the eve of first contact with the enemy. The fact that the men are still wearing Highland shoes with khaki dyed spats rather than the boots, hose tops and puttees issued to kilted troops in the field early in 1915, and Second Lieutenant Murray is carrying a broadsword suggests this picture was taken immediately before departure or more likely very shortly after arrival in theatre in late November 1914.

This photograph is the nearest thing to a Section nominal roll that exists because infantry subunits then – as now – are not fixed in terms of personnel for any length of time as promotions, sickness and casualties occur. In fact, on occasion the number of men in the Section is given as 28 and 25, but the number of High School FPs serving in the Section at some point was probably nearer 35 as new men like Private Neil Campbell joined.[8]

NUMBER 4 (HIGH SCHOOL) SECTION
F Company. 1/5 Battalion, The Black Watch
Arbroath High School Magazine, March 1915 *(Head Teacher, Arbroath High School)*

Even so, there can be little doubt that the composition of the High School Section on mobilisation would have raised a few wry smiles amongst the old soldiers of the 5th Battalion. The school janitor Sergeant Christie was platoon sergeant, which would have come as a shock for the six former Arbroath School Board teacher members, but that was as nothing compared with the pre-war promotion to lance corporal of two of the four current pupils serving. Although Lance Corporal Bonnyman was detached to the 5th Black Watch Second Line still in training, Lance Corporal J L Gibb served with the Section from the beginning of the war, so that for a brief period the former Head of Science, Dr A J McKenzie was outranked by his pupil.[9] The Section also appears to have been unusual in that several of the junior NCOs going into action were far younger than the men they gave orders to, a situation requiring a degree of military maturity not always found in Territorial soldiers in the early part of the war. Nevertheless, the men of the Section appear to have bonded into a unit very well.

As the 5th Battalion settled down to prepare for deployment, on 26 September, a group of around 300 men who had volunteered for foreign service – the vast majority of whom had not reached the age standard – were drafted to Forfar to form the nucleus of a second-line battalion. Even so the three current pupils remained with the Section and deployed with them when the 5th Battalion entrained for Southampton on 29 October. However, even when the battalion had reached the frontline, the problem of underage and overage soldiers had not been fully resolved, for in a letter home published on 9 January 1915 Sergeant Hugh Hunter described a parade of around 50 men aged either under 19 or over 50 from his double company. The sergeant commented he 'expected trouble soon' and 'Poor lads, they stick it well, but should never have been here'.[10] Nevertheless, one current pupil, Private J Guthrie, was 16 when he was wounded weeks later and given the maximum age a pupil could attend school, the other three current pupils were also under the age standard. A further two, Lance Corporal Crowe and Private Nicoll had only passed their Higher exams in July 1914 and so must also have been underage when they went to France where they remained until commissioned in 1915.

'THOSE THAT REMAIN AFTER THE LAST SCRAP'
[Arbroath] High School Section 5th Black Watch
Private J A Davidson, Lance-Corporal W M Davidson, Private D J A Neish,
Lance-Corporal C Crowe, Private N J Gibson, Private A Dewar, Private J Scott
Arbroath Herald, 18 June 1915

In terms of pre-war occupations, the Section produced no great surprises. Teacher FPs working in the town were the largest single group, but their decision to go to war was not as straightforward as might have been thought. After all, they were employees of the Arbroath School Board and as teachers were directed by the Scottish Education Department (SED), a body which kept a strict oversight of all schools in Scotland in receipt of public funding. In fact, the first communication of the war from the SED to schools, *Circular 464* dated 24 August 1914 and the only *Circular* marked 'Very Important' during the war, summed up the SED position regarding how school boards and their teachers should approach the war:

Very Important

The first and most obvious duty of managers is to see that the education of the children is not unnecessarily interrupted. They can best serve their country during this critical period by straining every nerve to ensure that the work of the schools proceeds as far as possible on absolutely normal lines.[11]

The largest single group of 16 SED *Circulars* out of a wartime total of 60 concerned teachers and all of these appear to have been aimed at helping maintain staffing stability in some way.

Shortly after the issue of *Circular 464*, the *Arbroath Guide* reported on a gathering at Arbroath High School when the teachers of the town met 'for the purpose of considering their position in regard to the war'.[12] Mr L'Aimee, languages teacher from the High School, and Mr Pirie of Keptie Public School were elected to explain to a meeting of the Arbroath School Board that under certain conditions about 20 Arbroath teachers were willing to offer their services to their country. Some of the teachers had already served with the Territorial Forces at some point and were 'willing to repay the country for their training in the present crisis'.[13] The delegation was received in private when the teachers were commended by the Provost for their patriotism, promised half pay for the duration of their service and given an assurance that they would return to their positions at the end of the war.

Other occupations also appeared: mercantile and other clerks, bank workers, a stockbroker, booksellers and a draper were all represented. It was also the case that in the ways of that time, and before the development of university courses in management studies or accountancy, at least some of these men were the equivalent of modern management trainees. They were trained 'in house' and like Private N Smith were 'on the staff' thus indicating their status. Others, like the brothers M G and J A Hood or Private Savege were involved in their family businesses. Apart from the four men who were current pupils of Arbroath High School, these were exactly the sort of jobs FPs would have been expected to have taken, for this was very much an aspiring or more accurately, an established middle-class group.

When the addresses of the High School Section men shown in their own separate listing in the Arbroath papers were checked, these tended to be located in the west end of Arbroath where property was generally more expensive than elsewhere in the town. The middle-class nature of the Section was further confirmed by the entries in the *Arbroath Roll of Honour* for the six men killed in action.[14] The prominence given to their obituaries in both local papers indicated the respect in which both they and their families were held in the town.

DEPLOYMENT AND LETTERS HOME

From the earliest days of the war, High School Section men wrote long, well-constructed and detailed letters home which then found their way into the columns of the *Arbroath Guide* or the *Arbroath Herald* and even the *Arbroath High School Magazine*.

One article appeared in the *Arbroath High School Magazine* of June 1915 entitled 'Sunshine and Shadow' written under the name of 'One of the Jocks'. It described amongst other things a night relief in the line, a procedure which had to take place every few days, but which was a relatively complex manoeuvre requiring a high standard of discipline and training to be carried out effectively and without excessive casualties. When the account is examined closely the procedure described followed the sequence of events infantrymen would recognise even today, and his description of the treatment of a casualty caused by harassing fire was entirely believable. The identity of the author, 'One of the Jocks', remains unknown except that he was commissioned during the war. However, other school magazines also published articles from serving FPs which were much more revealing; and should never have passed the unit censor. That led in turn to SED *Circular 486 Accidental Disclosure of Military Information*, the only *Circular* of the war to be marked 'Confidential' on 15 December 1916 to all schools. Although it was ignored far more often than it should have been in schools, the existence of *Circular 486* correctly identified the extent to which this material was accurate and had an intelligence value.

Odd snippets of information and concerns would also appear. One worry seems to have been about whether the Section men were tough enough to stand the terrible conditions in France, but that soon died away. The ability of the Section men to speak some French was also commented on and perhaps that was because Arbroath High School had something of reputation for excellence in languages. Inspectors' reports of the pre-war years frequently contained comments such as 'the Higher candidates make a very good appearance under oral examination' in French while in German 'Higher candidates converse freely' appearing regularly. This linguistic talent translated into excellent relations with one particular local family in Vielle Chapelle which, before they all died in a German bombardment, appears to have provided a home from home for the Section.

Letters published in both Arbroath papers from the Section men contain details of long forgotten operational methods and are of interest for that reason alone, but they also contain something of how Section men saw the war as well as the conditions behind the lines. In fact, from arrival in France until the fight at Aubers Ridge in May 1915, hardly a week passed without a letter or some communication from a Section man being published, so it is possible to cover this period in their own words. Thereafter, partly because of casualties and promotions to other units as well as increasingly effective censorship, published letters dropped off in numbers.

One early letter came from Corporal Hugh Hunter, who had rejected an immediate commission in the Seaforth Highlanders, but later accepted a second lieutenancy in The Black Watch. He wrote to the editor of the *Arbroath Herald* while still in Scotland with 'A Call to High School FPs', published on 23 October 1914 demanding of High School FPs in Arbroath, 'Are we to have another squad or not?' and told wavering FPs that they should 'Buck up' and join. It was a hard life but a healthy one he assured them. After all, he continued, the High School Section had upheld the honour of the school and now it was their turn to do the same adding the promise that if enough men joined to form a squad he had been assured they would be taken into 'F' Company.

There was an awareness too among some members of the Section at least that their activities were of interest to potential recruits, particularly members of the Arbroath sporting fraternity. When a picture which appeared in the *Arbroath Herald* on 27 November 1914 sent in by a Section man taken very shortly after its arrival in France subtitled 'Arbroath Amateur Footballers at The Front', of the seven men in the photograph, five were Section men. The sender also wrote of the picture, 'it may do something to encourage recruiting'.[15]

The first letters home from members of the Section were fairly restrained, but that would change quite quickly. One letter to a teacher in the High School published in the *Arbroath Guide* from Private C Crowe stated that they had 'had some thrilling experiences and had been in a few tight corners', but as Private A Neish remarked, 'The High School fellows are liking it alright'.[16] There were other communications too, often subtitled 'Cheery Letter from the Front' or similar, like one from Private Neil Campbell who joked that he would never be unemployed again after having worked as a gravedigger, general porter and erector of barbed wire. But lurking behind the jokes was an understanding of what was to come. He ended the letter with 'our division will retire for a rest, then we may go back to something livelier'.[17]

A number of the letters from the Section men were sent to Arbroath in acknowledgement of gifts sent to individual men. The High School pupils began raising money in support of their own FPs from the first days of the war and time and again, news of their efforts and the amount of monies raised were published in both local papers. Letters of thanks from the Section men and others were sent to the school and these were read out at formal assemblies, and any occasion where parents were present such as school concerts. Unfortunately, none of these have survived. However, one letter of thanks from Sergeant Hugh Hunter to the Women's Guild of St Margaret's Parish Church written on 20 December 1914 was published in the *Arbroath Guide*. The sergeant complimented the ladies of the Guild on their choice of contents of his parcel as well as assuring them of how welcome these 'luxuries' were but for him the most important aspect was the moral effect on him of their arrival: 'It is not the value of the presents...It is that the people at home are with us...'. Sergeant Hunter, like the other letter writers was very open about the day-to-day activities of his unit. He went on to describe how recently while in reserve the battalion had to 'stand to in full marching order' all night to the sound of a bombardment, then heavy rifle fire followed by 'silence – ominous silence', and were finally given the order to escort German prisoners to a reception area seven miles behind the lines. He ended with a comment echoed time and again by Section men: 'Up there it is not the fighting that tires you out but the weather conditions'.[18]

The full extent of the havoc wrought on the entire 5th Battalion by the weather can be seen in the comment in Wauchope's *History of the Black Watch in the Great War* that in December 1914 the 'Right Half Battalion' could only muster 150 men fit for duty.[19] The extent to which comforts helped the Section men at this time was acknowledged in a letter reproduced in the *Arbroath Guide* from Private W M Soutar to his brother James who was a draper in Arbroath. The letter appeared under the heading 'Keep on Knitting' and subtitled 'How Comforts Sent From Home Are Appreciated' asking in particular for 'knee caps' made of wool which protected the bare legs from inflammation caused by mud and wet great coats rubbing on bare skin, and socks which he said were in short supply.

One of the most useful letters was written by Private N J Gibson, an Arbroath man turned stockbroker in Aberdeen commissioned into the Gordon Highlanders in 1915.[20] This letter outlined the activities of the Section from embarkation at Southampton until New Year's Day 1915 when the letter was written. Gibson described a period of measured activity including transport arrangements, inoculation, billeting and night-time trench digging close enough to the frontline to be aware of the crack of random rifle fire. His description of being 'gey flegd' as they took cover in a muddy ditch the first time they came under fire of that kind and how some Regulars walking along told them that 'the _ _ _ _ couldn't hit you with a shovel' was quite comical, but also made the important point that since then they had toughened up, and now marched that way many times, often in daylight and thought nothing of it. The letter also described the first night in the frontline trenches which at that point were about 200 yards from the Germans, as well as the eerie sight of German searchlights playing across no-man's-land and the crash of German rifle volley fire directed at any target the searchlights settled on.

The final section of Gibson's letter is far less discreet, and although it is known from other letters from the battalion that censorship was in place, the content suggests it was a completely uncensored letter. He explained how the battalion had moved to billets within three miles of the frontline a few days before, and so any military reader would have known they were now seen as of a quality good enough to be placed as a tactical reserve, available for immediate counterattack. He also noted how 'people at home have not the slightest idea the horrors some of the men here are suffering. It is hell on earth for most of them...'. His final remark suggests he had not completely accepted the opinion out there that 'the Germans are about played out'. As he said, 'I hae ma doots'.

In a letter to Reverend A Douglas of the Abbey Church in Arbroath dated 21 December 1914 and published in the *Arbroath Herald* on Ne'er Day 1915, Private Savege described some of the endless administrative tasks on which the infantry was engaged when not in the frontline. These included night-time ration delivery and trench digging duties in terrible conditions and often under enemy artillery bombardment and sniper fire.[21] This particular letter is interesting in that it is the first letter from a High School Section man which shows evidence of censorship at work, and because Savege writes far more about trench conditions than that he had been presented to the King and Prince of Wales who wanted to see the winter kit issued to soldiers. He described the experience as 'a few words with His Majesty and the Prince of Wales – a very few words. In fact, "Yes Sir" and "No Sir" and a few smiles was all that I had time for'.[22] Whether

Savege was embarrassed or even shy about mentioning this experience is unknown, but what was clear from his letter were his immediate concerns.

Another Section man who observed the whole show took a more cynical view.[23] Private W M Soutar wrote that they had no idea who most of the King's entourage were 'because of the infrequency with which we meet such military aristocracy'. Nevertheless, 'We duly inspected the King and his colleagues, and the Black Watch were very pleased with them,' Private Savege and the others were like 'Teddy bears in fur coats,' he wrote, but he did think that the Arbroath lady who made Private Savege's scarf would be pleased to know the 'King cast covetous eyes upon it'. However, the same letter ends with a description of a first sight of the German lines then 70 yards away, and after a night of activity, the first sight of the German dead in no-man's-land. On a purely practical – but human level – he also noted the speed with which at dawn firing slackened as all thoughts on both sides turned to breakfast.

The same edition of the *Arbroath Herald* published excerpts from a second letter from Private Savege to his father under the headline 'Christmas Day at the Front' in which he described the events of Christmas Day with some disapproval. 'War has its funny side', he wrote. 'On Christmas Day the Germans were out on top of their trenches and our boys were over shaking hands and exchanging souvenirs. I couldn't get over it...I wouldn't trust the beggars'.[24] Private Savege was not alone in that opinion: Sergeant Hugh Hunter told the *Arbroath Guide* in a letter published a week later that in the British trench there were 'men standing to arms ready for any dirty tricks'.[25] On the other hand, Captain J D Duncan who returned to Arbroath when interviewed by *The Courier and Argus* and other papers described it as 'quiet in the firing line' and the truce as 'an armistice by arrangement' when the dead were buried.[26]

DEATH AND DECORATIONS

When the first deaths occurred, detailed accounts of how the six men killed in action had died also appeared. These spared the readership nothing in terms of the random nature of death and wounds on the Western Front and contradicted any assumptions people at home may have had that men only died in the great battles of the war. Private Savege's own death along with four men of another regiment he was working with was caused by a what appears to have been harassing shellfire, while Private N Smith was killed by a bullet which passed through a loophole on the trench parapet. On the other hand, Lieutenant N J Gibson, who by the time of his death on 21 November 1917 had been commissioned into the Gordons, was killed in the final stages of the 4th Gordons' assault on a German strongpoint at Cantaign.[27] The sixth member of the original Section to fall, Corporal E Thompson died of wounds sustained at Neuve-Chapelle.[28]

Private N J Gibson wrote home describing being in the reserve at the action at Neuve-Chapelle and what being in the reserve battalion of the attacking brigade actually entailed. As the 5th Battalion passed over the German lines:

> We prepared to dig ourselves in, but before we got started the Germans turned a machinegun on us...This went on all day and fairly thinned our ranks. One of my best chums, John Dundas was killed within a yard of me...[29]

Gibson also explained the other tasks assigned to the reserve units such as securing prisoners and the burial of the dead, in this case a task they stuck at for seven days. Uncharacteristically he also mentioned, but did not dwell on, the upset he had endured in attempting to identify the dead, describing the process as 'heart rending'. He was also clearly appalled by the numbers of officers lost in some units but stopped short of commenting on the effects that would have on command and control of the units involved.

A few days later in Arbroath at a memorial service held for Private Dundas in Princess Street Church led by The Reverend James Murray, further details of how he had died were read out to the congregation. Reverend Murray was the father of Lieutenant Murray who was the original officer assigned to the High School Section, so it is at least reasonable to suggest that the letter from 'an officer who was with John at his last fight' was in fact the minister's own son. The letter provided more details of Private Dundas' death including how he died having been shot through the lungs, but that because of the danger a stretcher party could not be sent out to recover the body. Nevertheless, the writer assured the congregation that Private Dundas had had a decent burial and that his grave had been properly marked with his name and regiment. As was the custom, Lieutenant Murray as Section officer wrote a letter of condolence from the regiment to the family, assuring them of their deepest sympathy and that 'Johnny fell asleep quietly and without pain'.[30] It is also worth mentioning that similar letters appeared when the other Section men and others were killed and very similar memorial services took place. In view of this, it may well be that while the families of the dead may not have fully appreciated the full extent of the hell that was the Western Front, at least they had something approaching a factual understanding based on the contents of published letters.

The description of the action at Aubers on 9 May 1915 was equally blunt. The 5th Battalion was ordered to reinforce the attacking line which an Arbroath officer described as requiring the unit 'to cross two fields swept by rifle, machine gun and shrapnel fire'. A second officer wrote:

> Altogether we had 150 men knocked out – we have only about 350 left now out of the original fighting strength. I cannot describe the horrors of these two nights and a day. You should have seen the brave fellows of the 5th – never a quiver, and they fell like ninepins.[31]

Private Gibson described the defensive bombardment the Germans dropped on the 5th Battalion:

> For sixteen hours it was hell upon earth…Even after coming out we were not in the region of safety…a shell burst in the middle of our chaps, and poor Geordie Miller was killed… Maitland Hood is missing…[He ended the letter]…The Arbroath High School Section is now eight strong – it was once twenty eight.[32]

Sergeant Geordie Miller was an assistant teacher at Inverbrothock Public School who had joined the High School Section as a private on the outbreak of war. A colleague who had been standing beside him as they both watched the Arbroath companies march off to war, told the May monthly meeting of the Arbroath Branch of the Educational Institute of Scotland how Sergeant Miller had some experience with the Officer Training Corps, but deliberately chose to join the High School Section. Promotion came quickly and shortly before he was killed he had been told by the commanding officer that his name had been forwarded for the Distinguished Conduct Medal for 'gallant work in front of the parapet under heavy rifle and machine gun fire'.[33] This work was carried out in no-man's-land in front of The Black Watch front wire and involved loosening the entanglements ready to be drawn back to make way for the assault troops attacking at Aubers on the 9 May 1915. At that point in the war, there was no posthumous award of that medal, so Sergeant Miller's gallantry was never formally acknowledged.

One other Section man who was more fortunate and not only lived to collect his medal, but survived the war was Lieutenant Murray. The award of his Military Cross was announced in the *London Gazette* on the 25 January 1917 and repeated in the *Arbroath Herald* a week later with the citation: 'For conspicuous gallantry in action. He displayed great courage and initiative in reorganising his company under very heavy fire. He previously carried out several reconnaissances under fire'.[34]

END GAME

A second Arbroath High School Section picture appeared; this time published in the *Arbroath Herald* of 18 June 1915 showing seven of the nine men who were still fit for duty out of the 34 men named on the earlier picture. The two absentees, Lieutenant J Murray and the newly promoted Company Sergeant Major J Mathewson were still with the 5th Black Watch, but not present that day.

An accompanying article briefly spelled out the fate of those absent: five had been killed in action, another 11 had been wounded and were in hospital in France or Britain and a further four had been invalided home.

Another two men, Sergeant Hunter and Sergeant E L Wood, had been commissioned as second lieutenants into The Black Watch and the Gordons respectively, and Sergeant J Davidson, also believed to have been commissioned shortly afterwards, had been transferred to the Telegraphic Section.

For the majority of the wounded, the future held recovery and a return to the battlefields, but for some like Private Kinnear their wounds required amputation of a limb or for Captain Wilson, who succeeded Captain Duncan, the loss of an eye. Of those invalided home, mostly due to extreme exposure of the first terrible winter of the war before conditions improved in the trenches, they appear to have recovered sufficiently to return to some form of uniformed service. Of those who survived and returned to full duty, a group of eight were commissioned en-masse at Christmas 1915 and by the end of the war of those 20 surviving Section men who could be commissioned, 15 had begun the progression from second lieutenant onwards.[35]

After Aubers in May 1915, only the Bombers of the 5th Battalion took part in any major fighting including action at Chapel Farm during the diversionary attack at Loos, and later in support of the Royal Berkshire Regiment at Angle Point. The 5th Battalion, now so reduced in numbers and desperate for reinforcements which never came, took on the role of a Pioneer battalion in October 1915. One company became miners taking part in the war underground while other companies constructed winter quarters.

Finally, on 25 February 1916, the 4th and 5th Battalions amalgamated forming the 4/5th Black Watch, thus formally ending the existence of the old High School Section.

POSTSCRIPT

In 1939, with the threat of war imminent, the decision was taken to virtually double the strength of the Territorial Army and throughout Britain a campaign was launched to achieve the increase in recruitment required. Along with the usual recruiting marches and advertising campaigns an article and two advertisements appeared in the *Herald* which called for the resurrection of the old High School Section as part of 'C' Company, 4/5th Battalion, The Black Watch, commanded by Captain J A Oliver.[36]

The article began:

> It is felt that the Territorial Army up to now has not given much opportunity of service to a large section of young men [employed in offices, banks and other similar situations] who must now feel anxious to help their country and for whom National Service in its other forms holds no place.

The intention, therefore, was to form a platoon or larger unit along the same lines as the old High School Section. Many of this group of FPs and other middle-class young men were expected to know each other already, so that if a platoon or larger unit could be formed, it would be arranged that they could stay together both in training and at annual camp. A meeting to discuss this was held at The Black Watch Drill Hall in Marketgate the following week, along with a display of the new weapons and equipment on issue including the new Bren light machinegun, mortars and anti-tank guns. In the end, a 'High School Platoon' of sorts did go to war in 1939, but this was not a rifle platoon, rather a group of individuals who in the words of Colonel John McGregor, 'did sterling work' throughout the war in the administration of the 5th Battalion as company clerks and the Company and Regimental Quartermaster Sergeants.[37]

1   Victoria Schofield, *The Black Watch: Fighting in the Front Line, 1899-2006* (London: Head of Zeus, 2017); A G Wauchope, *A History of the Black Watch in the Great War, 1914-1918*, Volumes 1-3 (London: Medici Society, 1925-6).

2   Wauchope, *History*, Volume 2, p44.

3   *Arbroath High School Magazine*, Local Studies Section Holdings, Arbroath Library.

4   Peter Simkins, *Kitchener's Army: The Raising of the New Armies1914-1916* (Barnsley: Pen & Sword, 2007), pp82-83.

5 *Arbroath Guide*, 19 July 1913.

6 *Arbroath Herald*, 11 April 1913.

7 *Arbroath High School Magazine,* June1913.

8 *Arbroath Guide*, 22 May 1915.

9 *Arbroath High School Magazine*, June 1915. Another two current pupils serving were Private J Guthrie and Trooper A F D Carrie, Fife and Forfar Yeomanry.

10 *Arbroath Guide*, 9 January 1915.

11 Scottish Education Department, Scottish National Archives, ED/44/1/8.

12 *Arbroath Guide*, 8 September 1914.

13 *Arbroath Guide*, 8 September 1914.

14 *Roll of Honour: Arbroath & District 1914-1919* (Arbroath: T Buncle & Company, 1921).

15 *Arbroath Herald*, 27 November 1914.

16 *Arbroath Guide*, 28 January 1915.

17 *Arbroath Herald*, 20 January 1915.

18 *Arbroath Guide*, 2 January 1915.

19 Wauchope, *History*, Volume 2, p43.

20 *Arbroath Guide*, 9 January 1915.

21 *Arbroath Guide*, 1 January 1915.

22 *Arbroath Guide*, 1 January 1915.

23 *Arbroath Guide*, 12 December 1914.

24 *Arbroath Herald*, 12 December 1914.

25 *Arbroath Guide*, 9 January 1915.

26 *The Courier and Argus*, 7 January 1915.

27 *Roll of Honour: Arbroath & District.*

28 *Roll of Honour: Arbroath & District.*

29 *Arbroath Guide*, 27 March 1915.

30 *Arbroath Herald*, 2 April 1915.

31 *Arbroath Herald*, 21 May 1915.

32 *Arbroath Guide*, 22 May 1915.

33 *Arbroath Herald*, 21 May 1915.
   (Copy of letter to the parents of Sergeant Miller, 7 May 1915.)

34 *Arbroath Herald*, 2 February 1917.

35 *Arbroath Herald*, 3 December 1915.

36 Later Brigadier Oliver.

37 John McGregor, *The Spirit of Angus* (Chichester: Phillimore & Company Ltd, 1988), p2.

ALFRED ANDERSON (1896-2005)

Reverend Neil N Gardner

BUST OF ALFRED ANDERSON
The Black Watch Castle and Museum, Perth
(The Black Watch Castle and Museum)

T O BE HONEST, I'd never heard of Alfred Anderson until September 1998, when after seven years as an army chaplain, more than half of them with The Black Watch, I was inducted as minister of Alyth, Perthshire. It was six weeks or so before the Remembrance season, when the church and the nation would be marking the 80th anniversary of the Armistice that marked the end of the First World War in November 1918. It was not long before I learned that we actually had living in my new parish a rare survivor of that war, and not just any veteran but a Black Watch veteran! So I arranged to meet him. At that stage, as the twentieth century was drawing gently to a close, to shake the hand of a man who had fought in the Battle of Loos would have been more than enough for me. And it was as much as I could hope for. 'He doesn't talk about the war', I was told. That was not necessarily surprising as the same could be said of plenty other survivors of harrowing conflicts.

As it turned out, it was not entirely true in this case. Within minutes of my ringing the bell at his own front door, a spritely Alfred – already aged 102 – was reminiscing enthusiastically about setting off from the Tay Bridge railway station as an 18-year-old with the 5th (TA) Battalion in 1914, about crossing the Channel in a cramped troopship on his first trip overseas, and about arriving in France and approaching the frontline. I remember interrupting him, reluctantly. I wanted him to know that whilst I could happily sit there all day and all night avidly listening to his recollections, if it might upset him or disturb him to rake over memories he had put to the back of his mind all these years, then he should stop, and leave it at that. I did not want to be the one to bring it all back, when as they kept telling me, he didn't talk about the war. And yet, I will never forget his response. 'I can tell you're interested', he said, 'and you were in The Black Watch, so I know you understand'. Those were his exact words, and with them we began a friendship that would last for the rest of his extraordinary life.

Over the years, I got to know his war stories well, because as the number of British survivors inevitably dwindled away to a handful, Alfred was increasingly in demand for photographs and interviews with journalists, makers of TV documentaries and military historians. I suppose I acted as his agent (unpaid!) and he came to rely on my advice and support as he became more and more a figure of public interest. By the time of his death in 2005 at the age of 109, he was easily the oldest man in Scotland and the last Scottish survivor of the First World War. But he was also reckoned to be the last survivor of the British Expeditionary Force that sailed for France in 1914 and possibly the last man in the world to have been present on the Western Front during the famous Christmas Truce of 1914. Alfred did not play football with the Germans in no-man's-land that night, or swap cap badges and buttons. His platoon was stood down for a rest in a barn somewhere behind the frontline. Nonetheless, he retained a clear memory both of the guns falling silent, and of their starting up again on Christmas Day.

He also remembered briefly serving alongside a young officer, Fergus Bowes-Lyon, who was killed in the Battle of Loos in September 1915 and whose older sister Elizabeth would become The Queen Mother and Colonel-in-Chief of The Black Watch. Alfred himself was seriously wounded in 1916 when he was hit by shrapnel while stationed at a listening-post far out beyond the trenches. He had to wait until darkness fell so that he could be safely stretchered back to a field dressing station. Alfred spent the rest of the war training soldiers in Yorkshire, preparing others to brave the dangers that he had experienced all too vividly for himself. By the time the Second World War came around, he was too old for active service, and ran the Home Guard at Newtyle, Angus.

In September 2002, six months after his grandmother Queen Elizabeth had died, Prince Charles paid a private visit to Alfred's home in Alyth, the most high-powered of all the encounters I helped to arrange. When Alfred, by then 106, was sitting waiting for his royal visitor to arrive, and I was pacing the floor of his living room rather anxiously, he suggested there was no need to be nervous and we should just treat His Royal Highness like any other senior officer. 'How very sensible' said the Prince, as he strode up the garden path. And in so many ways that's exactly what Alfred Anderson was. Sensible and straightforward, modest and unassuming. He did not have a particularly remarkable war. He just lived to tell the tale, for longer than anyone else. He never forgot the friends he lost on the battlefields of France and he knew he was one of the lucky ones. Those of us who counted Alfred Anderson as a friend, we know we were the lucky ones.

AN EARNEST FRIENDSHIP
'FRIENDS ARE KNOWN IN THE HOUR OF BATTLE.'
THE 19TH REGIMENT OF INFANTRY OF THE FRENCH ARMY AND THE BLACK WATCH

Roddy Riddell

I N MAY 1745, the Highland Regiment – as The Black Watch was then known – was part of the Allied Army (Pragmatic Army) in France during the War of the Austrian Succession (1740-8) when, on 11 May, it fought at the Battle of Fontenoy against the French. Indeed, it was a French victory but one in which the new regiment of Highlanders was to perform with great courage. A contemporary French report of the battle stated:

> The British behaved well, and could be exceeded in ardour by none but our officers, who animated the troops by their example, when the Highland furies rushed in upon us with more violence than ever did sea driven by a tempest.[1]

It was from this report that the regiment earned the nickname, the 'Highland Furies'. Wars against France continued during the eighteenth and early nineteenth centuries and it was not until the Crimean War of 1853-6 that the British and French armies fought as allies. Sixty years later, they would fight as allies again and a particularly strong relationship would be formed between the Territorials of the 6th (Perthshire) Battalion, The Black Watch, and the 19th Regiment of Infantry.

The 6th Battalion entrained at Bedford on 2 May 1915 and arrived in Boulogne in the early hours of 3 May, and so began the battalion's involvement in the Great War that would lead to a long-lasting and enduring respect between The Black Watch in general, and the

6th Battalion in particular, and a regiment of the French Army.

A G Wauchope has detailed the first meeting:

> On August 1st [1915] the Battalion had the interesting experience of taking over a sector of the line from the French, when the 6th went into the firing line in front of La Boisselle. Here the trenches were dug in the chalky soil to a depth of fifteen feet and were provided with deep and roomy shelters, a great contrast to the shallow, ditch-like lines of breast-works at Festubert. With such protection it was possible for the battalion to remain for several weeks in one sector without relief, and this was to be the experience of the 6th for the next five months.
>
> Everywhere there was evidence of the prodigious energy and ingenuity of the French engineers and infantry. Their officers took a just pride in these famous lines, and displayed an intimate knowledge not only of their own sector, but also of the enemy lines in front; this knowledge they took great pains to pass on to their successors. They were especially anxious that points to which they had clung tenaciously – such as 'Ilot' and 'Duhollo' – although only hopeless masses of wreckage, should not be abandoned, and they never were.
>
> The French troops relieved by the 6th were the famous 19th Regiment of Infantry, a splendid body of men drawn from Brittany. At one point the Highlanders were addressed by a sturdy Poilu[2] in the broadest Scotch, and later it was discovered that in pre war days he had been employed selling onions in the streets of Perth![3]

The quality of the French lines was demonstrated within hours of occupying this position, for as the entry in the *6th Battalion War Diary* for 2 August 1915 stated:

> Enemy fired 20 bombs into ILOT SECTION. Little damage. Work done – Repaired damage done by trench mortars. Casualties – Nil.[4]

For the next 12 days, until relieved by the 7th Black Watch, the 6th Battalion lived through a period of mining and countermining by German and French engineers, including the explosion of mines by both sides. On 8 August, the explosion of a mine beneath The Black Watch position buried alive a whole platoon of C Company in their dugout and blew one man across no-man's-land into the German lines where he later died. Rescue came quickly in the form of a digging party led by Captain Pullar, but casualties were remarkably light with only one man killed, one missing and 14 wounded, most 'lightly'.[5] Meanwhile the defence of the position was led by Major Alexander who won a Distinguished Service Order for his work, and the clearing and rebuilding of the damaged section of the frontline by Captain Innes. By daylight, the work was complete, and the line restored, and casualty numbers remained low.

This relief by the 6th Battalion of the 19th Infantry Regiment in 1915 must have had a profound effect on the two units, as in 1936, a proposed pilgrimage to the battlefields of France and Flanders in September that year, was to include a meeting with veterans of the 19th French Infantry Regiment. M Pierre Massé, Honorary Secretary of the French Regiment was the moving force behind the meeting. The *Red Hackle* recorded:

> We have an old Celtic adage which says: 'Friends are known in
> the hour of battle'. The Bretonach found this out as we did
> ourselves, and the gesture of the extended hand of friendship
> between us is to be cherished and supported, and will do more
> towards international understanding and peace than a century
> of political activities.[6]

The *Red Hackle* also recorded that on 9 September 1936, the veterans of The Black Watch and the 19th Regiment met at La Boisselle:

> After the exchange of friendly greetings between Pilgrims and
> Anciens Combattants, to the accompaniment of the pipes
> which made everyone feel at home – (the 19th, being raised in
> Brittany, where they have a similar Celtic instrument, known
> as the 'cornemuse') – that party proceeded to Albert, where in

the reconstructed Basilica – known to wartime soldiers as
'Church of the Leaning Virgin', they were received by his
Grace The Archbishop of Amiens, who gave his blessing and
sang a Te Deum in honour of the occasion.[7]

No mention is made of an exchange of gifts that took place during the
pilgrimage, when one urn containing the soil of Aberfeldy and La
Boisselle and another urn, the soil of Le Folgöet and La Boisselle, were
filled and exchanged as a 'souvenir of the brotherhood of arms of the
Celtic people at La Boisselle'.[8]

M Pierre Massé also wrote a poem in 1936, called 'Ecosse – Armor'
in honour of the occasion.[9] The original is in rhyming couplets, the
translation is not:[10]

SCOTLAND – BRITTANY
TO MY DEAR FRIENDS OF THE BLACK WATCH

From the low and high ground
Of Scotland with its snowy peaks
To Brittany along its coastline
Flowers the same blue thistle

Your motto is almost identical
To that of the yellow gorse
Whoever provokes you will get pricked
As both have proved many times before

In the binious and bagpipes
The same voices can be heard
Those same that inspired the Muses
The Celtic muses of long ago

In our mesmerising histories
Our young queens have played a role
Anne was an offering to your king
And Mary Stuart lived amongst us

Our proud soldiers of the past
Loyal to their solemn oath
Lived through cruel struggles
But for the same freedoms

The sons of Scotland and Brittany
Assembled with common accord
On the soil of Picardy
To save their great homelands.[11]

In April 1937, the *Red Hackle* was publicising another pilgrimage to take place in July 1939, to commemorate the 200th Anniversary of the regiment and to include a reunion with the Amicale of the 19th French Infantry Regiment in the Somme area.

In July of that year, the regimental journal recorded that:

The Black Watch urn is being deposited with much ceremony, in the old church of Le Folgöet, in Brittany, on 27th June. Permission has been received from the Commissionairs des Monuments Historiques, to place a granite slab on the wall of the church beside the urn. The Dowager Lady Moncrieffe of Moncrieffe has kindly given a flag similar to the Pilgrimage Flag, to the Amicales des Anciens Combattants due 19c Reg. Inf., for use at this ceremony.[12]

The October 1937 edition of the *Red Hackle* reported that:

An interesting Ceremony took place at Le Folgöet on 27th June, when the Amicale of the 19th French Infantry deposited the urn, exchanged with The Black Watch Pilgrimage last year, and unveiled a marble plaque in the Notre-Dame. The procession to the War Memorial and the church was headed by the school children of Le Folgöet and the tricolours of the various bodies of ex-servicemen, among which was the St Andrew's flag, kindly gifted by the Dowager Lady Moncrieffe of Moncrieffe.

A large number of local dignitaries, members of the 19th French Infantry Regiment Amicale as well as the British vice-consul (M Mignon) gathered in the church of Notre-Dame which was described as the pride of Brittany. The plaque was unveiled and consecrated and after the service a social gathering and celebration was held. The author of the report was William Buchanan 'Tug' Wilson from Aberdeen, the Honorary Secretary of The Black Watch Pilgrimage Committee and an ex-sergeant in the regiment.[13]

In July 1939, the *Red Hackle* published the detailed itinerary for the proposed tour in August that year, but no report records the success of the pilgrimage as Nazi Germany invaded Poland on 1 September and the regimental journal was not published again until 1946.[14]

The October 1947 *Red Hackle* reported the death of M Pierre Massé in Brest on 16 August 1947.[15] A letter from William B Wilson the Honorary Secretary of The Black Watch Pilgrimage Committee was published in a later edition of the regimental journal:

> The 1939 Pilgrimage saw the Amicale of the 19th R.I. meeting The Black Watch Pilgrimage and the 19th Belgian Infantry Association on the old battlefield of Waterloo just a week before the 1939-45 War broke out. It was a memorable occasion and all thought out by the late M Massé, though rumours of war threw a certain gloom over the proceedings.

The letter also encouraged members of the regiment to donate money to erect a plaque to the memory of M Massé and said, 'He was a good friend of Scotland and The Black Watch'.[16]

The memorial plaque was unveiled in Le Folgöet on 30 April 1950 and Wilson recorded the event in great detail. He played a pipe tune called 'Lament for the Only Son' during the service and the plaque was placed directly above the Celtic urn.[17]

Wilson remained in touch with his friends and in particular with M Massé's sister Mme Boutelier but as the veterans of the Great War died, the links between the two organisations faded. The lasting memorial to the brave men of both regiments should be the words 'the gesture of the extended hand of friendship between us is to be cherished and supported, and will do more towards international understanding and peace than a century of political activities'.[18]

Sadly, following the visit of the late Joe Hubble to La Boisselle in 2012, and the publication of his account of his visit in the *Red Hackle* we can no longer assume that the urn in Brittany is still on display in the church in Le Folgöet and has most probably been lost.[19] Nonetheless, we do know that The Black Watch 'Brittany Urn' is treasured and displayed in the regimental museum in Perth, 105 years after the 19th Regiment of Infantry handed over the trenches at La Boisselle to the 6th (Perthshire) Battalion, The Black Watch, in August 1915.

THE 'BRITTANY URN'
The Black Watch Castle and Museum, Perth
(The Black Watch Castle and Museum)

1   Victoria Schofield, *The Highland Furies: The Black Watch 1739-1899* (London: Quercus Publishing plc, 2012), p33.

2   'Poilu' in the literal sense means 'hairy'. The generally accepted etymological theory is that French soldiers in the trenches were called 'poilus' because they were often unable to shave off their beards or cut their hair.

3   For a detailed account of the action at the Second Battle of the Marne see A G Wauchope, *A History of the Black Watch in the Great War, 1914-18*, Volume 2 (London: Medici Society, 1926), p132.

4   *6th Battalion War Diary*, 2 August 1915.

5   *6th Battalion War Diary*, 8 August 1915.

6   *Red Hackle*, April 1936, p41.

7   *Red Hackle*, October 1936 pp47-8.

8   *'En souvenir de la fraternité d'armes des peuples celtiques à la Boisselle.'*

9   *Red Hackle*, October 1936, p49. Armor is particularly the northern coast of Brittany, but the whole of it is referred to by Bretons as Armor. The name has nothing to do with love (*amour* in modern French).

10 The poet has altered the flow of a natural sentence to achieve the rhyme whereas the translator, Major (Retired) T J O Carmichael, has returned it to a logical sequence not reliant on grammar to make sense of its parts.

11 Binious are reedy chanters that accompany the pipes in Breton bands. Anne of Brittany was a highly respected fifteenth-century princess, ever loyal to her Breton roots. No immediate link to having been a consort of a Scottish king has been found. Henry VII of England was in strategic alliance with her against the French. In her own right, she was Countess of Richmond through her father's line.

12 *Red Hackle*, July 1937, p2.

13 William Buchanan Wilson fought in both the First and Second World Wars. He enlisted in 1908 and served in both the 1st and 2nd Battalions during the Great War winning a Military Medal in 1917. Leaving the Army in 1921, he rejoined the Colours and fought with the 6th Battalion during the Second World War and was badly wounded at Monte Cassino. He was described as a 'Remarkable Person – dedicated soldier, historian, poet piper, Gaelic scholar, athlete, *shikari*!'. He died in August 1966 and his obituary appeared in the *Red Hackle* of December 1966 (pp5-6).

14 *Red Hackle*, July 1939, pp47-48.

15 *Red Hackle*, October 1947, p2.

16 *Red Hackle*, April 1949, p4. The pilgrimage was cut short and the group returned to Scotland earlier than planned.

17 *Red Hackle*, July 1950, p12.

18 *Red Hackle*, April 1936, p41.

19 *Red Hackle*, May 1914, p14.

FROM THE FORTH DEFENCES TO THE *DINNA FORGET BOOK OF THE 7TH BLACK WATCH*

Bob Scott and Fraser Brown

O N 31 JULY 1914, in what was termed a 'Preparatory Movement,' a Special Service Section drawn from the 7th Battalion consisting of three officers and 117 other ranks arrived at Kinghorn to occupy the Kinghorn Fort, which with the heavily fortified island of Inchkeith formed an integral part of Number 3 Section Forth Defences. The following morning the *Fifeshire Advertiser* reported the event in a single terse paragraph:

Mobilization

Kinghorness Battery has been fully manned with members of the Territorial Forces. On Thursday, within three hours of the mobilization notices being issued, the garrisoning of the town was completed. The men of No. 1 and 4 Companies of the Forth HGA, at present in camp at Kinghorn, took positions at the Battery, while men of the 7th Battalion The Black Watch Royal Highlanders, drawn from various parts of Fife, marched into the town and took up strong defensive positions. Sentries were on duty overnight. Civilians were greatly interested in the mobilization, and commented freely of the quick transformation of the scene of a quiet town being turned into a military centre.[1]

On 2 August 1914, the Special Service Section of the 7th Battalion drawn from C Company (Kirkcaldy) and B Company (Lochgelly) marched to Kinghorn under command of Captain G W McIntosh and by the evening of 7 August, the entire 7th Battalion had been deployed in its war station. At that point, D Company and one machine-gun section were stationed at Burntisland and the remainder of the battalion with the second machine-gun section were deployed at Kinghorn. Almost immediately, the men of the battalion began to dig the first trenches on Crying Hill overlooking the Pettycur Battery and set up guard posts wherever required.

BLACK WATCH TRENCHES AT KINGHORN IN
THE EARLY DAYS OF THE WAR
Captain Herd MC, photo album

Three years later, with battalion casualty lists of a size unimaginable before the war, with the fights at High Wood, Beaumont Hammel, Arras, Third Ypres and Cambrai behind them and a year of hard fighting still to come, the service and the men of the 7th Battalion were celebrated in *The Dinna Forget Book of the 7th Black Watch*. This free pictorial supplement to the Fife edition of the daily *Dundee Advertiser* appeared on 5 January 1918 as one of a set of three battalion 'Dinna Forget' books for the 4th (Dundee), 6th (Perthshire) and 7th (Fife) Battalions. Its main purpose appears to have been to act as the introduction to a series of over 20 articles published daily in each local edition of the *Dundee Advertiser* describing the experiences of each battalion up to that point.[2]

The 'Dinna Forget' books all followed a similar structure. The Black Watch tartan front cover displayed a sketch of a Black Watch sniper and his observer drawn by Joseph Gray, a former employee of the *Dundee Advertiser* and member of the 4th (Dundee) Battalion, and by 1917 an established war artist. All three supplements contained 12 pages of very good quality pictures printed on equally good quality paper showing officers, senior NCOs and men of the different battalions as well as individual groups like the transport and machine-gun sections, or district groups such as the men of Atholl or Cupar. Carefully posed pictures of officers and men on the eve of their departure for the Western Front in 1915, the Pipes and Drums of each battalion, and men under training waiting to join their battalions on the Western Front were allocated a page each so that quite literally hundreds of clearly identifiable men are shown.

7TH BLACK WATCH MARCHING ALONG THE DUSTY
FRICOURT-ALBERT ROAD IN JULY 1916 AFTER THE ACTION
AT HIGH WOOD LED BY THE PIPES AND DRUMS
Dinna Forget Book of the 7th Black Watch, Dundee Advertiser, 7 January 1918.
(Used by kind permission of D C Thomson & Co Ltd)

Nevertheless, the 7th Battalion book differs in two significant respects. First, its double centre page featured one of the most evocative pictures of Black Watch soldiers of the Great War ever to be published. It is entitled 'With Ranks Reduced But Hearts Undaunted' and shows the survivors of the 7th Battalion led by the Pipes and Drums immediately after the action at High Wood on 30 July 1916 as they marched past an embankment lined with Tommies. Second, it both celebrates and mourns a number of 7th Battalion 'firsts' by presenting a picture of the first officer and other rank to be killed, the first officer and other rank to be decorated, the first officer to be wounded and the most popular officer in the battalion, all placed around the central picture of Lieutenant-Colonel Allen, DSO, CMG, the first wartime commanding officer until wounded in July 1916. This short section sets out to examine the achievements – and fate – of the seven men whose photographs appeared on the 7th Battalion page of 'firsts'.

Allen led the 7th Battalion from mobilisation until wounded on 28 July 1916, two days before the attack on High Wood. He had served in the Indian Army until 1911, had been awarded the Distinguished Service Order for his work in the Zakka Khel and Mohmand Expeditions of 1908 on the Indian Frontier and had served in several other Frontier campaigns including those in Waziristan. He replaced Sir Ralph Anstruther in 1913, and as commanding officer of the 7th Battalion on mobilisation was responsible for the defence – against sabotage or a surprise attack from the rear by a German naval landing party set ashore elsewhere in Fife – of Number 3 Section of the Forth Defences including the Kinghorn and Burntisland Batteries.[3] In 1915, he was in command of the 7th Battalion when it went first to Ripon and then to France, and apart from a short period in hospital in May 1916 remained with it until he was wounded at the end of July 1916. He returned to the 7th Battalion briefly before he finally left the firing line having been retired from frontline service at the age of 50.[4]

During the war, local newspapers generally made a specific point of identifying the first local man to be killed in action, and in that sense *The Dinna Forget Book of the 7th Black Watch* was no different. In fact, Sergeant Charles Nisbet of the old D (Cowdenbeath) Company who had been associated with the Territorials and the old Volunteers for 16 years, and regarded as 'one of the brightest and best' by his company commander, Major Guthrie, was the first man of the 7th Battalion to be killed.[5] His death on 22 May 1915 occurred during the battalion's first tour of the trenches in the Festubert Sector where they relieved the 6th Battalion in an area under constant shellfire and where the battlefield had not been cleared of dead, and discarded and damaged weapons and equipment still lay around. Nisbet's death from shrapnel wounds was described in some detail some weeks after the event in an article in the *Fifeshire*

Advertiser entitled 'Racy Narrative of Fife's Own' written by a Private Adams from Convalescent Company HQ, 51st Highland Division.[6]

Even so, while the account of Nisbet's death by Adams was graphic in detail, the death of Lieutenant A C Westwood the first officer to be killed, was seen by the *St Andrews Citizen* at least as containing something of a 'pathetic coincidence' in that:

> Condolence on the death of the first Cupar member of the 1/7th Black Watch who fell at the front, Private John Pratt, Castlefield, should have been conveyed to his mother by Lieutenant Westwood, while Lieutenant Westwood was the first Cupar officer to fall.[7]

Westwood, who fell while reconnoitring a better position for his machine-gun team, was well known in Cupar. He had attended Bell Baxter High School before going on to George Watson's College in Edinburgh, and was in business with his father Alexander Westwood JP, a well-known local book seller and publisher with business premises at Crossgate, Cupar. While at Watson's, Westwood had been a member of the school cadet corps, and a few years before the outbreak of war had enlisted in the 7th Battalion before being commissioned in 1914. Westwood was also something of a local sportsman and in addition to his being an enthusiastic hockey and rugby player, he was also a member of the Cupar Cricket Club and a keen motorcyclist.

The first Distinguished Conduct Medal awarded in the 7th Battalion was reported in the *Fife Free Press* under the heading 'Fife's Own First DCM Distinction For Dysart Soldier' on 25 September 1915.[8] That contrasted sharply with the amount of coverage of the award of the Military Cross (MC) to Lieutenant Fullerton-Carnegie in the Fife newspapers which mentioned his connection to the old Carnegie family of Angus of which the Earl of Southesk was the head. Strangely, no mention was made of how he won the MC On the other hand, letters home from men in the 7th Battalion, which were often printed in local newspapers, ensured that most of Fife knew all about the gallantry of Sergeant John Patterson long before the presentation of his medal. One such letter from an anonymous comrade dated 14 September 1915 appeared in the *Fife Free Press*:

> This has been a memorable day for the 7th, our first DCM being presented today. He is John Patterson. He went down a mine and rescued two men who were lying gassed at the foot. He was overcome bringing the second man up. He is a plucky fellow and deserves the medal...[9]

PAGE OF FIRSTS. "DINNA FORGET BOOK OF
THE 7TH BLACK WATCH"
Dundee Advertiser, 7 January 1918
(Used by kind permission of D C Thomson & Co Ltd)

As everyone in Dysart would have been aware, Patterson was a pre-war Territorial soldier of the 7th Battalion, a former miner working in the Frances Pit who lived in Fraser Place, Dysart. Fortunately, all three men lived to be taken off to hospital for treatment, and it seems they all survived.

Equally fortunate was Lieutenant W B Brown, the first officer to be wounded. Brown's wife received a War Office telegram at their home in

Orwell, St Andrews, with the news that he had been wounded; and this information appeared in the next editions of all of the Fife local newspapers. The *East of Fife Record* explained that Brown had been associated with the 7th Battalion for a number of years and that he was cashier in the office of Major J L Macpherson, a solicitor who was serving with the 2/7th Battalion.[10] Two days later, a letter from an anonymous Cupar private soldier who had witnessed the event appeared in the *Fifeshire Advertiser.*[11] It explained how Brown had been wounded by shrapnel in the arm and leg and that another ten men had been wounded and one killed by the same shell burst. By the end of May 1917, Brown had recovered, been promoted to captain and had returned to the 7th Battalion.

The very popular Captain Donaldson however, wounded in the same engagement as his great friend Lieutenant Westwood was killed, lost an eye on that occasion and was invalided home. On recovery, he was posted to the 3/7th Battalion, which was then the training and reinforcement unit and began to request to be sent on foreign service. When he returned to the 7th Battalion, it was very clear why the *Dinna Forget Book* claimed he was 'idolised by the Seventh' for as the *Fife Free Press* account stated, 'His reception was remarkable and showed the great feeling and regard the men entertained for him'.[12] Donaldson was also very much respected with the civilian population while stationed at Kinghorn where his record of service as a private in the Second Anglo-Boer War (1899-1902) in the Bankers Company of the Queens Edinburgh Volunteers attached to the Royal Scots was well known. It was also clear from the tributes paid by the Fife newspapers that this was a man deeply involved in his local community: he was in turn agent of the British Linen Bank in Falkland, a member of the Town Council, the local School Board, the Parish Council Secretary to the YMCA and the Curling Club, and days before his death at Arras while serving with the 9th Battalion, the Black Watch, became one of the new JPs for the county.

Finally, it is worth asking whether the pictures have any larger significance than that of a simple a pictorial record. Perhaps, and if it does, that significance lies in the sense that it represented the old 7th Battalion. All the men pictured as 'firsts' had been in it before the outbreak of war.

All the officers and senior NCOs, apart from one or two were Fife men, but the new 7th Battalion, as represented by the draft in training picture and group photographs of officers and senior NCOs taken in 1917 was of a different stamp. Some of the old 7th Battalion men were still there, but the Military Service Act of 1916 meant that conscripts rubbed shoulders with pre-war volunteers. Perhaps the greatest change of all, however, is evidenced by a remark made in the caption of a picture of the draft in training which made the point that most of the men were from the industrial west and not the old 'Kingdom'. The 7th Battalion which would endure despite the *Kaiserschlacht* and the other great battles of 1918 would be a very different battalion to the one that left Kinghorn in 1915.

1   *Fifeshire Advertiser*, 1 August 1915.

2   No similar supplement exists for either the 5th (Angus) Battalion or the composite 4/5th Battalion formed in March 1916.

3   The three lines of landward defences constructed by the 7th Battalion near Abden and Grange Farm, outside Kinghorn, in the first days of the war were part of the response to that threat.

4   *Dundee Advertiser*, 7 January 1918.

5   *Leven Advertiser & Wemyss Gazette*, 27 May 1915.

6   *Fifeshire Advertiser*, 19 June 1915.

7   *St Andrews Citizen*, 26 June 1915.

8   *Fife Free Press*, 25 September 1915.

9   *Fife Free Press*, 25 September 1915.

10 *East of Fife Record*, 3 September 1915.

11 *Fifeshire Advertiser*, 5 June 1915.

12 *Fife Free Press*, 1 September 1917.

THE 7TH BATTALION AND THE
SCHOOLCHILDREN OF FIFE

Fraser Brown

IT IS CLEAR from the Fife wartime press as well as from entries in surviving school logs and magazines that from the outbreak of the Great War the schoolchildren of the county had chosen to do their bit to help the 'sodgers' in whatever way they could. Press coverage of girls spontaneously contributing their Saturday pennies to war funds, Boy Scouts manning Coast Guard stations watching for German warships off the Fife coast or Girl Guides acting as cooks and military messengers (as they did in Dunfermline) was widespread, if somewhat discreet.[1] In short, schoolchildren of all ages and classes all across the 42nd Regimental Area – including Fife – had 'self-mobilised'.[2] But what made Scottish children's war support work all the more remarkable was that unlike in England and Wales, where the authorities encouraged war support work to be done in schooltime, in Scotland, the Scottish Education Department ensured that it was done after school, on a purely voluntary basis and within local by-laws governing the employment of minors. This short section looks at some aspects of the relationship between schoolchildren and their local Territorial unit, the 7th (Fife) Battalion.

Dozens of little stories of children's efforts written in gravely approving tones were published in the local papers. Short snippets in the local press about local children abounded: Miss Work, the newsagent at Collessie, Fife, when describing the contributors to the collection for the 7th Battalion observed, 'even the little children brought in their message earnings to help swell the fund'.[3] The village and district had 140 men fighting, so the level of personal involvement amongst local children with The Black Watch and the soldiers in general is not hard to imagine, and in fact it endured for the rest of the war.

By the end of 1914, all over Fife the extent and range of pupil support work in aid of the 7th Battalion had grown massively in scope. Generally, these initiatives were organised by adults, but invariably driven by a pairing of the children's apparent overwhelming need for involvement in the war effort, and an inner personal drive to support the soldiers as kith and kin.

SPAGNUM MOSS GATHERERS:
One of the many ways Fife children worked in support of the war effort.
(After processing the moss was used in wound dressings.)
People's Journal (Fife Edition), 27 April 1917
(Used by kind permission of D C Thomson & Co Ltd)

In Cellardyke, the working out of one case of this combination began in earnest on 5 and 6 February 1915, when the pupils of the school gave two concerts for around 2,000 spectators in Anstruther Town Hall. When the takings were tallied it was found that they had raised £58/15 in order to buy the Cellardyke men a Christmas present and to provide a comforts parcel for all of them.[4] In fact, along with the usual comforts, each man received a present of a highly desirable, sturdy clasp knife with a tin opener attachment.

The school received letters of thanks which were read aloud to the entire school and three of these were published in the *East of Fife Record*. One letter was from a trooper in the Fife and Forfar Yeomanry while another was from a Scots Guardsman, and from the tone of both letters it was very clear that the contact and the gifts had left both a 'grand feeling' of not being forgotten by those in 'oor ain toon' as well as a very definite emotional impact on these men. The third letter was from Captain G M Black of

2nd Supernumerary Company, 2/7th Black Watch who was at the Royal Pavilion at Brighton, then a military hospital where his unit was on guard and general duties, was of a different stamp. It began, 'My Dear Bairns' and set out in simple but inclusive terms not only his gratitude, but also how he was doing his 'little bit' just as the children were doing theirs. He also expressed his confidence that 'I know you will continue to do so until this terrible war is ended'. He told the children of the sad sights he had seen on the wards and alluded to the plight of the 3,000 Indian wounded at Brighton and very frankly asked the children for their continuing help for all wounded. Finally, he appealed to them to remember that, 'In as much as ye have done it to the least of these my brethren, ye have done it unto me'. Captain Black's letter was not particularly unusual at that time in touching on those matters it covered, or in its religious undertones, but it is a particularly good example of the child being asked to take on the previously near exclusively adult role of so-called 'responsible' worker.[5] Yet even this invitation to responsibility appears to have constituted a very effective motivational driver, because for the remainder of the war the children of Cellardyke never faltered in their support as their contributions to war funds and savings schemes testify.

The idea that a young person, still in full-time education, could be a valuable volunteer war worker capable of assuming responsibility for locally important fund-raising projects was a fairly novel concept for many adults at the beginning of the war, but very quickly a different view took hold. In Anstruther, in what appears to have been near desperation, the organisers of several fund-raising projects turned to the senior girls of Waid Academy. Amazingly, this group now ran all street collections in Anstruther for wartime causes ranging from Scottish Women's Hospitals and Serbian Relief to Black Watch Flag Days from October 1915 until at least October 1917. At that point they disappear from the columns of the local newspaper, when the print acreage of the local paper shrank due to lack of newsprint and only the final accounts of monies raised were published. It is also important to state that the Waid Academy girls were not alone: the *Dunfermline Press* reported in glowing terms on the Lochgelly Guides operation of the Russian Red Cross Flag Day in May 1917.[6] Even more surprising – given pre-war thinking – Bell Baxter

High School girls formed an autonomous branch of the Cupar Volunteer Workers Association and appear to have achieved formal government recognition on terms of equality with the other Fife branches, continuing to make 'bomb bags', gloves for men on the minesweepers, supported a prisoner of war and made standardised comforts for The Black Watch till the end of the war.[7] Similar examples can be found all over the 42nd Regimental Area from the first months of 1915 onwards, and as always, the letters of thanks from grateful soldiers appeared to drive forward children's efforts.

Another feature of the support for the soldiers across Fife was that the actual numbers of children reported in the local press as involved in these fund-raising events in aid of the 7th Battalion were always substantial. In March 1917, for example, the Sunday School soirée of the Lochgelly Parish Church was addressed by Major MacDuff of the 7th Battalion who told the children present very directly how many of their male Sunday School teachers were in the trenches, how grateful the men of his company were that they had not been forgotten, and how much they appreciated their presents from the Lochgelly children. During the soirée, of the 400 children attending Sunday School in the town almost all were present that evening either as performers, Scouts demonstrating their skills, or in the audience.[8]

Interestingly too, this high level of attendance was to be found elsewhere particularly in after-school activities in support of the war effort in general: an appeal to all the head teachers in Fife to organise the pupils of their district to dig up dandelion roots at a particular point in the plant's life cycle drew a massive voluntary response from pupils. These roots were desperately required to provide a home-grown supply of *taraxacum*, an active ingredient in contemporary diuretics and liver treatment of bed-ridden wounded since the world price had rocketed due to serious wartime shortages. There was a massive response later to a request to children to gather broom shoots for similar use in treating kidney problems common amongst the wounded, for by 21 June 1916, within two days of receiving the request, the children of Castlehill School in Cupar had sent off the first batch from Fife of two hundredweights to Duncan & Flockhart, organic chemists in Edinburgh for distillation.

In addition, comments such as 'The pupils of Fife schools are lending invaluable assistance to the Cupar Volunteer Workers Association' appeared regularly in local papers while news from the villages noted specific events such as that Balmerino School had sent off dried roots for processing, or that children from Falkland or Cupar were picking sphagnum moss in large quantities.[9] Their efforts were frequently acknowledged in both print and in a number of cases by the appearance of a picture in the local press, and on many occasions by letters of appreciation from the military authorities – including Black Watch officers – addressed directly to the children.

Of course, school pupils' practical support for the soldiers did not end there and a full discussion of their contribution to the war effort is well beyond the scope of this short section. Nevertheless, taken as a whole, child mobilisation in Fife – as throughout Scotland – rapidly and effectively adapted to the needs of the nation at war. It achieved levels of coordination and efficiency seldom mentioned in current accounts of civilian life on the Home Front, although both military and civil authorities at the time gratefully acknowledged both the quality and volume of children's work.

---

1   *Fife News,* 3 October 1914; *Cowdenbeath & Lochgelly Times,* 27 November 1918; *Arbroath Guide,* 25 December 1914; *East of Fife Record,* 5 November 191; *Perthshire Constitutional & Journal,* 10 November 1915; *Brechin Advertiser,* 14 January 1916.

2   *Perthshire Constitutional & Journal,* 27 March 1916; *Forfar Herald,* 17 December 1917; *Arbroath Herald,* 10 May 1918.

3   *Fife Herald,* 8 December 1915.

4   *Cellardyke Public School Log,* 5 February 1915.

5   This aspect is covered in Manon Pignot, 'Children', in Jay Winter (ed), *The Cambridge History of the First World War* (Cambridge: Cambridge University Press, 2013), p32.

6   *Dunfermline Press,* 19 May 1917.

7   Bomb bags were grenade satchels.

8   *Cowdenbeath & Lochgelly Times,* 7 March 1917.

9   *Cowdenbeath & Lochgelly Times,* 13 September 1916, 14 November 1917.

THE HEIRS OF HUGH MACKAY

BLACK WATCH PIPERS IN THE GREAT WAR

Alistair Duthie

EVER SINCE the earliest days of The Black Watch, in peace and particularly in war, the pipers have always brought something to regimental life that the ordinary soldier might find difficult to define, but which everyone understood was always present. A G Wauchope's *A History of the Black Watch in the Great War, 1914-18* described that presence as being the result of 'the power of the pipers to touch the spirit of the regiment'.[1] When the duty piper sounded the routine calls of barrack and peacetime soldiering, Black Watch soldiers went about whatever duty the calls demanded: every call from reveille, defaulters and mess calls to lights out was answered. The piper was also both the celebrant and bearer of a cultural tradition born of regiment, recruiting district and a wider Scottish identity as they played for dancing, at mess nights and led regimental celebrations. Generally, their contribution to the development of The Black Watch regimental culture was by way of individual performance, and at times their musical creativity extended the regiment's great store of pipe music through original composition. These original compositions could record cause for celebration, or remembrance, or even some truly insignificant but memorable event like 'The Orderly Man Spilled the Coffee Oh!'.

In wartime, pipers often led the way in the attack, frequently at great cost; they cheered men on the march and lifted men's spirits in hard times, but always acted as a constant reminder to The Black Watch men of the Great War of who they were and what was expected of them. At times too, the idea of the piper playing his regiment into action became something larger than a man doing his duty – often with fatal consequences – and far more of a symbol of his regiment, or of the Scottish soldier in general. Of course, with the Great War came much more detailed newspaper reporting on the fate of ordinary soldiers, and with that came additional assessment of the piper as an individual rather than as a functionary carrying out a prearranged role. Pipers were always what was known at the time as 'men of character', generally led by a Pipe Major who was also something of a 'character', and whose influence with them invariably appears to have gone well beyond the musical direction and application of a strict disciplinary code expected of any bandmaster. Today, courtesy of digitised newspaper archives, much more evidence is available as to exactly who these men were.

It was also the case that no matter what century he lived in, the piper was nothing if not a very visible and much drawn, painted and photographed soldier, especially when in company with the drummers. Half a century before the outbreak of the Great War, the American Civil War (1861-5) introduced still photographs of soldiers' daily lives and the realities of the battlefield to the public. For the first time in history, the civilian at home did not have to rely on the war artist for information about what their armies and the places they fought in actually looked like. During the Great War, the number of still photographs taken by official photographers and released to the press, as well as pictures taken against orders by individual soldiers with illicit private cameras then pasted into private and regimental scrapbooks, was simply enormous. For the first time, the pipers could be seen by the general public as they really were, stripped by the wartime still photograph and the moving picture of the war artist inspired romanticism of previous conflicts. Even so, the painter Charles 'Snaffles' Payne's sketch 'There Cam a Piper Oot o' Fife' is still a wonderful depiction of the power of the piper to command an audience. Snaffles apart, with much more detailed information available, and more access to moving and still images of pipers available than ever before, even previously apparently impenetrable pipe band group photographs become more 'approachable'.

Within that mass of moving and still pictures, every Scottish regiment could find its own set of abiding and near iconic images, and in the majority of these the pipers were strongly featured. The film of the 15th Battalion, Highland Light Infantry, still dressed in their tramway uniforms marching to George Square in Glasgow in September 1914 to be named 1st Glasgow is one. The picture of the Seaforth piper leading four of his comrades back from the attack at Longueval in July 1916 which fronts Trevor Royle's *Flowers of the Forest* is another, and on both occasions, as in so many other similar pictures, these images have a good deal to say about the place and the role of the pipes and those who played them in the life of a regiment at war.[2] In this sense The Black Watch is no different to any other Scottish regiment. It can draw on an array of pictures, not least of which is of the 7th Black Watch marching along the dusty Fricourt-Albert road in July 1916 after the action at High Wood led by the Pipes and Drums and watched by rows of Tommies standing on the roadside. It should not be forgotten that it is in this environment of mass photography and accompanying mass publication of photographs in the press that the Great War piper – and sometimes also the drummer – existed.

Beyond these images of very real and often identifiable individuals, there is another image, or rather a stereotype of the Great War piper in the public mind and it is that of the mythical, near indestructible, invincible 'lone piper' leading the advance, striding out well ahead of his kilted comrades. But there was much more to pipers and piping during the Great War than that. Questions such as how pipers were employed when not actually playing, who led them, and how did the experience of war impact on their music are only a few. It might also be asked what effect their music had on their comrades, and what evidence is there to support the idea of an especially strong bond between members of the Pipes and Drums during the Great War. However, the first thing to be discussed is the reality or otherwise of pipers leading the advance and playing their companies into action during the war.

GREAT WAR PIPER:
STEREOTYPES AND REALITIES

The most comprehensive account of when pipers played men into action during the Great War is to be found in Sir Bruce Seton and Pipe Major John Grant's work *The Pipes of War*.[3] This book, published in 1920, contains the result of a statistical exercise initiated by Seton which collected information on the fate and the employment of pipers of a large number of Scottish and Imperial units where they served during the Great War. The initial undated *Circular Letter* sent to all units stated that information gathered was to be formed into a 'Record' of all pipers on field service 'with all proceeds devoted entirely to orphans of pipers killed during the war'.[4] The *Circular Letter* also specifically requested details of when men had distinguished themselves either as pipers, and separately if employed in any other role at the time. The result was an impressive compilation of nominal rolls of pipers by regiment and battalion, each accompanied by a note on employment of each battalion's pipers. However, from a purely regimental point of view the absence of any mention of the 3rd (Special Reserve) and 12th (Labour) Battalion pipers is unfortunate; as indeed is the absence of any mention of the Scottish Horse given that it became a Black Watch battalion during the war. It is also clear from other sources such as the Dinna Forget books of the 4th, 6th and 7th Black Watch, obituaries in local newspapers and the frequently published pictorial lists of The Black Watch men killed in action that many pipers appear to have been overlooked in the *Pipes of War* lists.[5]

In view of these omissions, this chapter therefore defines a piper as any Black Watch soldier including boy pipers who held that appointment at some point during the Great War, whether he was a member of his Battalion Pipes and Drums or not, and regardless of his final rank during that war.[6]

The first officially recorded occasion pipers attempted to play the 1st Battalion into action was at Cuinchy on 25 January 1915 on a day of very heavy casualties caused by atrocious ground conditions when the attacking troops advanced knee deep in mud. The 1st Battalion attack on Aubers Ridge on 9 May 1915 was led by company pipers and two, Pipers Wishart and Stewart, particularly distinguished themselves. Piper Stewart, who was a reservist and who had returned from Australia on the outbreak of war was awarded the Distinguished Conduct Medal (DCM) for his exploits that day which included playing the second line into the attack until he was shot down on the German parapet. According to Wauchope – although Seton and Grant stated otherwise – that was the last occasion the pipers of 1st Battalion led their companies into action as 'gas helmets were shortly to muffle the pipers'.[7] Gas, the pipers most recent and probably greatest enemy, however, had not finished with the 1st Battalion yet. A plan to celebrate the capture of Wassigny on 18 October 1918 by parading the Pipes and Drums through the town was upset by the effects of a single, stray gas shell which hit the billet of the battalion headquarters and not only put the runners and scouts there out of action, but also the entire pipe band.[8]

In the case of the 2nd Battalion, Wauchope explained in some detail how at Loos where that battalion was part of the Indian Corps diversionary attack at Mauquissart, the pipers played an important part in the action.[9] Piper MacDonald (1539) recommended for a Victoria Cross (VC) and sometimes referred to as the 'Other Piper of Loos', was noted by Wauchope as having 'showed a courage typical of all the Pipers of the Regiment in this action; played the charge at the head of his platoon through the first and second line of enemy trenches'.[10] Not content with that, according to Seton and Grant, as the platoon started to bomb their way along the German trench, he walked along the parapet playing until shot down. Unfortunately, Piper MacDonald lost a leg and was not awarded the VC but did get a DCM. His companion Piper Armitt played on, then joined the bombers for the rest of the battle, while Piper Simpson fell at the head of Number 1 Company. Once in Mesopotamia in 1916, pipers led their companies again, including at Sheikh Saad, when Corporal Piper MacNie who had won the DCM at Mauquissart the year before was killed.

When the nominal rolls of the Territorial battalions are examined, it is clear that their pipers also led the attack on occasion. The note accompanying the nominal roll of the 4th (City of Dundee) Battalion, The Black Watch (TF), for example stated that on 3 September 1916, the battalion was played into the attack, although by that time it had merged with the 5th Battalion to become the 4/5th Battalion. The 6th (Perthshire) Battalion was played into the attack at High Wood in July 1916 by Pipers Pirnie, Forbes, Mapleton and Tainsh, but this was an exceptional use of pipers in that battalion rather than the norm. Another piper of the same battalion was mentioned by Seton and Grant as having created a great stir in the German lines when, whether by way of a joke or reveille, marched from one end of the line to the other playing 'Johnnie Cope'. The Germans were not best pleased with this, and 'expecting an immediate attack, at once started a barrage. No attack was intended'.[11]

Of the other battalions, only the 5th (Angus) and 7th (Fife) Battalions are not specifically mentioned by Seton and Grant as having been led into the attack by pipers, however when interviewed in Jock Duncan's collection of recollections of the Great War published as *Jock's Jocks*, Albert Edwards of the 5th Battalion (later the Machine Gun Corps) was clear that 'Our Company Pipers piped us over to the attack many a time'.[12]

Of the 'New Army Battalions', however, Seton and Grant stated that the 8th was played into action at Loos and in many of the Somme engagements and lost heavily, but their band had the honour of heading the State Entry of King Albert into Brussels in November 1918. The 9th Battalion Pipers played their men into the attack at Hill 70, an action in which all but one member of the band were killed or wounded. Amongst the 9th Battalion Pipers to fall that day was Piper Duncan McLarty, born in Perth, Western Australia, the second Australian Black Watch man to be killed that day.

PIPERS AS COMBATANTS

When the public as a whole look at the Pipes and Drums on parade they are often unaware of the non-musical role they play in the life of the battalions they serve with. Regardless of regiment, all pipers are and always were combatants, so while like military musicians in general they are part of the ceremonial life of their regiments and corps, nevertheless in time of war, unlike military bandsmen these men were – and still are – soldiers and combatants. Today the Pipes and Drums of The Black Watch battalion are the Assault Pioneer Platoon, but at different times they have also been a Rifle Platoon and the Head Quarters Defence Platoon. During the Great War on the other hand, on mobilisation, all pipers except for the Sergeant Piper and five pipers reverted to the ranks and were then deployed at the discretion of the commanding officer.

In the Great War, that phrase 'deployment at the discretion of the Commanding Officer' meant pipers assumed a number of different roles, but there was a general tendency amongst the different Black Watch battalions to employ pipers as stretcher-bearers, and it was their work in that role that was often commended and acknowledged by awards of medals for gallantry. Piper G Swan, MM, of the 7th Battalion for example was but one piper killed while carrying out that task. During the Battle of the Somme, the 6th Battalion pipers came to be regarded by many of the wounded as the best stretcher-bearers they came across. The 4th Battalion men were also 'highly complimented for their gallantry at Neuve Chapelle' in March 1915 where Pipe Major Alex Low of that battalion was unsuccessfully recommended for the DCM for his work with the wounded. However, his role in the evacuation of the wounded was recorded some months later in a photograph showing him supervising training of members of the Pipes and Drums in the use of the 'short' stretcher for sitting wounded. A few months later in September 1915 at Loos, another 4th Battalion man, Piper (later Pipe Major) D McLeod won the Military Medal (MM) for bringing in his commanding officer Lieutenant-Colonel Walker who had been mortally wounded during the fight.[13] In an interview many years later, McLeod recalled how at Loos, the pipers had been deployed in pairs in what might be called today as a 'first responder' role with orders to stabilise the condition of the wounded, make them as comfortable as possible, then to leave them for the Royal Army Medical Corps stretcher-bearers to carry off the battlefield.

Later in the war, now promoted, Pipe Major McLeod won a Bar to his MM for his role in the organisation and leadership of carrying parties resupplying their battalion with everything from water to hand grenades, while Piper T Nisbet of the 7th Battalion won his first MM for gallantry while carrying out that task at Beaumont Hamel in November 1916.[14] As combatants serving in the frontline, pipers were expected to carry out the same duties as any other soldier, so that those men serving in the rifle companies took their place with the other Black Watch men where the same levels of military competence were expected of them as of any other soldier. The extent of that competence as well as the different ways pipers were deployed as combatants can be found in the citations which went with the medals they won.

Leaving aside those awards won for piping their battalions into action, awards invariably involved recognition not only of courage and personal risk, but also of military competence. Sergeant Piper J Keith was awarded his DCM in 1917, 'For gallant and distinguished service throughout operations' and also credited his good work with the pipers as the key to their excellent performance of their duties.[15] The award of the DCM to Acting Sergeant W Webster of the 5th Battalion was typical of its kind, acknowledging that he had entered an enemy dugout and taken an officer and 20 men prisoner and 'Later, he commanded the right half of his company with great skill'.[16] Lance Corporal McNie won his DCM in 1915 at Neuve Chapelle for gallantry and skill at arms 'in working a trench mortar gun in the Crescent with great effect on the enemy, whilst under heavy fire from them'.[17] Others like Piper J G Robb were part of the regimental signals when he won the MM for the dangerous and skilled job of repairing field telephone wires while under fire and Piper G Galloway won his MM as a runner – the most basic – and dangerous job in the transmission of information on the battlefield.

Another now long forgotten deployment of the Pipes and Drums is to be found in surviving fragments of 1st Battalion Part 2 Orders held in The Black Watch Castle and Museum, Perth. These describe band ceremonial duties such as piping for quarter guards and providing spectacle for visiting dignitaries and playing duty calls at both divisional and corps headquarters.

It has been claimed by Seton and Grant and shown convincingly by Thomas Greenshields that the pipers were kept from the frontline by some regiments because their loss would cause serious problems of unit morale.[18] However, given the number of decorations awarded, a casualty rate of 73 per cent amongst Black Watch pipers and a well-known aversion of anything that smacked of favoritism amongst the officers, it seems hard to sustain that argument amongst The Black Watch battalions. In any case, where pipers were deployed to headquarters areas for ceremonial duties, these were duties pipers had always been called on to perform.

At these times, pipers also had to teach newly arrived men the tunes required for duties such as guard mounts, mess calls, parades and to play for marching troops. Given the casualty rate for pipers this task was never ending, even to the extent that there was little time even for impromptu composition. Although it is believed that a number of tunes were composed at this time, many were 'of the moment' and were lost or have not yet been rediscovered. Only four tunes can be attributed to The Black Watch during this period: one each by Pipe Majors Keith (2nd Battalion) and Knowles (1st Battalion) and two by Corporal Piper David M Sinclair (8th Battalion).[19] Other regiments fared rather better and have archive collections of Great War music; and there is no Black Watch equivalent of 'Battle of the Somme' by Pipe Major Lawrie of the 8th Argyll and Sutherland Highlanders.

Some pipers looked to engage with the new weapons technology which came on stream throughout the war. A few, like Pipers T Cameron and J Carstairs joined the new Royal Flying Corps while Piper David McEwan transferred to the newly formed Machine Gun Corps, but the vast majority remained with The Black Watch. The Lewis light machine gun, first issued in significant numbers to infantry battalions by the end of 1915, when equipped with the new 97-round aircraft version magazine could be deployed very effectively in an anti-aircraft role, and according to Seton and Grant, the 7th Battalion pipers in particular appear to have been very successful in that area. A few pipers became snipers: Piper A Nicol of the 5th Battalion was wounded while engaged in that activity, while others were paired with individual snipers to act as their observers as was the tactical doctrine of the time.

As the war continued into its second year and beyond, a number of pipers moved on from the Pipes and Drums to warrant or commission rank, frequently demonstrating their skills as combatants and well as musicians. One of those was Corporal Piper Harry Redpath, a former tenter from Leven in Fife who won the DCM as Company Sergeant Major in the 8th Battalion.[20] His citation noted in particular his 'consistent gallantry and devotion to duty during the period 17th September [1918] to the close of active operations in the advance from Ypres to the Scheldt'.[21] The citation also made clear that this award was being given to a soldier capable of inspirational leadership by personal example, stating that the high morale and fighting spirit maintained in his company was 'in no small measure due to the splendid example of constant courage and cheerfulness set by this Warrant Officer'.

Outstanding talent also brought a commission and an interservice transfer for a boy piper of the 4th Battalion who was transferred to the Royal Navy. The career of 16-year-old Acting Sub-Lieutenant T W Paterson, C de G, EM, was pure *Boys Own Paper* material. His story was reported in the local press in Perth and Dundee where he had attended both Dundee's Harris Academy and Perth Academy as well as having been a member of a local scout troop. When he joined The Black Watch as a Boy at the age of 14 on 18 June 1915 on the hundredth anniversary of Waterloo, he had already 'won distinction as a boy piper' in civilian life.[22] Boy Paterson was initially something of a recruiting draw and within days was taking his turn at the Depot as duty piper. However, he also became involved in signalling, trained as a wireless telegrapher and was so good he was made first an instructor, then commissioned into the Royal Navy so he could be deployed as a radio officer on a hospital ship in the Dardanelles. At that point, his situation changed completely: unlike the Army, the Navy had no qualms about sending teenage midshipmen and lads like Jack (Boy) Cornwell, who won a VC at the Battle of Jutland, aged 16, into action at sea. Some time later, while in Berne, Paterson saved the life of a French general who was in immediate danger of drowning, which earned the recently commissioned Sub-Lieutenant Paterson the *Croix de Guerre*. He saved another man's life at sea, but not in action, and so was awarded the Edward Medal and by 1917 his promotion to lieutenant had been confirmed. Paterson survived the war and died in Kirkwall in 1976.

A less spectacular ascent from piper to commissioned rank took place in the case of Piper R Mapleton of the 6th Battalion who was one of the four pipers who played their battalion into the attack on High Wood on 14 July 1916 during the Battle of the Somme. He was commissioned into the Gordons and taken prisoner during the German offensive in 1918. Piper Mapleton had been Pipe Major of the Glenalmond College Cadet Corps and was a very competent rifleman as his scores at the Darnley Rifle Meet and Bisley for the Glenalmond Cadet Corps in the 1910 and 1912 shoots reported in the *Perthshire Advertiser* indicate. He, like Kenneth McLean and William Wilson, the other two former pipers who were also commissioned from the ranks, survived the war.

PIPE MAJORS

Of course, the Pipe Majors were very prominent figure both within their own battalions and the wider piping world. A significant number of Pipe Majors, as well as rank and file pipers, who had no ambitions beyond playing, also had a record of very long service in various piping roles, and this was particularly the case amongst the men of the Territorial battalions. A good number of these men had been young pipers in the Regular 1st and 2nd Battalions, had taken their discharge and joined civilian bands or joined the old Volunteer Battalions Royal Highlanders (VBRH) then went over to the new Territorial Force units. Many of these men had significant teaching careers, passing on the music and tradition of the pipes to the next generation of players and composers, some of whom were their own family members. There were a number of examples of this, both before and during the Great War, but perhaps the most famous example of this trend were the Bain brothers, sons of Donald Bain, the 'Piper of the Alma'.

Donald Bain, the patriarch of the family won fame at the Battle of the Alma in 1854 and again in India at the Relief of Lucknow in 1857, while his son William Bain who enlisted in 1880 fought at Tel El Kebir and was Acting Pipe Major between 1884 and 1888, then permanently between 1889 and 1899.[23] William was in uniform again during the Great War but did not serve overseas, no doubt on account of his age, but instead was a Company Sergeant Major and Pipe Major in the 10th Battalion when it was formed. Another brother James enlisted in the 10th Forfarshire Rifle Volunteers in 1886, later serving with the 3rd (Dundee Highland) VBRH. On the outbreak of war, he was appointed Pipe Major of the 3/5th Battalion (a position he held until 1916). Like his brother William, he did not serve overseas, but instead brought to bear their vast experience in the training of troops for the reinforcement drafts so desperately required throughout the war. Two further brothers, Alexander and David Bain, were in turn Pipe Majors of the 3rd VBRH.

Yet interesting as the Bain father and sons grouping are from a family history viewpoint, there was a deeper significance to this practice of father teaching son than is first apparent. The lineage of teaching that began with Donald Bain which passed to his son William, passed next via William as instructor to a significant group of Great War Pipe Majors: Albert E Crowe (5th Battalion, The Black Watch), Thomas Clark (1st Battalion, The Black Watch), Richard Matchett (8th Battalion, The Black Watch), Henry Brand (Highland Cyclists), James Burns (13th Battalion, CEF) and James Reid (10th Battalion, The Black Watch).

With this teaching lineage to draw on, the Pipe Majors of the Great War generation went about their duties. They, as all Black Watch Pipe Majors, and others in the Highland regiments always taught the members of their band, whether they could play before enlistment or not, and as their immediate military superior it was their interpretation of the music, influenced by those who taught them which prevailed. The Pipe Major also fulfilled other roles. They set the tone of the Pipes and Drums and regulated pipers' conduct both in the musical and disciplinary sense, encouraged creativity amongst those who wanted to compose and acted as critical friend, but above all they were custodians of the relationship between the music and the glories and tragedies of the past, and between Black Watch regimental identity and the demands of the present. In a war where over 50,000 men would join The Black Watch, and in which research shows no fewer than 516 pipers, as defined earlier, served, of whom 382 were in frontline battalions, where 78 were killed, and another 103 wounded along with six taken prisoner, this was no mean task.

Other Pipe Majors also brought a wealth of experience derived from regular or long service in the Volunteers or Territorial Forces to the New Armies and Second Line Territorial battalions forming all over Scotland. Donald Kennedy of the 4th VBRH, which became the 6th Battalion, was one, and remained at home with the 2/6th Battalion as Pipe Major. When the 2/6th and 3/6th were merged into the 4th Reserve Battalion between 1916-19, he remained as Pipe Major. It is also fair to say that there is a clear sense in which it is far too easy to underestimate the importance of Donald Kennedy and other clearly overage pipers to The Black Watch and even Army piping tradition. It was after all, due to his work and that of others like him, that The Black Watch men in training were kept in touch with the sound of the pipes – one of the fundamental aspects of Black Watch and Scottish soldiering in peace and war. The sound of the pipes, always present from the first day of service onwards was one very important entry point for new soldiers into the regimental esprit de corps, and in that sense it was also a first step towards moulding a coherent regimental identity amongst volunteers of the New Army units and amongst conscripts after the application of the Military Service Act 1916. It is also important to remember that because like so many other Pipe Majors his piping interests were diverse and included being Pipe Major to the Gaelic Society of Perth between 1899-1925, he and other Black Watch men provided a highly effective cultural bridge between civilian and military piping.

POWER OF THE PIPES

The power of individual pipers, or the Pipes and Drums playing together to 'lift men' as it was termed at that time, appears to have been largely about the sound of the pipes, though that idea was challenged in the BBC documentary *Pipers of the Trenches* first released in October 2014. In an experiment designed to recreate the sound conditions of a Great War battlefield, it was found that the actual sound of the pipes could not be heard over the din of artillery, trench mortar and machine-gun fire. Instead it concluded that the power of the piper lay in his visibility to the men going forward.

On the other hand, it has to be said that a Great War barrage was not a simple wall of sound as it appeared to be in the experiment, but instead came in waves when for example guns shifted targets in the creeping barrage. Besides, recordings were used which means the harmonics of the experimental barrage were different to those of real artillery firing outdoors, and that affected the way sound travelled in the experiment. Unfortunately, there was also no way of telling from the programme whether the pipes used were of Great War vintage, an important point here because their drone pitch was lower and so the sound was different and would have travelled further. No mention was made of weather conditions which can also change how far the sound of the pipes travel. Taking all of this into consideration, the results of *Pipers of the Trenches* sound experiment are less convincing. On the other hand, the finding that the power of the piper lay in his visibility to the men going forward is easier to agree with – at least in part.

The anonymous author of the 2nd Battalion chapter in Wauchope's *A History of the Black Watch in the Great War, 1914-18* also touched on that same point:

> In many battles men have followed where the Pipers led, and great was the service though heavy the toll rendered playing the way along the smoke hidden trenches in France or putting fresh life into men during the hard fought battles near Kut and Baghdad.[24]

In some cases, at least, the power of the piper came from the tune that was played, and what that meant to those who heard it. Two of the most eloquent writers The Black Watch has ever produced, Linton Andrews and Eric Linklater, both produced detailed accounts of this phenomenon, but other soldiers who appreciated the pipes and what they meant also described the effects of both the sound and the music on men of the regiment in time of war. Private Peter Baigrie of the 6th Battalion described his experience in the broad Doric of his Peterhead home:

> Wir pipers played us on the merch and even oot of the line fin we gid back a bit. On a lang march wir heeds wis up an we were swingin awa fair fine, bit fin they stoppit playin we jist sloochit doon richt awa fair tired oot. The pipes brocht ye ti life – Christ Aye – it helpit![25]

Eric Linklater described another example of the power of the tune and all it stood for, when as a young Black Watch soldier he came out of the line in during a lull in the German offensive in 1918:

> We encountered a tattered fragment of a Battalion of the Foot Guards, and our piper puffing breath into his bag and playing so that he filled the air like the massed bands of the Highland Division, saluted the tall Coldstreamers who had a drum or two and some instruments of brass that made a gallant noise. Stiffly we passed each other, swollen of chest, heads tautly to

the right, kilts swinging to answer the swagger of the Guards, and the red hackle in our bonnets like the monstrance of some bruised but resilient faith.

We were bearded and stained with mud – The Guards, The fifty men that were left of a Battalion were button bright and cleanly shaven – we were a tatterdemalion crew of the coal mines of Fife and the back streets of Dundee, but we trod quickstepping to the brawling tune 'Hielan Laddie', and suddenly I was crying with a fools delight and the sheer gladness of being in such company.[26]

The power of 'Hielan Laddie' as a tune to lift soldiers was not confined to The Black Watch. The Glasgow Highlanders (9th HLI) which also had that tune as their regimental march experienced much the same feeling as they marched along the long dusty road to the Somme. Thomas Lyon, author of *More Adventures in Kilt and Khaki* described the effects of the tune:

Then the pipes set the heavens and earth dancing to the strains of 'Hielan Laddie – the regimental march of the Glasgows... but it was something more heartening than wine that put boldness in their step: it was the sense of the tradition and the honour of their regiment: the sense that they must on no account present other than a brave front to the world.[27]

It is also true to say that an understanding of the importance of the pipes to Scottish units was widespread across Scottish society and beyond at that time. The inhabitants of Liss in Hampshire where the 9th Battalion were stationed before leaving for France understood, probably because of the close relationship they had with The Black Watch men, for the parting gift of that village to the 9th Battalion in 1915 were sets of pipes.

An incident in Kirkcaldy High School in 1915 also indicated a similar level of understanding of the Scottish military culture, albeit amongst children. The school received a request from a newly commissioned former pupil and old member of their Officer's Training Corps (OTC) for help in acquiring a set of bagpipes for the 13th Royal Scots. In his letter, later published in the *Fifeshire Advertiser*, Second Lieutenant Mitchell admitted that while in peacetime the officers bore the cost of sets of bagpipes, their officers were all very young and without the private incomes of pre-war officers.[28] In a letter from the Head Teacher published in the same edition of the paper in support of Second Lieutenant Mitchell's request, the point was stressed that the pipes formed 'a very necessary part of the equipment of a Scottish Regiment preparing for the front'. The Head Teacher also wrote that a set was to cost £15 and would have a silver plate mounted on it explaining that these were the gift of the present and former pupils of the school and would be returned at the end of the war to the Kirkcaldy High School OTC as a 'prized possession'. Two weeks later the *Fifeshire Advertiser* announced that the sum raised was in excess of £32 and that two sets of pipes for the 13th Royal Scots could be viewed in the window of James Burt, Bookseller & Stationer, Kirkcaldy. The pipes did not return to the school and their fate is unknown, but those pupils who donated their pennies appear to have known not only what they were buying but why that was important.

THE PIPER AND THE
PHOTOGRAPHIC ARCHIVE

Far from the battlefield, other images of Black Watch pipers have survived and tell their own story, not only of individuals, but also of the Pipes and Drums as a group. Many photographs help illustrate and lend credence to the earlier remarks made by senior officers about the role of the piper during the war. Gritty and grainy as many of the original pictures are, and although generally the pipers do not appear in any way to have been positioned specially for the camera, nevertheless the best of these pictures still do lend a degree of authenticity to the claims made for the power of the piper. In these images, long forgotten incidents never formally recorded in regimental histories or battalion war diaries are preserved as potential evidence for some future research. When married up with findings from written research material, the photographic archive allows a degree of access to the very formal – and at first sight often near impenetrable –

group portraits of the different battalions' Pipes and Drums.

The group picture of the 4th (Dundee's Own) Battalion Pipes and Drums which appeared in the *Dundee Advertiser* in 1914 for example was typical of its kind. The members of the band were shown in service dress, formally seated by rank behind their stacked drums or standing at attention, but what these pictures could not show was the full extent of the closeness of the bond between band members or of an impending tragedy. Seated in the front row was Sergeant Drummer 'Archie' Troup, a well-known character in the 4th Battalion, tragically remembered today not so much as the big drummer of the band, but because of an incident following his death at Aubers Ridge in May 1915: his son who also served in the same battalion erected a cross for his father at the memorial service for the fallen a few days later. This ceremony which Wauchope regarded as 'unique in the annals of the regiment' also included Sergeant Major Pyott doing the same, but for his son who had been shot down as he picked up his company's marker flag during The Black Watch advance at Aubers Ridge after the subaltern carrying it was killed.[29]

THE 8TH BATTALION PIPES AND DRUMS PLAYING
AFTER THE CAPTURE OF LONGUEVAL, JULY 1916
A G Wauchope, *A History of the Black Watch in the Great War, 1914-18*, Volume 3 (1926)

Other pictures captured moments of respite, and no matter how much the Pipes and Drums needed time to rest and enjoy moments of quiet reflection, they played for their comrades. The photograph of the 8th Battalion Pipes and Drums standing in a circle playing for the troops after the capture of Longueval in July 1916 is one example of this. This action which was part of the larger Battle of the Somme began on the 8 July 1916 when the 8th Battalion took over the line from the 11th Royal Scots. It continued through the initial success of the attack on Longueval on 13 July, then near daily attacks, German counterattacks and heavy German shelling until 19 July. At that point, the 8th Battalion now reduced in strength to six officers and 165 men, were relieved by the 19th Durham Light Infantry and marched to the sand pit at Meaulte. Whether or not the picture discussed here was taken at the sand pit is a moot point, what is not in doubt is the attraction for the survivors of the fight at Longueval of their Pipes and Drums, indicating perhaps that with the music came a return to a sort of normality.

Other pictures like that of the 1st Battalion preparing to leave Oudenarde Barracks for France in 1914 showing the Pipes and Drums in its traditional position on the right flank of the battalion were taken as one 'last great hurrah' before the battalion marched off to war. Here was the last record of that battalion as a complete unit, for within days of that last parade, they would suffer their first casualties, and by Christmas 1916 but little of the Pipes and Drums would be left. The picture of the 9th Black Watch celebrating Hogmanay in 1917 in billets behind the lines on the Somme is one of a number of similar pictures of celebration and comradeship where the pipers lead. In spite of the mud-spattered kilt aprons, the muddy ground, and the open ditch between the huts, the broad smiles and laughter suggest the tune played might even have been 'Happy We've Been A' Thegither'. The photographic archive also shows the ubiquity of the pipes in The Black Watch during the war. The chapter on the 10th Battalion in Wauchope's *History* contains a dramatic picture of that battalion on the march to Ambarkoi in 1916, endlessly snaking through the low hills of Salonika in column of fours with the pipes playing on the march.

CONCLUSION

In the end what can be said of the pipers and their music? The last word goes to the author of the 2nd Battalion chapter in Wauchope's *History* who wrote:

> Even in peacetime men will turn out to see and listen to the Pipes and Drums, and in war their power is far more evident. Nothing scatters the gloom of a wet and cheerless billet so well as pipe music: on a long march they give life to a weary column. [And of their music:] Tradition and sentiment – how much is lost when they are neglected, how much is due to their magic; powerful factors towards victory, they are the essence of pipe music.[30]

10TH BLACK WATCH PIPE BAND
Sutton Veny Camp, Salisbury Plain, August 1915

1   A G Wauchope, *A History of the Black Watch in the Great War, 1914-18*, Volume 1 (London: Medici Society, 1925), p239.

2   Trevor Royle, *Flowers of the Forest* (Edinburgh: Birlinn Ltd, 2019).

3   Sir Bruce Seton and John Grant, *The Pipes of War* (Glasgow: Maclehose, Jackson & Company, 1920).

4   Scottish Horse Archives, Dunkeld Community Archive.

5   The Dinna Forget books were three 12-page booklets containing pictures of
    Black Watch troops in the 4th, 6th and 7th Battalions. *Dundee Advertiser*, 1917.

6   Piper signified an appointment and not a rank. Research by the author indicates
    appointment of Piper had disappeared by early 1915.

7   Wauchope *History*, Volume1, p37. Seton and Grant claimed that 'during the Somme
    fighting the Companies were frequently played to the attack by their pipers'.
    Seton, *Pipes of War*, p96.

8   See 'Wounded Evacuated (Gassed) 1st Battalion Part 2 Orders, 20 October 1918.

9   Wauchope, *History*, Volume 1, p194.

10 Wauchope, *History*, Volume 1, p194.

11 Seton, *Pipes of War*, p52.

12 Jock Duncan, *Jock's Jocks: Voices of Scottish Soldiers from the First World War*
    (Edinburgh: NMSE Publishing Ltd, 2019).

13 Seton, *Pipes of War*, p99.

14 Members of carrying parties were often described as 'bearers' suggesting they were
    stretcher-bearers.

15 *London Gazette*, 29 August 1917.

16 *London Gazette*, 26 January1917.

17 *London Gazette*, 3 June 1915.

18 Seton, *Pipes of War*, p30; Thomas Greenshields, *Those Bloody Kilts*
    (Warwick: Helion & Company, 2018) – see Chapter 7.

19 Specifically, P M Keith – 'Baghdad', P M Knowles – 'Lt. Col. J.G.H. Hamilton's
    Farewell to The Black Watch', Cpl Sinclair – 'Black Watch Welcome to Nigg' and
    'Major Hugh Thurburn of Crausley'.

20 Tenters were loom tuners.

21 *London Gazette*, 11 March 1920.

22 *Perthshire Advertiser*, 12 September 1917.

23 Sandy Cram, Alistair Duthie, Alistair Irwin, and Scott Taylor,
    A Collection of Pipe Music of The Black Watch (Royal Highland Regiment)
    (Perth: Balhousie Publications, 2012), pxxi.

24 Wauchope, *History*, Volume 1, p239.

25 Duncan, *Jock's Jocks*, p195.

26 Eric Linklater, *The Man on my Back: An Autobiography*
    (London: MacMillan & Company Ltd, 1947).

27 Thomas S Lyons, *More Adventures in Kilt and Khaki*
    (Kilmarnock: Standard Press, 1917), p182.

28 *Fifeshire Advertiser*, 7 November 1914.

29 Wauchope, *History*, Volume 2, pp13-14.

30 Wauchope, *History*, Volume 1, p239.

Young Soldiers and Underage Soldiers

Fraser Brown

THROUGHOUT the four years of commemoration of the Great War, one aspect of the war which was regularly discussed was the seemingly enormous number of young men who fought as underage soldiers. It appeared at times as if almost every family could lay claim to an underage soldier who had volunteered to serve, and of course it was true that a significant number of underage boys did fight, die and suffer life-changing wounds. However, what is often not understood is that The Black Watch along with other regiments did take action to prevent this. First, on the outbreak of war, the 1st Battalion did not send men under the age of 19 to France with the British Expeditionary Force, and second, trawls of Black Watch battalions looking for underage troops led to at least one mass removal of soldiers from the Western Front who – underage or not – were valuable, experienced personnel The Black Watch battalions could ill afford to lose.

'TOO YOUNG TO FIGHT FOR THEIR COUNTRY'
Underage soldiers return from the Western Front
The Courier and Argus, 19 June 1915

To some extent it had been near impossible to prevent these young men donning khaki in 1914. The rush to war, the need to process enormous numbers of volunteers in an age when barely half of the population had birth certificates, when recruiters were paid bounties for each man enlisted, and a large percentage of young men were determined to join, all created a perfect environment for administrative errors to flourish. Also close to the heart of this discussion, however, is a fundamental lack of civilian understanding of the difference between young soldiers serving their country perfectly legally, and underage soldiers fighting overseas.

As far as military law was concerned, the situation was clear enough. *Queen's Regulations 1895* (Section VII, Paragraph 177) and *Volunteer Regulations* 1901 (Section II, Paragraph 118) stated that although boys could be enlisted in the Regular Army at 14 or enrolled as Volunteers and Territorials at 13, they were not to be considered adult soldiers until they were 18 and could not be sent overseas to fight before they were 19. The Military Service Act of 1916, which introduced conscription, confirmed that age standard, but the situation changed in 1918 when young men of 18 were in the frontline in every theatre of war. The service of the five young men outlined in this section is intended to show the difference between those serving as young soldiers, and those who went to war as underage soldiers.

One example of a young soldier as opposed to an underage combatant was Boy Wardlaw. In a well-publicised case reported in the *Dunfermline Press* and elsewhere, Mrs Wardlaw of Victoria Terrace, Dunfermline was called before the local school board in September 1915 to explain the non-attendance at school of her son.[1] She appeared with the 13½-year-old Alexander, who as a Boy of the 7th Black Watch and a Territorial enlisted for home service, appeared in his uniform. The board enquired if he was 'doing well' and confirmed he was attending Continuation Classes through the army, then congratulated him on his patriotism, wished him speedy promotion and dismissed the case. In fact, the war was over before he was eligible to fight, but he was able to take on many of the other duties previously done by older men.

The case of Drummer Matthew Currie of the 5th Black Watch, of 3 Bolders Close, Brechin, who appeared in the *Brechin Advertiser* under the heading 'A War Veteran at 16' and his friend of the same age, Drummer

Walter Keyes McCallum, was rather different. They were both properly enlisted Territorial Boys, but both went to war with the 5th Battalion in direct contravention of *Queen's Regulations 1895* and *Volunteer Regulations 1901* before McCallum was wounded at Aubers Ridge and Currie was identified as underage and sent home. Drummer Currie may be one of the people in a published photograph of underage Black Watch soldiers arriving at Dundee railway station from France after having been 'spotted' as underage. How they were able to get to France in the first place can only be guessed at, but administrative 'error' or a nod and a wink in the right direction was clearly enough to get a place on the boat. Even so, when Currie was old enough, he returned to France, this time as a lance corporal with the Gordons, but was killed during the *Kaiserschlacht*. McCallum appears to have survived.

On the other hand, the case of Private John McKinnon, DCM, and holder of a Wauchope Medallion for his conduct at Loos was rather different. He really was an underage soldier who joined the 2nd Battalion aged 15, but as his mother said, he was a 'strapping lad' who looked older than he really was. Until he was wounded and recovering in an English hospital, his parents in Leith were unaware he was anywhere near the 'Front'. They wrote to the commanding officer of 2nd Battalion, The Black Watch, and eventually he was sent home. In many ways he was typical of so many of the underage soldiers: he was a highly competent and experienced trench soldier who understood exactly what was expected of him. He was also more than capable of showing initiative when required, for as his Distinguished Conduct Medal citation recorded, not only did he hold a 'block' for two hours but 'for two hours he used enemy bombs and an enemy rifle, his own having failed'.

In the instance of Private McKinnon – as no doubt was also the case with the other underage soldiers – he possessed a highly adventurous streak in his character; but in his case at least more detail is known of his life after discharge from The Black Watch. No sooner than he was released from the Army than he slept through a Zeppelin raid in Leith, then told the local newspaper he had slept through worse. Next, he went off to join the Royal Navy but was refused as too young and so joined the Merchant Service and was torpedoed while crewing an oil tanker later in the war.

After the war, he sailed to Antarctica on the *Discovery*, but lost part of one hand in an accident at sea. At one point, an undated article from the *Scottish Daily Express* lamented the fact that his injury meant he could not work and with money scarce, he had been forced once again to pawn his medals.

Private McKinnon survived the war, but one other young man who was not so fortunate was Private Scott Oram from Arbroath of 1st Battalion. It is not clear precisely how he was able to get to France, but – according to the local press at the time and the *Roll of Honour: Arbroath and District* – he was taken prisoner at Mons before he was 15, spent the rest of the war in eastern Germany and the captured Russian territories and after what was described as 'many trying experiences', on the eve of repatriation, he became a victim of the influenza epidemic and died in Schneidemuhl Hospital Camp, 23 December 1918.[2] A number of letters from Private Oram to his old teacher in Arbroath were published in his local newspapers over the course of the war, as were Drummer Currie's story and news of Private McKinnon's medal award.

That level of press exposure helps explain one other aspect of the Great War on the 'Home Front' – the voluntary involvement of children in efforts to support the serving soldiers. Pictures appeared in the local press showing smart young soldiers in uniform, so that suddenly children might well look not only to fictional characters as heroes and role models, but often to young soldiers very close to their own age. In these circumstances, it is unlikely to be a coincidence that children all over the 42nd Regimental Area dug deep into what little ready cash they had to send comforts to their local Black Watch battalions, and to respond so generously to the Boy Cornwell VC appeal, often earning for their school a special colour picture of Jack Cornwell, mortally wounded, but still standing by his gun at Jutland.

---

[1] *Dunfermline Press*, 4 September 1915.

[2] Although there is evidence that Oram became a prisoner of war, the exact location of his capture may not have been Mons given The Black Watch were not in action at Mons in 1914.

LOS VOLUNTORIOS ESCOSESES

BLACK WATCH MEN FROM
LATIN AMERICA

Fraser Brown

THE PUBLICATION in 2014 of Stuart Allan and David Forsyth's book *Common Cause: Commonwealth Scots and the Great War* was a timely reminder to the Scottish public of both the mass military return migration of Scots and their descendants to fight in the First World War, and the price paid by those men who returned.[1] Allan and Forsyth concentrated on the contribution of Australians, Canadians, New Zealanders and South Africans of Scottish birth or heritage who returned to fight in the armies of these countries – largely, but not always – in Scottish titled units. However, as Sir Tom Devine pointed out, a comparatively large part of the Scottish population had always migrated and the Scottish diaspora was 'wide in its spread and very long lasting', but those Scots who returned from countries outwith the British Empire were hardly mentioned in *Common Cause*.[2] This short section attempts to address one small part of that deficiency by looking at The Black Watch element in a group of returnees known as the British Latin American Volunteers (BLAV).

This group consisted of men of British birth or heritage whose existence was eventually officially recognised in 1918 by the issue of a special patch, and their inclusion in the great Victory Parade of 1919 where they were permitted to march as a formed body under their own banner. The Black Watch element of the BLAV were almost all born in Scotland or in Latin America of Scottish heritage and were men who returned to Britain to fight in the Great War. Because the Derby Scheme and the Military Service Act of 1916 introducing conscription had no force in Latin America, these men were either occasionally Black Watch reservists or far more often men who volunteered to serve in the regiment on arrival in Britain.

As for the strength of The Black Watch element, following research in both Scotland and Latin America by this author, the total strength is estimated at around 110, of whom at least 21 are known to have been killed. The number of dead is almost certainly an underestimate given the ratio of men killed to those who served, which for the Scots of the Argentine Republic recorded on the Scottish War Memorial in Buenos Aries was 22 per cent. The number of BLAV men in The Black Watch may have been higher than in some other regiments, particularly after the conversion of the Scottish Horse and Fife and Forfar Yeomanry to infantry as the 13th and 14th Battalions of The Black Watch added a number of former *estancia* men to The Black Watch total, although by that time many of them had been commissioned into other regiments. At times Latin American men with specialist skills enlisted in the regiment but were almost immediately 'poached', particularly by the Army Remount Service and the Royal Engineers. The calculation of the true strength of the BLAV is extremely difficult, but from an examination of the main sources an estimate of between 9,500 and 11,000 men seems fair.[3] The Scottish element of the BLAV may have been as high as 15 per cent of the whole.

When it comes to identifying Black Watch men of the BLAV, evidence of their presence is at best fleeting. Only one, Company Sergeant Major (CSM) Palmer, from Chile, of the 2nd Battalion was identified as such in A G Wauchope's *A History of the Black Watch in the Great War, 1914-1918*.[4] However, the main difficulty in identification is caused by the fact these men returned as individuals, not as members of a formed unit with a clear identity, defined military purpose and a place in the British Order of Battle, therefore no trail of unit war diaries or official history exists to remind posterity of their contribution to the war effort.[5] Instead, during the war their presence was confirmed in reports of their departure from Latin America and their arrival in Scotland in both the local Scottish and Latin American English language press such as the *Buenos Aires Herald* and the *South Pacific Mail*.

Identification of some Black Watch men was possible only because of announcements of gallantry awards, wounds sustained or their deaths in action as reported in the Latin American press. One such was Captain Hamish Dey, MC, 7th Seaforths, who had first enlisted in September

1914 in the 4th Black Watch. The Black Watch connection only came to light when news of his award of the Military Cross was reported in the *Standard* where it was also mentioned that he had been on the staff of the London and River Plate Bank in Buenos Aires and had enlisted in The Black Watch on his return home.[6]

Second Lieutenant Thomas H Bell of the 11th Battalion, and an employee of the same bank did not survive, and was killed in May 1917, but while his death was reported in Argentine newspapers, the *Standard* and *Buenos Aires Herald*, it does not appear to have been reported in the local press in Scotland. Similarly, no report of the death in action in August 1916 of Lieutenant J F Crichton of the 8th Black Watch has ever been found in the Scottish press. Nevertheless, perhaps because he was regarded as a senior member of management at La Plata Cold Storage, Buenos Aires, his passing was reported in both the *Buenos Aires Herald* and the *Standard* and like the others mentioned his name appears on the Scottish War Memorial in St Andrew's Scots College in the city and again on the war memorial brass tablet in St Andrew's Scots Church on Avenida Belgrano in Buenos Aires.

LIEUTENANT J W DUNLOP *(Left)*
SECOND LIEUTENANT OSWALD STANLEY BROWN *(Centre)*
LIEUTENANT JOHN FAIRWEATHER CRICHTON *(Right)*
Arthur L Holder, *Activities of the British Community During the Great War 1914-1919*
(Buenos Aires Herald, 1920)

Nevertheless, other Black Watch men left their mark in the Scottish press. Company Quartermaster Sergeant (CQMS) George Moncrieff was typical of the three types of Scot who went to Chile: engineers, shepherds and commercial and banking men. Moncrieff was an engineer hired by Williamson, Balfour & Company, a Scottish firm founded in 1851 by two men from Fife – Alexander Balfour from Leven and Stephen Williamson of Cellardyke – to trade with the Pacific states of South America. Moncrieff, like Williamson whose father had been a local ship owner, was a native of Cellardyke, but whether that had eased Moncrieff into a position in Chile is not known. In any case, that sort of patronage would not have been unusual at that time within the Scottish-Chilean community – particularly amongst the sheep-rearing areas around Punta Arenas whose returnees overwhelmingly from the northern counties of Scotland joined the Queen's Own Cameron Highlanders and the Seaforth Highlanders.

Moncrieff first appeared as a BLAV man in an article in the *Fifeshire Advertiser* in May 1915 when a report on the 3/7th camp at Bridge of Earn described him as an 'exceedingly popular officer engaged in Chile' who had come home to enlist. The same article explained Moncrieff's rapid promotion in terms of having had previous experience with the Fife Territorials under Major Murray. A few months later, the *East Fife Record* reported a 'crack' or conversation in the trenches when CQMS Moncrieff now of the 4th Battalion met another Cellardyke man, Private Thomas Martin of the 2nd Battalion in France.[7] Shortly after that, however, Moncrieff was wounded by shrapnel in two places near the spine and was subsequently invalided out of the Army and returned to Taltal, Chile, whereby all accounts he resumed work for Williamson, Balfour & Company.

As might be expected, the famous Williamson, Balfour & Company had a number of commercial rivals, one of which was another Scottish company, Duncan, Fox & Co, with interests in mining, shipping and marine and other insurance. Amongst their employees were a significant number of Scots including Second Lieutenant Oswald C Fraser, 9th Battalion, who was involved in the insurance side of the business, first in Chile and a few months before the war began, in a major promotion to Inspector of Insurance in the company office in Rio De Janeiro, Brazil. He had attended George Heriot's School between 1892 and 1896 and on return to Edinburgh was offered a commission in an English regiment but turned that down and waited until he could be commissioned into The Black Watch. He was wounded at Arras on 9 April 1917 and was killed as he was being stretchered off the battlefield.

CSM Palmer mentioned earlier had served 21 years in the regiment retiring with the rank of sergeant in 1912, then found new employment in the Punta Arenas region of Chile. A G Wauchope's *History* described him as a storekeeper on a cattle ranch in Patagonia but according to his obituary in the *South Pacific Mail*, like so many Highland Scots from the Punta Arenas region of Chile he was involved in sheep farming.[8] On the outbreak of war, he resigned and paid his own passage back to Britain on the British flagged SS *Oronsa*. That action was not without serious risk because at that point the German warship *Dresden* was operating off the Chilean coast. That said, he survived the voyage to be killed in action with the 2nd Battalion at Istabulat on 21 April 1917.

South America had always attracted an adventurous type of Scot, so whether returning volunteers had been Patagonian sheep farmers, gold prospectors from the Andean foothills, cattle men from the estancias, or bankers from Buenos Aires, The Black Watch would make the acquaintance of at least a few of them on their return home. In these circumstances it will come as no great surprise to find that The Black Watch had its own South American revolutionary in the shape of Captain The Hon C Edwardes, 13th Black Watch, who moved to the Tanks just before his death in action on 20 November 1917. He was a son of the 4th Baron Kensington who also turned out to have been a long-term South American hand, having first surfaced in Paraguay where he had been involved in at least one failed revolution. Later he fought in the Second Anglo-Boer War (1899-1902) with the Imperial Yeomanry and returned to Argentina to go *on estancia* before leaving for Britain on the SS *Aragon* in 1914 and immediately enlisted in the Scottish Horse, a favourite destination for *estancia* men from Uruguay, Argentina and Chile.[9] The Great War generation has gone in Argentina just as it has elsewhere, but Black Watch men who returned from both wars did form an Argentine

Branch of The Black Watch Association which was last mentioned in the *Red Hackle* in 1951 and again in 1952.[10] Importantly, The Black Watch men from Argentina are commemorated at the Scottish War Memorial in St Andrew's Scots College, Buenos Aires. On every second Armistice Day, the school turns out, those few remaining veterans of the Second World War attend, the school piper plays the 'Flowers o' the Forest' and along with the other Scots of the BLAV, The Black Watch men are remembered.

---

[1] Stuart Allan and David Forsyth, *Common Cause: Commonwealth Scots and the Great War* (Edinburgh: NMSE, 2014).

[2] T M Devine, *To the Ends of the Earth: Scotland's Global Diaspora* (London: Alan Lane, 2011), pp289-290.

[3] The leading Argentine authority, Dr M I Tato, in consultation with the Imperial War Museum, considers this the best available estimate.

[4] *A History of the Black Watch in the Great War, 1914-18, Volume 2* (London: Medici Society, 1926), p267

[5] Juan J Deverill, *Sus Nombres Viveran Eternamente* (Buenos Aires: Grupo Abieto Libros, 2016) covers the Argentine contingent in detail.

[6] *The Standard*, 10 September 1916. The Standard was formerly known as the *River Plate Standard*.

[7] *East Fife Record*, 21 October 1915.

[8] Wauchope, *History, Volume 2*, p267.

[9] An *estancia* is a ranch large enough to employ a *mayordomo* (general manager) and several other under managers, all commanding very large salaries and generally a share of profits.

[10] *Red Hackle*, July 1951, pp34-35, January 1952, pp26-27.

'AND MAN, YOU'RE A DAMN FINE TYPE'

PRIVATE CHARLES CRAIG, ONE OF 'DUNDEE'S OWN'

Derek J Patrick

THE 4TH (City of Dundee) Battalion, Black Watch, received its mobilisation orders on 23 February 1915. Described as 'a well-set-up, gritty battalion..."the Fourth" looked fit to rough it with the best of them'.[1] The battalion was unusual in that it recruited exclusively in Dundee. The other Territorial Force battalions of the regiment were recruited from the counties of Forfar, Perth and Fife, covering much larger areas. Consequently, the 4th Black Watch had a particularly intimate link with Dundee and its citizens, 'represent[ing] a Scottish city at war...[and] as the Battalion was successful or otherwise, so in great measure did the fortunes of war fluctuate in the opinion of the citizens of Dundee '.[2] In short, the 4th Black Watch was 'Dundee's regiment, and it carries with it the honour of the town'.[3]

Leaving Dudhope Castle in three detachments, the battalion marched via Garland Place, Constitution Road, Barrack Street, Tally Street, the Nethergate and Union Street to the West Station. The men were 'enthusiastically cheered by huge crowds in the streets, and every window held its quota of spectators. In the vicinity of the station the crowd was particularly dense, and but for effective policing the place would have been stormed'.[4] On reaching the station, the battalion encountered Thomas Abbot, a 74-year-old veteran of the 93rd Highlanders. He had served in both the Crimea and in the Indian Mutiny (First Indian War of Independence) of 1857-9, and now stood 'at the salute at the entrance gate':[5]

> 'Are ye no'comin' tae?' one lad asked, and there was a tinge of regret in the old man's tone as he told the 'Courier,' 'I sent in my papers to see if they could mak' ony use o' me, but I havna got an answer yet.'[6]

'Dundee's Own' represented all ranks of the city's society. The officers included several prominent citizens and the other ranks comprised men from all the city's main industries. On the outbreak of war, the battalion was 350 men short of its complete establishment. These were recruited within two weeks.[7]

This included several local journalists employed by the city's newspapers. William Linton Andrews, News Editor of the *Dundee Advertiser*, described his fellow volunteers as 'an extremely mixed mob'.[8] He soon discovered that men enlisted for different reasons. Outside the recruiting office Andrews encountered some difficulties:

> A gaunt man in a muffler towered over me. He looked down, and said, not without sympathy: 'Out o' work chum?'…I told the big man I had a goodish job. 'Then you make way for us lads wi' out jobs,' he said. And forthwith I was hustled to the edge of the crowd.[9]

On eventually joining the 4th Black Watch, Andrews learned that life in Bell Street Drill Hall could be rather challenging. The 'drill-hall, with all the dust, stirred up by the trampling, and with roysterers being sick at night where they lay, and many of them prematurely lousy, struck dismay into my heart'.[10] On his reporting the theft of an expensive pair of boots a sergeant gave him some valuable advice: 'Watch yourself, laddie', he said. 'They'll steal the milk out of your tea in this mob.'[11]

In addition to its new recruits, the battalion included several experienced volunteers, former Regular soldiers and servicemen. For example, Private Joseph Ferguson, 26 Whorterbank, Lochee, a fireman with Cox Brothers Ltd before the war, had served ten years in the Royal Navy.[12] Likewise, Lance Corporal John Loftus, 25 Temple Lane, a 37-year-old joiner, had previously served in The Black Watch for some ten years.[13] Private John Diamond, 12 Dallfield Walk, employed as a labourer in Dundee, had served in Egypt and India with the Argyll and Sutherland Highlanders.[14]

Corporal Robert Logan, 1 North George Street, a machinist with John Howe & Son, Fairmuir Turning Works, had experienced active service with the Gordon Highlanders in India and South Africa. Corporal Logan had 'been clear of the Reserves for some years...but the old martial spirit was rekindled in him, and he enlisted in the 4th Black Watch'.[15] Private Alexander Ettle, 7 Mid Street, employed by Mr John Mitchell, Italian warehouseman, Nethergate, was another veteran of the Boer War.[16] Several soldiers had served with the battalion for a number of years. Sergeant George Aird, 2 St David's Lane, claimed to be the oldest Territorial in Scotland. He joined the Seaforth Highlanders in 1875 aged little over 14, transferring to the Dundee Black Watch in 1882. When he went to France in February 1915, he had already served 39 years as a volunteer.[17]

The 4th Black Watch also included several much younger soldiers. Twenty-seven Dundee 'lads' were sent home being 'under the age fixed by the military authorities for combatants on the field of battle' in June 1915.[18] Sixteen-year-old Private Norman W Robb, 47 Carnegie Street, a dresser in Bowbridge Works, had already been hospitalised with a gunshot wound in his right foot.[19]

PRIVATE CHARLES CRAIG
Evening Telegraph, 7 October 1930
(Used by kind permission of D C Thomson & Co Ltd)

However, 'Dundee's Own' was not without an experienced cohort of veteran campaigners whose experience would be an obvious asset when the battalion reached France. One of the most seasoned veterans was Private Charles Craig, 3 Hilltown, Dundee.[20] Craig was 48 when war was declared and had spent 32 of those in the ranks of The Black Watch as both a Volunteer and Regular soldier. He joined the Perth Militia in February 1883. On joining, he claimed to be 19 but was in fact only 16. Following eight weeks' basic training, a young Charles Craig enlisted in The Black Watch. Within a matter of months, he found himself campaigning in the Sudan, marching 'fourteen miles a day, through knee-deep hot sand, on half rations – half a pound of hard biscuits and bully, and one pint of water per man per day'.[21]

Sudanese religious leader Muhammad Ahmad, the self-proclaimed Mahdi, had initiated a rising against Egyptian suzerainty. The Black Watch was part of the force charged with restoring order in East Sudan. Craig fought in the Battles of El Teb and Tamaii, where, on 13 March 1884, Osman Digna's 10,000 strong Mahdist army 'broke' the British infantry square which included The Black Watch. The regiment was in a right-angled formation, providing half the front face of the square, and half of its left.[22]

On approaching the enemy, The Black Watch was ordered to advance, but the main body of the Sudanese Army remained concealed in a ravine. Craig recalled how 'the Sudanese were on us too fast'.[23] The regiment was at once surrounded and the Mahdists were able to exploit the opening in the British square. Fierce hand-to-hand combat ensued as The Black Watch fought to regain its former position. Facing front and rear, and left and right, the regiment began to force its way back to the square. The fighting was frenzied with spears and swords against bayonets and claymores; rifles could not be used because of the British troops beyond the enemy, and anyone who fell was stabbed through repeatedly by the Sudanese, who themselves were bayoneted as they stabbed.[24]

Craig and another soldier, Peter M'Kew, were acting as stretcher-bearers when the Sudanese advanced. Faced with a large group of Mahdist tribesmen, Private Craig thought he was 'liable to die', but 'the adjutant's horse in front of us, suddenly rearing, knocked both of us and the stretcher flat on our backs, and the Sudanese ran right over us'.[25] The Battle of Tamaii was described by one participant as 'a veritable hell' and by another as a 'terrible, terrible fight'.[26] The Sudanese were routed but at considerable cost. The Black Watch suffered heavily with 61 men killed and another 33 wounded.[27]

Craig and his regiment joined the ill-fated attempt to relieve General Charles Gordon then besieged in Khartoum. On 10 February 1885, he participated in the Battle of Kirbekan, his regiment's third and last action against the Mahdist Sudanese, where his 'pal', Tommy Handy, was mortally wounded. Only a few days later it was discovered that Khartoum had fallen, Gordon was dead, and the expedition was ordered to return to Egypt. Craig claimed the rather dubious honour of being the last man of The Black Watch to board the Nile expedition's transports leaving the Sudan. He was loading kitchen equipment in preparation for the return journey when he swore in the vicinity of his commanding officer. The Colonel enquired as to his origin and Craig replied 'Dundee, sir'. He was subsequently ordered to remain 'on the bank, until everyone else [was] embarked'.[28] Consequently, Private Charles Craig would be the last man of the regiment to quit the Sudan campaign.

The years that followed saw Craig stationed in Malta and Gibraltar where he had ample opportunity to indulge his passion for football. He was the centre-forward for The Black Watch team which entitled him to certain benefits. The team was 'allowed off duty three of four weeks before any match, in order to get training'.[29] Sport was an integral part of army life and football would play a prominent part in the life of Charles Craig.

Following almost eight years' service overseas Craig was discharged at Perth barracks. He completed his service in the Army Reserve serving with the 1st Volunteer Battalion, Black Watch, which would become the 4th (City of Dundee) Battalion, with the creation of the Territorial Force in 1908.

On the outbreak of war in South Africa, Charles Craig, now resident at 3 Reid Street, offered his services. The volunteers of the Second Active Service Company left Dundee on 18 February 1901. Leaving the Drill Hall in Bell Street, the volunteers 'met with a tremendous ovation. A number of mill girls, who had left their work, preceded the procession, and, with mouth organs, set up a howling noise, which was scarcely drowned by the patriotic airs of the brass band'.[30] All along the route from Bell Street, into Euclid Crescent, Reform Street, High Street, Nethergate and Whitehall Street to the West Station, 'the streets were thickly crowded with people...the crowd assum[ing] immense proportions'.[31] The volunteers' enthusiastic send-off was followed by 18 months of relatively mundane active service. The war had entered its guerrilla phase, but Craig saw 'no fighting'.[32] He was employed as Captain Robert Main Christie's officer's servant. Christie was a well-known Scottish international footballer from Dunblane, Perthshire, who had represented Queen's Park in the 1884 FA Cup Final. Christie scored the 'Spiders' only goal as they lost to Blackburn Rovers in a closely contested match. For Craig, it 'was a dreary life' but he did have an opportunity to represent The Black Watch volunteers in a football match against their Regular counterparts: 'I played inside-right to Bob Christie on the wing'. Despite their best efforts the match was lost by two goals to nil.[33]

DEPARTURE OF THE 4TH BLACK WATCH FROM DUNDEE STATION
The Evening Telegraph and Post, 24 February 1915
(Used by kind permission of D C Thomson & Co Ltd)

The Second Active Service Company departed Cape Town on 10 May 1902, arriving at Southampton on 5 June.[34] The Dundee contingent reached Magdalen Green Station about 7.30pm that evening, and were greeted by 'the vociferous cheering of [a] huge crowd'.[35] The volunteers 'were "lionised" on the streets, and in most cases reached their homes surrounded by a crowd of admiring children'.[36] In recognition of their 'patriotism' and active service in South Africa, Craig and the Dundee volunteers were granted the freedom of the city and made honorary burgesses.[37] He felt it 'a bit rich at the time', but this was indicative of Dundee's relationship with her citizen soldiers.[38]

Given Craig's long and distinguished military career the 'stirring scenes of enthusiasm' he witnessed in Dundee on 23 February 1915 would not come as a complete surprise.[39] It was described as 'a wonderful expression of a city's feeling. Dundee was giving, and giving freely, of her best'.[40] The battalion's enthusiastic send-off would have been reminiscent of his leaving the city with The Black Watch volunteers some 14 years earlier. Then his destination was Cape Town and the Boer War. However, his experience of campaigning in the Sudan and on the South African veldt could not fully prepare him for the rigours of trench warfare on the Western Front.

The 4th Black Watch arrived at Le Havre at 9.30am on 26 February with a strength of 30 officers and 860 other ranks, subsequently joining the Bareilly Brigade of the 7th Meerut Division, Indian Army Corps. The battalion entered the trenches for the first time on 5 March and sustained its first casualty. Corporal Ralph Dick was a 19-year-old apprentice accountant in the service of Messrs Alexander Tosh & Son, Reform Street, Dundee. His platoon was receiving instruction on trench duties when he was shot and killed. Corporal Scott wrote:

> You can scarcely realise what the rest of us felt like after he dropped dead. He had just been asking me a few minutes before how I was enjoying myself, and it was after that we all began to realise how serious a position we were in.[41]

In a letter to Dick's parents Captain E Leslie Boase described how he was 'struck by a sort of stray bullet – it may have been a ricochet – which caught him in the head. He dropped and passed away at once'.[42]

'Dundee's Own' would suffer further losses over the coming days and weeks. On 10 March, the battalion moved up to a breastwork named

'Windy Corner', 'facing the shell-battered village of Neuve Chapelle'.[43] This would be its first general action. One Dundee Territorial described the conduct of the battalion as 'splendid...They behaved, officers and men, as Black Watch men are expected to, and got high praise from the Regulars, by whose side they fought'.[44] Craig described Neuve Chapelle as 'the heaviest battle that has been fought since the war started. There were a lot of our men knocked out, not many killed, but a lot wounded. I may say the 4th has got a good name since we came out here'.[45] Private Robert Gray, 159 Hilltown, was one of the six Dundee men reported killed in action.[46] His brother, Hercules, served in the same company. In a letter home he reported that while 'running across the field...our Bob was struck. I did not see him go under myself...I was told by one of the men running alongside him'.[47] Robert and Hercules Gray were not unique. 'Dundee's Own' included a considerable number of men whose close relatives, friends and workmates served alongside them in the ranks. It is little wonder that Dundee followed the fortunes of its 'Terrier' Battalion with 'the closest and most anxious attention'.[48]

Craig had been appointed personal servant to the commanding officer, Lieutenant-Colonel Harry Walker, describing him as 'the finest man I have ever met'.[49] Walker had a long association with the 4th Black Watch and was extremely 'popular with the men under his charge and the community from which the bulk of the battalion is drawn'.[50] In civil life he was a member of Messrs Harry Walker & Sons Limited, spinners and manufacturers, Caldrum Works, where Craig was employed before the war.[51]

In his role as Walker's personal servant Craig saw little fighting but he was slightly wounded near Neuve Chapelle. In an article that appeared in *The Evening Telegraph and Post* in October 1930, he recalled being struck by a piece of shrapnel 'which split my face rather badly'.[52] The same article mentioned how his duties occasioned an impromptu meeting with General Douglas Haig, the man who would command the British Expeditionary Force on the Western Front from late 1915. In Richebourg St Vaast he was approached by Haig and a group of his staff officers. The General looked sternly at Craig and pointed at the medal ribbons displayed on his tunic and asked:

Haig: Those decoration ribbons…are they yours?

Craig: Yes, sir.

Haig: Good…You've more of them than I have. How old are you?

Craig: [Forty-eight].

Haig: Well, well…what are you doing out here at your time of life? You're a daft old soldier. And man, you're a damn fine type.[53]

The 4th Black Watch was employed holding the line around Neuve Chapelle until May 1915 when it would participate in the Battle of Aubers Ridge. The first attack of the Indian Corps was launched at 6am on the morning of 9 May but proved a complete failure. The battalion was ordered to make ready for a second assault at 4pm and moved forward at 10.50am. It was almost impossible to negotiate the communication trenches which were blocked by soldiers who had participated in the morning's action, many of whom were wounded. One company of 'Dundee's Own' joined the attack but could make no progress.

Before reaching the enemy trenches the attacking platoons had to cross some 300 yards of flat open ground, through which ran a small stream too deep to wade. The only means of getting over this obstacle were a few narrow bridges, some of which were hidden; others broken, and others blocked with the bodies of those who had been killed and wounded in the earlier assault. Over the whole of No Man's Land the Germans concentrated a deadly machine gun fire.[54]

Most of the attackers were killed or wounded before they had covered a few yards. One officer and 38 others ranks were killed, and over 100 of 'Dundee's Own' were wounded.[55] One participant simply described his experience as 'awful'.[56] In a letter home another wrote that he was 'lucky to be alive'. He described how his company had sustained heavy casualties:

In the great attack the Fourth have been badly hit. Poor Walter Eltom is no more. He was hit by shrapnel and died almost at once…The poor chaps were lying thick all over the place. In all I think the battalion has lost about 160 killed and wounded. D Company have about 6 killed and 40 wounded. In 13 Platoon 'Chick' Wallace and two of the new draft that arrived the night before were killed, while Sandy Scott was wounded in the chest below the lung; Dod Edwards in the arm pretty badly, and __. M'Kenzie. Harry Fraser and some of the new men were wounded. Jimmy Scott got a bad one in the head. I was just a foot behind him when he got it, and Harry Fraser was just in front of him. Jimmy's head was in a terrible mess, and although he was alive four hours afterwards I do not know how he is getting on. It was a pretty bad case. I was a lucky man, I can tell you. In Platoon 14 Nor. Harley got a pretty bad one in the arm; J. A. Spark in the chest, arm, and legs; Walter Crosby a bad one in the leg; R. G. Sellars and R. Jack got shrapnel in the legs, and we had two of the draft with slight wounds, making a total of seven for the platoon. I was hit four times myself in the knee, leg, and hand, but the wounds are only scratches.[57]

The battalion's dead included Lance-Sergeant Archie Troup, 10 Watson Street, Dundee, and 17-year-old apprentice plumber, Private Donald Pyott.[58] Wooden crosses were erected over each grave. Private John Troup carried a cross for his father and Company Sergeant Major (CSM) Donald Pyott 'put up a little white cross for his boy'.[59] CSM Pyott's 'Good-bye, laddie' brought tears to more than one pair of eyes.[60] The ceremony was almost certainly unique in the long history of the regiment and helps highlight the intimate relationships which connected the men of the 4th Black Watch with Dundee and its battalion.

In a letter to The Reverend Dr Colin Campbell, 'chaplain of the battalion in its volunteer days', Colonel Walker reflected on the conduct of the 4th Black Watch. He offered 'a glowing tribute to the officers and men whom he commanded'. He wrote:

The 4th Battalion has certainly 'made good' since it came out, and although I was always sure they would do well they have far exceeded my expectations. The work which we are called upon in large part to undertake – trench work – is so different from anything we had been taught or led to expect that it was perfectly wonderful how soon the men became efficient. Much of this was due to the junior officers, who are splendid lot of boys. Many prophesied that trench warfare would take all the vim out of the men for an advance, but anyone who saw my boys go over the parapet on the 9th May must have admitted that the Black Watch, at any rate, are always ready for a fight.[61]

The battalion would soon have another opportunity to demonstrate its readiness. Charles Craig's post-war account of his service in the ranks of 'Dundee's Own' is largely focused on the Battle of Loos which he described as a 'ghastly affair'.[62] The action has become synonymous with Dundee and the fortunes of the 4th Black Watch. The battalion was part of a diversionary attack tasked with drawing German reserves from the districts east of Loos. The fighting strength of the battalion on the morning of 25 September 1915 was 423 men.[63] 'Rain was falling when the order to "Stand to" was passed down the lines.'[64] In preparation for the attack a mine was successfully detonated under the enemy frontline at 5.48am. This was followed by a 'terrific bombardment' of the enemy positions, and chlorine gas and coloured smoke were released, making it 'impossible to see more than a few yards in front of our own parapet'.[65] The wind was constantly changing and many British and Indian soldiers were put out of action before they could adjust their gas masks.

The attack was launched at 6am. 'Dundee's Own' made steady progress across no-man's-land but had barely left their trenches when they were met with a steady fire from the German lines:

Men stopped in their stride to pitch forward and lie motionless on the ground. Many others were wounded, and either lay where they fell or, if still able to walk, struggled on until their strength gave out and they too fell.[66]

Major Elmslie Tosh, second-in-command, was wounded about 60 yards from the British frontline.[67] Sergeant Petrie 'carried him towards our lines on his back, but unfortunately the Major was again hit by a piece of shell and mortally wounded'.[68] Captains Norman Crawford Walker and Stanley Lee Watson, and Lieutenant Sidney Herbert Steven were killed as the battalion advanced on the German frontline trench. Walker 'led his company with great dash and skill...He was actually killed during the first charge, leading his men as he would with great dash and cheerfulness. He died immediately he was hit'.[69] CSM Thomas Bowman, 35 St Peter Street, Dundee, a veteran of the Second Anglo-Boer War (1899-1902) who had been awarded the Distinguished Conduct Medal for gallantry at Neuve Chapelle in March, recalled events in a short article published in *The Courier and Advertiser* in September 1933. He doubled across a battlefield 'swept by rifle fire'.[70] It was, he noted, 'a very hazy morning and you couldn't see far ahead. We had to keep close together to keep in touch with each other'.[71] He had only gone a short distance when he saw 'a Highlander lying prostrate beside a tree...It was my brother'. [72] Sergeant John Bowman's right leg had been shattered by a bullet. 'You can't do anything, Tom', he said. 'Go on.' [73] The brothers shook hands and CSM Bowman re-joined the battalion. Both men survived the battle, but John Bowman's leg was amputated as a result of his wounds.[74]

Corporal William Linton Andrews wrote:

> [our] Companies moved steadily into the enemy's front line. Those Germans who survived surrendered in batches. Most of them were young and well built, but pale compared with our weather-beaten veterans...Although it was still very misty, and shells kept knocking out parties of our men, the Black Watch pressed forward at good speed.[75]

A Seaforth Highlander recalled hearing 'amongst the strange noises and the panting a magnificent yell of "On the ball, Dundee"'.[76] 'Dundee's Own' captured the German frontline and support trenches, but the Bareilly Brigade's flanks were unprotected and the men were subjected to increasingly heavy German artillery fire and counterattacks.

Lieutenant-Colonel Harry Walker ordered his battalion to consolidate the captured trenches, but the situation had become critical. The 4th Black Watch had lost almost half its strength and most of the officers were killed or wounded. 'Many of the men's rifles had become unworkable owing to clogging up with mud, and the bombs were finished. The enemy advanced in great masses and bombed our advanced position.'[77] To hasten reinforcements, Colonel Walker attempted to reach brigade headquarters, but fell mortally wounded. The battalion was forced to withdraw from its forward positions. 'Stand after stand was made, the men of the 4th halting and firing as they retired.'[78] On the eve of the 18th anniversary of the battle, CSM Bowman wrote:

> Men were falling thick. I realised we had to retreat. I jumped into the open with the intention of making a race for our own trenches. Immediately there was a burst of fire…Afterwards we realised how serious were the losses sustained by the 4th Black Watch.[79]

The battalion's *War Diary* records that on the morning of 25 September 1915 its total strength was 21 officers and about 450 men. Its losses during the action were 20 officers and some 240 other ranks killed, wounded and missing. 'It had been a grand advance but at great cost.'[80] On hearing that Colonel Walker had been badly wounded Craig spent several hours searching for his officer. He later discovered that Walker had been taken to the casualty clearing station at La Gorgue where he succumbed to his wounds.[81] He is buried next to the battalion's second-in-command, Major Elmslie Tosh, at Pont-du-Hem Military Cemetery. Describing the scene, a member of the battalion wrote:

> They were laid to rest, in a pretty little orchard within range of the guns. What a difference to-day looking around the ranks of dishevelled, war-worn, sad men compared to the boisterous enthusiasm of the 1100 who paraded in Dudhope Square that afternoon in February when we marched off to the front. I remember yet the pride in the Colonel's eye that day when he

addressed us from the steps of the Castle and the cheery smile of the Major as he led the half battalion off the square. How strangely different to-day! There we stood in the little orchard with our Colonel and Major lying side by side at our feet. It was their last parade. The service was the short, simple service of the Presbyterian Church, and the bodies were lowered into the grave by the senior non-commissioned officers and the deceased officers' servants.[82]

Reflecting on the loss of the Colonel one of his non-commissioned officers likened the battalion to 'a house without a father, for the Colonel was a fatherly man, ever interested in the welfare of his regiment'.[83] Home on a short furlough, the battalion's medical officer, Major James S Y Rogers, paid tribute to Colonel Walker and the officers and men of 'Dundee's Own':

The deeds of the 4th Black Watch on 25th September may been equalled but they have never been excelled. The bravery and gallantry of the officers and men were an example to all, both fighting men and civilians in this country. I cannot speak too highly of the behaviour of the officers and men. The battalion did magnificently. The only man I will specially mention is Colonel Harry Walker – than whom a braver and more able man never lived.[84]

Loos had a huge impact on Dundee. On 6 October 1915, a memorial service was held in St Mary's Parish Church, a day 'consecrated to the fallen heroes of the 4th Black Watch, "Dundee's Own"'.[85] Reverend A W Fergusson described the collective loss that the city had suffered. He said:

[they] were assembled for the consecration of certain great common feelings, thought and purposes that they all had in their hearts. They were assembled in a common sorrow, such a sorrow as had never fallen on Dundee in one day and generation, and they came impelled by a great human sympathy for those who mourned their beloved dead.[86]

In Dundee Loos was considered 'our fight' and the city was united in mourning its 'gallant sons'.[87]

Loos was effectively the battalion's last act as a separate entity. On 7 February 1916, it received news that it would be amalgamated with its sister 5th (Angus and Dundee) Battalion. It also signalled the end of Charles Craig's military career. The veteran soldier 'was pronounced too old for fighting, and came home'.[88]

Craig returned to Dundee where he resumed civilian life and his long-standing association with Dundee Violet Junior Football Club. When not on active service, Craig had represented Dundee Wanderers as both a player and trainer before his connection with Dundee Violet which spanned 22 years.[89] On 23 September 1933, he attended a Scottish Junior Cup match between Arbroath Victoria and Dundee Violet at Gayfield Park. On the return journey he complained of feeling ill and left the train at East Haven. It is surmised that he attempted to walk along the line to Carnoustie where he hoped to catch a train to Dundee. However, he had only gone a short distance when he was knocked down and killed.

Craig's body was discovered near East Haven station. Judging from his injuries it was assumed that he had been struck by two trains. 'The body was so badly mutilated that the only means of identification was by a wartime identity disc, which deceased had in his possession at the time.'[90] Charles Craig, 13 West Dock Street, Dundee, was 68, and survived by his wife and family. The veteran of El Teb, Tamaii, Kirbekan, Neuve Chapelle, Aubers Ridge and Loos had lost his life in tragic circumstances only a few miles from home. 'It [was] a pathetic coincidence that his death should take place so tragically practically on the eve of the Loos anniversary.'[91]

He was buried in Dundee Eastern Cemetery on 27 September with full military honours. Large crowds gathered outside his home and at the cemetery gates. 'The coffin was borne from the house to the hearse by six soldiers from the Black Watch Depot at Perth…The lament was played by Piper Davis, and the 'Last Post' sounded by Bugler Wilson, both of Perth'.[92] Three days earlier, the beacon on the Law memorial was lit and a crowd of some 500 men and women assembled in a rain-drenched Dudhope Park to mark the 18th anniversary of the Battle of Loos. One observer reflected on the long passage of years and the bridging of time by memory.[93] The city's and Craig's memories of the Great War were intrinsically linked with the service of 'Dundee's Own'. His death may have occurred almost 18 years after Dundee's worst day, but he was no less one of her gallant sons. The fact that he still wore a military identity disc, on his person when he died, materially demonstrates how this connection endured. Charles Craig never forgot his time serving in the ranks of the 4th Black Watch, nor his comrades, Dundee's citizen soldiers, many of whom never come home.

1 *The Courier and Argus*, 24 February 1915.

2 A G Wauchope, *A History of the Black Watch in the Great War, 1914-18*, Volume 2 (London: Medici Society, 1926), p3.

3 *The People's Journal*, 27 February 1915.

4 *The Courier and Argus*, 24 February 1915.

5 *The People's Journal*, 27 February 1915.

6 *The Courier and Argus*, 24 February 1915.

7 Wauchope, *History*, Volume 2 (London: Medici Society, 1926), p4.

8 W L Andrews, *Haunting Years: The Commentaries of a War Territorial* (London: Hutchinson, 1930), p14.

9 Andrews, *Haunting Years*, p11.

10 Andrews, *Haunting Years*, p14.

11 Andrews, *Haunting Years*, p15.

12 *The Courier and Argus*, 9 July 1915.

13 *The Courier and Argus*, 22 March 1915.

14 *The Courier and Argus*, 19 May 1915.

15 *The Courier and Argus*, 8 April 1915.

16 *The Courier and Argus*, 11 October 1915.

17 *The Evening Telegraph and Post*, 24 February 1915; *The Evening Telegraph and Post*, 18 October 1918.

18 *The Courier and Argus*, 19 June 1915.

19 *The Courier and Argus*, 17 June 1915.

20 *The Courier and Argus*, 27 March 1915.

21 *The Evening Telegraph and Post*, 7 October 1930.

22 Eric and Andro Linklater, *The Black Watch: The History of the Royal Highland Regiment* (London: Barrie & Jenkins, 1977), p127.

23 *The Evening Telegraph and Post*, 7 October 1930.

24 Linklater, *The Black Watch*.

25 *The Evening Telegraph and Post*, 7 October 1930.

26 Victoria Schofield, *The Highland Furies: The Black Watch 1739-1899* (London: Quercus Publishing plc, 2012), pp 523-524.

27 Schofield, *The Highland Furies*, p525.

28 *The Evening Telegraph and Post*, 7 October 1930.

29 *The Evening Telegraph and Post*, 7 October 1930.

30 *The Courier and Argus*, 19 February 1901.

31 *The Courier and Argus*, 19 February 1901.

32 *The Evening Telegraph and Post*, 7 October 1930.

33 *The Evening Telegraph and Post*, 7 October 1930.

34 *The Courier and Argus*, 5 June 1902.

35 *The Courier and Argus*, 6 June 1902.

36 *The Courier and Argus*, 6 June 1902.

37 *The Muster Roll of Angus 1899-1902: South African War, 1899-1902: A Record and a Tribute* (Arbroath: Bridie & Salmond 1903), p231.

38 *The Evening Telegraph and Post*, 7 October 1930.

39 *The Courier and Argus*, 24 February 1915.

40 Wauchope, *History*, Volume 2, p5.

41 *The Evening Telegraph and Post*, 26 March 1915.

42 *The Courier and Argus*, 11 March 1915.

43 Wauchope, *History*, Volume 2, p7.

44 *The Evening Telegraph and Post*, 25 March 1915.

45 *The Courier and Argus*, 27 March 1915.

46 The National Archives, WO 95/3948/2.

47 *The Evening Telegraph and Post*, 22 March 1915.

48 *The People's Journal*, 27 February 1915.

49 *The Evening Telegraph and Post*, 8 October 1930.

50 *The People's Journal*, 2 October 1915.

51 *The People's Journal*, 28 August 1915.

52 *The Evening Telegraph and Post*, 8 October 1930.

53 *The Evening Telegraph and Post*, 8 October 1930. The Commander-in-Chief, Sir John French, accompanied by Sir Douglas Haig, inspected the battalion on 10 April 1915. He addressed the battalion as follows: 'I cannot find words to express my admiration for the courage, the self-denial and the splendid fighting spirit of the Territorials in this war'.

54 Wauchope, *History,* Volume 2, p12.

55 *The Red Hackle*, October 1923, p40.

56 *The People's Journal*, 29 May 1915.

57 *The Evening Telegraph and Post*, 17 May 1915.

58 *The People's Journal*, 22 May 1915.

59 *The People's Journal*, 12 June 1915.

60 *The People's Journal*, 12 June 1915.

61 *The Courier,* 2 October 1915.

62 *The Evening Telegraph and Post*, 8 October 1930.

63 Wauchope, *History*, Volume 2, p15.

64 Wauchope, *History*, Volume 2, p17.

65 The National Archives, WO/95/3948/2.

66 Wauchope, *History*, Volume 2, p17.

67 *The Broughty Ferry Guide and Carnoustie Gazette, Monifieth and Tayport Advertiser*, 12 November 1915.

68 The National Archives, WO/95/3948/2.

69 *The People's Journal*, 16 October 1915.

70 *The Courier and Advertiser*, Saturday, 23 September 1933.

71 *The Courier and Advertiser*, Saturday, 23 September 1933.

72 *The Courier and Advertiser*, Saturday, 23 September 1933.

73 *The Courier and Advertiser*, Saturday, 23 September 1933.

74 *The Courier*, 18 October 1915.

75 *The Leeds Mercury*, 4 March 1930.

76 *The People's Journal*, 9 October 1915.

77 The National Archives, WO/95/3948/2.

78 Wauchope, *History*, Volume 2, p20.

79 *The Courier and Advertiser*, 23 September 1933.

80 The National Archives, WO 95/3948/2.

81 *The Evening Telegraph and Post*, 8 October 1930.

82 *The Courier and Argus*, 4 October 1915.

83 *The Courier and Argus*, 12 October 1915.

84 *The Broughty Ferry Guide and Carnoustie Gazette, Monifieth and Tayport Advertiser*, 29 October 1915.

85 *The People's Journal*, 9 October 1915.

86 *The Evening Telegraph and Post*, 6 October 1915.

87 *The People's Journal*, 2 October 1915.

88 *The Evening Telegraph and Post*, 8 October 1930. By the Armistice, Craig had four sons at the front. James and William served in the artillery, Charles in the 4th Black Watch, and David in the American Army.

89 *The Courier and Advertiser*, 25 September 1933.

90 *The Evening Telegraph and Post*, 25 September 1933.

91 *The Courier and Advertiser*, 25 September 1933.

92 *The Courier and Advertiser*, 28 September 1933.

93 *The Courier and Advertiser*, 25 September 1933.

Joseph (Johnston) Lee

THE BLACK WATCH POET

Ron J Scrimgeour

THINK OF DUNDEE or ask Dundonians near and far for iconic images of the city and you are almost certain to get the Law Hill as first or second in the list, before or after the famous Dundee 'peh'! Regular listeners to Radio Tay will have D J Ally Bally's words thundering in their ears, 'Law means hill so you cannot say Law Hill! Let's play safe and refer to the volcanic plug as 'the Lah'. Probe a little further and ask how many Dundonians have been to the 'Tap o' the Lah', and the numbers will reduce greatly. There is no doubt that familiarity breeds various levels of contempt – or at the very least, apathy. Ask Dundonians or the wider public if they know who Joseph Lee was and the answer is likely to be a disappointingly low number.

Ask how many schools, colleges or universities include the works of Joseph Lee in their lesson or lecture plans and once again the results will disappoint. To end this already laboured point, it is worth posing the question as to how many Black Watch Association dinners, suppers, church services and Remembrance Day parades include a line or two from the regiment's very own 'Fighter Writer'?

The roll call of indifference to Joseph Lee is all the more disappointing because in the 77 poems in his two war poetry books, *Ballads of Battle* and *Work-A-Day Warriors*, Lee puts war under the forensic glare of artist and poet, cynic and cartoonist. In his poems, we are there with the frontline soldier or the prison camp inmate; for writing in the dugouts and trenches, Lee captured the horrors of war and its consequences for the combatants with singular simplicity.

On the first day of the Battle of the Somme, the statistics for bombardment and casualties were distressingly huge. On 1 July 1916, several truces were observed to recover wounded from no-man's-land on the British front, where the Fourth Army had suffered 57,470 casualties, 19,240 of whom had been killed. The British artillery fired more than 1.5 million shells during the preliminary bombardment, more than in the first year of the war. On 1 July, the first day of the main assault another 250,000 shells were fired; the guns could be heard on Hampstead Heath, 165 miles away.

Yet to my mind, Lee captured the horrors of war far more simply and directly than these eye-watering statistics. In 'The Bullet', Lee wrote with great candour and simplicity:

THE BULLET

Every bullet has its billet;
Many bullets more than one:
God! perhaps I killed a mother
When I killed a mother's son.[1]

In a similar vein, who can compare the sterile Army Form B 104-82 sent to the next of kin with possibly Lee's most touching poem, 'The Mother'.

Army Form B 104-82 begins:

Dear Madam,
It is my painful duty to inform you that a report has this day been received from the War Office notifying the death of...

Then follows a 'fill-in-the-blank' type of activity reminiscent of a primary school homework exercise where the name, rank and regiment of the dead soldier was added with anaemic accuracy. The cause of death, usually 'killed in action' was handwritten. Compare that most impersonal of Despatches, informing of the most personal tragedy a family could suffer, with 'The Mother':

THE MOTHER

Mother o' Mine: Mother o' Mine
My mother rose from her grave last night,
And bent above my bed,

And Laid a warm kiss on my lips,
A cool hand on my head:
And, 'come to me, and come to me,
My bonnie boy,' she said.

And when they found him at the dawn,
His brow with blood defiled,
And gently laid him in the earth,
They wondered that he smiled. [2]

The sketches Lee included in his journals were honed to perfection from the very early 1900s. Lee attended art classes at the local YMCA and then travelled to the most unlikely places for a working-class lad at that time, but always refining his creative art. Lee visited Europe including Gibraltar, the Black Sea including Istanbul, Sebastopol, the battlefields of the Crimean War (1853-6) and a cattle ranch in Canada. Landscapes, churches and farms gave way to 'people-scapes' of Dutch girls carrying heavy pails of milk and Russian women washing clothes in streams. The natural and raw talent that saw Lee able to capture the trench life of the mud-stained soldier was perfected through an apprenticeship as a cartoonist and then further study at Heatherley School of Fine Art.

JOSEPH LEE SKETCHING BEHIND THE LINES
People's Journal (Dundee Edition), 13 May 1916
(Used by kind permission of D C Thomson & Co Ltd)

Lee had both an artist's eye for detail and a poet's heart for sentiment. He excelled in both showing a hundred times or more that the pen is mightier than the sword and that the charcoal was mightier than both. Yet the question remains, why is Joseph Lee largely the 'Forgotten Poet'?

History Extra, the official website for a number of internationally acclaimed and influential magazines – *BBC History Magazine*, *BBC History Revealed* and *BBC World Histories Magazine* – lists its five great First World War poets in this order. Number one is Hedd Wyn (real name Ellis Humphrey Evans) a Welsh poet, followed by Siegfried Sassoon, Rupert Brooke, Wilfred Owen and Rudyard Kipling. Missing from the list is, of course, Lee. And yet, Kipling, less of a war poet and more of a jingoistic imperialist whose fervour for war resulted in him jettisoning his son Jack into the Battle of Loos in 1915, to be killed aged 18, is included. In addition, Joseph Lee is notable for his absence within most Great War poetry anthologies. How do we account for this grave omission?

Is it because Lee is not an archetypal hero poet? He was older than most on enlistment, from a working-class background and was an observer and narrator rather than an idealist and critic. Is it because he was from Dundee? Dundee is that great industrial cul-de-sac, a grim monument to man's inhumanity to man, wrote Hugh MacDiarmid in his poem 'Dundee' (1934). Would Lee and the 'band of brothers' that made up 4th Battalion, 'Dundee's Own', fall into the category of 'expressionless lumps' that Wilfred Owen referred to his own men as in a letter to his mother?

Could it have been because Lee was Scottish and more in the tradition of Robert Burns than John Keats? Who can forget the blunt exchanges between Lee and the recently appointed Poet Laureate, Robert Bridges? In 1914, Bridges castigated Burns for lack of depth and profundity with the lines:

> Thou art a poet Robbie Burns
> Master of words and witty turns
> Of lilting songs and merry yearns
> Drinking and kissing
> There's much in all thy small concerns
> But more that's missing.[3]

Was Lee relegated to obscurity because he did not use his poetic voice to rail against the war and to idealise the slaughter of 'doomed youth'? Was Lee also found to be wanting by the intellectuals and that there was 'more that's missing'. Could it be that because Joseph Lee actually survived the Great War and the Second World War and went on to live a productive if unpretentious life that he is overlooked? Is survival and ordinariness a crime among the war poet literati?

Whatever the reasons for the omission of Lee from war poet league tables and anthologies, it was not because of the quality of his poetry or his sketches. Both have stood the test of time and the forensic glare of present-day academia. I am sure that Lee would not wish us to waste time, effort and energy trying to rationalise the irrational. However, he may silently applaud our efforts to reverse the trend and reawaken interest in his life and work, particularly in his home town.

A good beginning is to follow the lead set by Kenneth Baxter, Caroline Brown and Matthew Jarron, stalwarts of Dundee University's archive and museum, who have promoted exhibitions of Lee's work and displayed his archived artefacts. They were instrumental in the installation of a plaque identifying a former residence of Lee in Airlie Place, which forms part of the university precinct. In 2014, the University of Dundee published *Poems from the Great War* to provide a fresh starter reader to those unfamiliar with Lee's poems, songs and sketches.

The Black Watch Association has also rekindled interest in its warrior poet by including Lee's 'Home Coming' in the Association's 100th Anniversary Service at the regimental home, Balhousie Castle, Perth, in June 2019. Major Colin Grey brought a sobering note to the service by his reading, particularly the last verse:

> When Te Deums seek the skies
> When the Organ Shakes the Dome,
> A dead man shall stand
> At each live man's hand
> For they also have come home.[4]

It is time to apply some creative thinking to help bring Joseph Lee out of obscurity and into the light of the twenty-first century. Is there anyone more deserving of such energy than Dundee's very own 'Fighter Writer'?

1   Joseph Lee, *Ballads of Battle* (London: John Murray, 1917), p21.

2   Baxter *et al*, *Poems from the Great War*, p67.

3   Robert Bridges, 'To Robert Burns: an Epistle on Instinct', *Monthly Review March 1902*, pp157-163.

4   Lance Corporal Joseph Lee, *Ballads of Battle* (Plymouth: Classic Reprint Series, Forgotten Books, 2012), p44.

'I AM PROUD TO BELONG TO THE 8TH BLACK WATCH'

LOOS, 25-27 SEPTEMBER 1915

Derek J Patrick

THE 8TH (Service) Battalion, Black Watch, was raised in August 1914. Formed at Albuhera Barracks, Aldershot, it was the senior battalion of the 9th (Scottish) Division, the first division of Lord Kitchener's 'New Army'.[1] Its commanding officer, Lieutenant-Colonel Lord Sempill of Fintray, considered his men 'a body of excellent soldiers'.[2] The battalion had a backbone of Regular and ex-Regular officers (most of whom had served in The Black Watch), and a number of non-commissioned officers were serving soldiers or ex-soldiers.[3] 'They came…from city offices and the plough, and it was wonderful to see how they all adapted themselves to the work of training to become efficient soldiers.'[4] They represented the 'pick of a large number of men'.[5]

The 8th Black Watch arrived in France in early May 1915 with a strength of 29 officers and 1,007 other ranks.[6] The men would soon experience life in the trenches, but the Battle of Loos would be the battalion's first general action.

The 9th (Scottish) Division was tasked with capturing a series of heavily defended German positions beginning with the formidable Hohenzollern Redoubt. Only 200 yards from the Scots' trenches and set forward from the German frontline, the redoubt had a commanding view over no-man's-land both north and south. Behind the redoubt lay a pit head, 'Fosse No8', a large slag heap, and a small mining village, the east part of which was known as the Corons de Maroc and the Corons de Pekin.[7] The 8th Black Watch would be in support of Lochiel's 5th Cameron Highlanders.

The preliminary bombardment began on 21 September 1915. The battalion's *War Diary* records that on the morning of 25 September 'after 40 minutes of gas, smoke candles, artillery and machine-gun bombardment, at 6.30am [the] British attack was launched'.[8] The light westerly wind carried gas and smoke towards the German trenches as 26th Brigade, including the 8th Black Watch, attacked the redoubt and eastern extremities of Fosse No8.

Lochiel's Camerons came under close enfilade machine-gun fire from the left flank and suffered heavy casualties. Private James Laidlaw, 5th Cameron Highlanders, a native of Penpont, Dumfriesshire, wrote:

> [we] lost heavily during the advance. When we started we were eleven hundred strong. We returned with 261...that will give you an idea of what we had to face. It was a terrible scene on the battlefield. The noise of the shells bursting and the cries of the wounded were terrible to listen to. A trench we occupied on our left flank had been strongly protected with barbed wire entanglements, and scores of our brave Camerons were slain here...In some places the dead were lying five deep – Camerons on the top of Germans and Germans on the top of Camerons. It was awful to march over the bodies of our own comrades, but we had to go on.[9]

Lieutenant-Colonel Sempill observed that 'when it came to the turn of the Red Hackles the men wanted no leading, and in spite of a terrific fire the men advanced steadily, though many a poor lad fell the moment he was over the parapet'.[10] Private Robert Blelock, 8th Black Watch, writing to friends and family in Perth, recalled that at the moment the battalion advanced 'it seemed as if hell had been let loose'.[11]

By 7am the Hohenzollern Redoubt had been captured and the 8th Black Watch and 5th Camerons were advancing on Fosse No8, but both battalions had sustained heavy casualties.

Lieutenant-Colonel Lord Sempill was wounded after crossing the second line of German trenches near Fosse No8. Paralysed and unable to move he lay on the battlefield for several hours attended by his orderly, Corporal Smith, before stretcher-bearers could carry him back. The pair were exposed to almost constant enemy shell fire 'but by the mercy of Providence we got nothing worse than some showers of earth and clods'.[12]

Despite heavy losses, Fosse No8 and the Corons de Pekin had been secured by 9.30am. The 26th Brigade had no support on either its right or left flank and 'telephone communication with our rear had completely failed'.[13] The line was held until 1.30am on 26 September 'under heavy shell fire and a considerable amount of rifle and machine-gun fire', when The Black Watch and Cameron Highlanders were relieved by 73rd Infantry Brigade, 24th Division.[14] The division had only just arrived in France and had no frontline experience.

'AN INCIDENT AT LOOS'
Rab Simpson
(The Black Watch Castle and Museum)

On the morning of 27 September, it became clear that the 73rd Brigade was in difficulty and falling back.[15] Fosse No8 was recaptured, and the enemy now threatened the Hohenzollern Redoubt. Captain Fergus Bowes-Lyon, 8th Black Watch, fourth son of the Earl of Strathmore, and older brother of the late Queen Mother, with a composite force of Black Watch and 5th Camerons, was sent forward at 8.30am to secure the ground and rally any men seen retiring from the redoubt. Bowes-Lyon and his small force of 70 Black Watch and 30 Cameron Highlanders successfully stopped the German advance but he was killed in a bombing attack at around 10.30am.[16] Captain Bowes-Lyon was 26. The precise location of his grave is unknown, and Bowes-Lyon was originally commemorated on the Loos Memorial. However, in November 2011, his grandson supplied information concerning his original burial place. Consequently, he is now commemorated in Quarry Cemetery, Vermelles, Pas de Calais, France, where a headstone is inscribed with his details.

The redoubt was successfully held under heavy shrapnel fire until 9.30pm when the battalion was eventually relieved. Lieutenant-Colonel Sempill wrote, 'our brigade had done all that men could do, and it was through no fault of theirs that Fosse 8 and part of the Hohenzollern Redoubt were recaptured by the enemy'.[17] In three days' fighting the 8th Black Watch lost 19 officers and 492 other ranks killed and wounded, almost 75 per cent of its total strength.[18] Recalling the action Lieutenant-Colonel Sempill wrote, 'I always felt confident that my Blue Bonnets would do well, which a letter I received later from our Brigadier, General Ritchie, confirmed, in the words – "Your lads were splendid"'.[19] Sergeant John Smellie, 8th Black Watch, a veteran of the Second Anglo-Boer War (1899-1902) who was awarded the Distinguished Conduct Medal for 'conspicuous gallantry' at Loos, simply wrote, '[our] regiment fought as it always does'.[20]

In a letter to friends in Perth, a Black Watch soldier wrote, 'there is only one thing I should like to say. I am proud to belong to the 8th Battalion, which has kept up the traditions of the famous Black Watch. Scotsmen proved their worth last Saturday, Sunday and Monday'.[21] Reflecting on the losses incurred in the battle he was similarly bullish: 'I am only sorry to say that Scotland paid heavily for the advance, and so did some of the English regiments, but the Scotsmen died fighting'.[22]

In December 1915, the *Dunfermline Journal* published a short poem which had been sent home by Private James Jones after the Battle of Loos. Before the war, Jones was a miner in the Aitken Pit, Kelty. He joined The Black Watch on 27 August 1914 and was an original member of the 8th Battalion. He was killed by a sniper on 28 November 1915, aged 19. The verse stands as a fitting epitaph to his comrades in the 8th Black Watch:

THE 8TH BLACK WATCH

Here's tae the lads of the 8th Black Watch–
tae the lads whas valour has nae match.
Their equal canne weel be found,
On ony famous battle ground.
They're the pick o' Scotland's men;
Born and bred in hill and glen,
Whaur ilka cairn tells aye the story
O' some famed deed for Scotland's glory.
Aye, Jim ma lad, A'm prood tae ken,
That you're among this pick o' men,
Ready, aye, ready tae do or die –
'Scotland for ever,' your battle cry.[23]

———————————

1   A G Wauchope, *A History of the Black Watch in the Great War, 1914-18*, Volume 3 (London: Medici Society, 1926), p3.

2   *Aberdeen Weekly Journal*, 9 June 1916.

3   Wauchope, *History*, Volume 3, p3.

4   *Aberdeen Weekly Journal*, 9 June 1916.

5   Wauchope, *History*, Volume 3, p3.

6   Wauchope, *History*, Volume 3, p3.

7   Wauchope, *History*, Volume 3, p9.

8   The National Archives, WO95/1766/1.

9   *Dumfries & Galloway Standard and Advertiser*, 6 October 1915.

10 *Aberdeen Weekly Journal*, 9 June 1916.

11 *The Evening Telegraph and Post*, 21 October 1915.

12 *Aberdeen Weekly Journal*, 9 June 1916.

13 The National Archives, WO95/1766/1.

14 The National Archives, WO95/1766/1.

15 Wauchope, *History*, Volume 3, p13.

16 Wauchope, *History*, Volume 3, p14.

17 *Aberdeen Weekly Journal*, 9 June 1916.

18 Wauchope, *History*, Volume 3, p15.

19 *Aberdeen Weekly Journal*, 9 June 1916.

20 *The Berwickshire News*, 28 December 1915.

21 *Perthshire Advertiser and Strathmore Journal*, 9 October 1915.

22 *Perthshire Advertiser and Strathmore Journal*, 9 October 1915.

23 *The Dunfermline Journal*, 11 December 1915.

'A Remnant of a Regiment'

The 9th Black Watch at Loos,
25 September 1915

Derek J Patrick

O N THE MORNING of Saturday, 25 September 1915, the men of the 9th Black Watch, waited on the order to advance. The battalion would attack at 6.30am. Major John Stewart, second-in-command, noted that the men were as 'keen as mustard.'[1] In the forward trenches, Lance Corporal Donald McLean described his comrades as 'confident and cheerful', but knowing what lay before them, 'brought out the portraits of their nearest and dearest – wives, mothers, sweethearts, as the case might be – and said to each other as they gazed upon the faces that were to them an incentive and inspiration, "Better let's have a last look at them, boys"'.[2] The Battle of Loos was preceded by an artillery bombardment that began on 21 September and intensified as the men prepared to advance. Stewart described it as the 'devil's own row'.[3] Chlorine gas was discharged at 5.50am but the 'lack of sufficient wind, and its uncertain direction, minimized the results expected'.[4] On hearing that he would be 'going over' in half an hour, Private George Craig 'began to shake a bit, but they came round with a tot of rum, which warmed us up'.[5] In the minutes before the attack was launched Craig's officer addressed his men:

> Now, lads, this is our chance of getting hand-to-hand with the enemy. I want to say that I am only too proud to be at your head, and the 9th Black Watch has got the honour of taking this position. Give them [hell], and remember the Lusitania![6]

Private George Roddick recalled how the officers were 'standing waiting with their eyes on their watches, and at 6.30 the word passed along – 'Mount the parapet'.[7] Moments later the leading platoons crossed the parapet and advanced on the German frontline. Major Stewart had

THE BLACK WATCH AND THE GREAT WAR

gone forward to observe the opening stages of battle:

> I must say the men went marvellously well, they were cheering,
> laughing and joking as they went up and passed through our
> wire entanglements. Our casualties started directly we showed
> ourselves.[8]

The 9th Black Watch was formed at Albuhera Barracks, Aldershot, on 6 September 1914.[9] The ranks of the 8th Black Watch, the first of the regiment's Kitchener or 'Service' battalions, were filled by 3 September 1914. Subsequent drafts leaving Perth would join the 9th Battalion which was up to strength after only a few days. Command was assumed by Lieutenant-Colonel Thomas Owen Lloyd of Minard, a Black Watch veteran of the Second Anglo-Boer War (1899-1902) who had retired in August 1910.[10] The first priority was turning recruits into soldiers and during its first months the battalion carried out intensive training. 'At first ten hours a day, including Sundays, was the rule.'[11] Describing his experiences, Company Quartermaster Sergeant (CQMS) William Darling wrote:

> We rose at dawn and formed fours, marched in column, formed
> on the left, closed column of platoon and other manoeuvres, ad
> infinitum. We did physical exercise – running before breakfast,
> square drill in the forenoon, attempted manoeuvres if the
> weather permitted it in the afternoon, and attended instruction
> lectures at night. We ate what we got and how we got it.[12]

Private James Brewster shared his experiences in a letter to his workmates in Bo'ness. 'I am in Aldershot, and getting on first-rate. The heat and the marching are telling on my tender feet; otherwise I am well.'[13] Due to the unprecedented expansion of Britain's military and the War Office's limited resources, Kitchener's Second Army were, at first, 'nobody's child'.[14] Equipment was in great demand but short supply. The battalion's first uniform was described by Darling as a 'civilian overcoat, red tunic, blue trousers with the red stripe, and a postman's hat'.[15] More serviceable attire arrived piecemeal with kilts, khaki tunics and greatcoats eventually issued in late January 1915.[16]

Despite the inevitable difficulties encountered in the autumn of 1914, the new recruits approached their training with 'enthusiasm and [an] entire absence of grumbling.'[17] CQMS Darling identified 'an ardent willingness to train for battle, and to get into it with the least possible delay'.[18] 'The task of instruction was easy, and it was not long before the 9th became what it was throughout the war – a smart and well-disciplined Battalion.'[19]

This success was due in no small measure to Lieutenant-Colonel Lloyd and his regimental staff, and was even more impressive considering he had so few experienced officers at his disposal. Major John Stewart, Lloyd's second-in-command, was a Boer War veteran who had just retired as a serving officer with the 1st Black Watch. Captain Alexander Kelty McLeod, the only Regular officer in the battalion, joined as adjutant. The Quartermaster, Lieutenant William Clark, commissioned in September 1914, would become a mainstay of the battalion for the duration of its war. Clark was a keen and efficient soldier, who began his martial career at the early age of 16, when he enlisted in the Royal Scots.[20] His was an invaluable appointment:

> In the early days it was by no means easy to clothe and feed the Battalion, but apart from his very thorough knowledge of the Regulations (and ways round them) Clark's priceless gift of ever seeing the bright and humorous side of any situation was of the greatest value.[21]

The original company commanders were also not without experience. Captain John Gilchrist had served with the Gordon Highlanders for over 20 years:

> [He] saw much active service in India and Africa, rising to the rank of colour-sergeant...He retired several years ago, but on the outbreak of the European War re-enlisted as a private soldier. He was immediately made quartermaster-sergeant, however, and was promoted to a Captaincy within a month.[22]

9TH BLACK WATCH OFFICERS

BACK ROW: 2nd Lieut. O. L. Bearn; 2nd Lieut. L. G. Morrison; 2nd Lieut. R. Andrew;
2nd Lieut. W. J. Leslie; Lieut. E. R. Wilson; 2nd Lieut. J. Campbell;
Lieut. S. Norie-Miller; 2nd Lieut. A. Sharp; 2nd Lieut. W. S. McIntyre.

CENTRE ROW: 2nd Lieut. J. Millar; 2nd Lieut. D. J. Glenny; 2nd Lieut. L. Murray-Stewart;
Lieut. J. C. Henderson-Hamilton; 2nd Lieut. R. H. Robertson; 2nd Lieut. R. Stirling;
2nd Lieut. J. D. G. Miller; Lieut. G. A. Rusk; 2nd Lieut. A. O. Dennistoun;
Lieut. J. Crighton; Lieut. W. Story-Wilson.

FRONT ROW: Capt. J. M. Bell; Lieut. and Q.M. W. Clark; Capt. J. H. Stewart-Richardson;
Capt. A. K. McLeod; Major J. Stewart; Lieut.-Col. T. O. Lloyd;
Lieut. and Adjutant R. E. Harvey; Capt. J. Gilchrist; Capt. S. D. Stevenson;
Lieut. F. A. Bearn, R.A.M.C.; Capt. D. N. H. Graham.

SEATED: 2nd Lieut. R. W. Reid
Parkhouse Camp, Salisbury Plain, June 1915

Gilchrist assumed command of C Company, 9th Black Watch. Major
Michael William Henderson, joint agent of the Linlithgow branch of
the Commercial Bank, had served as a volunteer officer in South Africa,
and in 1914 commanded the 10th Royal Scots, 'one of the best Territorial
units in the Kingdom'.[23] However, 'his personal desire, which rose to
passionate eagerness, was to reach the actual scene of hostilities'.[24]
Resigning his commission he secured a position with Lloyd's
9th Black Watch. Described as a 'natural soldier', Henderson commanded B Company. Captain Donald Hatt Noble Graham, commanding
A Company, had spent 14 years in India as a partner in the firm of

Messrs Graham & Company, Glasgow.[25] 'He had had military training and experience during his long residence in Bombay.'[26] Captain John Murray Bell, commanding D Company, was another enthusiastic 'amateur' soldier. A chartered accountant from Edinburgh, he was 'always greatly interested in the OTC'.[27] He was a volunteer in his school days and a captain in Edinburgh University Officers' Training Corps.[28]

Regular officers were a scarce commodity by September 1914 and Kitchener's Second and Third New Armies were much more reliant on retired officers or 'dug-outs'. Few battalions in the 15th (Scottish) Division possessed more than four officers on formation. The average number of Regular officers with the division was less than one per battalion.[29] Nearly all company officers in the 9th Black Watch were initially gazetted as second lieutenants. 'Few had any military experience at all and it was a difficult matter to select company commanders and their seconds-in-command, but Colonel Lloyd accomplished this difficult task with rare discrimination, and after the first few weeks, hardly a change was found necessary.'[30]

The 9th Black Watch was fortunate in being able to secure the services of a number of former Regular soldiers whose experience would prove invaluable. Few New Army units contained enough competent re-enlisted soldiers to fill all their non-commissioned ranks and officers had no option other than to choose promising candidates to fill vacancies.[31] Lieutenant-Colonel Lloyd and Major Stewart ensured that the 'few old – and some were very ancient – non-commissioned officers were, of course, at once given acting rank, the remaining vacancies being filled on the recommendation of company commanders'.[32] Remarkably few mistakes were made and the 9th Black Watch was the first battalion in the 15th (Scottish) Division to report that it had filled its share of Company Sergeant Majors (CSMs) and Quartermaster Sergeants.[33] Perhaps the most auspicious appointment was that of Regimental Sergeant Major (RSM) George Dunn Bedson. He was born in Fort Garry, Canada, and had joined the regiment at Edinburgh on 14 April 1882, aged 21. Bedson had served through the Egyptian campaign and was twice wounded at Tel-el-Kebir. He had been exempt from recall with the reserve for several years but 'was one of the first to answer Lord Kitchener's call for men'.[34]

Bedson re-enlisted at Dundee on 12 September 1914, aged 53 years and 138 days. He almost immediately received a senior non-commissioned rank. RSM Bedson was responsible for maintaining standards and discipline in the battalion. However, he would fulfil an equally important role in the raising of the 9th Black Watch:

> It very soon became apparent that, in his quiet and unostentatious way, he was busy inculcating into the newly appointed non-commissioned officers and men the pride in the traditions of the regiment in which he himself had served so long.[35]

Regimental Quartermaster Sergeant Thomas Hampton and Orderly Room Sergeant John Lindsay completed the battalion's staff. Both had been long-serving Black Watch Colour Sergeants and discharged their duties with consummate professionalism.[36]

Similarly, all four CSMs were veteran soldiers. William Butter McLaren, a native of Luncarty had joined the Black Watch in 1882, completing nearly 28 years' service with the Colours. Before retiring he had been described as 'the handsomest soldier in the Black Watch'.[37] John McAinsh had served 12 years in the regiment including service in South Africa. 'At the outbreak of the present war he re-enlisted as a private, and by his abilities and experience was quickly promoted.'[38] William Murdoch was another who saw service in the Boer War:

> He had served 21 years in the Army, and re-enlisted on Kitchener's appeal, being attached to the 9th Black Watch. For many years, when connected with the 2nd Black Watch, he was resident in Perth Barracks.[39]

David Grieg was similarly experienced. He joined the New Army at Seaforth, Lancashire, on 3 September 1914, aged 49 years 340 days.

The 9th Black Watch included several non-commissioned officers who could boast similar service. Pioneer Sergeant Edward Henry Barnes had served over 15 years in the regiment and was a veteran of the Nile

Expedition, 1884-5. Some had participated in the ill-fated Battle of Magersfontein in December 1899. Sergeant David Riddle, Lorne Street, Lochee, had been twice wounded in the engagement, but 'refusing to be invalided home through lameness as a result of his wounds, he joined the Mounted Infantry until the end of the war, then went to India with his regiment'.[40]

9TH BLACK WATCH SERGEANTS,
STAFF-SERGEANTS AND WARRANT OFFICERS
Parkhouse Camp, Salisbury Plain, June 1915

Sergeant Daniel Godfrey, a beetler (linen worker) with Messrs Lumsden & Mackenzie, Stormontfield, Perth, was made a prisoner of war in the same action.[41] Several of the battalion's non-commissioned officers served in South Africa. Sergeant Robert Munro, head porter at Bridge of Allan railway station, had re-enlisted 'and was for a period drilling troops in England'.[42] Likewise, Sergeant Alexander Cumming had 'served eight years with the 2nd Black Watch, and fought on the Indian Frontier and in the South African campaign'.[43]

Others were promoted on the basis of their relevant experience or abilities. Sergeant William Hector White had never served in The Black Watch but was indisputably a son of the regiment. He was the only son of long-serving Colour-Sergeant Hector White who had served with the regiment in the Third Anglo-Ashanti War (1873-4) and had lost an arm at El-Teb in the Sudan in 1884.[44] Sergeant White had been born in Edinburgh Castle and although he had not chosen to become a professional soldier he 'had previously seen much of the soldier's life'.[45] In comparison, CQMS Darling had no regimental antecedents. In his autobiography he wrote:

> I would like to record that I owed my promotion to my military qualities or distinction as a soldier, or at least expectation of distinction in the military sphere, but I have to admit in this sober and solemn chronicle of fact that it was not these qualifications which secured my promotion.[46]

Darling was an educated man of no mean ability and could 'add a column of figures, and keep that intricate piece of military accountancy, the pay and mess book'.[47] CQMS Darling added:

> [that his] colleague, the Company Sergeant-Major, a reservist of twenty-one years' service and more, had all the military merits, but could not count; and with that wise distribution of talent of which the Army is the master, controller and director, it was considered more appropriate, and I did not disagree, that he should address himself to the instruction of recruits, while I, with my arithmetical if not academic gifts, should attend to the administration and accounts.[48]

Bedson and his non-commissioned officers, a significant number of whom had served with the regiment on the battlefields of Egypt, the Sudan and South Africa, not only helped add a professional edge to the new battalion but their shared experience of army life would help instil the traditions, history and identity of the 'regiment' in Lloyd's 9th Black Watch.[49]

Shortly before the battalion left for France in July 1915, an incident occurred in Aldershot that illustrated how a sense of tradition and regimental identity were assumed by New Army battalions. CQMS Darling was called to intervene in what he described as 'a riot of soldiers and civilians, both men and women'.[50] On enquiring as to its cause, he discovered that it was a result of regimental reputation:

> Some time in an Egyptian war, the Black Watch, with the Gordon Highlanders, had been jointly engaged in some forgotten action. It was alleged by the Gordon Highlanders that the Black Watch 'broke the square' at this action... some teacher, draper, miner, now a soldier in the Gordon Highlanders, had either read or had been told or had in some way heard of this episode, and in a public house met one who also had only recently been a teacher, draper, miner and was now a soldier in the Black Watch, whose regiment had broken the square. The Black Watch man resented this imputation and, on behalf of the fame of dead comrades on the Egyptian battlefields, challenged the Gordon Highlander and all the Gordon Highlanders to withdraw or justify the assertion. Thus the riot had begun.[51]

CQMS Darling wrote:

> It very moving that these men, who lately owed no allegiance to anyone...had somehow accepted the reputation of their recently not even self-chosen regiment as something for which they had a special responsibility, something for which they were prepared, at any rate immediately, to fight, and as events showed something for which when the time came in France and Flanders they were prepared to die.[52]

The men who would fill the ranks of the 9th Black Watch in September 1914 were all volunteers. The regiment had no problem securing recruits as thousands answered Kitchener's call. Each day a large number of recruits would report to The Black Watch Depot in Perth. Describing the scene at the depot a local newspaper correspondent reported:

From all parts of the country have come strapping young fellows – from America and from Canada and from other colonies. Perhaps the most interesting feature of the extraordinary rush to the Black Watch colours is the large number of Welshmen.[53]

RECRUITMENT DRIVE, PERTH
(Likely Princes Street railway station) *c.* September 1914
Photographer James Kelly

He wrote that 'probably at no time in its history has the popularity of the regiment been so emphatically demonstrated'.[54] Its popularity, and the appeal of kilted regiments in particular, was closely linked with the reinvention of Scotland in the nineteenth century, and the appeal of a romantic 'Highlandism'. Highland regiments occupied an important place in public imagination and their exploits on innumerable battlefields had made them synonymous with Britain's martial achievements. However, *The Tatler's* 'FAMOUS REGIMENTS' series considered The Black Watch a class apart:

There is not a man in all bonnie Scotland whose heart does not beat more proudly at the mention of the Black Watch. Every

Scotsman glories in the Greys, the Gordons, the Cameronians, the 93rd, and many another proud regiment, but the Black Watch seems to stand out separate and distinct as the National Regiment. Where other corps represent counties and clans "Am Freiceadan Dubh" represents Scottish chivalry as a whole.[55]

Not to be outdone, *The Courier and Argus* described the Black Watch as 'the premier Highland regiment by virtue of age and actual extent of fighting service. It is impossible in circumscribed space to do credit to the marvellous feats of this world-famed corps'.[56] Likewise, F A M Webster's *Britain in Arms*, a short volume intended 'to bring the man in the street into closer touch with his soldier-brother behind the barrack-gate', and encourage recruitment, considered the Black Watch 'Scotland's oldest and best-beloved regiment'.[57]

Throughout the period of voluntary enlistment Scotland produced over 320,000 recruits, the highest percentage of enlistments in the UK. It is difficult to attribute the 'recruiting fever' that swept Britain in late August and early September 1914 to a specific reason.[58] Some were moved by patriotism and duty while others' options were shaped by economic necessity. Whatever the reasons behind their decision to answer Kitchener's call, the men of the 9th Black Watch were recruited from across Scotland, with significant cadres representing England and South Wales. The regiment's traditional recruiting areas that comprised Perthshire, Fife, Dundee and Angus, were a valuable source of manpower for its New Army battalions. Based on an analysis of the original members of the 9th Black Watch the industrial central belt was also important with at least 30 per cent of recruits enlisting in Lanarkshire and over 10 per cent from the Lothians. CQMS Darling found himself in charge of a barrack-room including 'Scots, English, Welsh and Irish – and all proud of it, too!':

> The English as usual were tolerant and acquiescent of their allies. From opposite corners of the barrack-room on our first night...national songs were sung. The Welsh led with Land of my Fathers, and the Scots from a more varied but less musical repertoire offering a competing entertainment.[59]

The Welsh contingent included two 'pals' from Pontycymer, South Wales. Privates William T Nicholas and Peter Kear 'were always together, enlisted together, trained together, left for France at the same time, and both fought for the last time in the great battle of Loos'.[60] Before the war both had been miners in Ffaldau Colliery. The battalion included a number of men who enlisted alongside relatives, friends or workmates. However, it was not a 'Pals' battalion of which Scotland had comparatively few. There were instances of this phenomenon in the 9th Black Watch (and in other New Amy units) but it was localised and on a much smaller scale.

Private Andrew Matthew, 'the well known Harp F.C. half-back' was one of several Perth footballers who joined the 9th Battalion.[61] He served with Corporal Willie Macpherson who had represented St Johnstone and East Fife:

> [Described as] a versatile lad on the football field. He could fill almost any berth in the team but as centre-forward he seemed to find his true position. Possessed of a fine turn of speed 'Mac' could shoot with telling effect and while robust in his methods he always played the game.[62]

Private Thomas Maconachie Galloway, well known in Perth Junior football circles, would also join the battalion. These local sporting connections almost certainly explain why St Johnstone 'sent [the 9th Black Watch] a set of old jerseys' while the battalion was stationed at Aldershot.[63] Joining the Perth contingent was Private Duncan Ritchie, the 'Newcastle United, Renton, Derby County, Raith Rovers, and Dumbarton football player'.[64] The footballers also included Private David Skene who played right-back for Forfar Athletic for several seasons before the war. He was considered 'a defender in whom implicit faith could be imposed, his play being characterised by steadiness and fearlessness'.[65] Given the talent in the 9th Black Watch Private Matthew was reasonably optimistic about the battalion's footballing prospects. In a letter to a Harp FC official he wrote, 'We have some good players in our team...Give my regards to all the boys'.[66] Andrew Matthew, Willie Macpherson, Thomas Galloway and David Skene were killed in action at Loos. In a tragic coincidence, Private James Doig, the 25-year-old calendar (textile) worker who replaced Skene in the Forfar Athletic team, would lose his life while serving with the 4th Black Watch, 'Dundee's Own', in the same action.[67]

The 9th Black Watch also included small groups from Kinneil Colliery and the Forth Shipbreaking Company, both Bo'ness.[68] Likewise, several co-workers employed on the Brodick Castle estates enlisted at Ardrossan. Sergeant George Gouldthorpe, a Royal Navy veteran of the Boxer Rebellion, was one of three killed at Loos who are commemorated on the Brodick war memorial.[69] However, associations of this nature were not unusual in the New Army or Territorial Force.

Irrespective of their origins, within a few weeks the men began to assume a new allegiance and identity. CQMS Darling wrote:

> We were in the Army, and we were in the Black Watch, the Royal Scots, the Gordon Highlanders, or the Argyll and Sutherland Highlanders. Civilian loyalties and allegiances were lost in these traditional and all-embracing arms.[70]

The physical fitness of recruits in 1914 was a significant issue with desperately overworked recruiting staffs lowering standards to help speed the enlistment process and civilian practitioners paid a bounty for every recruit examined. However, regular training would weed out the physically unfit and forge the remainder into effective units. Major Stewart described the men as a 'really wonderful lot',[71] adding, 'I must say I think our 9th Battalion compares very favourably with the 1st [Battalion] not only as regards officers'.[72] The battalion was deemed ready for active service and on 4 July 1915, the 9th Black Watch, 44th Brigade, 15th (Scottish) Division, received orders that it would soon embark for France.[73]

The 9th Black Watch left Folkestone on 8 July reaching Boulogne later that evening. The 15th (Scottish) Division were ordered to join General Sir Henry Rawlinson's IV Corps then holding the line between Grenay, Pas-de-Calais, and La Bassée Canal, near Lens.[74] The battalion's first weeks in France were spent attached to various units with the objective of becoming more familiar with the routine of trench life. It would take over a portion of the frontline for the first time on 2 August 1915. Lieutenant-Colonel Lloyd and Major Stewart were understandably apprehensive about how the 'training of the past eleven months would stand the test', but after observing how well the men performed, Stewart wrote, 'I'm not one bit afraid of them now and am sure they will face anything'.[75] Reflecting on the battalion's first experience of holding a frontline trench he wrote:

> I think the men have done splendidly considering that this was our first tour of the trenches, after the first day neither [Lloyd] or I saw a single man of our lot that was not shaved and properly clean after 10am even in the actual trenches themselves, and they were always cheery and bright.[76]

9TH BLACK WATCH REGIMENTAL STAFF
R.Q.M.S. T. Hampton; Lieut. and Q.M. W. Clark; Major J. Stewart; Lieut.-Col. T. O. Lloyd;
Lieut. and Adjutant R. E. Harvey; R.S.M. G D. Bedson; O.R.S. J. Lindsay
Parkhouse Camp, Salisbury Plain, June 1915

It was during this period that the battalion would also receive the Red Hackle. Major Stewart had heard that Colonel Charles Edward Stewart, 1st Black Watch, would object to the hackle being worn by a Kitchener battalion. Stewart recorded in his diary that 'I think it will be exceedingly silly if he objects to the rank and file wearing them. [Lloyd] has written to him and St John Harvey [2nd Black Watch] about it, personally I would not have asked'.[77] Following Lieutenant-Colonel Lloyd's intercession, permission was granted, and on 6 September Stewart reported, 'Our hackles, or rather 500 of them, arrived last night and I served them to A and [two-thirds] of B, and HQ [Company]'.[78] Nevertheless, Lieutenant-Colonel Lloyd was informed that while the divisional commander, General McCraken, had no objection to the 'emblem' being worn behind the line, he considered it too conspicuous, and had decreed that it must not be worn when the battalion was in the trenches.[79] Lieutenant-Colonel Lloyd dined with General McCraken some days later and 'took the opportunity of explaining what the "Red Hackle" meant to every Black Watch man…[the General] immediately withdrew his veto'.[80] By 12 September 1915 every man in the 9th Battalion had been issued with a Red Hackle.

The battalion's attention was now focused on an imminent British offensive. The 15th (Scottish) Division would attack the high ground north of Loison-sous-Lens with its 44th Brigade on the right and 46th Brigade on the left. The leading brigades would attack in two columns, each consisting of one battalion, with a section of Royal Engineers and a platoon of the 9th Gordon Highlanders (Pioneers) in support.[81] The 44th Brigade would advance with 9th Black Watch on the right and 8th Seaforth Highlanders on the left, and 10th Gordon Highlanders and 7th Cameron Highlanders in support. The brigade's objectives were (a) the enemy's first- and second-line trenches, (b) Loos village, (c) Puits 15, (d) Hill 70, (e) Cité St Auguste and (f) the high ground north of Loison-sous Lens, some two miles further east.[82] The battlefield is immediately north of the mining town of Lens, in the heart of the industrial area of north-east France. The ground is open and undulating, and the enemy held the high ground east and south of Loos. Thus the advantage as regards ground clearly lay with the enemy, and, so long as he held Loos under observation, neither guns nor reserves could be safely brought up to assist a further advance.[83]

The most formidable point on the German frontline, the heavily fortified Lens Road Redoubt, was immediately on the battalion's front. Major Stewart was under no illusion as to the size of the task but felt optimistic about the battalion's prospects. On 21 September he wrote:

> I hiked out to the school house in Maroc to have a look at a
> certain part of the 'hay field' that will be of interest to us
> shortly, a really very interesting sight. The Hun wire is darned
> strong and will take some crossing but I don't think there will
> be very much left of it when once we get to work with our guns.[84]

Major Henderson shared a similar opinion of the German defences.
In a letter to the Linlithgow school board dated 13 September he wrote:

> I dare not go into details, and even if I could, and wrote down
> the bald details of what we have to get through, in order to
> break the German line, you would, I fear, only put me down as
> a far-away liar who could not be brought to book. [The
> German line] is a mass of palisade, barbed wire, and *chevaux-
> de-frise*, and their trenches have overhead cover, with machine-
> gun emplacements made of concrete, with steel cupolas
> flanking their own trenches and wire. Theirs is defence, pure
> and simple, and I have little doubt the line can be broken,
> though at a price, of course. Passive defence never won any
> game, and we are going to smash these swine.[85]

Sergeant Joseph Miller Barber, cashier in the Elgin Bleach Works,
Dunfermline, drafted a letter to his parents, dated 24 September, which
reflected the mood in the battalion. 'We are expecting great things and
everyone is in great spirits.'[86] Major Stewart observed 'everyone is fit and
well and we are all eagerly waiting the jump off'.[87] He described the
officers and men as living on the 'tip toe of expectation,' adding 'it will
perhaps be difficult to hold them back when we get going'.[88] Brigadier-
General M G Wilkinson, 44th Highland Brigade, hoped to foster this
offensive spirit with his 'Special Order' published on 23 September:

> The attack is to be pushed home to the fullest possible extent
> and I am certain that the high state of discipline and the
> keen feeling now maintained will enable the Brigade to give a
> good account of itself when dealing with the enemy. I feel

confident that all ranks will prove to the Scottish nation that they are able to worthily uphold the glorious traditions of the Highland regiments they now belong to.[89]

Stewart, reflecting on the task that now lay ahead, noted in his diary, 'Providence is with us and we will get through all right'.[90] The leading waves of A Company, 9th Black Watch, mounted the parapet and advanced at 6.30am on Saturday, 25 September.

From his vantage point Major Stewart watched the attack develop:

> The enemy's M[achine] Guns got to work and our men dropped right and left, but they never wavered for a second, on they went line after line, into and over the German front line trenches, on into the second and third lines and bang into Loos itself, nothing stopped them; it was a perfectly magnificent show but alas, alas, it was only a remnant of a [Regiment].[91]

A Perth man serving with the 9th Black Watch man wrote, we 'could see nothing but shells and bullets flying over our heads'.[92] Despite their heavy casualties, Stewart described the battalion's steady and disciplined advance. 'There was no sensational charging; they kept touch in distance and marched solidly across the "hayfield".'[93]

> There was no shouting or hurry; the men moved in quick time, picking up their 'dressing' as if on a ceremonial parade. The distance to be crossed varied from 80 to 200 yards, and, despite the fierce fire, not a line wavered or stopped.[94]

Major-General Sir John Burnett-Stuart, 15th (Scottish) Division, described the battalion's advance on the German first line as 'the finest sight he had ever seen':[95]

> It seemed impossible to realize that these lines of disciplined soldiers had been, twelve short months before, almost all

civilians. Perfect steadiness prevailed, regardless of the heavy fire which, coming more especially from the 'Lens Road Redoubt,' swept the ground over which they had to cross.[96]

Private Maxton Mackinlay, a native of Crieff, recalled these opening moments in a letter to his parents. 'Our men were met by a terrific fire of machine guns, bombs, grenades and shrapnel shells, and many fell between the two lines of trenches.'[97] Within five minutes of 'going over' the 9th Black Watch had taken the Lens Road Redoubt, German front and support trenches. However, this success came at a high price. It was estimated that over 200 officers and men had been killed, and nearly all remaining officers and a large number of other ranks had been wounded.[98] The dead included three of the four company commanders and all four CSMs.

Major Henderson's last words to his company were 'Keep going'.[99] Captain Bell 'fell a few yards from the German trenches, rose to his feet, ran a few yards forward, and then fell and died at once. He was the finest type of soldier that any one could hope to see'.[100] Seven officers died within 50 yards of Stewart's position in the British frontline trench.[101] Captain Richard Ernle Harvey, who had replaced Captain MacLeod as Adjutant, was mortally wounded as he carried instructions to the different companies.[102] He was shot in the chest as he stood at the side of Lieutenant-Colonel Lloyd. On walking the field, a day or so after the battle, Brigadier-General Henry Fleetwood Thuillier, left a graphic account of the scene:

> In front of the remains of that work known as the 'Lens Road Redoubt'...the dead Highlanders, in Black Watch tartan, lay very thick. In one place, about 40 yards square, on the very crest of the ridge, and just in front of the enemy's wire, they were so close that it was difficult to step between them. Nevertheless, the survivors had swept on and through the German lines. As I looked on the smashed and riven ground...I was amazed when I thought of the unconquerable, irresistible spirit which those newly raised units of the 'New Armies' must possess to enable them to continue their advance after sustaining such losses.[103]

On 30 September, Captain Alastair Drummond Carmichael organised a burial party which recovered the bodies of six officers and some 70 men of the 9th Black Watch who had fallen in the short distance between the British wire and German frontline trench. His efforts were hampered by German artillery and he was eventually obliged to abandon the task.[104]

Despite these heavy losses, the advance continued. Lloyd and Stewart helped dress the wounds of Lieutenants Richard Stirling and Godfrey Scott Pearse, who were lying just beyond the British wire, and joined their men as the battalion advanced.[105] Corporal George Hannah, Maxwelltown, previously employed in the motor department of Arrol-Johnston Limited, described how, in the initial assault, the 9th Black Watch 'lost men…it was an awful charge, and I will never forget it as long as I live':

> As soon as we got to the German first line trench the enemy held up their hands. We left them and went straight ahead for the next trench. Again the enemy surrendered, and we started again for the third line trench, where we had hand to hand fighting. I tell you we gave them what for, as we were all like madmen by this time. We pushed through their third line and made for the town of Loos.[106]

The advance was led by the battalion's pipers who played their companies into action. The band had been raised in October 1914 and fully equipped from subscriptions raised by friends of the battalion.[107] Piper William James McCann, who had been employed by a firm of booksellers before the war, 'was shot down while playing "Highland Laddie" when his battalion went into action'.[108] Describing the scene a correspondent wrote:

> The Black Watch went into action with their pipers playing 'Highland Laddie,' and the enemy have every reason to remember their terrible dash through trench after trench amid the smoke of exploding bomb. The pipers paused at the first German trench, still playing as the position was cleared of the

enemy. Two of them at least mounted the parapet, and the defiant skirl of their pipes could be heard above the crash of bombs. One piper was shot down; his companion did not move, but continued playing as though on the barrack square.[109]

It is believed that William McCann was the Black Watch piper who died on the German parapet.[110] Lance Corporal Robert MacDougall, 'a piper and stretcher-bearer in C Company', would also fall. MacDougall was a native of Aberfeldy, and before enlisting had worked on the Highland Railway at Blair Atholl. Piper William Pert, born in Dairsie, Fife, was another railwayman. The 33-year-old assistant linesman was employed in Glasgow but well known in Perth where he enlisted on 6 September 1914.[111] Piper Duncan Keith McLarty was born in Perth, Western Australia, but had enlisted in Cardiff. He was killed in action aged 24. McCann, MacDougall, Pert and McLarty have no known graves and are commemorated on the Loos Memorial. Piper William Robertson, Galashiels, was wounded.[112] Piper casualties were extremely heavy 'and the whole band, except one man, was killed or wounded'.[113]

Shortly before reaching the village 'a treacherous act on the part of the enemy increased the fury of the Black Watch'.[114] Lieutenant Sharp, a partner in the firm Messrs Graham & Finlayson, Solicitors, Crieff, was shot and killed in regrettable circumstances. Stewart wrote that 'Poor' Sharp was killed after lowering his revolver 'when a Hun officer held up his hands'.[115] Private Mackinlay described how the lieutenant encountered a German officer who offered to surrender:

> He was taking him prisoner when this officer's servant shot Mr Sharp through the head. But the servant did not live long. Oh! they are a cowardly lot of men. They wouldn't show fight at close quarters at all, but laid down their rifles and asked for mercy, saying – 'Comrade, comrade, me English.' And they got mercy! Our fellows killed many of them, and, risking every-thing, regardless of their own lives, started to use the German bombs, and caught many like rats in the village of Loos.[116]

By 7.50am Lieutenant-Colonel Lloyd and Major Stewart had reached the edge of the village:

> [There was] scarcely a house left standing, communication trenches ran up every street connecting with cellars, and these had been filled with Germans – they were filled with Germans as we passed, but they were all either dead or wounded – our men had done the work exceedingly well, methodically working from house to house with bombs never giving the enemy any rest.[117]

Loos village was the scene of some desperate hand-to-hand fighting. The battalion's medical officer, Captain F A Bearn, who had been wounded in the nose and gassed, established a dressing-station in Loos, but had to relocate on three occasions because of shellfire.[118] Throughout the day he was ably assisted by a young Frenchwoman, Mme Émilienne Moreau, better known as the 'Heroine of Loos'. When the dressing-station came under fire from one of the houses opposite, Moreau commandeered a revolver and went to deal with the threat:

> A few seconds afterwards two shots, and two only, were heard, and almost immediately the girl returned, laid down the revolver, quietly remarking 'C'est fini,' and continued her work of attending to the wounded as if nothing had happened.[119]

Captain Bearn later confirmed her story. Interviewed in 1944, Moreau said:

> I was indignant to see two Germans amusing themselves firing from a cave on wounded Scots, so I seized a revolver and crept up and killed them. Afterwards I showed the Black Watch where the enemy strongpoints lay. I guided them through the mined areas.[120]

Despite being only 17 in September 1915, '[Moreau] displayed the courage of the bravest of the brave'.[121]

Still on the outskirts of the village Lieutenant-Colonel Lloyd and Major Stewart waited to hear from the battalion but no news arrived.

They discovered afterwards 'that the reason why messages did not come back was that all officers by this time were either killed or wounded'.[122] Picking their way through Loos a wounded Black Watch man informed them that the remnants of the battalion were on Hill 70. On clearing the last of the houses, they could see 'the remainder of the Highland Brigade holding on to the crest of the hill'.[123] The position was precarious at best. However, the Highlanders fought with a 'dour heroism'.[124] Due to the nature of the fighting in the village the four battalions of 44th Brigade were hopelessly intermingled:

> Our right rested on the extreme East-South-East edge of the crassier or slag heap, and was very lightly held by a few men of the 9th Black Watch. This point is immediately in front of a strong German position at Dynamitière.[125] The line continued towards the North-East along the slope of Hill 70 up to and around a half-finished German work at the extreme North-east end of the Hill.[126]

Both flanks of the 15th (Scottish) Division were exposed as neither the 1st Division on its left nor 47th (London) Division on its right had made significant progress, and reports indicated that the German defenders were preparing to redouble their efforts against the Scots' right. Lloyd and Stewart sent any available men, with the exception of runners and signallers, to reinforce the flank which was held by Corporal J Connely and some 20 men. This left only a handful in reserve in the event of any counterattack. Stewart felt that it was 'a perfect marvel that the Germans did not make some attempt to out-flank us from the crassier, as the result of a counter-attack with one Company and four machine guns would have forced us all off the Hill at any minute of the day'.[127]

On the left the Scots made repeated attempts to take and hold the half-finished redoubt on the summit of Hill 70. Some six or seven times the men of 44th and 46th Brigades stormed and took the work but, on each occasion, they were driven back by heavy machine-gun and rifle fire. There was a strong wire entanglement to the front of the redoubt, and 'although our men were able to penetrate into it time after time, it was open

9TH BLACK WATCH PIPES AND DRUMS
Parkhouse Camp, Salisbury Plain, June 1915

to an attack from the German side, and our men had in each case to fall back through the German wire'.[128] Of those who went over the hill and reached the Dynamitière few if any returned. The Germans were aware of the strategic significance of Hill 70 and were determined that it should not fall into British hands. 'Redoubling their efforts, the enemy swept the crest of the hill with artillery, rifle, and machine-gun fire.'[129] The embattled Scots were eventually compelled to withdraw a short distance and dig in just below the western slope.[130] Private Liddell, 7th Cameron Highlanders, the 'Shiny Seventh', compared 44th Brigade's tenacious defence of Hill 70 with one of the greatest examples of Scottish military valour:[131]

> The Thin Red Line was a glorious thing but the thin line of
> the Brigade on Hill 70 was as glorious if not, more so, holding
> at bay thousands of Germans…We stuck on the Hill for
> 14 hours, and I lived many years in that time.[132]

Lance Corporal Isaac Green, C Company, 9th Black Watch, a native of Old Kilpatrick, employed by Messrs Napier & Miller, shipbuilders, was awarded the Distinguished Conduct Medal (DCM) for his gallantry on Hill 70.[133] He received an accidental bayonet wound in the right calf as he crossed the first German trench but refused to retire. He recalled how, 'That got my blood up'.[134] The original citation for his award describes how he took part in the fighting in and around Loos, on Hill 70, and the advance beyond. On retiring to the western slope, Green was the only non-commissioned officer left. In an interview with a local newspaper he remarked that he would 'never forget the Loos fight. The carnage was terrible. It is his opinion that if a soldier came through that battle safely he will not be killed in this war'.[135] Digging in on the reverse slope with a small group of seven survivors, Green was joined by another 23 including Lieutenant Eric Ronald Wilson.[136] With the exception of Lieutenant-Colonel Lloyd and Major Stewart, Lieutenant Wilson was the only 9th Black Watch officer left on the field.[137] He had been shot through a shoulder, had it dressed, and been ordered to go to the field ambulance, but managed to elude the medical officer and return to Hill 70.[138] He was described as exhausted 'owing to the cold and want of food'.[139] It was then that Lance Corporal Green, notwithstanding the heavy artillery, machine gun and rifle fire, covered 'hundreds of yards…to gather in the men of the 9th'.[140] In all he managed to rally about a company from what had been a new battalion.[141]

Green was one of two men in the battalion to be awarded the DCM at Loos.[142] The other, Lance Corporal William Bell, a booking clerk at Baillieston Station, 'attended to the wounded indefatigably till late in the evening, and then, although himself wounded and suffering great pain, brought another wounded man back to the dressing station'.[143] His wounds rendered him unfit for further active service.[144]

Three other men serving with A Company were also recommended for gallantry awards on account of their actions. Before the battalion had 'gone over' a Royal Engineer responsible for releasing chlorine gas had been overcome by fumes from two damaged cylinders. Lance Sergeant Walter S Turnbull, 'went forward followed by [Lance Corporal Samuel] Surgeon, found a key and turned off [the] leaking cylinder, thus stopping the flow of gas into the trench'.[145] Surgeon then took the key and turned off the second cylinder. When the battalion advanced, Private Robert Napier had led a party of bombers through the German trenches and into

Loos, 'doing splendid work'. 'He had not been originally selected as one of a bombing party as he had only received instruction in the use of bombs on the two days previous to the attack.'[146] The third, Private George Boak, was knocked over by a shrapnel shell outside Loos suffering flesh wounds in both legs:

> He continued to advance, killed a bomber who was throwing bombs among our men as they advanced and then assumed command of a party of men, leading them through Loos, on to, and over Hill 70. On finding that his party was too far advanced for our artillery, he then led them back to be safe from our own shells.[147]

Boak was mentioned despatches. However, the nature of the fighting at Loos meant that many acts of gallantry went unrecorded. Lance Corporal Green highlighted the actions of Private Gordon Hossack, a well-known footballer with St Bernard's and Bo'ness. He believed Hossack would have won the Victoria Cross (VC) had he lived. He 'caught the bombs like a goalkeeper and returned them to the Huns time after time, there to do their deadly work. It is just what those who knew Gordon expected of him, for he was a brave lad and a good sport'.[148]

It was rumoured that Private Tom Fletcher had been recommended for the VC having 'killed 18 Germans and an officer in the charge at Loos'.[149] Describing the action in a letter to his brother he wrote, 'we fought like true Scots of old, and you know I was in it…I was one of the brave in that charge', adding, 'I am down for honours. I don't know how it will go'.[150] Private Fletcher received no official recognition for his actions at Loos.

It would be impossible to chronicle each act of extraordinary bravery performed by the men of the 9th Black Watch on 25 September, nor the sacrifices they made. Their courage is exemplified by the conduct of Sergeant Thomas Rutherford, a blacksmith from Ladybank, who received a shrapnel wound in the thigh 'while rallying his men for rapid firing after a bayonet charge. He retired to the dressing-station, where his wound was treated, but he insisted on going back to the fighting line'.[151]

It was believed Sergeant Rutherford was killed during the capture of Hill 70. The many instances of selflessness are demonstrated by the anonymous platoon sergeant of D Company who died dressing the wounds of Lance Corporal Lewis Davidson from Coatbridge during the retirement from the half-finished German redoubt on the summit of the hill. One of Davidson's comrades described how the sergeant 'stayed with Lewis, and was bandaging his wounds when he got three bullets in him, and was killed instantly'.[152]

The losses incurred in taking Hill 70 were great. In a letter home an anonymous Perth man wrote that this was 'where we lost half our men… There is very few of our regiment left'.[153] Brothers, David and James Walker, employed by Kipps Brickworks, Coatbridge, before the war, were among the men of the battalion who lost their lives on the hill. Private James Nimmo wrote to the brothers' parents:

> I lost poor David on Saturday morning. He was with me from the German trenches right up to Hill 70…We were lying close together on this hill, and were only about a quarter of an hour there till David got the shot on the forehead, and just as he got it his last words were 'Jimmy, Jimmy, my head.' I looked at him and was just going to dress him when I saw he was dead. The bullet must have stayed in his head, and I was making sure he was away before I left, but it was right. He has gone, but died a hero, poor fellow. Then we got the order to retire, and I had to leave him. Jimmy is missing. He was seen last on the same hill where David and I were, but away on the right. He was wounded, and must have been taken prisoner on the order to retire. This is Wednesday afternoon, and nothing of Jimmy yet.[154]

Other families would be similarly affected by the Battle of Loos. Mrs Grieve, Denbeath, received a letter from Sergeant Nisbet, stating that her son, Sergeant Peter Izatt, 9th Black Watch, had been 'blown to pieces'. Nisbet wrote, 'I knew your son's worth as a Sergeant in the regiment, in which he was well liked'.[155] Mr Grieve's son, Private Walter Grieve, was wounded, and a son-in-law Private John Christie, Kirkcaldy, a machineman in the Pannie Coal Pit, was killed in action.[156]

The remnants of the 44th and 46th Brigades now stubbornly held the western edge of the hill. Matters remained like this practically all day. 'Everything was at a standstill – no reinforcements came up, as we had been led to expect, and we did not know at what moment a German counter-attack would drive us off Hill 70.'[157]

Lieutenant-Colonel Lloyd, senior battalion commander in the 44th Brigade, sent a message to headquarters at noon asking for urgent reinforcements. The reply came at 1.25pm informing him that the artillery had been moved to its new forward positions and reinforcements were coming up. This was welcome news, but it was some time before they arrived. Six motor machine guns appeared at 3pm. Stewart wrote that 'I was never more glad to see anything in my life'.[158] Two were immediately sent to reinforce the lightly defended right flank and the remainder to the centre.[159]

It would be another hour before further reinforcements arrived to support the left and around 4.45pm before men of the 47th (London) Division appeared in sufficient number on the right. Lieutenant-Colonel Lloyd now asked that 44th Brigade be relieved. Its strength was approximately 500 men having started the day some 4,000 strong.[160] Colonel Sandilands, 7th Cameron Highlanders, informed Lloyd that he had only around 100 men left. Colonel Wallace, 10th Gordons, could not estimate his casualties. Lloyd received no reply from the 8th Seaforth Highlanders. The 9th Black Watch had barely 90 men left in action. It was agreed that the 44th Brigade would be relieved by the 62nd Brigade during the night. Stewart was of a mind that they had 'hung on by the skin of [their] teeth'.[161]

On the morning of 26 September, at around 1.30am, the 9th Black Watch was relieved by half a company of the Northumberland Fusiliers. In his diary, dated Thursday, 30 September, Major Stewart wrote, 'Just think, the remnants of a battalion, who went into action over a thousand strong, were relieved by half a Company!'.[162]

Only 98 men of the battalion returned to Philosophe in the early hours of 26 September, 'which we reached dead done, too tired and anxious even to sleep...By God's good grace alone we stood it'.[163] Lance Corporal Green described how, when the battalion 'got back to Quality Street (where the charge started) the Guards thought they were a company of some regiment. When told that they were all that remained of a battalion tears could be seen in many a stalwart Guardsman's eyes'.[164] Over the next day or so men who had become detached from the battalion re-joined it at Mazingarbe where the battalion was accommodated in what would become known as 'Black Watch Farm':

> Here [Monsieur] Henniquet and his daughter [Mademoiselle] Henriette, contrived to carry on within three miles of the front...It was to this farm at 4.30pm on September 24, 1915, that the 9th Battalion the Black Watch came to stack their kits before the attack. Mlle Henriette saw them march away in the dusk – 940 stalwart young men, the cream of their generation, scarcely one of whom a year before had dreamed of being a soldier.[165]

Before the battle the farm had been scarcely large enough to billet a single company.[166] Henriette 'watched with compassion' as the battalion called the roll.[167] Taking stock, Major Stewart recorded that:

> In all, counting transport, details on other jobs etc., we mustered 8 officers and 326 men; out of the officers only two came back ([Lloyd] and myself) the other six we had were made up of the 4 we had left behind, the [Quartermaster] and the Transport Officer, and out of our 326, about 250 had been through the battle and about 60 of these had slight wounds; we went into action 20 officers and about 900 other ranks, but though our losses were heavy, we did our job all right and the [Kitchener Battalion] of The Black Watch well upheld the traditions of The [Regiment].[168]

In all Lloyd's 9th Black Watch suffered some 700 casualties on 25 September 1915. Brigade headquarters recorded 10 officers killed and 11 wounded; and 68 other ranks killed in action, 292 missing and

319 wounded.[169] These were the worst losses ever incurred by a battalion of the regiment in a single action.[170]

Reflecting on the action a Perth man serving with the 9th Black Watch wrote:

> You will have learned by this time that I have undergone my baptism of fire. Personally, I should consider it much more appropriate if it was called a deluge of fire. The only battle that I had seen prior to the great fight was in a picture palace, and, with due respect to the cinema artist, the real thing is a bit more exciting. So far as I am concerned I have no special desire to gain any further experience, and I have a sneaking feeling that Mr German will be equally delighted to admire the gentlemen in 'petticoats' at a respectable distance. I have no intensions of giving you a description of the great fight. I want to forget it as quick as possible, but when I look along the line and see so many faces gone I am afraid it will be well-nigh impossible.[171]

Private John Hammond, Bo'ness, was struck on the wrist by a bullet and a piece of shrapnel tore a hole in his kilt. He told his sister:

> It was hell let loose, for there was nothing but shells and bullets flying around, doing their deadly work...how I came out alive I cannot imagine. It must have been God that saved me, and I shall never forget the sights I saw on that battlefield as long as I live...I hope and trust I shall never see the like again.[172]

Private Tom Fletcher, Airdrie, shared similar sentiments in a letter to his brother. 'We led the charge, and it was an awful sight. If ever I prayed in sincerity it was on that battlefield.'[173] Describing the aftermath of his battalion's advance a Crieff man recalled:

> Our lads had German helmets, rifles, and bayonets, and other things too numerous to mention. It was an awful sight – the

wounded that came down the line – a pitiful sight, and one
which I hope I will never see again.[174]

However, there was also a sense of accomplishment in what the
9th Black Watch had achieved. Private Maxton Mackinlay was of the
opinion that the battalion had 'upheld their grand name' and 'gained
such a fine victory'.[175]

Similarly, John Hammond wrote, 'There can be no doubt about it,
the [9th] Black Watch did their duty and took Hill 70, and advanced
three miles'.[176] In a letter to a friend in Carriden, West Lothian, Private
Andrew Black described how 'we routed the Germans out of four lines of
trenches which they had held for seven or eight months…We proved
ourselves to be of the right Scottish stuff, and kept up the good name of
the Black Watch as "bonnie fechters"'.[177]

Likewise, Private Thomas Brown, a Dumfries soldier, wrote 'the
Germans have a terrible dread of the Black Watch boys. When they see us
they either run as hard as they can or hold their hands up'.[178]

The 9th Black Watch, with the 44th Brigade, had captured four lines
of German trenches, Loos village, and had reached the crest of Hill 70, a
distance of some five miles. The 15th (Scottish) Division, without support
from adequate reserves, made the farthest advance of any British division
between the outbreak of the war and the Battle of Cambrai in November
1917.[179] General McCraken's instructions 'to push forward to the utmost
were obeyed to the letter…Unaided, mortal men could have done no
more than did his Division at Loos, and in the performance of those
orders the 9th Black Watch well upheld the credit of its parent regiment'.[180]
The men received the recognition of the corps and divisional commanders,
and the congratulation of Colonel Stewart, 1st Black Watch, 'a very much
treasured compliment'.[181] Lloyd was of the opinion that is 9th Battalion had
'more than maintained the traditions of its parent battalion [that] day'.[182]

In a letter to his son, written on 29 September, Major Stewart
considered the part played by the battalion:

Here I am, safe and sound after having been in what I suppose
is the biggest fight the world has ever seen. We had a very

rough time and have lost a lot of our officers and men...BUT WE HAD DONE OUR JOB all right and the enemy know what The Black Watch can do. We took nearly 200 prisoners, and our Brigade took altogether 1500 and 2 Field guns a whole lot of machine guns and other things. It was "some fight" old boy.[183]

To his wife he wrote:

The Regiment was absolutely magnificent and they've written a page of [Black Watch] History that will rank with Ticonderoga.[184] I cannot write details now dear heart but believe me you've reason to be PROUD of [Kitchener's] Highland [Brigade] and the Germans know us well too by now.[185]

On 1 October, Lieutenant-Colonel Lloyd addressed the remnants of his battalion in a similar fashion:

When, just about a year ago, we were first formed into a battalion, we hoped to be able, by our conduct, to prove ourselves at any rate worthy descendants of our two great parent battalions, the 42nd and the 73rd. And now, whenever you look back on Saturday, the 25th September 1915, you will do so with conscious pride, that not only have you proved yourselves trustworthy, and upheld those great traditions, but that on the very first day the 9th Battalion went into action they themselves wrote a fresh and glorious page in the history of the regiment; and what more could man desire?[186]

The 9th Black Watch had suffered devastating losses during the Battle of Loos. The battalion had taken almost a year to build but had been all but destroyed in a single action. However, what it achieved that day was remarkable. In acknowledging its accomplishments and the many men who fell, it seems appropriate to leave the conclusion to Major John Stewart. Reflecting on the battalion and its casualties on 25 September 1915, he wrote:

They will be remembered as long as the [Black Watch] is a Regiment. Ah 42nd, you have reason to be proud of your 9th [Battalion].[187]

---

1 Major John Stewart's Diary, Friday, 24 September 1915, The Black Watch Castle and Museum Archives, BW25/2/9, p29.

2 *The Perthshire Advertiser and Strathmore Herald*, 16 February 1916.

3 Major John Stewart's Diary, Thursday, 30 September 1915, p30.

4 A G Wauchope, *A History of the Black Watch in the Great War, 1914-18*, Volume 3 (London: Medici Society, 1926), p124.

5 *The Strathearn Herald*, 23 October 1915.

6 *The Perthshire Constitutional and Journal*, 18 October 1915.

7 *Dumfries and Galloway Saturday Standard*, 20 November 1915.

8 Major John Stewart's Diary, Account of the Battle of Loos, p37.

9 *The Red Hackle*, April 1921, p32; Wauchope, *History*, Volume 3, p107.

10 Neil McMicking, *Officers of The Black Watch 1725 to 1925* (Perth: Thomas Hunter & Sons, 1952), p55.

11 Wauchope, *History*, Volume 3, p109.

12 Sir William Darling, *So It Looks To Me: The Autobiography of Sir William Darling* (London: Odhams, 1952), p127.

13 *Linlithgowshire Gazette*, 18 September 1914.

14 Wauchope, *History*, Volume 3, p108.

15 Darling, *So It Looks To Me*, p127; Wauchope, *History*, Volume 3, p109.

16 Wauchope, *History*, Volume 3, pp111-112.

17 Wauchope, *History*, Volume 3, p108.

18 Darling, *So It Looks To Me*, p127.

19 Wauchope, *History*, Volume 3, p109.

20 *The Scotsman*, 5 November 1947.

21 Wauchope, *History*, Volume 3, pp107-108.

22 *The Evening Telegraph and Post*, 2 September 1915.

23 *Linlithgowshire Gazette*, 4 December 1914.

24 *Linlithgowshire Gazette*, 8 October 1915.

25 *The Scotsman*, 6 October 1915.

26 *The Manchester Courier*, 5 October 1915.

27 *The Evening Telegraph and Post*, 5 October 1915.

28 *The Scotsman*, 5 October 1915.

29 Peter Simkins, *Kitchener's Army: The Raising of the New Armies 1914-1916* (Manchester: Manchester University Press, 1988), p218.

30 Wauchope, *History*, Volume 3, p108.

31 Peter Simkins, 'The War Experience of a Typical Kitchener Division: The 18th Division, 1914-1918', in Hugh Cecil and Peter H Liddle (eds), *Facing Armageddon: The First World War Experienced* (London: Leo Cooper, 1996), p471.

32 Wauchope, *History*, Volume 3, p108.

33 Wauchope, *History*, Volume 3, p108.

34 Wauchope, *History*, Volume 3, p108.

35 Wauchope, *History*, Volume 3, p108.

36 Wauchope, *History*, Volume 3, p108.

37 *The Post Sunday Special*, 17 October 1915.

38 *The People's Journal*, 13 November 1915.

39 *The Scotsman*, 18 November 1915.

40 *The Courier and Argus*, 10 November 1915.

41 *The Dundee Advertiser*, 15 October 1915.

42 *The People's Journal*, 13 November 1915.

43 *The Courier and Argus*, 11 November 1915.

44 The Marchioness of Tullibardine and Jane C C MacDonald, *A Military History of Perthshire 1899-1902* (Perth: 1908), p186.

45 *The Courier and Argus*, 5 November 1915.

46 Darling, *So It Looks To Me*, p127.

47 Darling, *So It Looks To Me*, p127.

48 Darling, *So It Looks To Me*, p127.

49 The National Archives, WO95/1937/2, 30 August 1915. On 30 August 1915, the battalion received a draft of 30 men, some 'having been home wounded'. These were primarily veterans of the 1st and 2nd Battalions and had participated in the fighting of 1914. They brought additional experience to the 9th Black Watch.

50 Darling, *So It Looks To Me*, p128.

51 Darling, *So It Looks To Me*, p129; Eric and Andro Linklater, *The Black Watch: The History of the Royal Highland Regiment* (London: Barrie & Jenkins, 1977), p127. This riot was a result to the controversy surrounding the 'broken' square at the Battle of Tamai, 13 March 1884. Linklater described how a fight could be started in any pub in a garrison town where a Black Watch battalion was stationed simply by calling for 'A pint of Broken Square'. At that, belts would be flailed, and knuckles bloodied.

52 Darling, *So It Looks To Me*, p129.

53 *The Courier and Argus*, 14 September 1914.

54 *The Courier and Argus*, 14 September 1914.

55 *The Tatler*, Volume LIV, Number 693, 7 October 1914.

56 *The Courier and Argus*, 21 October 1915.

57 F A M Webster, *Britain in Arms* (London: Sidgwick & Jackson Ltd, 1914), p125.

58 Simkins, *Kitchener's Army*, p64.

59 Darling, *So It Looks To Me*, p126.

60 *The Glamorgan Gazette, (Bridgend and Neath Chronicle and Central Glamorgan Gazette: Incorporated)*, 29 October 1915.

61 *Perthshire Advertiser and Strathmore Journal*, 23 January 1915.

62 *Perthshire Advertiser and Strathmore Journal*, 6 November 1915.

63 *Perthshire Advertiser and Strathmore Journal*, 30 December 1914; *The Dunfermline Journal*, 9 October 1915. The 9th Black Watch's sporting contingent included well-known Fife cricketer, Private Robert Boyd, who suffered a severe shrapnel wound on 25 September 1915. Boyd was one of 12 Dunfermline men who enlisted together in September 1914. Nine were wounded and three reported missing at Loos.

64 *The Glasgow Herald*, 1 October 1915.

65 *The Forfar Herald and Kirriemuir Advertiser*, 22 October 1915.

66 *Perthshire Advertiser and Strathmore Journal*, 23 January 1915.

67 *The Forfar Herald and Kirriemuir Advertiser*, 22 October 1915.

68 *The Edinburgh Evening News*, 2 October 1915.

69 James C Inglis, *Brodick-Arran and the Great War 1914-1918* (Edinburgh: Oliver & Boyd, 1919), p43.

70 Darling, *So It Looks To Me*, p128.

71 Major John Stewart's Diary, Saturday, 21 August 1915, p17.

72 Major John Stewart's Diary, Wednesday, 21 July 1915, p8.

73 Wauchope, *History*, Volume 3, p114.

74 Wauchope, *History*, Volume 3, p116.

75 Major John Stewart's Diary, Friday, 13 August 1915, p16.

76 Major John Stewart's Diary, Friday, 13 August 1915, pp15-16.

77 Major John Stewart's Diary, Sunday, 25 July 1915, p9.

78 Major John Stewart's Diary, Monday, 6 September 1915, pp22-23.

79 Wauchope, *History*, Volume 3, p119.

80 Wauchope, *History*, Volume 3, p119.

81 Wauchope, *History*, Volume 3, pp121-22.

82 Wauchope, *History*, Volume 3, p122.

83 Wauchope, *History*, Volume 3, p122.

84 Major John Stewart's Diary, Tuesday, 21 September 1915, p27.

85 *Linlithgowshire Gazette*, 8 October 1915.

86 *The Evening Telegraph and Post*, 5 November 1915; Victoria Schofield, *The Black Watch: Fighting in the Front Line 1899-2006* (London: Head of Zeus, 2017), p79.

87 Major John Stewart's Diary, Thursday, 23 September 1915, p28.

88 Major John Stewart's Diary, Saturday, 18 September 1915, p25.

89 Major John Stewart's Diary, Thursday, 23 September 1915, p28.

90 Major John Stewart's Diary, Tuesday, 21 September 1915. p27.

91 Major John Stewart's Diary, Thursday, 30 September 1915, p30.

92 *The Perthshire Constitutional and Journal*, 6 October 1915.

93 Major John Stewart's Diary, Account of the Battle of Loos, p36.

94 Wauchope, *History*, Volume 3, p124.

95 Wauchope, *History*, Volume 3, p124.

96 Wauchope, *History*, Volume 3, p124.

97 *The Strathearn Herald*, 9 October 1915.

98 Wauchope, *History*, Volume 3, p124.

99 Wauchope, *History*, Volume 3, p124.

100 *The Scotsman*, 5 October 1915.

101 Major John Stewart's Diary, Account of the Battle of Loos, p36.

102 *Sussex Express, Surrey Standard, and Kent Mail*, 8 October 1915.

103 Wauchope, *History*, Volume 3, pp128-129; Major John Stewart's Diary, Tuesday, 1 February 1916, p54. On 1 February 1916, Major Stewart, Major A H O Dennistoun, whose son, Lieutenant Alexander Oakley Dennistoun, 9th Black Watch, had been wounded at Loos, and Captain F A Bearn, visited 'the old historic spot where the 9th [Black Watch] jumped off on that memorable day; it was sad work'. They visited the graves of the officers and walked the battlefield. Stewart 'picked up two hackles which had lain there ever since that day'.

[104] Major John Stewart's Diary, Thursday, 30 September 1915, p34; Wauchope, *History,* Volume 3, p131.

[105] Major John Stewart's Diary, Account of the Battle of Loos, pp36-37; *The Strathearn Herald*, 23 October 1915.

[106] *Dumfries and Galloway Standard and Advertiser*, 13 October 1915.

[107] *The Red Hackle*, April 1921, p32; Wauchope, *History,* Volume 3, p110.

[108] *The Scotsman*, 5 November 1915.

[109] *The Fife Free Press*, 30 October 1915.

[110] R H Crawford, *Floo'ers o' the Forest: Fallen Pipers of the Great War* (Duntroon Publishing, 2014), pp67-68.

[111] *The Perthshire Constitutional and Journal*, 15 November 1915; Crawford, *Floo'ers o' the Forest*, p63.

[112] *The Jedburgh Gazette and Border Courier*, 8 October 1915.

[113] Brevet-Colonel Sir Bruce Seton and Pipe Major John Grant, *The Pipes of War: A Record of the Achievements of Pipers of Scottish and Overseas Regiments during the War 1914-18* (Glasgow: Maclehose, Jackson & Co, 1920), p104.

[114] Wauchope, *History,* Volume 3, p125.

[115] Schofield, *The Black Watch*, p85.

[116] *The Strathearn Herald*, 9 October 1915.

[117] Major John Stewart's Diary, Account of the Battle of Loos, p38.

[118] Major John Stewart's Diary, Thursday, 30 September 1915, p34.

[119] Major John Stewart's Diary, Saturday, 6 November 1915, p46.

[120] *The Press and Journal*, 16 August 1944.

[121] Major John Stewart's Diary, Saturday, 6 November 1915, p46.

[122] Major John Stewart's Diary, Account of the Battle of Loos, p37.

[123] Major John Stewart's Diary, Account of the Battle of Loos, p37.

[124] *The Scotsman*, 21 December 1921.

[125] The Dynamitière was a group of houses on the southern bottom of Hill 70 originally used to store explosives for the mines.

[126] Major John Stewart's Diary, Thursday, 30 September 1915, p31.

[127] Major John Stewart's Diary, Account of the Battle of Loos, p40.

[128] Major John Stewart's Diary, Account of the Battle of Loos, p39.

[129] Lieutenant-Colonel J Stewart and John Buchan, *The Fifteenth (Scottish Division) 1914-1919* (Edinburgh: William Blackwood & Sons, 1926), p 38.

[130] Wauchope, *History,* Volume 3, p126.

[131] Robert Burns, *Once a Cameron Highlander* (West Sussex: Woodfield Publishing 2000), p41.

[132] *Daily Record and Mail*, 12 October 1915.

[133] *The Evening Telegraph and Post*, 25 February 1916.

134 *The Post Sunday Special*, 27 February 1916.

135 *The Post Sunday Special*, 27 February 1916.

136 *The Post Sunday Special*, 27 February 1916.

137 *The Aberdeen Daily Journal*, 23 September 1916. Lieutenant Eric Ronald Wilson was awarded the Military Cross for gallantry at Loos.

138 Major John Stewart's Diary, Account of the Battle of Loos, p39.

139 *The Post Sunday Special*, 27 February 1916.

140 *The Post Sunday Special*, 27 February 1916.

141 *The Post Sunday Special*, 27 February 1916.

142 Wauchope, *History,* Volume 3, p130; *The Kilmarnock Herald*, 17 December 1915. In addition to other gallantry awards earned by men of the battalion, Lance-Sergeant David Ramsay McKellar, Dundonald, Ayrshire, received the *Croix de Guerre* for 'conspicuous bravery' on 25 September 1915.

143 *Supplement to the London Gazette*, 14 January 1916.

144 *The Coatbridge Leader*, 10 June 1916.

145 Major John Stewart's Diary, A Company, 9th Black Watch, Return of men recommended for gallantry in the field, September 1915, p29.

146 Major John Stewart's Diary Return of men recommended for gallantry, September 1915, p29.

147 Major John Stewart's Diary Return of men recommended for gallantry, September 1915, p29.

148 *Linlithgowshire Gazette*, 3 March 1916.

149 *The Airdrie and Coatbridge Advertiser*, 23 October 1915.

150 *The Airdrie and Coatbridge Advertiser*, 23 October 1915.

151 *The Dundee Advertiser*, 11 November 1915.

152 *The Airdrie and Coatbridge Advertiser*, 16 October 1915.

153 *The Perthshire Constitutional and Journal*, 6 October 1915.

154 *The Airdrie and Coatbridge Advertiser*, 20 November 1915.

155 *The Leven Advertiser and Wemyss Gazette*, 21 October 1915.

156 *The Evening Telegraph and Post*, 2 November 1915.

157 Major John Stewart's Diary, Account of the Battle of Loos, p40.

158 Major John Stewart's Diary, Account of the Battle of Loos, p40.

159 Wauchope, *History,* Volume 3, p126.

160 Major John Stewart's Diary, Account of the Battle of Loos, p40.

161 Major John Stewart's Diary, Account of the Battle of Loos, p40.

162 Major John Stewart's Diary, Account of the Battle of Loos, p41.

163 Wauchope, *History,* Volume 3, p127; Major John Stewart's Diary, Thursday, 30 September 1915, p32. The National Archives, WO95/1937/2, 'Reference order to furnish a short report on operations of 25-9-15', Houchin, 29 September 1915. Lieutenant-Colonel Lloyd estimated that he reached Philosophe with about 150 men at 3am on the morning of 26 September.

164 *The Post Sunday Special,* 27 February 1916.

165 John Maclennan, *Scots of the Line* (Edinburgh: W & R Chalmers Ltd, 1953), p99.

166 Wauchope, *History,* Volume 3, p128.

167 Maclennan, *Scots of the Line,* p101.

168 Major John Stewart's Diary, Thursday, 30 September 1915, pp32, 34.

169 WO95/1934/1, 27 and 30 September 1915.

170 Linklater, *The Black Watch,* p145.

171 *The Perthshire Constitutional and Journal,* 6 October 1915.

172 *Linlithgowshire Gazette,* 8 October 1915.

173 *The Airdrie and Coatbridge Advertiser,* 23 October 1915.

174 *The Strathearn Herald,* 9 October 1915.

175 *The Strathearn Herald,* 9 October 1915.

176 *Linlithgowshire Gazette,* 8 October 1915.

177 *Linlithgowshire Gazette,* 8 October 1915.

178 *Dumfries and Galloway Saturday Standard,* 9 October 1915.

179 Stewart, *The Fifteenth (Scottish Division),* p51.

180 Wauchope, *History,* Volume 3, p129.

181 Wauchope, *History,* Volume 3, p129.

182 The National Archives, WO95/1937/2, 'Reference order to furnish a short report on operations of 25-9-15', Houchin, 29 September 1915.

183 Major John Stewart to 'My dear old Boy', Wednesday, 29 September 1915.

184 Linklater, *The Black Watch,* pp31-32; *The Courier,* 19 September 1914; *The Courier,* 21 October 1915. During the desperate fighting at Fort Ticonderoga on 8 July 1758, the regiment lost eight officers, nine sergeants, and 297 men killed; 17 officers, 10 sergeants, and 306 men wounded. The Black Watch, 'loth to retire though ordered to do so, continued fighting desperately', demonstrating 'unequalled courage'. Despite losing over half its strength, Linklater described the battle 'not as a disaster, but as a triumphant display of Highland gallantry'.

185 Major John Stewart to 'My Darling', Monday, 27 September 1915.

186 *Dumfries and Galloway Saturday Standard and Advertiser,* 20 November 1915; Major John Stewart's Diary, Monday, 4 October 1915, p35.

187 Major John Stewart to 'My Darling', Monday, 27 September 1915.

TALES OF THE GREAT WAR
TOLD TO ME BY MY GRANDFATHER
A PERSONAL RECOLLECTION

C B Innes

M Y GRANDFATHER, Colonel Sydney Armitage Innes, DSO and Bar, who was born in 1879, joined The Black Watch in 1898, and shortly afterwards was posted with the 2nd Battalion out to South Africa to take part in the Second Anglo-Boer War (1899–1902). He was wounded at the Battle of Magersfontein in 1899 and was later invalided back home. He then served in India for many years during the years of peace after the Boer War, later becoming Adjutant of the Highland Cyclist Battalion (TF) in Fife before the outbreak of World War I. He was widely known as Colonel Syd.

COLONEL SYDNEY ARMITAGE INNES, DSO

Promoted to major in 1915, he was given command, as a temporary lieutenant-colonel, of the newly formed 9th Service Battalion of The Black Watch, just after they had taken part in the Battle of Loos. He commanded the battalion with great distinction from then until early 1918, by which time had had been awarded the Distinguished Service Order and Bar. By then the 9th Battalion had fought through the dreadful trench warfare battles of the Somme (1916-17), Arras and Ypres. Over the course of the war the 9th Battalion suffered appalling casualties so that at the end it had to amalgamate with the 4/5thTerritorial Battalion of the regiment, at which point in May 1918 only one officer and 83 other ranks of the original 9th Battalion were still serving.

The day-to-day pressures of command borne by officers commanding infantry battalions during the war in those dreadful conditions must have taken a toll upon my grandfather, particularly given the length of time he was in command of the 9th Battalion. Still, he was rewarded with a fine posting after the war and from 1930 until 1939 was the Commandant of Queen Victoria School, Dunblane, before he was again called-up to become the Deputy Assistant Adjutant General at the 51st Highland Division headquarters in Perth until he finally retired in 1940.

I often used to visit my grandfather who lived at Fairmount House on Kinnoull Hill overlooking Perth. When I was very young, during the Second World War, I remember the house was visited by many serving regimental officers, still in uniform, back on leave from the conflict and keen to visit their old commanding officer, or to stay with my grandparents who made Fairmount open to all. I was then only between three and eight years old and so I did not quiz him much about his wartime experiences at that point, but I did later on when I thought that I would follow my father and my grandfather into the regiment, and I wanted to know more regimental history.

Now I must mention my father, Lieutenant-Colonel Berowald Alfred Innes, who joined up in 1924 and was posted out to India and the 2nd Battalion, The Black Watch, which was commanded by his father, Colonel Syd, stationed at that time in Quetta. My father served throughout the Second World War, later commanding the 4th Battalion in Gibraltar before taking over the 7th Battalion from my (soon to be) father-in-law, Lieutenant-Colonel Charles Cathcart, DSO, before the Rhine Crossing. At the end of the war, my father was given command of the 1st Battalion in Duisburg.

So, in about 1952, aged about 16, and hopefully heading to join the regiment, I began to ask my grandfather about his service in the Second Anglo-Boer War (1899-1902) and in the Great War. He was then about 73 and probably had not talked about both wars for many years. He was not all that forthcoming to begin with but later warmed to the subject and began to recount some tales.

During the Boer War, he said that he had lost several great officer friends in battle but a much greater number of other ranks, some of whom had been in his platoon or in his company. On return to Scotland, he said that he made a point of visiting the relatives of those whom he had known very well and tried to describe to them the lie of the land in South Africa and where their sons had perished.

He also mentioned his having been being wounded at Magersfontein and being sent to hospital in Cape Town to recuperate. There he found himself alongside a fellow subaltern, Lieutenant Freddie Tait, who had also been wounded in the battle and who was later to be killed whilst storming the heights of Koodoosberg Drift, near Kimberley. Nevertheless, before his death at the age of 30, he had won the Amateur Golf Championship twice (in 1896 and 1898). He and my grandfather were good friends and had played some golf before the war, though Freddie Tait was by far the better golfer.

We then discussed the Great War. Again, he was reluctant to speak openly to start with, as were so many of his generation after experiencing the horrors of that five-year conflict. But he did talk about the mud and the snow and shelling and the almost total destruction of the landscape and the major towns and villages. He said that he had left the line once, totally exhausted, but had been allowed two days rest and recuperation, after which he was ready to take up command of his battalion once again.

Once again, when back in Scotland, my grandfather spent much time visiting relatives of those who never returned or who had been badly wounded. He was much involved with the formation of The Black Watch Association in 1919, the centenary of which welfare organisation was celebrated in 2020 and which was formed to keep in touch with all those who had fought so gallantly during the war and to care for the widows and other relatives of those who had fallen. He seldom missed a regimental dinner or gathering and wore his Red Hackle in his bonnet as a staff officer at the 51st Highland Division headquarters in Perth when he was called-up for the third time in 1939. In many ways too, he showed by his involvement in the regimental association and his visits to the families of those men of all ranks who did not return, that he stood within the tradition of a continuity of comradeship which cut across the years and which lies at the heart of The Black Watch regimental family.

Colonel Syd was a gentle and much-loved soldier and a very well-known regimental character. I was always very fond of him and I admired him greatly.

———————

SALONIKA

Ronnie Proctor

COMMONWEALTH WAR GRAVES COMMISSION
MARKER FOR PRIVATE JACK GIBSON, SALONIKA
(Ronnie Proctor)

I **FIRST BECAME** interested in the Salonika Front during a family
visit to Thessaloniki in 2003. The immediate focus of my interest was
the coincidence that the first grave we found at Mikra British Cemetery
on the eastern side of the city, was that of a Black Watch man, Private
John (Jack) M Gibson of the 13th (Scottish Horse) Battalion, The Black
Watch, from my home town of Kirriemuir. My long-term interest in
the campaign, however, was largely due to reading *Under the Devil's Eye*
by Alan Wakefield and Simon Moody.[1] This book amounted to a reassess-
ment of the importance of the Salonika Front, once thought of as little

more than a sideshow led by the French and reluctantly supported by the British. As the authors indicated, opinions have changed, and it is now recognised as an area of some importance, particularly because of how success in Salonika fitted into the chain of events which led first to the Bulgarian Armistice, then the collapse of Turkey, Austria and finally of Germany. In a regimental context, the Salonika campaign is also of interest because of the role played by the vagaries of weather, initial logistical shortcomings on arrival in theatre and medical factors in limiting the capabilities of Black Watch battalions during this campaign.

When I read the accounts of the 10th and 13th Battalions, both of which served in Salonika, in A G Wauchope's *A History of the Black Watch in the Great War, 1914-1918,* I was conscious that logistical difficulties and the appalling weather meant there was something of an echo of the Crimea in their experience, particularly about the 10th Battalion's first weeks in Salonika.[2] But even more serious was the extent to which sickness, and particularly malaria could drain manpower. As Wakefield and Moody pointed out, 'Throughout the campaign, disease, rather than the enemy, would claim the most casualties, the chief cause being malaria'.[3]

The extent to which sickness played a role in the lives of The Black Watch men during the campaign is best summed up in the opening lines of Chapter III in Wauchope's history of the 10th Battalion:

> All this time malaria was raging. Many remedies were tried
> unavailingly. Between July 3rd and August 26th [1916] there
> were 140 cases in the Field Ambulance including a third of the
> transport men.[4]

During their time in theatre, both the 10th Battalion and the 13th (Scottish Horse) Battalion attempted to lessen the risk of this plague by draining marshy ground when appropriate, issuing such mosquito nets as were available and taking to wearing shorts with special turn-ups which could be turned down to protect the legs from mosquito bites at night.

Unfortunately, too, other dangers also lurked: water chlorination tablets were issued, everyone was inoculated against paratyphoid then given a second inoculation against cholera and every man was given ten grains of quinine twice a week. Sickness and general debility could strike battalions very quickly so that in mid-October 1917 after a third of the 10th Battalion were forced to fall out during a three-mile march, the medical officer reported officially that it would be a month before the majority of these men would be fit for duty again. The 13th (Scottish Horse) Battalion fared little better during their time in Salonika. At one point in the summer of 1917, the situation was so bad that the forward line was dismantled and moved back to the south of the Struma River to less mosquito-infested ground. From the time of their arrival in October 1916 until their departure, summers brought malaria and sandfly fever, for even as the 13th Battalion prepared to leave Salonika in June 1918, the effects of influenza and malaria meant that on average 100 men a day were attending sick parade.

Although only one percent of those admitted to hospital died of malaria, reinfection was common and did not require a second bite to set off symptoms of the disease. Nevertheless, it appears that Private Gibson who came from Kirriemuir and whose grave marker I found at Mikra, was one of those who died of the disease. He was 24 when he enlisted at Dunkeld, the youngest son of a family of seven living at 1 High Street, a house in the centre of Kirriemuir. It still exists today as a dwelling house and overlooks the statue of Peter Pan. By 1895, his mother Betsy (née Ogg) had died in Anstruther, Fife, and there was no record of his father David in Kirriemuir in the 1901 Census. (David Gibson had been a temperance hotel keeper.) In addition to his eldest sister who was 20 years older than him and was an assistant teacher, there were four other sisters and a brother who was two years older.

Sadly, Jack Gibson was not alone in succumbing to malaria. Wauchope lists the death of each Black Watch man in their battalion's Nominal Roll followed by date and cause of death under subheadings: 'Killed in Action', 'Died of Wounds', 'Died at Home' and 'Died'. Wauchope also specifically mentions in the headings to the Nominal Rolls that men who died of disease were included. Because Wauchope does not include accidental or any other classification, it is reasonable to assume that of the 18 officers and 151 other ranks of the 13th (Scottish Horse)

Battalion who died in the Great War, the two officers and 12 other ranks listed simply as 'Died' were the deaths from various diseases including malaria contracted in Salonika.

[1] Alan Wakefield and Simon Moody, *Under the Devils Eye* (Barnsley: Pen and Sword, 2010).

[2] A G Wauchope, *A History of the Black Watch in the Great War, 1914-1918*, Volumes 1-3 (London: Medici Society, 1925-6).

[3] Wakefield, *Under the Devils Eye*, p168.

[4] Wauchope, *History*, Volume 3, p223.

'NOT VERY GLORIOUS BUT OF DEFINITE VALUE'[1]

THE 12TH (LABOUR) BATTALION OF THE BLACK WATCH

Stewart Coupar

DUE TO the protracted nature of the fighting during the Great War and the rapid growth of the British Expeditionary Force (BEF), it became apparent to the British government early in the conflict that a large labour force would be required to maintain the infrastructure needed by their armies on the Western Front. That in turn presented the British General Staff with a problem of manpower allocation that endured throughout the war: how could the Army find men to maintain existing infrastructure and build new capacity without weakening their operational capability?

Under pre-war planning arrangements, the French government had agreed to provide the labour required to support the BEF, but it was soon clear they could not do so. The railways and roads of France and Belgium – those great supply arteries of the BEF on the Western Front, which were key targets for destruction both from enemy artillery and later from the air – required men for repair and maintenance, yet somehow the numbers of men required for the great British offensives of the war still had to be found. Part of the answer to this dilemma was found in the recruitment of foreign labour so that by the end of the war, the presence of the Chinese Labour Corps in France along with labour from India, Egypt, South Africa, Fiji and other countries indicated how desperate the labour situation had become for the British Army. The photographic archives of the Imperial War Museum contain a mass of evidence not only of how diverse this labour force was, but also how wide was the spread of their activities.

One solution adopted by the British Army was to create labour battalions within the existing regimental structures. One of these new formations was the 12th (Labour) Battalion of The Black Watch, which was raised in Blairgowrie in May 1916. The *War Diary* of the 12th Battalion opens on 18 May 1916 with the appointment of Major H Jennings-Bramley, and then describes in detail day by day the formation of the battalion.[2] The men were described as 'of the "B" (the vast majority of these "B2") and "C" classes, and, as a whole were elderly and none of them physically very strong', but were 'of good character' and drawn from the 3rd Battalion, The Black Watch, and other Scottish regiments.[3] While there was a sprinkling of old soldiers in the ranks, the rest were described as 'practically raw'.[4] After training, on 26 June 1916, they entrained at Blairgowrie for Southampton, landed at Le Havre and were on their way by troop train to Bailleul two days later. At this point, the battalion was composed of 12 officers, six warrant officers and six sergeants, and 1,022 other ranks.[5] On 4 July 1916, the battalion suffered its first casualty while carrying out some entrenching work near La Clyte.

THE 12TH (LABOUR) BATTALION OF THE BLACK WATCH
WIDENING THE ROAD AT FRICOURT
Outside 48th Division headquarters, 1916
(IWM Licence LIC-24826-S1C4C6)

Service on the Somme, in the Ypres Salient and in the area around Arras followed. The work was arduous, the men often having to work under shellfire, and as with all labour battalions, the weather took a heavy toll of the older, less fit men. Their work at Montauban in road maintenance was vital in keeping the supply routes open and in January 1917, they were involved in building a light railway from Noyelle-Vion to Warlus when they were described as a 'hard working, willing Battalion. Have done good work'.[6] However, it was at Arras in April 1917 that they sustained most casualties, almost all from shellfire, until on 11 May 1917, the 12th (Labour) Battalion, The Black Watch, ceased to exist. The commanding officer, adjutant and Quartermaster became HQ, 44 Labour Group and the remainder of the battalion became 5th and 6th Labour Companies.[7]

It is not known how many Black Watch men were transferred to the Labour Corps during the war, but a search of the Medal Index Cards shows over 5,000 soldiers as transferred, including many previously fit and relatively young men who had been medically downgraded due to wounds or sickness during the course of the war. Large as this number is, the demand for labour behind the frontlines by 1918 was so great that this appears to be a reasonable estimate. The new regiment, The Labour Corps, contained individual companies which were to perform all labouring tasks required by the Army such as dockside cargo handling, salvage, supplies depot work and even provided agricultural labour. It was also the case that Labour Corps men who were overwhelmingly fully-trained and experienced infantry soldiers, could be relied on to defend themselves, so that during the German 1918 Spring Offensive, many Labour Corps units, particularly entrenching battalions, were used as infantry to help plug gaps in the frontline where the enemy had broken through.[8]

In general, the Labour Corps' ranks were made up of soldiers who earlier in the war would have been discharged as no longer being fit for active service due to wounds or sickness, but who under the Military Service Act 1916 could be kept in the Army and redeployed and only discharged if found to be no longer fit for any manual work. Two examples of Black Watch men whose service was retained in that way are William Carr and Stewart Maconachie.

William Carr was born in Bridgend, Perth, in 1877. His father, like many in Perth, was employed in the cloth dying industry. On leaving school, Carr found employment with Pullar's Dyeworks and became a dyer's finisher. He must have been of a military bent as he was a member of the 4th Volunteer Battalion, whose headquarters were on Tay Street in Perth. In July 1895, Carr decided to enlist as a Regular in The Black Watch. For the first two years, he served with the 2nd Battalion which was based within the Home Command area. Later in 1897, he was posted to the 1st Battalion which was stationed in India. With this battalion, Carr found himself fighting the Boers in South Africa in December 1901. He decided to take his discharge in 1902 on completion of seven years' Colour Service when his battalion was posted back to Britain. Carr's surviving documents show that he had worked for six months as a mess waiter and had also been a regimental policeman for two and a half years; so, he must have been a good, trusted and smart soldier.[9]

Carr returned to Perth and found employment as a ploughman on a farm outside the city. This life did not appeal to him and in 1904, he sought permission to re-enlist and to complete 12 years' service with the Colours. He found himself back in India with the 2nd Battalion and was one of the 'guard of honour' for the King and Queen during the Delhi Durbar celebrations in 1911, receiving the Delhi Durbar Medal. He stayed in India until being posted to the 1st Battalion then based at Edinburgh Castle in 1912. When war was declared, Carr was serving with 'A' Company of the 1st Battalion in Aldershot and went to France with the BEF in mid-August 1914. Carr stayed with his battalion through the retirement from Mons, the Battles of the Marne and Aisne, the fighting around Ypres at Black Watch Corner and the campaigns of 1915, until the Battle of the Somme the following year. However, on 21 August 1916, when serving in the support trenches at the Quadrilateral, near High Wood, he was wounded in the neck and thighs by a bursting bomb, probably dropped by an enemy aircraft.

Carr was sent to a hospital in 'Blighty', and after his recovery was posted to the 3rd Battalion, then based in Nigg and stayed with the battalion when it moved to Ireland. In September 1918, while the battalion was at Newtownards, in Ireland, he was transferred to the 655th (Home Service) Employment Company of the Labour Corps, because as a consequence of his wounds he had been medically downgraded to class B2 meaning that he was not fit for active service. The company was also based at Newtownards, and it is probable that Carr's company served alongside the 3rd Battalion carrying out tasks for it. As a member of an employment company, he could have been employed as a batman, cook, storeman, orderly, clerk, policeman or sanitary man. Carr was discharged in 1919 after 23 years' service. He settled in Perth after the war and married and raised a family. Carr died in Perth in 1957 aged 79 and is buried in Wellshill Cemetery.

The second former Black Watch man is Stewart Maconachie. His records show he was born in Dundee, but by the time he volunteered to enlist in September 1914, he was a labourer living in Kirkcaldy.[10] Maconachie was then 32 and had previously served with the 3rd (Militia) Battalion, The Black Watch, from 1900 to 1909. He was quickly posted out to the 1st Battalion in France in early 1915, probably because of his previous service, and was wounded in March 1915. This must have been a slight wounding as he did not return to Britain. However, during the opening day of the Battle of Loos on 25 September 1915, Maconachie was wounded again. This time it was much more serious, being hit on the arm and both thighs and this time he was sent to hospital in Britain.

Private Maconachie did not return to France until December 1916 where he was posted onto the strength of an infantry base depot. This was standard practice at this stage of the war as these base depots were used as holding units and would form men into drafts when replacements were required by battalions serving at the front. The members of the infantry base depots would undergo additional training to learn new fighting techniques in current use at the front and would also be used as labour in the base areas, which were always on the coast and next to harbours and railheads where demand for additional labour was high. While there, Maconachie was medically downgraded because he had not fully recovered from his wounds and was transferred to the Base Depot Battalion, which was made up of similar men who had also become unfit. On the formation of the Labour Corps, he was transferred to the 278th Employment Company, and then in May 1918, he was posted to 755th Agricultural Company where he remained until being discharged in early May 1919.

On return to Kirkcaldy, Maconachie decided to re-enlist into the Labour Corps and was posted to the Labour Corps Scottish Command centre in Blairgowrie. In June, he was posted to France to join a grave registration unit tasked with finding and exhuming battlefield remains and helping lay out and establish the war graves which exist today. Maconachie was discharged from the Army in April 1920 and died in Kirkcaldy in 1929, aged just 56.

After the war, it was decided the valued service of the Labour Corps should not be forgotten, particularly because so many men had passed through its ranks and because the unit would not survive into the post-war period. It was decided that a monument to commemorate the unit should be placed in Blairgowrie, the site of their Scottish command headquarters. The memorial took the form of a stained-glass window designed by the artist Robert Anning Bell RA and was installed in the Riverside Methodist Church, in Rattray.[11] (The church held a special place in the memory of members of the Labour Corps as the site of a wartime social club.) The window was unveiled on 2 December 1922 by Mrs Hay Wilson, Major-General G S Sinclair-McLagan, CB, DSO, commander of the 51st Highland Division and Colonel A B Robertson, CMG, DSO, General Staff, Scottish Command.[12]

1   A G Wauchope, *A History of the Black Watch in the Great War, 1914-18*, Volume 3
    (London: Medici Society, 1926), p286.

2   *12th (Labour), The Black Watch Battalion War Diary*, 18 May 1916.

3   Wauchope, *History*, Volume 3, p285.

4   Wauchope, *History*, Volume 3, p286.

5   *12th (Labour), The Black Watch Battalion War Diary*, Appendix 4, June 1916.

6   *12th (Labour), The Black Watch Battalion War Diary*, Appendix 4, February 1917.
    'Progress Report' by Captain R Couper, OC, Royal Engineers, Royal Anglesey Train.

7   Wauchope, *History*, Volume 3, p288.

8   Charles Messenger *Call to Arms: The British Army 1914-1918*
    (London: Orion Publishing Group, 2005), pp239-240.

9   William Carr: War Office Soldiers' Documents First World War, 'Burnt Documents',
    The National Archives, WO363.

10 Stewart Maconachie. War Office Soldiers' Documents First World War,
    'Burnt Documents', The National Archives, WO363.

11 The church was closed some years ago, but the building has since reopened as a
    restaurant, where the current owner is keen to look after and promote the story of this
    historic window.

12 *The Courier and Argus*, 4 December 1922.

COMBATANT MINISTERS AND SONS OF THE MANSE IN THE BLACK WATCH

Reverend John C Duncan and Fraser Brown

T HE MINISTERS MEMORIAL located in a special chapel area at the front of St Giles' Cathedral, Edinburgh, records the 115 names of those ordained ministers, serving both as chaplains to HM Forces and as combatants as well as those probationers and students of divinity of the Church of Scotland, the United Free and Free Churches of Scotland, killed in action during the Great War. A few, like Major F C Scougall, MC, of the Cameronians came from Manchuria and other Church of Scotland overseas missions, but the overwhelming majority came from Scottish parishes and served as commissioned officers in Scottish infantry regiments. A large number had also enlisted in the ranks some time before the passage into law of the Military Service Act 1916 which meant that while conscription was imposed on all single British men aged between 18 and 41, ministers of religion along with men in several other categories were exempt from military service. It is important to state clearly that those ministers named on the memorial along with those many unnamed ministers who served and survived were all volunteers, not conscripts.[1] Not since the 'Killing Time' of the late seventeenth century and the death of the Presbyterian Colonel Cameron at Dunkeld in 1689, had so many Scots Presbyterian clergymen chosen to go to war as combatants.

On the outbreak of war in 1914, the group of 18 commissioned Presbyterian chaplains serving with the Regular Army was composed of nine from the Church of Scotland, four from the United Free Church of Scotland, three from the Presbyterian Church in Ireland and two from the Presbyterian Church of England. The outbreak of war however led to a 'a glut of applications for the limited number of temporary commissions that were available' and as The Reverend Dr J A McClymont, Convenor of the General Assembly's Committee on Chaplains to HM Forces, commented, 'the "difficult and delicate task" of selecting ministers to be chaplains had to be managed carefully'.[2]

Nonetheless, by 1915, the number of Church of Scotland chaplains serving had doubled to 36 and by 1916 the number of Presbyterian chaplains in total stood at 175. However, although the shortage of chaplains had been identified as early as 1915, of the ministers of the Church of Scotland serving in 1916, those serving as chaplains were outnumbered by those serving in other unidentified roles by 85 to 83.[3] By the end of the war, 282 ordained ministers, probationers and students of divinity of the Church of Scotland served as combatants while 113 served as Chaplains to the Forces. Of these, nine chaplains were killed and 38 of the combatants fell. Sadly, searches of the National Records of Scotland and National Library of Scotland catalogues indicate comparable statistics are not available for either the United Free or Free Churches of Scotland.

The men named on the Ministers Memorial plaques of all three Presbyterian denominations were spread across the Scottish infantry regiments with a few more serving with the Highland Light Infantry and the Gordon Highlanders than other regiments. A few found their way into other units such as the Machine Gun Corps, the Royal Flying Corps and the Royal Army Medical Corps. They also tended to have been commissioned officers and when The Black Watch contingent of 14 combatant ministers is examined, it is found that all ended the war as commissioned officers spread across almost all battalions.

In a number of ways, Lieutenant Reverend William Urquhart, Minister of Kinloch Rannoch, described in A G Wauchope's *A History of the Black Watch in the Great War, 1914-18* as 'one of the many gallant men who left the Scottish Ministry to fight for their country' was a typical example.[4] He was a much-respected officer in his battalion and very popular with his brother officers who had nicknamed him 'Charlie Chaplin'. Urquhart had trained at Aberdeen, taking both his MA and BD at that university, and while a student was one of the first to join the newly formed Aberdeen University Troop of the Scottish Horse. He was given permission to enlist by his presbytery in the Spring of 1915, first joined the famous McRae's Battalion of the Royal Scots and was commissioned

LIEUTENANT REVEREND W URQUHART
Minister of Kinloch Rannoch. *The Courier and Argus*, 24 August 1916
(Used by kind permission of D C Thomson & Co Ltd.)

into The Black Watch in 1916. Urquhart, like many of his fellow combatants had also achieved a degree of academic success at university where he had won the Gladstone Memorial Prize for Philosophy and had been the Brown Scholar of 1909.

Second Lieutenant Robert Stevenson, 9th Battalion, The Black Watch, licensed to preach by the Dunfermline Presbytery also enjoyed significant academic success while studying at Glasgow University where he won the Cleland and Rae Wilson Gold Medal for Hebrew and the Glasgow Oriental Society Prize for Arabic in 1909-10. He also won the Black Fellowship which allowed him to study at the highly prestigious University of Göttingen in Lower Saxony. It is also interesting to note that Stevenson arrived at the 9th Battalion as part of a draft of 38 other ranks and 12 officers on 8 May 1917 in the company of Second Lieutenant William R Tovani, after the war ordained as an Anglican priest. No doubt they enjoyed the massed Pipes and Drums of the 15th Scottish Division playing at the close of the Division Horse Show a few days later at

Le Cauroy. By August 1917, Stevenson was acting signalling officer, and was at battalion headquarters located in an abandoned German concrete dugout in the former German frontline when a shell landed at the entrance and killed or wounded almost all the headquarters staff just as the 9th Battalion were attacking Gallipoli Farm (at Arras on 23 August 1917).[5] Stevenson was amongst the dead, having served less than four months on the Western Front.

Second Lieutenant Peter Ross Husband, 1st Battalion, The Black Watch, who was one of two brothers serving with the regiment survived for only three weeks before he was killed on 25 September 1916 with 'C' Company in an attack on the Flers Line during the Battle of the Somme. Before graduating from Edinburgh University and taking his theological course at New College Edinburgh, Husband had been a pupil and gold medallist of Dundee High School and would have been a contemporary of Second Lieutenant J Whittinghame Robertson, 7th Battalion, who was also a pupil there at the same time. Robertson had enlisted as a private in the Argyll and Sutherland Highlanders, was promoted to sergeant, then commissioned into The Black Watch. He fell at Arras on 23 April 1917. Like a number of the other men on the Ministers Memorial both were 'sons of the manse'; in Robertson's instance, the son of The Reverend Dr Robertson, Clepington Parish Church, Dundee, and the brother of the Minister of Little Dunkeld.

Nevertheless, the largest number of 'sons of the manse' to serve in the Great War were not the men on the Ministers Memorial or even the survivors of that group. Rather these were sons of the Scottish Presbyterian clergy who were not involved with the ministry in any way. In the case of the Church of Scotland, reliable figures can be derived from the *Roll of Honour of Sons of the Manse* presented to the General Assembly of the Church of Scotland in 1915 which named 450 'Sons' who together amounted allegedly to 90 per cent of the total number of existing 'sons of the manse'.[6] As the war continued, the total grew to over 900, who were identified in a second edition entitled *The Muster Roll of the Manse 1914-1919*.[7] This book named all Church of Scotland ministers as well as sons and daughters of ministers who had served, included missionaries and sons of missionaries, and ministers of overseas Church of Scotland congregations within the Empire. Field Marshal Haig, no doubt noting the Victoria Cross, 27 Distinguished Service Orders, 92 Military Crosses and 72 'Mentions in Despatches' won by this group was deeply touched by this level of commitment and sacrifice which he, as a staunch Presbyterian, saw as 'worthy of a Church which had always been foremost in the fight for religious and political freedom'.[8] In fact, Haig's comment on meeting his favoured chaplain, the recently ordained Church of Scotland minister Reverend George Duncan, that he was 'earnest and impressive, quite after the old covenanting style' would appear to support the idea that he was at ease with the idea of the combatant minister.[9]

When Black Watch sons of Church of Scotland manses are identified in *The Muster Roll of the Manse 1914-1919*, the total number involved was 62, and of these, while 14 were combatant ministers, another nine ministers were Chaplains to the Forces. All 39 remaining sons of the Church of Scotland manses except six were commissioned officers, but many of these had enlisted as private soldiers early in the war. Apart from two who enlisted as privates and were appointed to chaplaincies, all were combatants. As a group, they also appear to have been effective soldiers, particularly given that 16 were promoted to captain, while the most senior was Lieutenant-Colonel T D Murray, DSO, from the Anstruther Easter manse. Even so, it is important to remember that the United Free Church and Free Church of Scotland men are not included, and given that the ratio of Church of Scotland members to United Free and Free Churches of Scotland was around 6:4, the real number of Black Watch combatant ministers would likely have been around 20 and the number of Black Watch 'sons of the manse' closer to 100.

Of course, not all combatant ministers, probationers and students of divinity in The Black Watch or other units were killed, but their service is less well known. Occasional snippets of information surface such as the arrival home on leave from France in 1917 of Lieutenant C E Duff, Minister of St Vigeans, near Arbroath, at the same time as the former Church Officer, also of The Black Watch. While on leave, Duff who had been commissioned into the 6th Battalion and remained with it from December 1916 until the end of the war, preached from his old pulpit.[10]

Duff was from Islay and was himself a 'son of the manse', Dux of Glasgow High School and winner of several academic honours at Glasgow University. In 1958, he retired after 46 years in the ministry – first at St Vigeans then as Minister of (the joint charge of) St Vigeans and Auchmithie.

The Reverend D Logan Blair of Scone who also survived joined the 6th Black Watch as a private soldier, and like many others kept in touch with his old parishioners by letters written in France and published in the local newspaper. After over a year in the frontline, he was appointed to a chaplaincy outwith the regiment.[11] Blair survived and returned to Perthshire where he was actively involved in Black Watch affairs including acting as chaplain to the 1936 'Vimy Pilgrimage to France', and was present at the great 'Church Parade' of the Perth Branch of The Black Watch Association in June 1937, when the Pipes and Drums of the 6/7th Battalion led the march past and Major-General Marindin of Fordel took the salute.

To some extent too, the service of Reverend Blair who enlisted as a private and accepted a chaplaincy demonstrates the multi-faceted nature of the clergyman-soldier who served either by the sword or by the ministry of the Gospel, and whose value to his regiment transcended both denomination and religious hierarchy. The much loved Captain Herbert John Collins, Roman Catholic chaplain to the 44th Brigade, attached to the 9th Black Watch, who carried out burial services under machine-gun fire, dished out cigarettes to all ranks and 'most of all, when conditions were bad, did his cheery presence enhearten all ranks' was one such.[12] Reverend A Silver was another. He had been a Church of Scotland missionary from Madras who was attached to the 2nd Battalion and was present first at Mushaidie, and later at Istabulat when his fellow minister, Second Lieutenant Dugald MacArthur of the 2nd Battalion, and Minster of New Ardrossan was killed. Silver returned to missionary work in India after the war.

The famous Captain J M Hunter, CF, of the 6th and 7th Battalions and Minister of Abbotshall, Fife, who with Padre Gordon scoured the battlefield after Beaumont Hammel under continuous shellfire identifying the dead was another clergyman-soldier. Their selfless work meant that every missing man was accounted for and next of kin were spared the dreadful uncertainty suffered when men were posted as missing in action. Clearly valuable work could be done both as a chaplain and as a combatant, yet why did so many ministers choose the combatant role?

In a very general sense, Michael Snape's work *The Royal Army Chaplain's Department: Clergy Under Fire* which is a history of the Department from 1796 until 1953 offers one broad explanation:

> Chaplains were volunteers by definition and their fixed term contracts served as a further means of self-selection; consequently, whether they saw the war as a judgement on the modern world, or in a more liberal vein, a painful harbinger of the Kingdom of God, virtually all could agree on Germany's depravity and culpability and on the need to fight the war to a successful conclusion.[13]

In a broad sense too, according to A W Fergusson writing in *Sons of the Manse* there was a degree of historical consistency in the behaviour of the Presbyterian ministry during the Great War, for he saw the acceptance by ministers of a combatant role as 'in strict accord' with the history of the Kirk.[14] Fergusson pointed out that in both the 1715 and 1745 Jacobite risings, many Presbyterian clergy were 'commissioned officers of the militia,' including Ebenezer Erskine, the seceder-in-chief who was the moving spirit in the formation of the Defence Corps in Stirling in 1745.[15] Even Thomas Chalmers, leader of the Great Disruption of 1843, rejected a chaplaincy and procured instead a lieutenant's commission in the St Andrews Corps when the country was in danger of Napoleonic invasion.[16] It was also the case that following the establishment of the university Officer's Training Corps, students of Divinity joined in significant numbers.

At an individual level, one common element appears to have been that for some at least, like Acting Captain John Cargill, Assistant Minister at Scoonie, near Leven in Fife, combatant service was a matter of duty. The report of his death at Arras on 27 April 1917 in the *Leven Advertiser & Wemyss Gazette* explained his motivation for fighting as 'he concluded that the proper place for a fit man in a crisis in his nation's history was in the ranks beside his fellow countrymen'.[17] Cargill had enlisted in The Black Watch early in 1915 and had been in action at Loos before being commissioned into the 7th Battalion in 1916.

A more detailed reasoning of why an ordained minister would make the decision of become a combatant can be found in the published sermons of Reverend W N Monteith, Minister of Elie Parish Church, Fife, who enlisted in the Fife and Forfar Yeomanry on the outbreak of war, was commissioned into the Rifle Brigade and killed at Loos in 1915. The Reverend Monteith's son, Bill Monteith, born after his father's death, explained that he was deeply concerned that he was expected to encourage his parishioners to enlist while he stayed safely at home.[18] This reasoning was very much in line with the contents of a letter published in *The Times* in September 1914 in which Professor W P Paterson of Edinburgh speaking for the Church of Scotland declared 'there was no law on the subject save that of the individual conscience' and continued to write that 'each minister must settle that problem for himself'.[19] Paterson also refused to condemn any minister who having been called on to exhort others to take up arms, and who felt that it was their duty to practise what they preached. Paterson dispelled any lingering doubts or possible ambiguities with his final remark which he categorically declared to be the position of the Church of Scotland and the United Free Church:

> For any young minister who felt it to be his first duty to join the
> combatant ranks, the Presbytery, his ecclesiastical superior gave
> its permission, and its blessing along with that permission.[20]

It was also clear from The Reverend Monteith's sermon on joining the Army – delivered on 4 September 1914 – based on the text 'Shall your brethren go to war, and shall ye sit here?' that enlisting was no easy decision.[21] Nevertheless, it was a decision taken on the grounds that this was a 'war waged in the sacred cause of truth and justice' and that he too was not prepared to ask of others what he was not willing to do himself, and so he too would fight.

1　Amendments to the Act, first extended in May 1916 to include married men, and again in 1918 to include men up to the age of 51 did not alter their group exemption. Parliamentary Archives, HL/PO/PU/1/1916/5&6G5cl04.

2　Michael Snape, *The Royal Army Chaplains Department: Clergy Under Fire* (Woodbridge: Boydell Press, 2008), p197.

3　Snape, *Clergy Under Fire*, p198.

4　A G Wauchope, *A History of the Black Watch in the Great War, 1914-18*, Volume 1 (London: Medici Society, 1925), p58.

5　Wauchope, *History*, Volume 3, p162.

6　Reverend A W Fergusson, *Sons of the Manse* (Dundee: J P Mathews, 1923), p283.

7　Reverend Duncan Cameron, *Muster Roll of the Manse 1914-1919* (Glasgow: Hodge, 1919).

8　Reverend A W Fergusson, Sons *of the Manse*, p 284. Sadly, no equivalent statistics are available for the United Free or Free Churches of Scotland.

9　Gary Sheffield, *The Chief: Douglas Haig and the British Army* (London: Aurum Press, 2011), p155. Reverend Duncan, educated at Forfar Academy, Edinburgh University, Cambridge and St Andrews, was a distinguished scholar and theologian. Like a number of Scottish ministers, he pursued theological studies in Germany before the war – at the universities of Jena, Marburg and Heidelberg. He was also a Moderator of the General Assembly of the Church of Scotland.

10　*Arbroath Guide*, 16 June 1917.

11　*Strathearn Herald*, 6 October 1917.

12　Wauchope, *History*, Volume 3, p147.

13　Snape, *Clergy Under Fire*, p248.

14　Fergusson, *Sons of the Manse*, p282.

15　Ebenezer Erskine (1680-1754): Minister of Portmoak, Kinross-shire and founder with three other ministers of the Secession Church in 1733, which split from the Church of Scotland over the Lay Patronage (Scotland) Act 1711, which meant noble and other patrons, but not the congregation, chose the minister. The 1711 Act was the cause of significant civil disorder: new ministers had to be installed by armed troops in the pulpit for the first time. The same issue was the cause of the Great Disruption of 1843 led by Thomas Chalmers and the formation of the United Free Church of Scotland.

16　Fergusson, *Sons of the Manse*, p283.

17　*Leven Advertiser & Wemyss Gazette*, 3 May 1917.

18　'Collection of Sermons, Newspaper Articles and Pastoral Letters relating to Reverend Monteith', assembled by Elie Parish Church Guild (2008).

19　Fergusson, *Sons of the Manse*, p281.

20　Fergusson, *Sons of the Manse*, p282.

21　Numbers 32:6.

PIPE MAJOR ALEXANDER GRIEVE

THE BLACK WATCH, TRANSVAAL AND CAPE TOWN HIGHLANDERS

Sir Alistair Irwin

ORN IN Largo, Fife, in 1869, it is not known when Alexander
B (Sandy) Grieve started to play the pipes but by the time he was 18,
he was both a piper and a blacksmith. Both skills would have been enough
to give him satisfaction and employment for the rest of his life but on
24 November 1887 he was enlisted by Sergeant S Baker into the Second
Battalion, The Royal Highlanders. For the next 12 years, he and the
battalion were engaged in Home Service duties, experiencing a peripatetic
life flitting from Dublin to Aldershot via Belfast, Limerick, Glasgow,
Edinburgh and York. On at least one occasion, Grieve and the Pipes and
Drums performed for Queen Victoria at Balmoral.

These benign peacetime duties came to abrupt end with the outbreak
of the Second Anglo-Boer War (1899–1902). Grieve's battalion arrived in
South Africa on 23 October 1899 and on 11 December was part of the
doomed attack by the Highland Brigade on the Boer positions at
Magersfontein. Grieve was amongst the many wounded: he was shot by a
rifle bullet that passed through both cheeks touching neither tooth nor
bone but delivering a powerful shock, nevertheless. For anyone, this
would have been, if not fatal, at least distressing. For a piper, the doubts
about his ability to continue playing, even after they had healed, with two
additional holes in his mouth must have added to his dismay. To make
matters worse, he contracted enteric fever. Grieve remained in South
Africa recovering from wound and disease until 21 June 1900, when he
returned to Scotland. He was then discharged from the Army after
13 years and 18 days with The Black Watch.

Had that been the end of the story, Grieve's name might have remained
familiar only to his family. For seven unrecorded years after his discharge,
he and his family lived a contented but unexceptional life in Scotland.

Then, in 1907, he decided to emigrate with his wife and young son to South Africa. There he joined the Transvaal Scottish, a regiment with strong links to The Black Watch not least by being proud wearers of the Red Hackle. In 1915, Grieve was appointed Pipe Major of the 4th South African Infantry as it prepared to take ship for the Western Front. Consisting largely of volunteers with a few Regular officers and NCOs, it was formed of four companies: two from the Transvaal Scottish, one from the Cape Town Highlanders and one from the Caledonian Societies of the Free State and Natal. So, at the age of 46, Grieve proceeded once more to war.

On arrival in France, the 1st South African Brigade was assigned to the 9th (Scottish) Division, which included just one Black Watch battalion, the 8th (Service) Battalion. The 'Springboks' saw their first major action on the Somme. Delville Wood lay on the edge of Longueval Village and it was into this that the South Africans launched their assault on 15 July 1916. For more than four days fierce fighting gradually reduced both the wood and the South Africans to near destruction. Fierce hand-to-hand fighting combined with doubly fierce artillery bombardments caused enormous casualties. When the leading elements of another brigade finally managed to link up with the South Africans on 20 July, they found the severely battered remnants of a brigade still clinging defiantly to the positions it had so expensively taken from the Germans. So moved were the men of the Royal Welsh Fusiliers, Suffolks and the Berkshire Regiment that they formed a guard of honour as the South Africans handed over the line to them and marched to the rear. It is said that of the 121 officers and 3,032 men of the 1st South African Brigade who had launched into Delville Wood five days earlier only 140 emerged. They marched past their brigade commander, Brigadier-General Henry Lukin, weeping as he saluted these brave men. They were led out of the wood by Pipe Major Grieve who had been present throughout the battle. He was accompanied by his own pipers and by pipers of the 8th Black Watch.

Grieve remained on the Western Front with the South African contingent for the rest of the war and finally returned to his family in 1918. They moved to Cape Town where, still not content with his military service so far, he joined the volunteer Cape Town Highlanders as its Pipe

Major. Shortly after the end of the war, a memorial service was held at Delville Wood. Grieve was there and played the tune 'Delville Wood' which he had composed both to mark the event and to honour his many fallen comrades.[1]

Grieve was still in uniform when war once again broke out in September 1939. By now, he was 70 and surely too long in the tooth to go to war for a third time. Not according to Grieve, nor surprisingly either to his wife or to the military authorities. He volunteered for full-time service and with the mobilised regiment he remained in South Africa until June 1941. They then joined the 1st South African Division in the Western Desert in the wake of the failure of General Wavell's Operation Battleaxe. An unwelcome result of that failure was that Wavell was replaced as Commander-in Chief Middle East by General Auckinleck. The South Africans now had some time to prepare for their major role in Operation Crusader, the ultimate purpose of which was to raise the Siege of Tobruk. Grieve was present, and no doubt played his pipes, throughout the series of rapid movements and battles that lasted from the middle of November until the end of the year. Aged 72, he will have heard and experienced yet again the noise and dangers of battle as the Afrika Korps with their Italian allies contested mastery of the North African coast with British and Imperial forces.

Operation Crusader was followed, after some further limited actions, by a period of stalemate, both sides regrouping and replenishing; a respite that was to be broken violently with the opening of the Battle of Gazala on 26 May 1942. Grieve would have heard news of the battle on his way home to Cape Town, for he and his commanding officer had by then bowed to the inevitable conclusion that the field of battle was no place for a 73-year-old, no matter how determined or brave he might be. And so, it was that a remarkable record of military service came to an end. Could it be that this redoubtable soldier, once a Black Watch man, wounded at Magersfontein, a survivor of the carnage at Delville Wood and a veteran of the fighting in the Western Desert in 1941, can claim to be the oldest Jock ever to have served on the frontline anywhere or at any time?[2] Could it be that he is the only Black Watch man of any age to have served in the Second Anglo-Boer War and both world wars? Whether or not he is unique in this way Sandy Grieve deserves the crispest of salutes from everyone who has ever proudly worn the Red Hackle for his sense of duty and, presumably, for his unquenchable love of soldiering.[3]

---

1   Delville Wood is the site of the South African National Memorial.
    It is opposite the Commonwealth War Graves Commission cemetery there.

2   A short film about Sandy Grieve can be seen at
    https://www.youtube.com/watch?v=jF-8vdl5QFw
    Further information can be found at
    https://samilhistory.com/2018/11/09/the-black-watch-and-the-delville-wood-lament/
    (Accessed October 2020).

3   The author is indebted to Richard Hunter, formerly Archivist at The Black Watch
    Museum for bringing Sandy Grieve to his attention.

MAJOR 'DADDY' STUDLEY
AND HIS SONS

Fraser Brown

O N 26 FEBRUARY 1916, Major Harry Studley, affectionately
known to the men of the 7th (Fife) Battalion, The Black Watch (TF),
as 'Daddy' died at his home in St Andrews aged 52. The Major had been
invalided home several weeks before, but while he had survived the
Egyptian Campaign and the war in South Africa unscathed, the strain of
preparing the Territorials of the 7th Battalion for overseas service had
told heavily on his health. For always the enthusiastic soldier, 'Daddy'
Studley had thrown himself into his work as Quartermaster with great
gusto. He was also the soldier patriarch of a family of five equally talented
martially minded sons, four of whom are in the photograph (overleaf).
Their story was chronicled by the *St. Andrews Citizen* over the course of
the war and is retold here.

Major Studley's funeral was conducted with full military honours: his
sword and feather bonnet rested on a coffin draped in the Union Jack,
first borne into St Andrew's Episcopal Church then onto an ammunition
wagon on the shoulders of a carrying party drawn from the St Andrew's
Machine Gun School and the Administrative Centre of the 7th Black
Watch. Large crowds witnessed 100 men of the Highland Cyclist Battalion
lead the funeral procession through the town followed by the Pipes and
Drums of the 2/7th Black Watch playing 'Land o the Leal', followed by
the officers of the 2/7th Black Watch and officers of other regiments, then
finally men of the Machine Gun School. The firing party under Captain
Lockhart fired the traditional three volleys.

Sadly, Major Studley was not the first of the Studley family to die in
the war. His son Logan, born in barracks in York and who had completed
part of his education at Madras College, St Andrews, died of his wounds
sustained at Ypres on 24 October 1914. Logan Studley had been a member
of the 7th Black Watch before the war and had joined as a Boy as permitted

by the King's Regulations then governing enlistment into the Territorial Army. He was not the only schoolboy in Scotland to have done this, and while he was noted for his fine solo in the Madras College performance of 'H.M.S. Pinafore' when he sang 'I am the Captain of the Pinafore' (the 'Captain's Song' as it is better known) and for his proficiency in shorthand, his obituary photograph in the school magazine showed him in his Black Watch review order uniform. He appears to have left school at 16 or possibly 17 then joined Alexandra, Princess of Wales's Own Yorkshire Regiment, better known now as the Green Howards, after being re-titled in 1920, where he was promoted lance corporal very quickly. On the outbreak of war, he was commissioned almost immediately into the East Yorkshire Regiment and died of his wounds aged 17 years and 10 months as Second Lieutenant Logan Studley, one of the first to be named on the Madras College Roll of Honour.

In August 1914, the eldest brother Harry was a bombardier in the Royal Horse Artillery, but very little appeared in the *Citizen* about his wartime career, although it is known that he was not killed. The soldier in The Black Watch uniform, Sergeant Thomas Studley, remained with that regiment until February 1914 when he applied to the Colonial Office for a posting as an instructor to the West African Forces. As someone who had passed the Musketry School, Swedish Drill and the Maxim Gun courses – all with very high marks – and was regarded as one of the best bayonet fighters in the regiment, his application was welcomed, and he was quickly accepted. However, no sooner had he set about learning an approved African language – a requirement for all British NCOs – than war broke out.

Thomas with his machine-gun section was involved in much of the fighting against German forces in Togoland and Cameroon, and he was recommended for a commission in early 1916. After a home leave in St Andrews he returned as a second lieutenant in The Black Watch seconded to the Nigerian Regiment. He was awarded the Military Cross as a lieutenant in 1917 for his work in an action against the German forces in Africa during which he was wounded. As the notice of his wounding in the *Citizen* stated, he was lucky to have survived because the bullet missed his spinal column by a fraction of an inch. In 1919, he was still in Nigeria, gazetted as temporary captain.

Richard Studley began the war as a corporal in the Army Service Corps, but by 1917 he had climbed the ranks and his service in that corps had been recognised by the award of the Meritorious Service Medal. The *Citizen* reported in November 1917 on the award and referred to Richard as Cadet Richard Studley who had been in France since the beginning of the war, and now had come home to study for a commission.

'A FAMILY OF FIGHTERS'
'Daddy' Studley and his Sons, *People's Journal*, *c.* October 1914
(Used by kind permission of D C Thomson & Co Ltd)

The youngest member of the family to serve is not shown in the photograph. He was Hector MacDonald Studley who in February 1918 was reported by the *Citizen* as having joined the Officers' Training Technical Corps for the Royal Flying Corps. It also reported how everything about soldiering interested him greatly and how he had been a prominent figure in the Volunteer Pipe Band where he had been the big drummer. Whether he had been part of the St Andrews Scout Defence Corps when he was a boy scout in St Andrews is unknown, but the corps was open to boys between 15 and 17 who were taught marksmanship and bayonet fighting by Sergeant MacThom. In 1915, when the corps was inspected by officers of the 7th Black Watch in the St Andrews Drill Hall followed by a drill parade at Madras College, it was 50 strong. A church parade in St Leonard's Church followed where The Reverend R R Wallace, a prominent member of the Boy Scouts Association, complimented the leaders on the good job they had done in training the boys 'for service in peace and war'.[1] Whether Hector MacDonald Studley served for long enough before the war ended to be commissioned into the new RAF is not known.

While the photograph is an excellent example of the type of 'family at war' picture much loved by local newspaper editors of the time, it also has a deeper significance. The fact was that by the end of the war the Studley brothers had achieved a great deal: two decorations, three commissions from the ranks and at least one had survived what could easily have been a fatal wound. Sadly, Second Lieutenant Logan Studley did not survive. In short, the significance of the picture is that taken together the Studley brothers are an excellent example of that reserve of military talent and experience previously lying dormant in the ranks of the pre-war Regular Army, but which was so desperately required as Britain grappled with the problems of creating a mass army and as officer casualties multiplied. When the pre-war Territorials, Kitchener's New Armies and finally conscription massively swelled the ranks, these men were available to assume positions of leadership and responsibility in what was by then a rapidly expanding army adapting to the needs of a battlefield that was in a constant state of tactical and logistical flux.

---

[1] *East of Fife Record*, 13 May 1915.

SECOND LIEUTENANT JAMES GRANT FERGUSSON

'FROM STANFORD AND A NEW MEDICAL CAREER TO THE 8TH BLACK WATCH'

Julie M Orr

DURING HIS DECADES as a Stanford University student, professor, and eventually Dean of Engineering, W M Kays remained intrigued by the memorial plaque he had chanced to notice in his institution's Memorial Court. It acknowledged James Grant Fergusson, Second Lieutenant in the 8th Black Watch, killed in action at Longueval, France, on 14 July 1916. Kays recognised there had to be far more to the young officer's story and retained his interest until circumstances allowed not only local research, but recruitment of friends and colleagues to pursue the story on both sides of the Atlantic. The result of his efforts was published in the Stanford Historical Society's journal *Sandstone and Tile* and provides the material for the recounting of Lieutenant Fergusson's life presented here.[1]

SECOND LIEUTENANT JAMES GRANT FERGUSSON MEMORIAL
Stanford University
(University of Stanford Historical Society)

Jamie Fergusson began his life in 1889, spending his early years at Ethiebeaton, his family's estate located on the north side of the Tay estuary, east of Dundee. The second son of Robert Arklay and Maud Allen Fergusson, he was one of three brothers and two sisters, all of whom would become enmeshed in the events of the war to come. In 1900, however, Ethiebeaton anticipated a visit from the children's uncle, Henry Ruston Fairclough, who was on sabbatical from Stanford University and would become a trusted companion and mentor to his ten-year-old nephew. Four years later, in response to Robert Fergusson's concerns over his son's restlessness while attending Charterhouse in Surrey, Jamie would find himself a member of the Fairclough household in California and, by the Fall of 1905, a student at Stanford. Medical studies followed, culminating at Johns Hopkins School of Medicine in Baltimore, Maryland, and a coveted assignment in surgery at New York's Roosevelt Hospital.

Plans changed abruptly with Britain's declaration of war in August 1914, prompting Fergusson to declare in a letter to Fairclough, 'My country needs me'. The promising doctor travelled first to Ethiebeaton, arriving three days before his father's death, attending the funeral, then following his two brothers, his brother-in-law and his other sister's fiancé into military service. Assigned to the Royal Army Medical Corps, he went initially to the military hospital at Netley, outside Southampton. Feeling he was 'not doing enough for my country; older men can do this medical work as well as I', Fergusson sought a commission in the infantry, was commissioned into The Black Watch as Second Lieutenant, and by February 1915 was training with the 10th Battalion on the Wiltshire Downs. Shortly after the Battle of Loos, Fergusson was attached to the 8th Battalion and wrote his uncle in October of his impatience to get to the front: 'We're very busy out there just now' he explained, 'and it would have been awful to have been in England any longer'.

As the winter progressed, Second Lieutenant Fergusson rotated through the trenches without witnessing major action. He was admitted to hospital on 17 March 1916, but rejoined his unit on 9 April, apparently having recuperated from a burst eardrum caused by an exploding German shell. He continued to correspond with the Faircloughs during these months, remaining positive and expressing the 'great fancy' he had taken to his company commander, Captain L G Miles of 'D' Company, complimenting the quality of medical care he had received and noting the 'good fellowship' behind the lines that was 'hard to find among Englishmen of all classes elsewhere'.

By July 1916, however, action had begun at the Somme and Fergusson faced very different circumstances. For a week, British troops, suffering extreme losses, had been relentlessly repulsed by the enemy while Fergusson's battalion, as part of the 9th (Scottish) Division, were held in reserve. Finally, recognising the initial line of German trenches had been breached along the southern portion of the front, the 9th (Scottish) was called forward. Fergusson's battalion reported 35 casualties following action on 8-9 July, the same period when Jamie was reported wounded. According to a letter written to his mother intended to pre-empt her seeing the news elsewhere, Fergusson said he had been hit by shrapnel. 'Only a scratch', he reassured her, crediting his steel helmet for its protection and adding 'we're very well off...resting again for a few days and having the time of our lives'.

By 12 July, the town of Longueval had become the focus of attention as four divisions, including the 9th (Scottish), were assigned to exploit a small breach along a ridge. Over a kilometre of exposed ground between the captured German line and the targeted rear trench favoured a surprise night-time offensive. Action was initiated at 3.25am on 14 July 1916.

It was to be the first and only major action for Fergusson as the resulting losses included not only four captains but eight second lieutenants, including Jamie Fergusson. Captain Miles, who would survive his own wounds, wrote to Maud Fergusson from his hospital bed informing her of her son's death and recounting his final interaction with his lieutenant. They had reached German frontlines within five minutes of initiating their advance, he wrote, and he had seen Fergusson among his men 'along a trench. He was splendid, absolutely cool and without fear'. Miles had then lost consciousness, never knowing what precisely happened afterwards.

Back at Ethiebeaton, Mrs Fergusson received a War Office telegram on 20 July notifying her of her son's death. Three days later, a letter followed from the 8th Black Watch written 16 July reiterating the sad news and explaining that Fergusson had been leading his platoon against the Germans and had been buried with three of his fellow officers in Longueval. After expressing condolences on behalf of the entire battalion, Major G Abercromby added that Mrs Fergusson's son 'was one of the best subalterns in the Battalion, and is a great loss to us both as an officer and a friend'.[2]

The life of James Grant Fergusson, although a mere 27 years, was notable for accomplishment and commitment.[3] Not only did he adjust to life on contrasting east and west coasts of the US, but he successfully completed studies at Stanford and Johns Hopkins, sacrificing a promising and much sought-after New York medical career to return home for the simple but profound reason that, in his own words, 'My country needs me'.

---

[1] W M Kays, 'The Death of Jamie Fergusson: The First Stanford Casualty of World War I' *Sandstone & Tile,* Stanford Historical Society, Volume 27:1 (Winter 2003), pp3-12. The article relies heavily on the autobiography of Fergusson's uncle and mentor *Warming Both Hands: the autobiography of Henry Rushton Fairclough, including his experiences under the American Red Cross in Switzerland and Montenegro* (Stanford University, California: Stanford University Press, 1941).

[2] Within two months, Mrs Fergusson was to receive additional tragic news. Her eldest son, Captain Allan Arklay Fergusson of the Coldstream Guards, had been killed only a few miles from where Jamie had fallen. Esmé, the youngest of the brothers, who relinquished an Oxford scholarship to join the military, would be severely wounded but survived the war, living until 1972. (Special thanks to Dr Fraser Brown and Tom McCluskey for the photograph of the Ethiebeaton monument clarifying Esmé's status.)

[3] Kays, 'The Death of Jamie Fergusson' contained the comment 'Apparently Fergusson had left more of an impression on campus than I first thought. The monthly *Stanford Illustrated Review* reported the death of "Jimmie" Fergusson, a Phi Beta Kappa student and notable "two-miler" on the track team, in its first issue after the summer 1916 holidays. Fergusson, they said, was "A Stanford Hero"', p12.

THE GELLATLY BROTHERS

A VERY PERSONAL JOURNEY OF DISCOVERY

William D Whytock

O N 27 JULY 2016, on the 100th anniversary of the death of
Private Robert Gellatly of the 6th Black Watch at High Wood, I
took Chrissie, one of Robert's two surviving nieces, together with my son
Robert, to the Wellmeadow Gardens War Memorial in Blairgowrie where
we held a short private service of remembrance. Far from Robert's grave
in Tyne Cot Commonwealth War Graves Cemetery in Belgium, flowers
were laid on the steps of the Blairgowrie War Memorial below the plate
where his name is listed. At that point remembrance was uppermost in
our minds. Later, as a nagging curiosity led me to research my own
family members who had been involved in the Great War, I began to
realise the wealth of information on both the soldiers who fought,
and the town they left behind that exists in our local newspaper, the
Blairgowrie Advertiser. There on its pages, side by side with important
articles about close relatives were fascinating little stories about events
that were suddenly worth recording simply because the country was
newly at war.[1]

Now, in 2020, some of the events reported in the *Blairgowrie Advertiser*
seem hard to imagine but they do show one thing – the Great War was
about much more than soldiers fighting far away. These stories from
wartime Blairgowrie, and many other places like it in Black Watch country,
are worth remembering in the story of The Black Watch during the
Great War because they really do open a window into the past and let us
'see the Regiment as others saw it'.

The *Blairgowrie Advertiser* of 19 December 1914 celebrated the
service of Robert Gellatly and his three brothers:

> Another local family enjoys the unique distinction of having
> four of its members in the service of the King. Four of the

Gellatly brothers, who are all well known in the Blairgowrie and Rattray Districts by reason of the interest they have taken in football matters, are now in the Army – Private Stewart Gellatly in the 1st Black Watch, Private James Gellatly in the Scottish Rifles, Private Robert Gellatly in the 6th Black Watch and Charles, who enlisted this week into the Scottish Rifles. They are all the sons of the late Mr Alexander Gellatly, Leslie Street, Blairgowrie, who also had seven years Army Service in the Scottish Rifles and their present home address is Grants Land, Old Rattray.

Private Stewart Gellatly, Black Watch served three years with the Colours and was nine years in the reserve. Called up at the beginning of the War, he has seen some hard fighting on the Continent and is now recuperating in Cheshire from the effects of shrapnel wounds in the arm and hand. James, who has been about a year in the Scottish Rifles has also been at the front but fever caught him and he had to be invalided back to London. He expects to get north to Rattray shortly. Robert has had considerable Territorial Service in the Highland Cyclist Battalion and the 6th Black Watch. All four brothers are keen footballers and it was no uncommon sight to see Stewart, James and Charles playing together in the 'Boys' or the Amateurs.[2]

'RATTRAY'S FAMILY RECORD', THE GELLATLY BROTHERS
Blairgowrie Advertiser, 19 December 1914

Family tradition also shows how reality had struck home amongst the Gellatly clan even in the first days of the war. My grandfather, Charles Gellatly, had wanted to enlist into The Black Watch, however, family members were not encouraged to serve in the same regiment in case the entire family was wiped out in one battle. With two brothers already in The Black Watch, he enlisted into the Scottish Rifles joining his brother James, but later all four brothers were to serve at the Somme in 1916 where Robert was killed.

The *Blairgowrie Advertiser* also described what the excitement and the rush to war in 1914 actually meant, not in faraway London, but in the middle of Perthshire: 'Blairgowrie Black Watch go to War' and the article that followed captured the mood of pride and silent fear:

MOBILISATION SCENES AT BLAIRGOWRIE
Departure of Military

A fervent patriotic spirit has pervaded Blairgowrie and District this week and memorable scenes have been witnessed demonstrative of the loyalty of the community and of the lively interest in the War.

The tidings of the momentous happenings on the continent and in London which arrived at intervals in the beginning of the week created great excitement and further items of news were awaited with the utmost eagerness.

Not since the South African War had such a wave of martial enthusiasm gripped the district as that which followed the issuing of the mobilisation proclamation on Tuesday Evening 4th August 1914 and accompanied the departure of the reservists, Scottish Horse and Territorials the next day.

On Wednesday 5th August 1914 The Black Watch who left at 5.45pm were the most numerous contingent of Military to leave Blairgowrie and a remarkable demonstration of patriotic enthusiasm and excitement marked their departure. In their serviceable khaki tunics and swinging kilts, the men looked splendidly fit for any call that might be made of them as they marched from the Drill Hall in Union Street to the Railway Station under the command of Colour Sergeant Instructor Wilson.

A special carriage was reserved for the use of 'E' (Blairgowrie) Company 6th Black Watch. Touching scenes took place at the carriage doors as the Territorials, some of them mere boys but all resolute and strong, bade farewell to their relatives and friends.

'May they all speedily return safe and sound' was the silent prayer in many an anxious heart. Who can tell whether all these brave lads, who so cheerfully set out to guard their country in her hour of great need, will again see their bonnie town that they love so well?

But the parting was far from being a sad one. The younger Territorials chatted and joked with the crowd, light hearted banter was exchanged and jolly laughter, punctuated the hum of conversation till the guard signalled the train to start. Then a deafening cheer was raised and handkerchiefs and bonnets were waved.

As the train moved slowly away to the accompaniment of a series of detonators, further ringing cheers were raised which continued till the train, carrying the majority of Blairgowrie's quota of our country's defenders, some of the pick of the young manhood of the town was well down the platform. As long as the train was in sight the crowd waved farewell to the gallant kilties, whom perhaps, they might never see again. But happily the British Fleet is on the high seas and with the power of Britain Navy as the country's first defence, it is problematical if the 6th Black Watch will ever see a German.[3]

That last sentence may have been naïve, but it would haunt the Gellatly family and the families of thousands of other Black Watch Territorials for the duration of the war.

Soon the war touched everything. The Blairgowrie and Rattray Horticultural Annual Show was cancelled in 1914 on account of the war. Colour Sergeant White was appointed Recruiting Officer for the district during the absence of Colour Sergeant Instructor Wilson who went off on duty with the Territorials. At a meeting of the directors of the National Bible Society of Scotland on 10 August 1914, it was decided to present each of the young men of Scotland who had been called to the defence of the country with a copy of the scriptures.[4] As there were 35,000 Territorials in Scotland, this would cost £250 to provide each with a New Testament.

The day after the troops mobilised, Provost Keay sat in court and dealt with a case of begging:

Begging

Thomas Quirk, berrypicker, was sentenced to 15s or 10 days for begging in Perth Street. The accused stated he had only asked for matches but evidence showed he had solicited money. The Provost told the accused he was not allowed to go about the streets begging. An able bodied man like him should be able to earn enough to keep him during the past three weeks in Blairgowrie.[5]

After all this was a stiff sentence indeed, but one cannot help thinking that an example was being made due to the state of the town's conscience regarding mobilisation.

Meanwhile, if Blairgowrie's newly mobilised Territorials were unaware before the war that they would be on the same footing as Regular soldiers and had the same responsibility towards a mobilisation order as a Regular soldier, they were quickly made aware of that fact. Refusal or failure to respond rendered them liable to treatment as a deserter.[6] They received the pay and allowances of the corresponding rank in the Regular Army and all ranks received an embodiment gratuity of £5 provided they were actually called upon for service. This met the cost of any necessary articles which were lacking in that part of his kit which individual Territorial soldiers had to supply. In addition, a payment of 10s was paid to each man who paraded at headquarters with his kit complete and in good order. Over and above what was supplied by the Territorial Association, each man had to provide a pair of ankle boots (or shoes in the case of Highland regiments) and a number of other items including a shaving brush, toothbrush, comb, a razor, two flannel shirts, two pairs of worsted socks and one spoon.

Of course, shirts and socks wear out and the local papers all show the great effort in providing comforts for troops at the front which continued throughout the war. Letters to the local press like this appeal from the wife of the commanding officer of The Black Watch Depot were common and were quickly and generously answered:

> Dear Sir
>
> I should be so much obliged if you could put a notice in your paper that grey socks (with small pieces of soap to prevent rubbing when marching) are needed for the Black Watch, also shirts and woollen helmets.
>
> I am collecting these garments specially for the different Battalions of the Black Watch and thought that should it come to the notice of relatives of soldiers in the Regiments, they would be glad to send.
>
> All articles will be received and dispatched by me.
>
> Yours
>
> Mrs Hamilton
>
> PS – My husband Major Hamilton commands the Black Watch depot.[7]

Recruiting never stopped. Men of Perthshire aged between 19 and 40 years were still required to bring the 6th Battalion up to strength. On 21 November 1914, the 6th Battalion Colours were laid up in the East Parish Church, Perth, under the custody of the Kirk Session prior to the battalion going on active service.[8] Private Robert Gellatly the footballer and his friends in the 6th Battalion were on their way to the Western Front where amazingly they would still be able to read Perthshire papers sent from home, and it is tempting to wonder what the Blairgowrie contingent would have made of the news of Blairgowrie Amateurs 7-0 defeat by St Johnstone.

All too soon the blood began to flow. Private James Moon, 1st Black Watch, eldest son of James Moon, Lower Mill Street, and a very close friend of Private Stewart Gellatly was killed in action at the Battle of Aisne.[9] In an age when every letter was censored by a platoon commander, Stewart wrote to Mr and Mrs Moon to tell them of the tragic news. By

Christmas 1914, Stewart would be back in Blairgowrie recovering from wounds to his right hand and arm received at Ypres. Luckily, he was ambidextrous and wrote all his Christmas correspondence with his left hand. It was not the last time that he would be wounded. Along with his brothers Stewart and James, my grandfather received two wound stripes for shellshock and shrapnel as well as being gassed and James, also in the Scottish Rifles, was medically discharged due to the wounds he received at the Somme.

Lance Corporal Robert Gellatly, 6th Black Watch, was killed in action on 27 July 1916 at High Wood during an enemy bombardment. Two others were killed and ten wounded that day according to the *6th Battalion War Diary*.[10] Strength was recorded in the 'Remarks' column as 43 officers and 962 other ranks. Paradoxically out of the four brothers who went to war, Robert was the only Territorial, and remembering that it was thought that none of the Territorials would ever see a German, he was the one to die.

Robert's brief obituary appeared in the *Blairgowrie Advertiser*:

> Reverend R. Stewart at the close of his sermon in St Marys Church, Blairgowrie on Sunday forenoon, paid a high tribute to the memory of the late Lance Corporal Robert Gellatly 1/6th Black Watch who was recently killed in action. He also referred to the courage and loyalty shown by the Gellatly family and the splendid service they had rendered to the country in its need, no less than four brothers and a brother in law having all been engaged fighting at the Front. Reverend Stewart also referred to the long connection the family had had with the church, their father and mother having been the first couple he had married on coming to Blairgowrie now many years ago.[11]

Robert was 34 and left behind a widow, Elizabeth Allan of McLagans Land, Old Rattray. A few years ago, I came into possession of a memorial card for him, presumably put together by the family. The verses on the card are short but very fitting:

Sleep thy last sleep
Free from care and sorrow
Rest where none weep
Till the eternal morrow

Relentless death amongst us comes
And bitter grief imparts
It takes the loved ones from our home
But never from our hearts

He left his home and wandered there
A foreign grave to fill
But Christ is there to watch and care
And call him home at will

Our loved one sleeps in a foreign land
His grave we may never see
As long as life and memory last
He will remembered be.

Thy Will Be Done

The war continued for another two years and like so many others who served, my relatives did not talk about their experiences. Nevertheless, a connection with the Gellatly brothers still exists in the shape of a small book of Burns poetry that my grandfather carried with him all through the First World War. I always have it with me when I attend The Black Watch Burns Supper. My brother has my grandfather's 1914 tobacco box, medals and cap badge, however whenever I was on operations (as a soldier in The Black Watch), I was given his cap badge which I wore inside my Tam o' Shanter back to back with the Red Hackle to keep me safe. Each time on my safe return it was put back in its brass box.

There is also a deeper connection that joins The Black Watch men of yesterday and today. It was intended that the wooden crosses that were placed on the memorial wall at Balhousie Castle over the period 2014-18 naming each Black Watch man killed in action would be burnt and the ash put into the River Tay during the 2020 Aberfeldy Muster Church

Service which marks the raising of the regiment at the place of its first muster on 10 May 1740. However, very sadly, due to the ongoing Covid restrictions on social gatherings, this event was postponed.

1 When I began my research into the Gellatly brothers, I was familiar with Blairgowrie & Rattray War Memorial – Behind the Names by Mark Duffy and Sir William Macpherson of Cluny (2006), which I consider to be essential reading for anyone researching Blairgowrie's war dead.

2 Blairgowrie Advertiser, 19 December 1914.

3 Blairgowrie Advertiser, 8 August 1914.

4 Blairgowrie Advertiser, 8 August 1914.

5 Blairgowrie Advertiser, 8 August 1914.

6 Blairgowrie Advertiser, 8 August 1914.

7 Blairgowrie Advertiser, 22 August 1914.

8 Blairgowrie Advertiser, 28 November 1914.

9 Blairgowrie Advertiser, 24 October 1914.

10 6th Battalion War Diary, 27 July 1916.

11 Blairgowrie Advertiser, 24 October 1914.

'THROUGH A DELUGE OF FIRE'

THE BLACK WATCH AT HIGH WOOD, 30 JULY 1916

Derek J Patrick

O N THE MORNING of Sunday, 30 July 1916, men of the 6th (Perthshire) and 7th (Fife) Territorial Battalions, The Black Watch, were preparing for an assault on High Wood, the heavily fortified German position that dominated the Bazentin Ridge, crowning a large upland almost 100 feet high. Since the beginning of the Battle of the Somme, there had been several unsuccessful attempts to capture High Wood. The Black Watch were now tasked with taking its western and eastern corners.

The preliminary bombardment was launched at 4.45pm with the attack scheduled for 6.10pm. The 6th Battalion would assault the German line running south-east from High Wood, while, on its left, the 7th Battalion was to advance northwards through the wood. However, the artillery barrage had proved insufficient to destroy the German trenches. The leading companies of 6th Black Watch were subjected to heavy machine-gun fire almost immediately. Despite mounting losses, the battalion managed to reach the German barbed wire some 25 or 30 yards from the enemy frontline trench.[1]

It was here that Captain John Hally, Ruthven Tower, Auchterarder, commanding C Company, was killed, while Captain Innes, commanding D Company, who before the war had been a member of the clerical staff with J Pullar & Sons, Perth, was wounded.[2] Their companies were all but annihilated; and the advance stopped.[3] The 6th Battalion's *War Diary* recorded that the survivors, 'finding that the 7th Black Watch on their left were held up in the wood they dug themselves in and held their ground till daybreak when they were ordered to return to [their] original front line'.[4] In total the battalion had suffered over 250 men killed, wounded and missing.[5]

The men of 'Fife's Own' 7th Black Watch were to encounter similarly stiff resistance. It was soon apparent that the artillery bombardment had

'had little or no effect on [the] German front line trenches', which were strongly held, 'the enemy being plainly visible lining their front line trench in large numbers with fixed bayonets'.[6] The enemy's fire was so intense that C Company could only cover a few yards with the advancing Highlanders forced to take up makeshift positions in shell-holes. Nearly all the officers of the two leading companies were killed but the men held on for some time before the survivors withdrew to their original position.[7]

Captain and Adjutant Andrew Currie Begg, a banker in civilian life, was the 36-year-old son of The Reverend Dr Begg, Abbotshall Church, Kirkcaldy. On the Sunday following the action, The Reverend Dr Begg made reference in his prayers to Second Lieutenant James Herbert Lockhart, another Kirkcaldy Black Watch officer, who had fallen on 30 July.[8] Lockhart had spent several years overseas having been engaged in the construction of the Aswan Dam.[9] Confirmation that Reverend Begg's own son had been killed on the same date did not arrive until the following morning. Captain Begg left a widow and five children.[10]

Captain Edgar Leslie Boase, a well-known figure in Fife and Dundee would also lose his life at High Wood. Boase was an experienced Territorial Army officer having served in France with the 4th Black Watch in early 1915. In a letter to his family, his death was described as 'an extremely gallant one, occurring during a more than plucky effort to prevent the instant death of the men under his command, and involving almost certain death to himself, of which he was fully aware'.[11] Captain James Gillespie, C Company, an architect from St Andrews, was killed immediately having crossed the parapet of the British trench.[12] Boase took his place and led Gillespie's company toward the German positions in High Wood. He volunteered to go forward and extinguish a fire that had broken out beside a stock of abandoned German ammunition which, had it exploded, would have inflicted heavy casualties on his men. One of his platoon commanders wrote:

> He handed over his revolver, took an empty Lewis gun-bag, [and] ran out into fierce enemy machine gun and rifle fire. He was warned that he would be hit, but still went on to put out the fire.[13]

Boase was shot by a sniper having accomplished his objective, one of nine officers of the 7th Black Watch killed on 30 July 1916. He was 48. In all, the 7th (Fife) Battalion suffered more than 140 casualties. These included Private Joseph Cavanagh, a veteran soldier who had served in the Second Anglo-Boer War (1899–1902). A miner at Dalbeath Colliery on the outbreak of war, Cavanagh left a wife and a ten-year-old daughter.[14] His brother-in-law, Lance Corporal William Kirk, also a miner at Dalbeath, was listed as missing the same day.[15]

Both battalions were part of the 51st (Highland) Division and had been in France since the beginning of May 1915. The men were familiar with the routine of trench warfare, but High Wood was their first experience of fighting on a large scale. In his account of the regiment's service in the Great War, A G Wauchope gave a succinct assessment of the fighting at High Wood: 'Unfortunately, the ground gained was disappointingly small compared to the losses incurred'.[16] Despite the outcome, however, no more could have been asked of the men of the 6th and 7th Battalions. Second Lieutenant Hubert William Strathairn, a Crieff officer, described his men as 'simply great', adding:

> They went over like men on parade, laughing and joking and talking, and never turned back. Most of them (Crieff boys) were in my platoon, and I can assure you no officer had a finer set of men than I had. But now many are lost and many wounded, and the loss of such fine fellows cuts very deep; but they did their duty nobly.[17]

A French observer described the 'magnificent Highlanders advanc[ing] like a whirlwind through the smoke, the flame, and the deadly hail of bullets...They carry themselves as superbly as the Old Guard'. Another account reflected on the ferocity of the action:

> The Germans met the charge with every weapon of destruction they could command, but it was to no purpose. Nothing would stop the onrushing kilties, and the Germans were so taken aback by the steadiness and courage that when some of us got

on to their parapet they were throwing bombs away before setting the fuses off...all agreed that officers and men had brought a new distinction not only on the regiment, but on the several districts to which they belong.[18]

MILITARY MEDAL AWARDED TO PRIVATE ARCHIBALD HAXTON
(Derek Patrick)

The two battalions' impressive list of gallantry awards for High Wood is testimony to the courage of the men. The 6th Black Watch alone received nine Military Medals for 'Bravery in the Field'. One recipient, Private Alexander Haxton, lost his left arm in winning his award. His younger brother, Private Archibald Haxton, church organist at St Paul's, Perth, was killed during the ill-fated attack.[19] His name appears on the Thiepval Memorial to the missing of the Somme, which commemorates over 72,000 officers and men with no known grave, including many of those who fell at High Wood. While the attack on 30 July failed to achieve its objectives the Highlanders who attacked the heavily defended German trenches behaved splendidly. In the words of a contemporary, the men of Perth and Fife 'acquitted themselves...in accord with the long and glorious traditions of the regiment'.[20]

1 A G Wauchope, *A History of the Black Watch in the Great War, 1914-18*, Volume 2 (London: Medici Society, 1926), p140.

2 *The Evening Telegraph and Post*, 7 August 1916.

3 Wauchope, *History*, Volume 2, p140.

4 The National Archives. WO95/2876, 30 July 1916.

5 Wauchope, *History*, Volume 2, p141.

6 The National Archives, WO95/2877/2, 30 July 1916.

7 Wauchope, *History*, Volume 2, p266.

8 *The Fife Free Press*, 12 August 1916.

9 *The Fife Free Press*, 12 August 1916.

10 *The Fifeshire Advertiser*, 12 August 1916.

11 *The Courier and Argus*, 7 August 1916.

12 *The Courier and Argus*, 7 August 1916.

13 *The Courier and Argus*, 11 August 1916.

14 *The Dunfermline Journal*, 19 August 1916.

15 *The Dunfermline Journal*, 19 August 1916.

16 Wauchope, *History*, Volume 2, p267.

17 *The Strathearn Herald*, 19 August 1916.

18 *The People's Journal*, 12 August 1916.

19 *The Perthshire Advertiser and Strathmore Journal*, 25 April 1917.

20 *The People's Journal*, 12 August 1916.

Private (Baron) Hubert de Reuter– 'Our Toff'

Victoria Schofield

Perhaps you'll say this was not love
May love not live in one heart alone?
Or must there be two fires that move
From two souls to make them one?[1]

O F THE 50,000 MEN who served in The Black Watch during the
First World War, the story of Private (Baron) Hubert Julius de
Reuter is unique. Aged 36 when war was declared in August 1914, he had
begun his military service in the Sportsman's Battalion, Royal Fusiliers
(City of London) Regiment. Instead of being drawn from the same
geographical area, these battalions consisted of 'pals': men who had the
same interests, mainly in sports but also the media. On 8 June 1915, de
Reuter gained a commission as a second lieutenant in the 3rd Battalion,
the Essex Regiment. But, instead of being sent abroad, as an older
member of the battalion, he was kept at the regimental depot because of
his 'steadying influence' on the younger men. Frustrated at his inaction,
he resigned his commission. At the end of 1915, he enlisted in The Black
Watch joining the 4th Battalion (City of Dundee) – known as the 'Fighter-
Writer' Battalion because so many of those who enlisted were journalists,
writers and artists from Dundee. 'I joined the army to fight the Germans,'
he told a friend; 'and this seems the best way of doing it'.[2] He later moved
to the 7th Battalion (Fife), The Black Watch, 51st Highland Division,
which was one of several Black Watch battalions fighting in the Somme.

De Reuter's service in The Black Watch on the Western Front did not
last long. In November 1916, he was killed, when the platoon in which he
was serving and another platoon of the 7th Black Watch, attached to the
6th Battalion, were engaged in severe fighting to take Y-ravine, 'a deep
gash in the ground almost at right angles to the line of advance' at

Beaumont-Hamel, a commune in the Somme department of Picardy.[3]

'He fell on November 13', recorded the *Perthshire Constitutional & Journal*, 'in a gallant fight in which he won high distinction for his adroitness, bravery and self-sacrifice'. He would have gained 'a very high decoration had he lived', recorded his commanding officer, Lieutenant-Colonel Cheape:

> The whole of the platoon went over the first line of German trenches into the second. De Reuter went down a 20-foot dug-out and shouted out in German asking if any men were there. No answer, so he threw two bombs round the corner and then again shouted – 'Anybody there' The answer came – 'One officer and thirty-five men.' These he made file out past him. He then found that some Germans had been passed over in the first line, and were shooting from behind and from the right rear, so he put the German officer on the parapet, threatening him with his bayonet and made him order the men to surrender. Sixty-two men came over.[4]

Reuter's 'gallant' action, which had shown 'courage and resource' meant that a platoon of one sergeant and 20 men had captured one officer and 97 German soldiers. Having carried back three badly wounded men to relative safety, under heavy machine-gun fire, he returned across no-man's-land for the stretcher-bearers, but was fatally wounded. Hubert was buried the next day; his resting place was Mailly Wood Cemetery on the outskirts of Mailly-Maillet village west of Beaumont-Hamel.[5]

But who was Hubert de Reuter? Why was he styled 'Baron'? Why did he speak German? So often in the course of writing military history we record the gallant death, but the family background and early adulthood are missing from the narrative.

De Reuter's background, however, is also what makes his story unusual. Already in early twentieth century Britain, 'Reuter' had become a household name. Thanks to the interest Hubert's grandfather, Paul Julius Reuter, had in telegraphy (having started with homing pigeons), what became the Reuters News Agency held a virtual monopoly of disseminating news and information more reliably and swiftly throughout the world than the traditional postal service.

PRIVATE (BARON) HUBERT DE REUTER

Born Israel Beer Josaphat – the son of a rabbi – in Kassel, Germany, Israel had moved to London in 1845. On his conversion to Christianity, he took the name Paul Julius Reuter, marrying the daughter of a German banker, Ida Maria von Magnus.[6] Soon afterwards, having returned to live in Germany and France (gaining experience working for the future Agence France-Presse), in 1851, he had set up his own private firm in London shortly before the opening of the undersea cable from Dover to Calais. Naturalised as a British citizen in 1857, four years later he restructured his firm as the Reuters Telegram Company.

Paul and Ida Maria had three sons: Herbert, George and Alfred. His eldest son and heir, Herbert, had a daughter, Olga Edith, born in 1877. Their only son, Hubert Julius, was born the following year. In the same year as Hubert's birth, his grandfather, Paul, retired and so his eldest son, Herbert, stepped into his father's shoes as managing director of Reuters; in time it was assumed that, his son, Hubert, would do the same.[7] Having been accorded the title Freiherr (generally translated in English as Baron) in 1871 by Ernest II, the Duke of Saxe-Coburg-Gotha – Prince Albert's brother – 20 years later Paul Julius Reuter's right to be styled Baron von Reuter as a member of the British nobility was confirmed by Queen Victoria.

After following in his father's footsteps, at Harrow School, North London, the young Hubert went to Wiesbaden in Germany to improve his German. He then lived in Lausanne, Switzerland, where he learnt French as well as enjoying climbing 'inaccessible peaks'. Returning to London, by 1901 Hubert was working as an editor in Reuters' office in Old Jewry, where one of his colleagues in the editorial department, the journalist Valentine Williams, described him as a 'gifted but erratic' young man who obviously did not get on well with his father.[8] Later, Hubert moved to Melbourne, Australia, and then Constantinople, then the capital of the Ottoman Empire. But he did not share his grandfather's interest in nor his father's commitment to newsgathering and the media. Having resigned his position, he took a job as a tutor and schoolmaster. In his spare time, he wrote poetry. In 1907, he published a collection of poems entitled *Gypsy Melodies*.

At the outbreak of war in August 1914, like so many millions of other young men, ordinary life was set aside as the commitment to fight for 'King and Country' took precedence. But as Hubert was acclimatising to military life, tragedy struck his family, when, on 15 April 1915, his mother, Edith, an invalid for many years, died. So grieved was his father that, three days later, he shot himself, both parents being buried in the same grave. Hubert became the 3rd Baron, which meant that when, later that year, he enlisted in The Black Watch he was known as Private (Baron) de Reuter.

His death at Beaumont Hamel without an heir in 1916, meant that the barony passed to his young cousin, Oliver, his uncle George's son, still only in his early twenties. Oliver died in 1966 but his widow, Marguerite, lived until 2009. Her death signified the last de Reuter link with the Reuters News Agency, which – had Hubert lived – he would have inherited. The previous year, the company had been bought by the Canadian newspaper conglomerate, Thomson Corporation, becoming Thomson Reuters. Since Olivier and Marguerite had no children the barony became extinct.[9]

A lasting remembrance remains. Before returning to the frontline for the last time, Hubert had dinner with Sir Roderick Jones, the new managing director of Reuters after Herbert's suicide.[10] Over dinner,

Hubert offered him an oil painting and a bust of his grandfather, Paul Julius Reuter, which Jones gladly accepted. The bust can still be seen in the office of Thomson Reuters at Canary Wharf, London; while the oil painting of his grandfather, by the English-German artist, Rudolf Lehmann, hangs in the offices of the Thomson Corporation, next to its Canadian founder, Sir Roy Thomson, at 3 Times Square, New York.

In memory of this unusual private soldier, Second Lieutenant William Tovani, who had known Hubert – or Harry as he was called – when both men were serving in the 7th Black Watch, wrote a poem, entitled 'Our Toff'.

OUR TOFF

We 'ad a toff in our platoon
a Baron's son was he,
a toff wot did his share of work
an' drank his Army tea
an' spent near all his handy cash
on chaps like you and me

He might have been a red-tab swell
that's wot he might have been,
but then we chaps that's coarser-like
would never quite ha' seen
the splendid man he was right through
a soldier – straight and keen

He's gone – like many another chap
an' we wot's out here still
when grey dawn breaks and men 'stand to'
when armies fight and kill.
We misses 'Arry, our star toff
who lies near Mailly hill

I ain't religious, but I'd like
to thank the God who gave
this world our Harry, Baron's son
who found a soldier's grave.[11]

1 Hubert de Reuter, *The Gypsy Melodies* (Wiesbaden: Carl Schnegelberger, 1906).

2 'Black Watch's Exploit', *Perthshire Constitutional & Journal*, 25 December 1916.
   See also John Entwistle, 'Romantic, idealist and no chip off the old block', *The Baron*,
   https://www.thebaron.info/archives/romantic-idealist-and-no-chip-off-the-old-block
   (accessed 5 May 2020).

3 A G Wauchope, *A History of the Black Watch in the Great War, 1914-1918*, Volume 3
   (London: Medici Society, 1926), p272.

4 Lieutenant-Colonel G R H Cheape quoted in 'Black Watch's exploit – How Baron de
   Reuter died', *Perthshire Constitutional & Journal,* 25 December 1916.

5 See Victoria Schofield, *The Black Watch: Fighting in the Front Line, 1899-2006*
   (London: Head of Zeus, 2017), pp114-115;

6 Baron Paul Julius Reuter, Baron von Reuter (1816-1899). Ida Maria von Magnus
   (1825(?)-1911). The 'von' was no doubt changed to 'de' in response to anti-German
   feeling prevalent in early twentieth-century Britain.

7 August Julius Clement Herbert de Reuter (1852-1915) married Edith (neé Campbell).
   Olga Edith de Reuter (1877-1941). She married John William Edward James Douglas,
   16th Laird of Tilquhillie and had a son John Sholto Douglas (born 1904).

8 Valentine Williams, *The World of Action* (Boston: Houghton Miffin Company, 1938),
   p66.

9 Oliver de Reuter (1894-1966); Marguerite, Baroness de Reuter (1912-2009).

10 Sir Roderick Jones, KBE (1877-1962) was managing director of Reuters, 1916-41.
   See Sir Roderick Jones, *A Life in Reuters,* (New York: Doubleday, 1951).

11 'H J De Reuter, 7th Royal Highlanders, 13/11/16',
   https://www.greatwarforum.org/topic/244861-h-j-de-reuter-7th-royal-
   highlanders-131116/
   (posted by Colin McNeil, whose grandfather, Private James McLeod McNeil,
   7th Black Watch, also fought at Beaumont-Hamel, later receiving the Military Medal,
   accessed 5 May 2020).

A VIOLIN AND A DIARY

PURGAVIE FAMILY SOUVENIRS OF
THE GREAT WAR

Alistair and Eric Stewart

O N 5 JANUARY 1917, Private James Purgavie who had volunteered for service under the Derby Scheme left Devonport, Plymouth, as part of a reinforcement draft for the 2nd Battalion, The Black Watch, then serving in Mesopotamia. At this point, he was already 39, a well-established local musician and a former gamekeeper from Redgorton, Perthshire, with a keen eye for wildlife and a willingness to record what he saw in a tiny, but beautifully kept, diary the size of an army field notebook. The diary, which ran with some gaps from the time he left Britain until the end of the war, recorded rumours, bitter complaints about food, the climate, the flies and how he was employed. It recorded his pursuit of his two great passions – musical performance and observing local wildlife – and described how he acquired a second family souvenir, a violin in a battered old case which not only survived at least two years of war but is also credited with saving his life long after the last shot had been fired. The main historical value of the diary, however, is that it is possibly the only known regimental account of the service of a Black Watch soldier assigned to logistical work in the base areas during the Mesopotamian campaign.

The diary itself consists of a field notebook with hard covers, three inches broad by four-and-a-half long, of a type familiar to anyone who served in the British Army. What is remarkable about it, however, is the style, quality and clarity of the handwriting for diaries kept in wartime and written in pencil tend to have large areas of 'smudged' and near illegible handwriting. This should not come as a surprise because calligraphy had been a pre-war hobby of Private Purgavie. The *Dundee Evening Post* wrote in the style of the time:

A remarkable calligraphic achievement has just been performed by Mr J Purgavie, gamekeeper, Battleby, Luncarty, near
Perth. Within the space that can be covered with a three-
penny piece this gentleman has succeeded in writing the
Lord's Prayer six times.[1]

What is perhaps more surprising is the overall legibility of the writing
and the general lack of smudging over the century that has passed since
the last entry on 9 March 1919.

The diary begins with an account of a nightmarish sea voyage aboard
an unnamed troopship in wartime from Britain via Sierra Leone, South
Africa and India to Mesopotamia. The first few days were spent sailing
through very heavy weather and all of the soldiers on board were very
seasick. A few days later, there was some sort of fever on board and all
personnel had to 'get a gargle' as a precaution. To compound matters,
there was a serious issue with the food and conditions on the ship at
times, and entries such as 'terrible rows about the food' appeared too
often. In addition, at one point, there was a fire in a coal bunker which ran
on for three days lengthening the journey significantly.

If all that was not bad enough, on 10 January 1917, a German U-boat
was seen, and the convoy altered course. In fact, this was a fairly dangerous
time for troopships sailing off the African coast: Germany had
reintroduced unrestricted submarine warfare and heavily disguised
German surface raiders like the SMS *Wolf* still operated off the coast of
Africa laying mines and capturing British flagged vessels. In spite of a
note in the diary on 20 January that the British had sunk a German raider
they had been after for some time, the entry for 27 January 1917 was
foreboding: 'Great excitement. All ships have stopped and turned right
about and are heading to the North. Wireless message from Cape Town
the Germans are waiting for us'.[2] Nevertheless, in spite of everything, on
1 May 1917, Private Purgavie arrived safely in Mesopotamia.

It was during the voyage that it became clear that Private Purgavie was
not in particularly good health, and on 11 January 1917, he was 'examined
by the doctor and failed to pass for [illegible – possibly 'gym'] again'.[3]
Other medical examinations followed, and when he passed A1 (he had

been D4 previously), he was listed for Mesopotamia. Although he arrived in Mesopotamia, there is nothing is his diary to say that he had joined the main body of the 2nd Battalion, but instead remained in the rear area working on the massive logistical operation required during the campaign to supply the army and it is entirely possible that his poor health and age were noted on arrival and he was assigned with other men in a similar condition to logistical support work. He may also have been suffering from malaria.

The full extent of the British logistical operation was described by Kaushik Roy in his study of that aspect of the Mesopotamian campaign and he specifically mentioned as an example that 'in January 1916, the 2nd Black Watch lacked stretchers (for removing the wounded) and blankets for the men'.[4] In any case, the demand for labour in the Basra area was immense and the *2nd Battalion War Diary* entries for the battalion's strength constantly record the large numbers of Black Watch men listed as 'employed in Corps Area', so it is at least reasonable to expect to find Private Purgavie there. However, it is when he described how he was employed that the full range of work expected of men involved in logistical support is made clear. On one occasion, he was employed in unloading bags of silver Rupees, and 'wished he had all that he carried', while on another occasion, he was on guard covering the guns and shells when there was a robbery at the other end of his beat and when a 'lot of silver was lifted', one man was shot and another escaped. On one other occasion (25 May 1917), he and his comrades were warned to stand by to surround the Egyptian Labour Corps camp with loaded rifles and fixed bayonets, but the trouble that had been expected never materialised.[5]

At the end of 1917, just as the 2nd Battalion was preparing to go to Palestine, an entry appeared in the Purgavie diary: 'I went to the Battalion and passed B4, so they have gone, and I am not going'. This entry coincides with another in the *2nd Battalion War Diary* for 21 December: 'Medical examination of weakly men held and 36 sent to join No 1 BB Depot as unfit to proceed with Battalion'.[6] Some time after the battalion left, Private Purgavie did go to Palestine, but again was deployed in the rear areas.

A large part of the diary is also devoted to Private Purgavie's great passion for observing local wildlife. His observations are invariably detailed and concise as he attempted to identify the genus or family to which the birds and insects he saw belonged. Some of his comments also showed that soldier or not, he still had a gamekeeper's eye for detail when he described flying fish which 'get up in coveys like partridges' or that the Tigris 'showed a fine rise at sunset'. Unfortunately, he was not in a position to go fishing at that point as he had done in Scotland when, for example his catches taken on behalf of Mr Coats from the Upper and Lower Redgorton water were published in the *Perthshire Advertiser*.[7]

Nonetheless, his passion for observation got him into what were two potentially fatal encounters with local wildlife. The first of these took place at Bangalore, India, when he unexpectedly came within a yard of what he called a rattlesnake, but which by his description was seven feet long and almost certainly a king cobra whose bite is invariably lethal. He described the encounter as 'the only time I have found my hair rising up'.[8] A similar encounter took place in Palestine when he found a beautiful silver snake about three feet long under a dead branch which was 'very quick in its actions, faced me up and hissed, with its head held up like a cock when it is fighting'.[9] Judging by the description given, he had almost certainly met a highly venomous Palestinian viper, but once again he was not harmed.

On the other hand, Private Purgavie's musical activities were much less dangerous. Before the war, he had been the conductor of the Monzie Orchestra in Pitlochry, a violin soloist and was a well-known and respected musician who was equally at home with 'A Night wi' Burns' or the overture to Alphonse Herman's 'La Diademe'. (Family tradition says that he spent several years in London before the war where it is thought he received some level of formal musical training.) He also played violin accompaniment to silent films before the advent of the 'talkies'. Newspaper reports of his performances appeared regularly from as early as 1889 and continued after the war, but the first indication he was performing on board ship came within days of leaving Devenport. On 22 January 1917, he wrote, 'Playing to the officers...Writing music for the band' and again three days later, 'Music concert tonight'. Sadly, no details of what he played or who he played with were given but family tradition related that he preferred to play classical pieces. Some of the concerts he played in took a slightly comic twist, particularly one at Be'itNa'ana (*sic*) where there were 'jackals howling around the place during the concert'.[10] In Bangalore, he went on church parade with the rest of the Scots troops and attended a church built by the Scottish community admiring greatly the singing; and he 'thought for a while he was back in Redgorton again'.[11]

It also appears that whilst on board ship, he played a violin drawn from what was probably a pool of instruments and several entries show how keen he was to have a violin of his own. He made more than one approach about this to Lady Cox, wife of the British Political Officer, who appears to have run concerts where he performed, but with no success. Nevertheless, on 8 December 1917, he noted in one sentence, 'Outbreak of smallpox' and in the next 'Tried fishing – nothing doing', and then, 'Have a fiddle to myself from Major Warburton' followed by 'Another visit to lady Cox'. After that meeting, the number of performances appeared to have increased again.[12]

Not all performances ended in requests for encores. One performance at the Sergeants' Mess at which a five-course dinner was served – and no doubt a good deal of alcohol was consumed – was particularly noteworthy:

12 January, 1918 Played at the Sgts Mess. 5 course dinner.
13 January, Hut 13, Police Huts, landed in nick 7 days.[13]

THE PURGAVIE VIOLIN IN ITS CASE
(Purgavie Family)

Nevertheless, at the end of the war, he still had his violin and the rather smart case that came with it, and it was then that it proved its real value, for one night while returning home on his bicycle from giving violin lessons he was struck by a car. By good luck, he had slung the violin case over his back with the broad end uppermost so that when he landed the violin case slid up his back and cushioned the blow to his head which almost certainly saved his life. The case and the violin given to him by Major Warburton which had survived at least two years of war were badly damaged, but James Purgavie survived – as does the precious violin, safe in the care of his grandsons.

1   *Dundee Evening Post*, 28 February 1905.

2   Purgavie Diary, p11.

3   Purgavie Diary, p3.

4   Kaushik Roy, 'From Defeat to Victory: Logistics of the Campaign in Mesopotamia, 1914–1918', *First World War Studies*, 1 (1), p41.

5   Purgavie Diary, p45.

6   *2nd Battalion War Diary*, 21 December 1917.

7   *Perthshire Advertiser*, 2 February 1910.

8   Purgavie Diary, p30.

9   Purgavie Diary, p53.

10   Purgavie Diary, p51.

11   Purgavie Diary, p33.

12   Purgavie Diary, p48.

13   Purgavie Diary, p49.

THE 9TH BLACK WATCH AT ARRAS

'THE CRUSHING DEFEAT OF THE ENEMY ON APRIL 9TH [1917] WAS DUE TO THE DISCIPLINE, HARD WORK, UNTIRING ENERGY AND MAGNIFICENT GALLANTRY OF ALL RANKS'[1]

Derek J Patrick

THE MEN of the 9th Black Watch began to advance at 5.30am on Monday, 9 April 1917. Their objectives were the German frontline and support trenches, and the rising ground known as 'Observation Ridge', designated the 'Black' and 'Blue' lines. The attack was to be carried out in successive stages with each limited to a particular section of the enemy's defences. Its second phase would see fresh brigades secure the tactically important village of Monchy-le-Preux, crucial to the success of the Battle of Arras, Britain's contribution to France's ambitious Nivelle Offensive.

The preliminary bombardment of the German trenches had begun on 4 April, and under cover of a creeping barrage of shrapnel and high explosive shells, the 9th Black Watch had reached its first objective by 5.45am with few casualties. On resuming the advance at 7.10am, the battalion encountered far stiffer resistance. Between the first and second objectives the heavily defended 'Railway Triangle' overlooked the ground westward. On its eastern face an embankment, some 50 or 60 feet high, was covered by a number of German machine guns, which enfiladed the ground to be crossed by The Black Watch. The battalion was delayed for approximately three hours, with snipers, machine-gun, and rifle fire exacting a heavy toll. The stalemate was eventually broken when the 7th Camerons and a tank, the 'Lusitania', were sent forward in support. The 'Blue' line was reached at 1.30pm and the men relieved several hours later, occupying Hermes Trench in brigade reserve. The rain that had started to fall as the advance began had turned to snow, and the work of consolidating the captured trenches was carried out in bitter cold and a strong gale. Despite the weather, it was observed that 'the knowledge of all they had accomplished...raised the spirits of all ranks', and that 'it [was] doubtful if at any period of its existence the morale of the Division was higher than it was on the night of April 9, 1917'.[2]

The day's operations were described as 'entirely successful', the battalion taking over 200 prisoners, and capturing four machine guns, a German trench mortar, ammunition, maps, plans and other materials.[3] In comparison with its losses at Loos on 25 September 1915, or the Somme in 1916, the battalion's casualties were relatively light. From a total strength of 19 officers and 618 other ranks, some three officers were killed and 12 wounded, and 38 other ranks killed, 12 listed as missing, 176 wounded; a total of 241 casualties. Fatalities included the battalion's Roman Catholic chaplain, Captain Reverend Herbert John Collins. Much admired, he had been attached to the 9th Black Watch since it left England in July 1915 and was responsible for many of the letters sent to the bereaved families of men who had fallen at Loos. Collins accompanied the battalion on each of its tours of the trenches, 'and was ever to be found in the front line with a haversack full of cigarettes, his own gift to the men'. He regularly conducted the funeral services of soldiers killed in the frontline, often under fire, 'and always, but most of all when conditions were bad, did his cheery presence enhearten all ranks'.[4] The regimental 'History' observed that no man was prouder of serving with the 9th Black Watch than Captain Collins. He was 35, and is buried in Cabaret-Rouge British Cemetery, Souchez, Pas-de-Calais.

The opening stages of the battle saw impressive territorial gains with the Canadian Corps capturing Vimy Ridge to the north, and General Allenby's Third Army in the centre making the furthest advances since trench warfare began. The 15th (Scottish) Division's successful advance on Monchy-le-Preux saw it take all its objectives and make gains of over two miles with relatively little loss. However, the second phase of the battle would prove more costly with a series of smaller-scale operations intent on consolidating the positions taken at the outset, and ultimately, helping relieve pressure on the French whose offensive had failed with heavy casualties.

CAPTAIN REVEREND HERBERT JOHN COLLINS, (far left)
With the officers of the 9th Black Watch at Burbure, April 1916
(Black Watch Museum)

In this second phase, the 9th Black Watch played an important part in the attempt to capture the village of Guémappe on 23 April. The initial advance at 4.45am made little progress, and subsequent attempts to carry the reinforced German first line were largely unsuccessful. Captain Leonard Graeme Morrison and a small party of some 70 men reached Hammer Trench and Dragoon Lane, north of the village, and held the position for four hours before being compelled to withdraw. Morrison, a 23-year-old medical student from St Andrews, made another attempt to recapture the lost ground at 6pm with a mixed force of Black Watch, Seaforths and Camerons.[5] The gallant captain was killed before he had gone several yards, but his party's attack was entirely successful. Much was owed to the bravery of Sergeant Joseph Gibb, a veteran Territorial soldier from Friockheim, Angus, who 'single handed worked his way round the end of the trench and destroyed an enemy machine gun and its crew who were holding up the advance'.[6] It was observed that the 'very gallant conduct of Captain Morrison and his devoted party that day added another leaf to the laurels of The Black Watch'.[7] For his actions, Gibb was awarded the Military Medal for 'Bravery in the Field', one of at least 15 gallantry medals received by officers and men of the 9th Black Watch for the Battle of Arras.[8]

The Battle of Arras lasted until 16 May 1917 and cost nearly 160,000 British and 125,000 German casualties. The 9th Black Watch suffered approximately 495 casualties from fighting spread over a 15-day period. However, this was very different to the battalion's baptism of fire at Loos. 'The spirit and fighting will of the Battalion was unquestionably the same', but here, the battalion was set a definite and achievable task.[9] The battle may have ended in stalemate but the improvement and innovations in artillery and tactics that marked the opening stages of the offensive emphasise the continued evolution of British operational effectiveness on the Western Front.

1 A G Wauchope, *A History of the Black Watch in the Great War, 1914-18*, Volume 3 (London: Medici Society, 1926), p152.

2 Wauchope, *History*, Volume 3, p147; John Stewart and John Buchan, *The Fifteenth (Scottish) Division* (Edinburgh: Blackwood, 1926), p121.

3 Wauchope, *History*, Volume 3, p147.

4 Wauchope, *History*, Volume 3, p147.

5 Wauchope, *History*, Volume 3, p149.

6 *The Scotsman*, 23 March 1915; Wauchope, *History*, Volume 3, p149.

7 Wauchope, *History*, Volume 3, p149.

8 *Supplement to the London Gazette*, 9 July 1917.

9 Wauchope, *History*, Volume 3, p150.

THE 9TH BLACK WATCH AT FREZENBERG, 31 JULY 1917

Derek J Patrick

T HE 9TH (SERVICE) BATTALION, The Black Watch, 44th Infantry Brigade, 15th (Scottish) Division, arrived in the Ypres Salient on 27 June 1917, in preparation for the Battle of Passchendaele (Third Battle of Ypres).[1] The coming weeks saw the battalion practise its part in the imminent attack over ground flagged out to represent the German trench system. Between 25 and 30 July, the 44th Brigade bivouacked one mile west of Ypres and companies made regular visits to the front in order to familiarise themselves with the terrain.

The 15th Division had been allocated three main objectives designated the 'Blue', 'Black' and 'Green' lines.[2] The 9th Black Watch would be on the right of the division's front alongside the 8/10th Gordon Highlanders, with orders to capture and consolidate the 'Blue' and 'Black' lines (the German front trenches and a second line some 500 yards further back). Zero hour was 3.50am on 31 July 1917, and by 4.45am the battalion had reached its first objective, advancing behind a creeping shrapnel barrage. Casualties in this initial phase had been slight and the leading companies were soon reorganised in shell-holes for the advance on the 'Black' line commencing at 5.30am.

The 'Black' line was a road some 300 yards east of Frezenberg village in front of which ran a trench strongly held by the enemy. Four tanks had been allocated to 44th Brigade for its attack on the 'Black' line but two were knocked out or had broken down before it was reached. Nonetheless, the remaining machines were of great assistance in capturing the trench and Frezenberg Redoubt, the 9th Black Watch advancing by sectional rushes. On securing its final objective at around 6.30am the battalion began to consolidate a line of shell-holes and concrete dugouts. Between 8.30am and 10am, the Germans attempted two counterattacks which were driven off with heavy loss.

The battalion, however, now occupied a precarious position on the eastern slope of Frezenberg Ridge under direct observation of the German positions some 2,000 yards away. The enemy had brought up fresh artillery batteries and their fire was exceedingly accurate. It was observed that 'the shell fire was very heavy, worse than any of us remember having received on the Somme, and this continued all day'.[3] Heavy shelling coupled with sniping and machine-gun fire which enfiladed part of the line, and dreadful weather, made reorganisation almost impossible. The 45th Brigade which had successfully captured the 'Green' line (the 15th Division's third objective) was compelled to withdraw at around 4pm due to the retirement of the 8th Division on the right and a strong German counterattack, but the newly consolidated line held. The 9th Black Watch was left holding the second objective until relieved by the 8th Seaforth Highlanders at approximately 10.30pm.

LANCE CORPORAL ALEXANDER W LAWRIE
Samuel Lindsay: *Coatbridge and the Great War* (Glasgow, 1919)
(Black Watch Museum Archive)

The first phase of the battle had gone reasonably well. The 15th Division had advanced some 2,000 yards and although the final objective had not been secured, the strategically important Frezenberg Ridge had been captured.[4] However, casualties had been heavy. The 9th Black Watch had gone into action with a strength of 18 officers and 520 other ranks. On relief it could only muster seven officers and 137 men (although many stragglers were still to come in). In all, some 20 other ranks had been killed, 45 were missing and 180 wounded.

Lance Corporal Alexander W Lawrie, who had been employed as a clerk in the Clyde Tube Works, was one of those listed as missing.[5] He had been with the battalion from its arrival in France in July 1915 and at the age of just 20 was already a veteran of Loos, the Somme and Arras. Lawrie was the youngest of three brothers all of whom would lose their lives in the Great War. He is commemorated on the Ypres (Menin Gate) Memorial with others of his battalion who fell at Frezenberg and have no known grave.

One officer, Second Lieutenant James Taylor, was killed, and 12 were wounded. These included Second Lieutenant Colin F I Neish, the only son of Major Neish, of Tannadyce House, near Forfar.[6] Captain and Adjutant Stanley Norie-Miller, well known in Perth, sustained a shrapnel wound in the leg, and the commanding officer, Lieutenant-Colonel Sydney Armitage Innes, who resided at Linder Bank, Perth, was wounded but both remained at duty.[7]

Second Lieutenant William Richard Tovani, who belonged to another Perthshire family, was awarded the Military Cross (MC) for conspicuous gallantry:

> When his company commander had become a casualty, he led his company forward with the utmost gallantry, although wounded in the face, and captured a machine-gun emplacement which was causing great hindrance to the advance. He continued to lead his company until he was wounded again and compelled to desist.[8]

Second Lieutenant Frederick Proudfoot, whose father was postmaster in Alloa, received a Bar to his MC at Frezenberg.[9] Like Tovani, his award was for assuming command of a company in particularly difficult circumstances:

For conspicuous gallantry and devotion to duty. When the officer commanding the attacking troops had become a casualty, he took charge and handled two companies in a most masterly manner. He led them with the utmost courage to the capture of all their objectives under heavy hostile fire of every description, consolidating his position through a strong counter-attack, which he beat off with heavy loss to the enemy and personally led at least two successful attacks on concrete gun emplacements which were delaying the whole advance. He displayed exceptional gallantry and fine leadership.[10]

In addition, a further two MCs, one Distinguished Conduct Medal (DCM) and 15 Military Medals (MMs) were awarded to men of the 9th Black Watch in connection with operations on 31 July 1917, several of whom were originally from Fife, Dundee, Angus or Perthshire. MM recipient Corporal Joseph Davidson was the first soldier from the Kinglassie area to be awarded a gallantry medal.[11] Sergeant Charles Ogilvie and Corporal Alexander Johnston, both from Methven, were also decorated. Johnston received the DCM for 'coolness and initiative': he 'collected a party of rifle bombers' and destroyed a German strong point that was holding up the advance.[12]

The 9th Black Watch was involved in several subsequent attacks in the vicinity of Gallipoli Farm with no real success. It was finally withdrawn from the front on 26 August, marching into reserve in pouring rain with a strength of just seven officers and 245 other ranks. This phase of the battle had been particularly trying with casualties in the region of 200 all ranks. General Gough, commanding the Fifth Army, inspected the remnants of the battalion and congratulated it on the work accomplished. In a letter copied to Lieutenant-Colonel Innes, Field Marshal Sir Douglas Haig also congratulated the men on 'their steady courage and determination in spite of bad weather and great hardship [which] has done much towards bringing us nearer to final victory'.[13] Nonetheless, a verse written by Lieutenant Tovani is a more fitting epitaph for those of the 9th Black Watch who died in the maelstrom of Third Ypres:

God, if it be my lot to lie
Under an alien-tented sky
Let me but share the soldier's shrine
A Wooden Cross.[14]

1 A G Wauchope, *A History of the Black Watch in the Great War, 1914-18*, Volume 3 (London: Medici Society, 1926), p155.

2 Wauchope, *History*, Volume 3, p158.

3 Wauchope, *History*, Volume 3, p159.

4 Wauchope, *History*, Volume 3, p160.

5 Samuel Lindsay, *Coatbridge and the Great War* (Glasgow: 1919), p118.

6 *The People's Journal*, 11 August 1917.

7 *The Perthshire Advertiser and Strathmore Journal*, 8 August 1917; *The Stonehaven Journal and Kincardineshire Advertiser*, 16 August 1917.

8 *Supplement to the London Gazette*, Wednesday, 9 January 1918.

9 *The Scotsman*, 10 September 1917.

10 *Supplement to the London Gazette*, 9 January 1918.

11 *The Courier and Argus*, 11 December 1918.

12 *The Post Sunday Special*, 30 September 1917, p5; *Supplement to the London Gazette*, 26 January 1918.

13 Wauchope, *History*, Volume 3, p163.

14 Torvaney, *Diverse Ditties*, (Edinburgh: Pentland Press, 1997), p71.

'WITH THE UTMOST GALLANTRY'

SECOND LIEUTENANT
WILLIAM RICHARD TOVANI, MC

Derek J Patrick

WILLIAM RICHARD TOVANI was born in Auchterarder, Perthshire, on 3 April 1893, the eldest son of The Reverend and Mrs William Thomas Tovani.[1] He was educated at Tonbridge School, Kent, and the University of St Andrews, where he was studying on the outbreak of war.[2] Tovani had an obvious talent for poetry and frequently contributed 'light verse' to the university magazine, *College Echoes*.[3] He was an accomplished scholar and was awarded the medal for Modern History for 1914/15. Tovani was a cadet-sergeant in the Officers' Training Corps when he received a commission in The Black Watch in June 1915.[4] Second Lieutenant Tovani first served with 3/7th Black Watch. In October 1915, he participated in a recruiting event in Leven, Fife:

> [Second Lieutenant Tovani] appealed to all men who were sportsmen to join in a far greater game than anything they had previously enjoyed, the sport of war. He had with him that evening some men belonging to the 7th Black Watch who were home wounded. His Colonel wanted more men of the same stamp, and he was there that evening to get them from the young men of Leven.[5]

He would soon have an opportunity to participate in the 'greater game' when he joined the 7th Black Watch in France in February 1916.[6]

Second Lieutenant Tovani joined the 9th Battalion in May 1917 and was wounded at Frezenberg on 31 July.[7] Here, he was awarded the Military Cross (MC) for 'conspicuous gallantry and devotion to duty'.[8] He was subsequently attached to the 6th Black Watch and received a bar to his MC in the battalion's last action of the war.

During operations of 24-26 October 1918, near Monchaux-sur-Écaillon and Famars, he displayed magnificent leadership in two attacks, in both of which his company did excellent work, capturing a large number of prisoners and machine guns. All through he showed a fine example of courage to his men and ability to deal with extremely difficult situations.[9]

Tovani was a prolific writer and his wartime experiences inspired several notable works. His poetry is not as familiar as that of Black Watch contemporaries Hamish Mann or Joseph Lee, but it is no less impressive. Tovani's 'Poppies of Cambrai' well represents his literary talents:

LIEUTENANT WILLIAM RICHARD TOVANI, MC
(The Black Watch Castle and Museum)

POPPIES OF CAMBRAI

Why do the poppies bloom so red
Along the Cambrai road?
Why do the cornflowers sway so fair
Where brave battalions strode?
Is it a tale they tell to me
To ease my load of pain?
Is it a hymn from earth to God
That sweetly quiet refrain?

Why do the roses blossom white
Athwart the cobbled way?
Why do they make my heart feel light
Though weary of the fray?
What is it here that fires the soul
That quickens each man's breath?
Is it a song they sing to me
Of deeds that live in death?

Red was the blood that dead men shed
Red are the poppies there;
White shone the light of steadfast souls
White bloom the roses fair;
Silent the host by the lone wayside
Noble the tale they tell
Of men who strode that Cambrai Road
To face the powers of Hell.[10]

Following the Armistice, Tovani remained in the Army serving with the Army Educational Corps. In October 1922, he was attached to the 2nd Lincolnshire Regiment at Poona, India. Here he announced that henceforth his surname would be altered to 'Torvaney'.[11] On leaving the military, he taught history and geography at Selkirk High School before attending the Theological College at Coates Hall, Edinburgh, in 1932.[12] He entered the Scottish Episcopal Church as Curate of Holy Trinity, Ayr, in 1933.[13] He moved to Montrose as Rector of St Mary's and St Peter's in September 1935.[14]

On the outbreak of the Second World War, The Reverend Torvaney served as a senior chaplain with the British Expeditionary Force. 'He served in France at the beginning of [the] war, was in the second last boat which left Dunkirk in the epic evacuation, and was an eye witness of the sinking of the *Lancastria*.'[15] The ocean liner, which had been requisitioned as a troopship, was sunk off St Nazaire on 17 June 1940 with the loss of some 3,000-6,000 lives, the largest loss of life in British maritime history. Torvaney helped pull survivors onboard his own vessel before it was bombed and set on fire.[16]

In November 1942, Torvaney was released from military duties and became Rector of St James's Episcopal Church, Holburn Junction, Aberdeen.[17] 'Here he not only ministered to his flock, but became as familiar and well known in Aberdeen as Union Street.'[18] In 1959, Torvaney was elected Synod Clerk of the Diocese of Aberdeen and Orkney, and Canon of St Andrews Cathedral.[19]

Torvaney was a member of the Aberdeen Branch of The Black Watch Association. In December 1950, he chaired the branch's tenth annual reunion which welcomed representatives of the 19th Belgian Infantry.[20] He was an avid reader, critic, freelance journalist and was described as 'no mean poet'.[21] In a long and varied career, he published several books, wrote a number of educational and theological articles, edited *The Scottish Churchman*, and during the Great War was a frequent contributor to the *Dundee Advertiser* using the pseudonym 'Red Hackle'. He also 'broadcast on numerous occasions'.[22] His hobbies were listed as tobacco growing and music.[23]

Torvaney retired as Rector of St James's on 30 September 1965 but had hoped to carry on until the beginning of December until his replacement was due to arrive. However, his health deteriorated, and he was admitted to hospital suffering with coronary thrombosis. Canon William Richard Torvaney died on 20 October 1965 aged 72. He was survived by his wife, Marion, two sons and a daughter.[24] Canon Torvaney was described as a 'kindly, friendly priest, who loved his fellow men'.[25] His was a life well spent. Torvaney was a devoted husband and father, a talented writer, well-respected cleric and decorated soldier. His service with The Black Watch is recorded in his poem, 'The Gallant Forty-Twa'.

THE GALLANT FORTY-TWA

You've heard the folk praise the Seaforths
Or laud the Gordons gay
The sturdy Scottish Rifles
Frae mony a Lowland brae,
But if ye see men marching
Wi' sober steady tread

The swing of kilts
Of sombre hue
Wi' hackle red
An' bonnet blue
In a' the land there's nane sae braw
As oor Black Watch, the Forty-Twa.

There's mony a lad frae Scotia's glens
That wears the bonnet blue,
An' mony a lad of valiant heart
Has braved a morn of rue
For glory of a nameless clan
Mid skirl of pipes while foeman ran
Frae swirl of kilts
Of sombre hue
Frae hackle red
An' bonnet blue
While brave men stand and brave men fa'
They're oor Black Watch, the Forty-Twa.[26]

1 H E Steed (ed.), *The Register of Tonbridge School from 1826 to 1910* (London: Rivingtons, 1911), p394.

2 *University of St Andrews Roll of Honour and Roll of Service 1914-1919* (Edinburgh, 1920), p106.

3 *The Citizen*, 11 October 1919.

4 *The Courier and Argus*, 14 July 1915; The Citizen, 25 August 1917.

5 *The Leven Advertiser and Wemyss Gazette*, 14 October 1915.

6 A G Wauchope, *A History of the Black Watch in the Great War, 1914-18*, Volume 3 (London: Medici Society, 1926), p323.

7 Wauchope, *History*, Volume 3, p185.

8 *The Citizen*, 25 August 1917.

9 *Supplement to the London Gazette*, Saturday, 4 October 1919.

[10] W R Torvaney, *Diverse Ditties* (Edinburgh: Pentland Press, 1997), pp90-91.

[11] *The Scotsman*, 9 October 1922.

[12] *The Evening Telegraph and Post*, 29 July 1939; *The Montrose Review*, 30 April 1959.

[13] *The Hawick Express*, 18 July 1935; *The Press and Journal*, 21 October 1965; *The Press and Journal*, 23 October 1965.

[14] *The Brechin Advertiser*, 18 June 1935.

[15] *The Brechin Advertiser*, 20 October 1942.

[16] *Montrose Standard and Angus and Mearns Register*, 28 June 1944.

[17] *Aberdeen Weekly Journal*, 8 October 1942.

[18] *The Press and Journal*, 23 October 1965.

[19] *The Press and Journal*, 21 October 1965; *The Press and Journal*, 23 October 1965.

[20] *The Press and Journal*, 2 December 1950.

[21] *The Press and Journal*, 23 October 1965.

[22] *The Press and Journal*, 23 October 1965.

[23] *The Press and Journal*, 21 October 1965.

[24] *The Press and Journal*, 21 October 1965.

[25] *The Press and Journal*, 23 October 1965.

[26] Torvaney, *Diverse Ditties*, pp44-45.

'A SEA OF MUD AND SHELL-HOLES'

THE 8TH BLACK WATCH AT PASSCHENDAELE, 12 OCTOBER 1917

Derek J Patrick

THE BATTLE OF PASSCHENDAELE (Third Battle of Ypres) is synonymous with much of what has characterised the Great War in Britain's collective memory. Fought between 31 July and 10 November 1917 with the objective of capturing the high ground to the south and east of the city of Ypres, shelling destroyed the fragile drainage system, and exacerbated by the wet weather, the waterlogged battlefield was likened to a 'sea of mud'.[1]

On 12 October 1917, the officers and men of the 8th Black Watch, 26th Brigade, 9th (Scottish) Division, were making final preparations for another attempt on Passchendaele. The 8th was a New Army battalion raised in August 1914, and had served with distinction at Loos, the Somme and Arras. At 7pm on 11 October, the battalion had left to take up its positions for the attack the following morning. From approximately 2am to 4am, the 8th was subjected to an intense gas bombardment, and, as a result, box respirators had to be worn. There was some confusion as A and B Companies had failed to locate any guides or markers and were unable to make contact with C and D Companies on the left, but all were in position by about 4am having suffered few casualties.[2] The battalion's *War Diary* records that at 'ZERO all four companies seem to have moved forward and got up close behind the barrage in their respective lines and advanced with it when it began to creep forward.'[3] From the outset, A Company was subjected to heavy rifle fire in the vicinity of Adler Farm. Shelling was heavy and as the company moved forward, it came under heavy machine-gun fire from both flanks, but making good progress reached its objective, where Captain Ian W W Shepherd ordered his men to halt and consolidate a line of shell-holes 'as far as the state of the ground would permit'.[4] B Company continued the advance under the command of Captain Peter James Alexander. Educated at Fettes and Baliol College, Oxford, he was the only son of James Alexander, Midfield, Perth, and had already received the Military Cross for gallantry.[5]

Pushing on to the final objective, B Company discovered a German pillbox, unmarked on the map, which was captured only after severe fighting. Captain Alexander was killed aged 23. His men endeavoured to 'dig in' but subjected to machine-gun fire from the front and both flanks, and with snipers active in the area, Second Lieutenant A L Milroy, the only remaining officer with the company, had few options and ordered the survivors to withdraw. That afternoon 'a small and apparently unorganised' German counterattack was driven off, but the new frontline was heavily shelled and machine guns and snipers were very active.[6] Milroy sent four messages to battalion headquarters as to his situation but none of the runners managed to get through.

On the left C Company was faring little better. The 'ragged' supporting barrage had caused several casualties, and after advancing 100 yards it was realised that the direction was wrong and too much to the left.[7] On reaching the enemy support lines the company was held up by snipers and machine-gun fire, which claimed a number of victims including the company commander, Lieutenant Hugh Barclay Dickson. Dickson was from Glasgow and educated at Glasgow Academy and Glasgow High School. He had been in Manila when war was declared but immediately returned to join the Army. Dickson was a well-known rugby player and had captained London Scottish. He was 29. His men managed to advance another 100 yards before consolidating a line of shell-holes 'it being realised that [any] further advance was impossible'.[8] No runners managed to get through to or from battalion headquarters until the morning of 13 October.

D Company had advanced 'half left' and lost direction as a result of 'there being no tapes or platoon discs and touch not having been gained with B Company on their right'.[9] Shortly after the advance began, the company was exposed to enfilade rifle and machine-gun fire from the direction of Oxford Houses. Lieutenant Alexander S Harper, with one section of 14 Platoon and Company headquarters, attempted to capture a German pillbox which was enfilading his command. All but the Company

Sergeant Major (CSM) were killed or wounded in the attempt.[10] The CSM reported the 'M.G. fire to have been the heaviest he [had] ever experienced and that the enemy offered the most determined resistance'.[11] Lieutenant Harper was the second son of William Harper, Tulliebelton, Perthshire, and had been educated at Elgin Academy and Aberdeen University, where he graduated with honours in Natural Science. He had completed his engagement in the Territorial Force before the war but re-enlisted on mobilisation in August 1914.[12] The remainder of his company consolidated what little ground had been gained, with C Company on its right.

The 8th's *War Diary* recorded several 'outstanding features of the attack'.[13] The battalion had lost direction, and companies had been unable to contact each other owing to the fact that it had been unable to assemble correctly. Heavy shelling had disrupted preparations for the attack and had caused severe casualties among the 'taping' party. Communications were a serious problem, and it had proved impossible to send runners either to or from battalion headquarters. The casualties among the runners were particularly heavy. It proved difficult, if not impossible, for the companies to recognise their objectives, 'almost all landmarks being obliterated by shellfire and everywhere and everything being a sea of mud and shell holes'.[14] The weather conditions were described as the worst of their kind. Heavy rain made movement extremely difficult, the ground being waterlogged and shell-holes more than half full of water. The battalion was much depleted and the medical officer, Captain G R B Grant, who had personally attended to the wounded in the open under heavy fire, estimated that it would be seven days at least before it would be in any state 'to undertake active operations'. He considered the supply of stretcher-bearers to be unequal to the demand, and their 'carry' was far too long considering the nature of the ground to be traversed.[15] The total casualties sustained by the 8th Battalion during the First Battle of Passchendaele were calculated at seven officers and 294 other ranks. This included three officers and 40 other ranks killed in action; four officers and 166 other ranks wounded; and a further 88 men listed as 'missing'. These figures were adjusted as wounded soldiers were recovered from the battlefield, and others succumbed to their injuries, with 25 suspected cases of shellshock added to the total.

The Commonwealth War Graves Commission records some three officers and 80 men of the battalion as having died on 12 October 1917. These include a large number from the traditional Black Watch recruiting districts of Fife, Perthshire, Dundee and Angus, with just over 60 per cent appearing to have some connection to at least one of these areas. These included 33-year-old Private Charles Rattray, a native of Dundee, whose father lived at 13 Miller's Wynd. Before the war Rattray was employed as a miner at Bowhill in Fife.[16] Private Alexander Cowper was born in Errol, Perthshire, and had enlisted in July 1916. Before the outbreak of war, he was employed at Stanley Mills, six miles to the north of Perth. Private Cowper had not been at the front a year when he was killed in action at Passchendaele aged 25.[17]

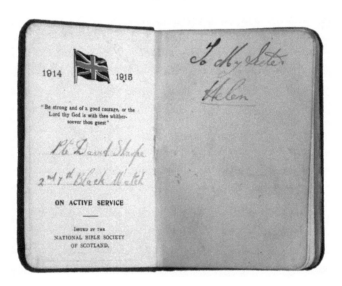

THE SOLDIER'S BIBLE PRIVATE DAVID SHARP GIFTED
TO HIS SISTER BEFORE LEAVING FOR FRANCE
(Derek Patrick)

Like the families of Privates Rattray and Cowper, my own would receive a War Office telegram bearing the news that a son and brother had lost his life on 12 October 1917. Private David Sharp, 8th Black Watch, a 19-year-old miner, from Melville Street, Lochgelly, Fife, had joined the army in 1914. His sister, my great-grandmother, received a letter from a second lieutenant in his company, describing the manner of his death. He wrote:

> From what eye-witnesses tell me, your brother's death must have been instantaneous and painless. He was killed by the concussion of a shell which exploded close where he was standing...Your brother had been in my platoon for several months and I had a most implicit confidence in him and his abilities, and if any special work requiring exercise of unusual care and skill had to be undertaken I always felt it could be left to him with the fullest assurance that it would be executed thoroughly and conscientiously and his knowledge and experience have been extremely useful to me on many occasions...I am sure he has met the kind of death he would have preferred and will leave behind him a memory of which all his relations may well be proud.

No photograph of David Sharp is known to survive, and like most of his comrades who fell on 12 October he has no known grave. His name appears on the Tyne Cot Memorial, West-Vlaanderen, Belgium, which commemorates some 35,000 British and Commonwealth soldiers whose graves are not known. David's *New Testament*, with its short dedication to my great-grandmother, a treasured family memento, is one of the few tangible reminders of one young man's sacrifice; one of almost 500,000 killed or wounded at Passchendaele.

[1] A G Wauchope, *A History of the Black Watch in the Great War, 1914-18*, Volume 3 (London: Medici Society, 1926), p46.

[2] Wauchope, *History*, Volume 3, p44.

[3] The National Archives, WO95/1766/2, 12 October 1917.

[4] Wauchope, *History*, Volume 3, p45.

[5] *The Stirling Observer and Perthshire Herald*, 3 November 1917.

[6] Wauchope, *History*, Volume 3, p45.

[7] The National Archives, WO95/1766/2, 12 October 1917.

[8] Wauchope, *History*, Volume 3, p46.

[9] The National Archives, WO95/1766/2, 12 October 1917.

[10] Wauchope, *History*, Volume 3, p46.

[11] The National Archives, WO95/1766/2, 12 October 1917.

[12] *The Aberdeen Daily Journal*, 24 October 1917.

[13] The National Archives, WO95/1766/2, 12 October 1917.

[14] The National Archives, WO95/1766/2, 12 October 1917.

[15] Wauchope, *History*, Volume 3, p47.

[16] *The Courier and Argus*, 4 December 1917.

[17] *The Courier and Argus*, 8 November 1917.

CAPTIVITY AND THE KAISERSCHLACHT

MAKING CONNECTIONS A HUNDRED YEARS ON

Gordon Millar

THERE WERE NEVER any Great War stories in my family or discussions about battle painting by the famous Scottish artist Robert Gibb, because by and large the war and paintings were not a common topic of conversation, yet in 2018 it turned out that both things were loosely connected in the story of our family. The only exception to all of that was a hazy recollection of my maternal grandmother who used to tell me a story of her father, Robert Balfour, having lumps of metal in his leg that as a girl she used to be able to touch and move about. She was the eldest of Robert's family of four daughters while the youngest daughter Margaret celebrated her 90th birthday in 2019.

My great grandfather Robert Balfour was born on 25 August 1897 in Kirkcaldy to parents, James and Janet Balfour who lived at 13 Glassworks Street. Prior to the outbreak of the Great War, Robert worked as an apprentice moulder with a local firm, Messrs Douglas & Grant. He enlisted in 1915, soon after his 18th birthday, as Private S/40729 Robert Balfour, 8th (Service) Battalion Royal Highlanders, The Black Watch, but according to his Medal Index Card he did not serve overseas until some time in 1916.

Over the years, my grandmother became aware of my growing interest in the Great War through my attendance at the Western Front Association meetings and gave me two old black and white posed photographs of Robert in his uniform: one of him with three comrades and one in uniform standing alone. The picture of Robert standing alone intrigued me most. It showed him wearing a bonnet with a feather on it and with two stripes on his arm. I now know the feather to have been a Red Hackle, and the two stripes on his left arm as I found out later were wound stripes.

My grandmother's story of her father having metal lumps in his leg accounted for one of the wound stripes, and while today it is assumed that any grenade or shell fragments would have been removed as a matter of routine, it seems that was not always the case. One incident of this practice was reported in the *Fifeshire Advertiser* after the fight at Aubers Ridge:

PRIVATE ROBERT BALFOUR
(Balfour Family).

Notes from the trenches

Corporal Robert L Brown, 1st Black Watch, Kinghorn (wounded on May 9) :- 'I am carrying a scrap iron heap about me as a result of a bomb wound in the right knee in five places, a shrapnel wound in the right arm and shoulder, and a bullet wound in the left leg'.

Once overseas, Robert joined the 8th Battalion in time to take part in the Battle of the Somme and appears to have been present at the action at Delville Wood:

14th July – Assaulted the village of Longueval at 3.25am.
At the SE corner of the village a strong-point gave trouble
and did not fall till 5pm. With this exception all objectives of
the Battalion were attained by 10am. By 18th July along
with the South Africans, Delville Wood fell into our hands.
Total 8th Battalion Black Watch casualties for July 1916:
Other Ranks Killed = 86: Wounded 370: Missing 71: Died of
Wounds 13: Total Casualties = 540.[2]

Private Robert Balfour survived the Battle of the Somme, but his
second wound was reported in the *Fife Free Press* in a brief announcement
in a style very familiar to the readers of local newspapers during the war:

Information has been received by Mrs Balfour, 13 Glassworks
Street, Kirkcaldy, that her son, Private Robert Balfour, Black
Watch, has been wounded by gunshot in the right arm and is
at present in Leicester hospital.[3]

There is scant surviving detail about Robert Balfour's service, but his
Medal Rolls shows he served with three different Black Watch battalions:
firstly, with the 8th Battalion, from which he was transferred to the 1st
Battalion and finally he served in the 7th Battalion. How long my great-
grandfather served with each Black Watch battalion is unclear, but it is
possible that his transfers were linked to his injuries. The only clue to
this comes from the *8th Battalion War Diary* in a note that four other
ranks were wounded on 13 March which is consistent with the newspaper
report of his wounding that appeared on 2 April 1917. After recovery, it is
likely that he would have been posted with a reinforcement draft to
whichever battalion needed them which would account for service in the
8th, then the 1st and finally the 7th Battalion.

Thereafter, we hear nothing of Robert until a letter in the *Fifeshire
Advertiser* of 4 May 1918 entitled 'Local Soldiers Missing'. Robert's parents
also received official intimation that he had been missing since between
21 and 26 March 1918. The earlier date was the beginning of the
German offensive known as the *Kaiserschlacht*; on that day at 5am a

German barrage of 'great violence and accuracy' fell on the whole forward area held by the 7th Battalion. The bombardment completely destroyed the frontline trenches and few survivors of 'C' and 'D' Companies were able to get back to the battalion's headquarters. As a member of 15 Platoon, 'D' Company, it is likely Robert was captured at that point.

News of his capture and survival was published in the *Fifeshire Advertiser* of 4 May 1918. A short article in the *Fife Free Press* (8 June 1918) stated that his mother had received a postcard from him to say that he was a prisoner of war and was in good health. He was taken to a POW camp at Parchim, North East Germany, and after one month was transferred to Friedrichsfeld, also in Germany. There he remained until he was released at the end of the Great War on 15 November 1918. A few days after Robert's capture, with an Allied defeat likely, and after he had begun the long march into captivity, Sir Douglas Haig issued his famous Special Order of the Day (11 April 1918) often known as the 'Backs to the Wall' order.

It is at this point that the second half of this piece begins. I had become aware through a newsletter sent out by Forfar Library in 1996 of the existence of Robert Gibbs' painting *Backs to the Wall*. Later, in 2014, at a meeting between the Angus Branch of The Black Watch Association and Angus Museums & Galleries to work out how the branch could help with the Great War commemoration in the county, one of the Angus Museums & Galleries officers insisted that the Association members view a big old painting in the store. That picture was in fact *Backs to the Wall*, the last battle painting by Robert Gibb commissioned by W J Webster of Denley, Arbroath, and gifted to the Arbroath Burgh Collection in 1932.[4] What the painting showed was the aftermath of the capture of Robert Balfour and what was required of those who survived the opening days of the *Kaiserschlacht*.

Later in 2014, I wrote to Arbroath Library to ask if *Backs to the Wall* would be displayed during the Great War commemoration and particularly in 2018, the centenary of the famous order of the same name. Sadly, the answer was no, mainly because exhibition space was required for displays centred on the centenary of the formation of the Girl Guides. After intervention by Major Ronnie Proctor, Chairman of the Angus Branch, the painting was exhibited in Arbroath Library, its original home.

For those who have never seen Gibb's *Backs to the Wall*, once seen it is unlikely to be forgotten. Gibb is best known for his paintings of Scottish soldiers – such as *The Thin Red Line* and *Forward 42nd* – and for showing Scottish soldiers formed up in line at a moment of decision when a fight can be won or lost. *Backs to the Wall* is very similar. A line of mostly Scottish troops, khaki aprons covering their kilts, stand defiant, bayonets fixed, rifles either at the on guard or ready position. It is clear that action is imminent: this is the moment of trial and judging by the wounded and dead Germans, an earlier attack had failed, but from the expressions on the faces of the men in the line the enemy is coming on again. In the background is what looks like a heavenly host watching the action; exactly who they are remains a mystery. Perhaps they were the 'Angels of Mons' who, legend tells, protected the British Army during the Battle of Mons, or the spirits of the fallen who had come to witness the last great battle. Looking along the ranks, the artist makes the viewer aware of just how young many of the men of 1918 were. That year manpower shortages were so desperate that the age a soldier could be sent overseas to fight was lowered to 18. The two men of the left of the painting give the distinct impression of being around that age. Even the wounded are manning the firing line. Even so, wounded, exhausted and ragged, the whole line reeks defiance, and in that sense their backs truly are against the wall.

In 2018, cleaned and restored to pride of place in Arbroath Library, a special public viewing of *Backs to the Wall* was held at which members of the Webster family were present, along with members of The Black Watch Association and pupils from the local schools which had been included in the Angus Branch school visits programme arranged on the day the Association members first saw the painting. As one of the spectators, and as an associate member of the Angus Branch and a member of the Tayside Branch of the Western Front Association, even at that point I was unaware of the connection between the *Kaiserschlacht*, the capture of Robert Balfour and the painting. It was only later, and after researching the story of my grandfather that the penny finally dropped – with an almighty clang!

1 *Fifeshire Advertiser*, 29 May 1915.

2 *8th Battalion War Diary*, 14 July 1916.

3 *Fife Free Press*, 28 April 1917.

4 A family member, Second Lieutenant Joseph F Webster, whose portrait hangs in the Webster Hall, Arbroath, was commissioned into The Black Watch in the first days of the war, then attached to the Gordons. He was killed in action on 30 October 1914.

'FIFE SOLDIERS ESCAPE FROM CAPTIVITY'

Derek J Patrick

T HE 7TH (FIFE) BATTALION, The Black Watch, had taken over the frontline trenches at Louverval on 1 March 1918. There were rumours of an imminent German offensive reinforced by increased activity behind enemy lines. The battalion anticipated action and, according to its official historian, 'all ranks were now eager for a fight and it was in that spirit that the 7th met the German offensive'.[1]

At 5am on the morning of 21 March, 'the enemy barrage fell with great violence and accuracy on the whole of the forward area'.[2] The intense bombardment, comprising high explosive and gas shells, all but destroyed the frontline trenches and only a few survivors of C and D Companies were able to withdraw to battalion headquarters.

The *War Diary* recorded that the 'morning was extremely misty and it was difficult at first to realise the presence of gas'.[3] German infantry was seen advancing at 10am by which time the frontline was 'practically obliterated'.[4] The Black Watch 'resisted gallantly' but outflanked and under increasing pressure, the survivors were compelled to withdraw to the Beaumetz-Morchies road, which was held by A Company, approximately 60 strong, and by the remainder of the battalion – some 30 men.[5]

On 22 March, the 7th Black Watch's position was subjected to a series of four bombardments, and an infantry assault shortly after 5pm. The battalion was again compelled to withdraw and occupied a line south of the Bapaume-Cambrai road. The 7th Battalion now numbered two officers, Colonel McClintock, DSO, and Captain Reid, MC, and only 30 other ranks.

In the coming days, the battalion with what remained of the rest of the 51st (Highland) Division would fight a series of actions as the German Army continued to advance. The division received a German message in recognition of its resilience, 'Good old 51st. Still sticking it?'.[6]

The 7th Black Watch had ceased to be a unit in itself and was now part of a composite '51st Division Force' until finally relieved at midnight on 25 March. The losses sustained during the German offensive were estimated to be in the region of 23 officers and 627 other ranks out of a strength of some 39 officers and 941 men.[7]

LANCE CORPORAL ANDREW HARROWER
(Erika Wilson)

The losses included Lance Corporal Andrew Harrower, Corporal David Mills and Private William Moyes who were listed as missing. Both Mills and Moyes had been captured by the advancing Germans on 21 March.[8] Moyes recalled the enemy attacking in 'overwhelming numbers, being mowed down terribly in his advance by machine-gun fire'.[9] Finding themselves cut off and outflanked Moyes and his surviving comrades had no option but to destroy their machine guns and give up. Harrower was taken prisoner the following day as he was having supper in a dugout: 'The Germans were at the entrance before we knew anything; one bomb was thrown down the stairs by them, and we had to surrender'.[10]

Taken to Villers-lès-Cagnicourt with some 600 British prisoners of war, the men experienced considerable hardship. At Wallers they were secured in 'an old dirty cotton factory'.[11] The conditions were poor: 'no bedding, very bad sanitary arrangements, not able to wash, no doctor...

one quarter of a loaf per day, and some coffee substitute, and a drink of barley soup, was our day's ration'.[12]

The camp at Marquion was no better. The captives were placed in a 'filthy barn' where it 'was so cold we had to keep fires going at night and sit round them in order to keep warm'. Food was in short supply: 'Some of the boys found a dead horse and cut it up and ate it, they were so hungry'.[13]

The conditions in the camp at Villers-lès-Cagnicourt were equally bad. The men were billeted in 'a church with a huge hole in the roof'. Harrower described it as being 'in a filthy condition; it had been used as a stable, and we had to clean out the dung and filthy straw before we could lie down'.[14] The camp held approximately 1,500 British prisoners who paraded at 5.30 every morning and were sent out in working parties. Harrower's job was 'salvage of shells and burying the dead' in the vicinity of Bullecourt:

> Most of our dead were mere skeletons with a few rags on, and
> had evidently been there for a very long time. All their boots
> had been taken and there were no discs on the bodies.[15]

SERGEANT ANDREW HARROWER, MM
In Home Guard uniform
(*Erika Wilson*)

He recalled burying the body of at least one Australian soldier, who had almost certainly fallen at Bullecourt in April 1917. Describing the work as 'very severe', Harrower and his comrades 'were all in an utterly exhausted condition from lack of food. It was no use going sick as there was no doctor nearer than four miles, and he did not strike one off work unless absolutely useless and done in'.[16] The captives worked from about 6.30am to about 2pm each day with artillery shells falling only a few hundred yards away. Mills and Moyes recalled 'men so weak from want of food, they were fainting every day'.[17]

The Bavarian Guards could be 'somewhat harsh in their treatment of the [prisoners]'.[18] Harrower remembered 'one big brute who thrashed some of our chaps pretty badly', and an officer who allegedly gave the order that any man who 'shirked work' should be shot.[19] There was no writing or receiving letters and the prisoners' cherished cigarettes were confiscated and sold back to them at 'enormous prices'. The guards were encouraged by the success of the offensive but, according to Lance Corporal Harrower, believed that 'they must have a complete victory within three months or they would be beaten on account of the food question'.[20]

This was the captives' daily routine until the evening of 18 April when, accompanied by Corporal Charles Mottershead, 9th Royal Welsh Fusiliers, the four men made their escape, reaching their own lines the following morning. Describing the escape, Moyes explained how 'two of them went out past the sentry telling him they were going to the well for some water. They energetically worked the pump until their other pal came out for the same purpose, and then made a bolt'.[21] Exchanging their kilts for discarded French civilian clothes they 'ran and walked and crawled' a distance of some 20 miles guided by the sound of the guns and occasional star shell.[22] At about 3.30am, the four fugitives were challenged by a sentry and immediately 'thought the game was up'.[23] However, as luck would have it, they had somehow managed to slip through the lightly defended German frontline and reach a Canadian outpost.

Shortly afterwards, the men were granted leave. Corporal Mills' parents, 69 Balsusney Road, Kirkcaldy, had not heard from their son since the start of the German offensive. Fearing the worst 'they got a huge surprise when the door opened and [their] missing son walked in'.[24] There were similar reunions when Lance Corporal Harrower, a Fife coal-miner, reached his home in Arthur Street, Cowdenbeath, and Private Moyes, only 19 and already wearing two wound stripes on his uniform sleeve, arrived at Dalgleish Street, Tayport.[25]

The remarkable story almost immediately appeared in the local press and the Fife escapees were lauded for their exploits. In recognition 'of [their] gallant conduct and determination displayed in escaping...from captivity', Lance Corporal Harrower, Corporal Mills and Private Moyes, 7th Black Watch, and Corporal Mottershead, 9th Royal Welsh Fusiliers were awarded the Military Medal.[26] The men of 'Fife's Own' had more than upheld the fine reputation of the regiment's Territorial soldiers.

1 A G Wauchope, *A History of the Black Watch in the Great War, 1914-18*, Volume 2 (London: Medici Society, 1926), p299.

2 A G Wauchope, *History,* Volume 2, p299.

3 The National Archives, WO95/2879/3, 21 March 1918.

4 The National Archives, WO95/2879/3, 21 March 1918.

5 The National Archives, WO95/2879/3, 21 March 1918.

6 A G Wauchope, *History,* Volume 2, p300.

7 A G Wauchope, *History,* Volume 2, p301.

8 The National Archives, WO/161/100/173.

9 *The Fifeshire Advertiser*, 4 May 1918, p7.

10 The National Archives, WO/161/100/171.

11 The National Archives, WO/161/100/173.

12 The National Archives, WO/161/100/173.

13 The National Archives, WO/161/100/171.

14 The National Archives, WO/161/100/171.

15 The National Archives, WO/161/100/171.

16 The National Archives, WO/161/100/171.

17 The National Archives, WO/161/100/173.

18 The National Archives, WO/161/100/173.

19 The National Archives, WO/161/100/171.

20 The National Archives, WO/161/100/171.

21 *The Fifeshire Advertiser*, 4 May 1918.

22 *The Fifeshire Advertiser*, 4 May 1918.

23 *The Fifeshire Advertiser*, 4 May 1918.

24 *The Fifeshire Advertiser*, 27 April 1918.

25 *The Fifeshire Advertiser*, 4 May 1918.

26 *Supplement to the London Gazette*, 30 January 1920.

THE AWARD OF THE *CROIX DE GUERRE* TO THE 6TH (PERTHSHIRE) BATTALION

Roddy Riddell

THE FRENCH *Croix de Guerre* (literally the 'Cross of War') was established on 8 April 1915 by the French government, to recognise acts of bravery by individuals and units in the face of the enemy, specifically mentioned in despatches. The different classes of despatch may be recognised by the emblem on the ribbon. For an 'Army Despatch', this was the *'palme en bronze'*. During the Great War, 12 units of the British Army received this award, of which two were Scottish: the 6th Black Watch and the 12th Argyll and Sutherland Highlanders.[1] The *Croix de Guerre* was awarded to the 6th (Perthshire) Battalion, The Black Watch, for the actions which took place between 20 and 30 July 1918.

Attached to the French 5th Army, as part of the 51st (Highland) Division, the 6th Battalion took part in the Second Battle of the Marne in 1918, when the advance of the German Army towards Paris was halted and turned into a hasty retreat.[2] The splendid deeds of the 6th Battalion under the command of Lieutenant-Colonel Francis Rowland Tarleton, DSO, during the period 20-30 July 1918, culminated after seven days of intense fighting, in the successful storming of a well-fortified and stubbornly defended wood. During the battle, the battalion was reduced to fewer than 140 (all ranks) and they suffered grievously. Twenty-six officers were listed as killed, wounded or missing and 428 other ranks were listed as killed, wounded or posted as missing. This battle was known as the Battle of Tardenois and was awarded as a regimental battle honour. The 6th Battalion was presented with the *Croix de Guerre* on 12 July 1919 in Paris when the medal was pinned to the regimental Colours by General Berdoulat, the Military Governor of Paris.

For many years, the officers and men of the 6th Battalion proudly wore the ribbon of the *Croix de Guerre* on the sleeve of their service dress jacket and as late as 1999, officers and men of the 3rd (Volunteer) Battalion, The Black Watch, wore the ribbon on the left shoulder of their service dress jackets; and officers and SNCOs wore the *fourragère* (a braided cord).

PIPE BANNER WITH CROIX DE GUERRE
Perth Branch, The Black Watch (Royal Highland Regiment) Association
*(Perth Branch President, The Black Watch
(Royal Highland Regiment) Association)*

The deeds of the 6th Battalion are commemorated annually at the '*Croix de Guerre* Dinner', which is organised and run by the Perth Branch of The Black Watch (Royal Highland Regiment) Association. In early 2018, the president of the Perth Branch invited Pipe Major Alistair Duthie to write a pipe tune to celebrate and commemorate the 100th anniversary of the battle. A centenary dinner was held in Perth on 29 September 2018 at which Pipe Major Duthie, carrying the 98-year-old pipe banner of the 6th Battalion, played the newly composed tune 'The *Croix de Guerre*'. Among the guests were the French Consul General in Scotland, Emmanuel Cocher, and Brigadier-General Hervé Bizeul, Deputy Commander 1st (UK) Division.

'THE CROIX DE GUERRE'
Pipe march by Pipe Major Alistair Duthie
(Pipe Major Alistair Reid)

1 Geoffrey Archer Parfitt, *The Award of the French Croix de Guerre, 1914-1918, to units of the British Army* (Shrewsbury: 4th Battalion KSLI (TA), 1963), np.

2 For a detailed account of the action at the Second Battle of the Marne see A G Wauchope, *A History of the Black Watch in the Great War, 1914-18*, Volume 2 (London: Medici Society, 1926), pp191-197, 202-203.

The *Croix de Guerre*, Buzancy and The Black Watch

Speech made at the Perth Branch of the Black Watch (Royal Highland Regiment) Association '*Croix de Guerre* Dinner' in the Salutation Hotel on 28 September 2018

by Lieutenant-General Sir Alistair Irwin

'PROVOST, M. le Conseil General, M. Le General de Brigade, ladies and gentlemen.

I am delighted to have been asked to say a few words before we eat, not only as a Black Watch man but also because by a happy coincidence my wife's father was himself the recipient of a *Croix de Guerre* in the closing stages of the Second World War – I have his medal here.

As we approach the climax of the centenary commemorations of more than four years of war, it seems more than appropriate that we should remember a great honour bestowed on only 11 other British battalions by the French 100 years ago. A year later, led by their commanding officer Colonel William Green, himself an officer of the Legion D'Honneur, a small party of Black Watch men attended the moving ceremony in Paris on 12th July 1919 at which the Military Governor of Paris, General Berdoulat, presented the *Croix de Guerre* in the presence of the French and Colonial troops assembled for the Victory March. The General pinned the Cross to the regimental Colours of the 6th Battalion and kissed the Colours before shaking hands with Colonel Green. Amidst much emotion the national anthems of our two great nations were played. It was an honour that meant a great deal at the time and which, as this dinner testifies, is quite rightly still considered a great honour to this day.

It is a powerful and treasured symbol of the close links that The Black Watch has had with our French comrades. In July 1918, at more or less the same time that the 6th Battalion was earning its *Croix de Guerre*, our 4/5th Battalion, along with the 8th Battalion, Seaforth Highlanders, took part in an attack at Buzancy near Soissons. A month after the battle General Horne commanding the British 1st Army received a letter from General Gassouin commanding the French 17th Division in which he stated that he had set up his HQ in Buzancy in which he said:

> I found there traces still fresh of the exploits of your Scottish soldiers and could see clearly what hard fighting you had to gain possession of the village. Wishing to leave on the spot some lasting tribute to the bravery of your soldiers I told one of my officers to erect a small monument. On it there are inscribed the words: '*Ici fleurira toujours le glorieux chardon d'ecosse parmi les roses de France*' ('Here the noble thistle of Scotland will flourish for ever among the roses of France.') The monument is erected on the highest point of the plateau where we found the body of the Scottish soldier who had advanced the farthest.

MEMORIAL AT BUZANCY
A gift from the 17th French Division to the 15th Scottish Division.
(Alistair Irwin)

The monument can still be seen in all its moving glory in the Commonwealth War Graves Commission cemetery in Buzancy.

There is a touching follow up to this. When our 1st Battalion was stationed in West Berlin in 1987 we made particular friends with the 11ème Chasseurs who had also been present at the battle for Buzancy. In a memorable ceremony in their barracks they named one of their AMX 30 tanks 'Buzancy The Black Watch'. It was a marvellous gesture which amongst other things resulted in the crew of that tank being presented to Her Majesty Queen Elizabeth the Queen Mother when she came to visit the battalion later that year.

So the sentiments associated with the *Croix de Guerre* have rightly lived on. They will perhaps come to our minds again when Pipe Major Alastair Duthie plays for us the tune he has especially composed for this occasion in memory of all ranks of the 6th Battalion who fought and of the great honour done to our regiment by France all those years ago.

———————

'HOSTILITIES WILL CEASE... AND TROOPS WILL STAND FAST...'

MONS, BELGIUM, 11 NOVEMBER 1918

Earl John Chapman

THE ALLIED SUCCESS at the Battle of Amiens (8-11 August 1918) led to an aggressive series of offensives on the Western Front known as the 'Hundred Days Offensive'. This campaign put the German armies into full retreat eastward out of France and Belgium, fighting as they gave back territory to their pursuers.[1] In the final weeks of the campaign, the Canadian Corps took the French town of Valenciennes after a vicious two-day battle. By 9 November, they were on the outskirts of Mons, a regional coalmining centre whose resources had helped fuel Germany's war effort throughout the conflict.

In the early days of the war, British troops had put up a fierce resistance around Mons in an effort to slow down the German advance towards Paris. After pushing the British out of Mons, the Germans had occupied the town for four years. Recapturing Mons now, at the end of the war, was of huge symbolic importance to the Allies.

The Canadian Corps, under the command of Lieutenant-General Arthur Currie, had been ordered to take Mons. To spare the city as much as possible, Currie ordered an encircling manoeuvre: the 2nd Canadian Infantry Division, moving around the southern outskirts, was to seize the high ground to the east; while the 3rd Canadian Infantry Division was to infiltrate into the heart of the city (this task was assigned to the 7th Canadian Infantry Brigade which included the 42nd Battalion, Royal Highlanders of Canada.[2] While the German Army may have reached 'the end of its metaphorical rope' in the summer of 1918, there were still plenty of grim, unbending soldiers willing to carry on fighting to the very end. Many German soldiers demonstrated an unbelievable resilience, contesting every yard of ground 'despite the dawning realization that their cause was hopeless', their sacrificed lives buying time for their comrades to continue the resistance.[3] Rumours also filled the Allied ranks of a possible peace treaty in the works, but until there was a formal armistice, the war would go on – but no-one wanted to be the last casualty.[4]

'TAKING A REST'
In the early morning hours of 11 November 1918, battle-weary soldiers of the 42nd Battalion, Royal Highlanders of Canada, rest in the Grand Place, Mons. For the 42nd Battalion, the war was over.
(Library and Archives Canada, PA-003570)

At about 11pm on 10 November, platoons of the 42nd Battalion and the Royal Canadian Regiment entered the Grand Place (the city's main square) – the first Allied troops to enter the historic square after more than four years of war.[5] By daybreak on Monday, 11 November, all four battalions of the 7th Canadian Infantry Brigade had penetrated the city and within a short period of time, Mons had been mopped up with out-posts established on the high ground on the eastern outskirts – all without the use of excessive heavy shelling. The pursuit of the retreating Germans continued without a stop, and Canadian troops were already eight kilo-metres to the northeast of Mons at the time of the Armistice at 11am.

Lieutenant Louis Hodgins Biggar, the 42nd Battalion's 21-year-old signalling officer, and Lieutenant Jordayne Wyamarus Cave, the battalion's 32-year-old scout officer, were the first officers to enter the Mons Hôtel de Ville (City Hall) where they established battalion headquarters and set up the battalion's telephone communication system.[6] In August 1916, Biggar had obtained a commission straight out of the McGill Canadian Officers' Training Corps contingent and had transferred to the 42nd the following year, while in June 1918, Cave had won a battlefield commission after long and meritorious service as a non-commissioned officer.

At about 9am, Lieutenant Biggar received telephone confirmation of the Armistice:

> Hostilities will cease at 1100 [hours] Nov. 11th. Troops will stand fast on line reached at that hour which will be reported to Brigade HQ. Defensive precautions will be maintained. There will be no intercourse of any description with the enemy. Further instructions follow.

Instructions were immediately sent out to the four companies of the 42nd, scattered about the city, ordering that no further offensive operations were to take place 'but all precautions would be taken to defend the line then held, outposts would be established, and the companies distributed in depth'.[7]

As the hour of the Armistice approached, a silence descended on the battlefield as guns ceased firing for the first time in four years. The general mood of the frontline troops 'was one of weary reflection, a distinct contrast to the celebrations that sent crowds spilling into the streets in cities farther behind the lines'.[8] No sooner had Lieutenants Biggar and Cave entered the Grand Place when the 'Gold Book' was taken out of the City Hall vaults 'where it had lain for over four years'.[9] The two officers had the distinction of being the first Allied soldiers to sign the book – the previous entry was that of King Albert of Belgium who had signed it in 1913 on his first visit to Mons after ascending to the throne.[10]

Interestingly, detachments of The Black Watch of Scotland had been near Mons at the beginning of the war, and as soon as the inhabitants saw the men of the 42nd Battalion in November 1918 they shouted out 'we knew you would come back'.[11] The following day, a funeral was held for those Canadians killed during the advance into Mons, including four soldiers of the Royal Highlanders of Canada who were killed on 10 November:

Lance Corporal Bernard Robert Jones, 418571
Private Thomas Mills, 228793
Private Joseph Andrew Daigle, 793792
Private Benjamin Brigden, 466663

All funeral arrangements were taken over by the city and in the words of the *42nd Battalion War Diary*, 'no other British soldiers had had such an elaborate and memorable funeral as these'. They were buried with all military honours, including a 25-man firing party; their graves placed in a commanding position on the right of the men of the 1st British Infantry Division who gave their lives in an effort to stem the German advance in the first days of the war. According to author C B Topp:

> Mons will always be a colourful name in the annals of the British Army. It is almost symbolic of the glory of the epic retreat of the 'Old Contemptibles' in the anxious days of August 1914, and by a strange coincidence the advance to victory had reached Mons when hostilities ceased. It was inevitable therefore that Mons should be the centre of popular interest in the swift moving events of the last hours of the war.[12]

Certainly, Mons will remain a cherished memory of Canada's Black Watch, what with the capture of the city by its 42nd Battalion and the ceremonies which followed:

> The pipe band played itself into the city about 07.00 Hours and created tremendous enthusiasm. Thousands of civilians lined the streets and the Grand Place, and the Battalion was given such a welcome as it had never seen before. Men, women and children vied with one another in expressing their hospitality – hot coffee, cognac and wines were distributed with the utmost generosity. Soldiers were everywhere embraced and kissed. In a few moments the whole city was bedecked with flags, flying from every window.[13]

'THE PIPE BAND PLAYED ITSELF INTO THE CITY'
Elements of the 42nd Battalion, Royal Highlanders of Canada, led by its pipe band,
proudly marches through the streets of Mons, 11 November 1918.
(Library and Archive Canada, PA-0035470)

'WELCOME TO MONS'
Officers of the 42nd Battalion, Royal Highlanders of Canada, are welcomed
by the Bourgmestre of Mons, 11 November 1918.
(The Black Watch Castle and Museum)

At 11am, the precise hour of the ceasefire, the Mayor of Mons (Bourgmestre Jean Lescarts) formally welcomed Brigadier-General John Clark, commander of the 7th Canadian Infantry Brigade, in honour of the capture of the city by units under his command. Elements of the brigade (as could be safely withdrawn from the line) were formed up *en masse* and after the ceremony there was a march past, led by the pipe band of the 42nd Battalion. Unfortunately, only one company, together with headquarters details, were able to participate in this parade as three companies were still holding the outpost line. According to the battalion's *War Diary*, 'the great square was filled with civilians and the troops got tremendous applause as they marched out'. Enthusiasm reached its zenith during the afternoon when General Currie rode into the city with his staff, escorted by the British 5th (Royal Irish) Lancers – the last British regiment to leave Mons in 1914 and the first to enter in 1918. Formed up in the Grand Place was a half-company of troops from every unit in the 3rd Canadian Infantry Division. Again, according the *War Diary*, General Currie's appearance 'provoked the wildest enthusiasm from the civilians who were packed solidly on the four sides of the square and crowded on the balconies and windows...the bands played the Belgian National Anthem which the people sang with great fervor'.[14] At this time, General Currie presented a Canadian flag to the city, appropriately tied to a lance. The final *War Diary* entry for 11 November reads:

> The day was the most memorable in the history of the 42nd Canadian Battalion by virtue of the fact that it was our good fortune to have the honour to capture the most historic city in the annals of the war.

On 27 November, the King of Belgium paid an official visit to Mons. A guard of honour was furnished by the 3rd Canadian Infantry Division, one battalion in each brigade providing 100 men. The 42nd was 'accorded the honour' of representing the 7th Canadian Infantry Brigade. At 11am on 5 December, His Majesty King George V passed through the city accompanied by the Prince of Wales and Prince Albert. There was no official parade but the 42nd Battalion 'lined both sides of the Grand Place' where the king received 'a rousing reception'.[15]

Finally, on 11 December, one month after the Armistice, the 42nd Battalion marched out of Mons heading to Bois-d'Haine, a distance of about 25 kilometres, where they went into billets. From this date until 11 March 1919, the 42nd were mainly concerned with the multitudinous duties involved in preparing for demobilisation. On 1 March 1919, in Liverpool, the battalion embarked on the White Star steamer *Adriatic*, arriving at Halifax nine days later. They immediately boarded a special troop train and after travelling most of the way through a heavy snowstorm, reached Montreal on the morning of 11 March, exactly four months after it had entered Mons on Armistice Day.

The 42nd had the good fortune to be the first of the Montreal-based battalions to return and was 'greeted with a moving demonstration of the heartfelt pride of the city in its achievements'.[16] Within 15 minutes of the train's arrival at the Place Viger Station, the battalion was on parade and soon to begin its last march through the city. The parade was led by the brass band of the 4th Garrison Regiment followed by a company of the 5th Regiment Royal Highlanders of Canada and the Highland

THE FINAL MARCH
The 42nd wheeling from St. Catherine Street
into Peel Street, Montreal, 11 March 1919.
(The Black Watch Castle and Museum)

Cadets; next were the veterans led by the 42nd's original commander, Lieutenant-Colonel George Cantlie, after whom marched the 42nd led by its pipe band. As the 42nd passed in review on the Champ de Mars, a dense crowd of 20,000 relatives and friends greeted it. The march continued along a cheering St James Street, up Beaver Hall Hill, left on St Catherine Street, and finally wheeling right on Peel Street to the Peel Street Barracks.[17] There, a last salute to the Colours was given, followed by Lieutenant-Colonel Royal Ewing's last command to his beloved 42nd, 'Dis-miss'. At once, the officers and men broke ranks and rushed to their families surrounding the building. Thus, passed out of existence the second expeditionary force battalion of the 5th Regiment, Royal Highlanders of Canada. The 5th Regiment, Royal Highlanders of Canada is today known as The Black Watch (Royal Highland Regiment) of Canada.

In 1927, an eight-foot bronze plaque, presented by the Canadian Battlefield Memorial Commission, was inaugurated under the porches of the Mons City Hall, honouring the soldiers of the 3rd Canadian Infantry Division which liberated the city on 11 November 1918:

> Mons was recaptured by the Canadian Corps on 11th November 1918: After fifty months of German occupation, freedom was restored to the City: Here was fired the last shot of the Great War.

The Canadian Corps had finished the war with a symbolic success, 'one which emphasized their status as one of the finest forces on the Western Front'.[18] Since 8 August, they had engaged some 68 German divisions, taken 31,537 prisoners, captured 623 guns, 2,842 machine guns and 336 trench mortars. They had also suffered some 45,830 casualties during the 'Hundred Days Offensive' – the *quid pro quo* of any assault force. Truly it was a magnificent achievement.

1 Canadians were to fight in Belgium on three separate occasions during the First World War, twice in the Ypres Salient and once on the way to final victory at Mons.

2 The 7th Canadian Infantry Brigade, the senior brigade of the 3rd Canadian Infantry Division, was commanded by Brigadier-General John Clark. The brigade consisted of four infantry battalions: The Royal Canadian Regiment, Princess Patricia's Canadian Light Infantry, 42nd Battalion, Royal Highlanders of Canada, and the 49th (Edmonton) Battalion.

3 Peter Hart, *The Last Battle: Endgame on the Western Front 1918* (London: Profile Books Ltd, 2018), px.

4 The last Canadian killed was Private George Lawrence Price of the 28th (Northwest) Battalion, tragically shot by a German sniper five miles northeast of Mons, just a few minutes before the Armistice.

5 On 10 November 1918, one company of the Royal Canadian Regiment had been temporarily attached to the 42nd Battalion. *42nd Battalion War Diary*, 10 November 1918.

6 The Hôtel de Ville is the heart or centrepiece of the sweeping Grand Place. Built in late gothic style, the first stone was laid in 1458 and since then has gone through numerous additions and modifications over the centuries. Its current appearance dates from the eighteenth century.

7 *42nd Battalion War Diary*, 11 November 1918.

8 Angus Brown and Richard Gimblett, *In the Footsteps of the Canadian Corps, Canada's First World War 1914-1918* (Ottawa: Magic Light Publishing, 2006), p127.

9 *42nd Battalion War Diary*, 11 November 1918. The 'Gold Book' is referred to by some historians as the 'Golden Book'.

10 A spirited controversy later developed between the RCR and the 42nd Battalion over who was the first to reach the centre of Mons. In the city's 'Gold Book' the signature of Lieutenant W M King (an officer of the RCR company attached to the 42nd) appears before those of the 42nd Battalion's Lieutenants L H Biggar and J W Cave. Biggar, however, disputed this evidence, averring that he signed well down on the page so that a suitable inscription could subsequently be inserted above. The *42nd Battalion War Diary* stated: 'As soon as they [Lieutenants Biggar and Cave] entered [the city hall] the 'Gold Book' was taken from the vaults where it had lain for over four years and they had the honour of being the first British troops to sign it...'. *42nd Battalion War Diary*, 11 November 1918.

11 Colonel Paul P Hutchison, *Canada's Black Watch: the first hundred years* (Montreal: Museum Restoration Services, 1987), p136.

12 Lieutenant-Colonel C Beresford Topp, *The 42nd Battalion, CEF Royal Highlanders of Canada in the Great War* (Montreal: Gazette Printing Company Ltd, 1931), p279.

13 *42nd Battalion War Diary*, 11 November 1918.

14 *42nd Battalion War Diary*, 11 November 1918.

15 *42nd Battalion War Diary*, 5 December 1918.

16 Topp, *42nd Battalion War Diary*, p308.

17 The former Montreal High School building on Peel Street was used as a military barracks during the Great War.

18 Peter Hart, *The Last Battle: Endgame on the Western Front 1918* (London: Profile Books, 2018), p344.

THE MAINS MEMORIALS IN DUNDEE

'ONE SAVED AND ONE LOST'

Tom McCluskey

IN LATE 2010, the Den o' Mains Memorial erected to the men of that district who fell in the Great War was under immediate threat of demolition and replacement by a commemorative plaque to be mounted on the wall of Mains Castle. At that point, there was no doubt that the memorial, located on the outskirts of Dundee, was in a dreadful state: pressure washing to remove graffiti had also removed some of the names, a new name plaque could not be added for technical reasons, it was the target of continuing vandalism and it was in a dilapidated and dangerous state. In fact, during initial discussions regarding its future, it was proposed that because it was regarded as beyond repair, it should be demolished. Nevertheless, a solution was found, the memorial survived, and in the process of saving it, research by a small group of enthusiasts revealed a number of aspects of the memorial that were long forgotten. Sadly too, the research process also revealed a previously unknown loss of a second memorial in the Mains district.

The group of enthusiasts I was invited to join to work for the preservation of the Mains Memorial was led by Ian Robertson and included Bob Paterson, then Chairman of the Western Front Association (Tayside), and George Webster from the University of St Andrews. The suggestion of demolition was not accepted by us because in our opinion the memorial, though battered and abused, was as much a part of the history of the Den o' Mains as its castle. In any case, it was agreed that the group would collaborate with Dundee City Council to reach a solution to preserve the memorial. However, Bob Paterson felt it necessary to have the memorial listed which he did the following day to ensure its future safety. This action slowed the progress but was nonetheless felt to be the right thing to do to secure the continuing existence of the memorial.

In the end, after two and a half years, thanks to the lead by Ian Robertson and the co-operation of Dundee City Council led by Derek Robertson (Head of Parks, Sports & Leisure) the conserved memorial was rededicated on 11 November 2011. Its new location in the Caird Park Stadium, formerly the King George V Arena and today the Ronnie Macintosh Athletics Stadium, was apt, as George V was the monarch at the time of the Great War and the first royal Colonel-in-Chief of The Black Watch. It was also only a short distance from its original position, placed in a quiet corner overlooking sporting activities dating back to classical times, but above all it was as safe from further damage as it could be.

MAINS MEMORIAL, DUNDEE
(Anne McCluskey)

Ten years later, looking back on our efforts three things are worth remembering. The first of these is that we did not know as much about the memorial as we thought we did when we started. The research that we did on the memorial showed its value when we discovered how unusual the memorial actually was in a Scottish setting:

> The Mains Parish War Memorial is an unusual example of a First World War Memorial. It was designed to incorporate a fountain. The form of the memorial is unusual in Scotland with its freestanding Corinthian columns and central stone domed roof. Few other examples of a freestanding memorial of this date are thought to include a decorative fountain. The setting of the memorial is appropriate to a building which is commemorating the dead. The setting within a sylvan location composed of trees and an adjacent stream evokes the Elysian fields through which in Greek mythology represented the resting place of the souls of the heroic and virtuous. The use of the Corinthian order for the column capitals is also a reference to classical Greek heroism as the Corinthian order was originally Athenian in origin.1

The research process also showed its value when, after a lot of work the group of 25 men – except for one – whose names had been partially obliterated by the power washing were identified by rank and regiment and was found to include 12 Black Watch men. In order to ensure this information was not lost again, where known, each man's name, rank, regiment and date of death was inscribed on a stainless-steel plate mounted on the side of the memorial. On Armistice Day 2011, a sombre and dreich day, the monument was rededicated at a ceremony attended by council representatives, council officials, members of The Black Watch Association and other interested parties. Lieutenant-Colonel Roland Rose TD opened the ceremony with a few introductory words. The short service of rededication was led by The Reverend David J Randall of Mains & Strathmartine Parish Church flanked by two standard bearers from the Dundee and Angus Branches of The Black Watch

Association. However, because of the involvement of The Black Watch Association and the annual Dundee Branch of The Black Watch Association Remembrance Parade on the Friday prior to Remembrance Sunday, the memorial has been erroneously called the 'Mains Parish WW1 Black Watch Memorial' at times.

The second point is that throughout the whole process vandalism was a constant problem. It seems that part of the reason for this was that the whole area had changed drastically since the memorial was erected in 1922, and while it made perfect sense at that time to site the memorial in its original position, that was no longer really the case. During one meeting we were asked by a lady from Historic Environment Scotland if the local community could be involved but the answer had to be 'No' as the population and settlement patterns had changed completely since the memorial was erected.

The fact was that in 1922 the Den o' Mains was an escape for the working class of Dundee from the abject housing conditions of the city as well as the long hours spent in the mills and factories. Besides individuals spending leisure time there, on high days and holidays gatherings were held at the Den o' Mains, particularly at Easter where families would gather to roll their eggs. This short excerpt from the *Courier & Advertiser* described the scene in 1939:

> 10,000 join in Den o' Mains frolics; more than 10,000 Dundonians celebrated Easter Sunday with the traditional whoopee at the Den o' Mains yesterday. Sliders [ice cream wafers] and chips were more conspicuous than the eggs commonly associated with the season.[2]

In good weather, young men would gather to play cards, a pastime frowned upon by the righteous. But as one commentator wrote, 'a young millworker is not invited to attend bridge parties at which good people play for money or other prizes'.[3] The reality, however, was that in 2010 it had been a long time since anyone could have honestly described the Den o' Mains as William Robertson did in 1911:

But Nature, with her wondrous charms,
Affords to jaded men
A rest and quietness from all strife
That soothes our aches and pains,
And makes us wish to spend our life
Beside the Den of Mains [4]

The urbanisation of the area began in earnest in 1946 when it was estimated that Dundee needed 20,000 houses. In the building programme that followed the Second World War, the memorial was surrounded by post-war housing estates and it seems that vandalism in the Den and to the memorial could be traced back to that time.[5] During the campaign each time a letter or article appeared in the papers about saving the memorial, more graffiti would be added. On one occasion, someone lit fires in the basins of the fountains, but over the years vandalism in the Den o' Mains area was not confined to the memorial: Mains Castle had been a regular target of vandalism, including fire raising on one occasion in 1955.[6] That incident led to an inspection of the damage by Dundee City councillors. The report of their visit in the *Courier & Advertiser* a few days later included a letter from an anonymous lady who summed up the situation:

> Dundee has not so many beautiful parks that this one should be allowed to go to ruin. Apart from the walk being a very lovely one, there is no pleasure in going there in the evening owing to so many hooligans being around.[7]

All of this led me to the personal conclusion that when a memorial and its surroundings clash – as was the case in the Den o' Mains memorial – the removal of the monument to a more secure location has to be considered. Happily, in this case removal was successful.

The third and final point to be made is this. Great War memorials can and do disappear overnight. During the course of our research, it was found that we were too late to save a second memorial in the local area. In 1922, on the weekend prior to the unveiling of the Den o' Mains Memorial, a stained-glass window dedicated to the memory of 50 young men of the Mains and Strathmartine Parish who died in the Great War, was unveiled by the Earl of Home.[8] The upper section of the window 'represented Christ bestowing the crown of glory on a faithful Christian knight' while the lower section recorded the names of the men of the parish who had fallen during the war.[9] In 1996, the church was sold and converted into five flats. Sadly, the fate of the beautiful stained-glass memorial window is not known.

[1] Historic Environment Scotland, http://portal.historicenvironment.scot/designation/LB51412.

[2] *The Courier and Argus*, 10 April 1939.

[3] *The Evening Telegraph and Post*, 10 May 1907.

[4] *The Evening Telegraph and Post*, 8 June 1911.

[5] *Courier & Advertiser*, 13 September 1946.

[6] *Courier & Advertiser*, 16 May 1955.

[7] *Courier & Advertiser*, 20 May 1955.

[8] *The Courier and Argus*, 15 May 1922.

[9] *The Courier and Argus*, 15 May 1922.

THE VISIT

Neil Hobson

AFTER I HAD TAKEN school parties on tours of The Black Watch Museum, I often used to wonder what they thought about what they had seen and heard in the Great War Room and what they really thought about the First World War in general. After all, they were always heavily supervised by teachers and school helpers on these trips, so a frank and full discussion of the First World War was never likely to take place during a visit. However, in late June, 2019, I was given an opportunity to see how school pupils reacted to exposure to Great War weapons and artefacts in a setting far away from The Black Watch Museum when I took part in a visit to a local high school by the a group from the Angus Branch of The Black Watch Association who have been visiting schools for many years.

The visit took place on the second last day of the school year and involved over 70 pupils from 4th and 5th years preparing for the Higher History course or National 4/5 as well as a small number of students from other year groups. As the sizeable class filed into the room, I realised this might just be a very tricky 110-minute long double period. Nevertheless, I remember how we all laughed about the modern languages teacher from the school who was arrested in France as a spy on the first day of war, how one former pupil serving with the Scottish Women's Hospitals for Foreign Service won the Order of St Sava for work with the Serbian wounded and the other who died of dysentery nursing British soldiers in Salonika. I watched the class reaction to pictures of pupils of that school handing over what few pennies they had to buy comforts for The Black Watch during the war and other pictures of the handover of two ambulances bought by the pupils of Perthshire on the South Inch in Perth. Every now and again individuals would straighten up and little sparks of understanding could be seen in their eyes when the pictures were shown and addresses read out of the men of the district who had been killed, and they realised these men would have been their neighbours.

The real gasp of surprise came when the picture of the wounded 15-year-old Ordinary Seaman of the Naval Division and veteran of France and Salonika from a neighbouring village was shown. Not even the sight of the Vickers machine gun on its tripod or the appearance of a 'tired, outstripped 5.9' German shell as described in Wilfred Owen's 'Dulce et Decorum est', a poem known to all the pupils, could compete with the effect of that picture on the class. In fact, the only thing that had more effect on the audience – and for me it was the biggest surprise of the day – were the two of the poems read aloud to the group as part of the presentation.

The first was Joe Lee's poem 'The Bullet'. It has been reprinted here because in my opinion any poem by a Black Watch soldier that has the effect this one did on school pupils deserves to be read again and again, for it was when I watched faces of the pupils as they listened to this poem that I saw how, one by one, so many pupils came to understand what this poem really meant:

THE BULLET

Every bullet has its billet;
Many bullets more than one:
God! perhaps I killed a mother
When I killed a mother's son. [1]

The second poem was by Second Lieutenant A J 'Hamish' Mann, 8th Black Watch, who was badly hit by shellfire while leading his platoon during the Battle of Arras on the morning of 9 April 1917 and died of his wounds the following day. It is reproduced here for the same reason as the first, for it too had a remarkable effect on those who heard it:

THE SOLDIER

'Tis strange to look on a man that is dead
As he lies in the shell-swept hell,
And to think that the poor black battered corpse
Once lived like you and was well.

'Tis stranger far when you come to think
That you may be soon like him...
And it's Fear that tugs at your trembling soul,
A Fear that is weird and grim!

Drop Alley Trench, The Somme, 1 October 1916[2]

The emotional effect of this poem on a number of pupils was obvious, because to my amazement more than one shed a very discrete tear.

The session ended, and at that point it was clear that whatever the last 110 minutes had been, it had not been a waste of time, that the three Black Watch veterans present had been treated with great respect, and that the pupils who had attended knew a good deal more about both the Great War and The Black Watch service in it that war than they did when they got up that morning.

---

1 Joseph Lee, *Ballads of Battle* (London: John Murray, 1917), p21.

2 Hamish (A J) Mann, *A Subaltern's Musings* (London: John Long, 1918), p18.

LIVING HISTORY AND THE ROYAL HIGHLANDERS

Ruadhán Scrivener-Anderson

HISTORICAL RE-ENACTMENT, or living history, is a very effective method of historical research, and of conveying information to the general public. In terms of The Black Watch during the First World War, this generally involves the portrayal of soldiers and officers, their uniforms and equipment. By bringing history to life in this way we can learn a lot about the past, arguably more than from a text or still photograph. However, this also means that living historians have a responsibility to present history in the most accurate way possible, for the purposes of both education and remembrance, and there are many difficulties faced in achieving this in the modern age.

When constructing a historical impression, I have adopted, through several years of experience, a process to achieve the highest possible levels of accuracy. When attempting to replicate the uniform of a Black Watch officer the first port of call was the 'Bond of Sacrifice Portraits', a collection of photographs in the Imperial War Museum, which consists of very detailed images of the uniforms of officers and men from the vast majority of regiments in service during the First World War. After a careful examination of a range of images of the uniform to be reproduced, I then turned to the *Dress Regulations for the Army 1911*, and the *1914 Clothing Regulations*, which between them detail the basic uniform worn by every rank and regiment during the First World War.[1] Specialist texts on badges, buttons and headdress were also consulted at this point, to ascertain the exact patterns correct for the period. In the case of The Black Watch officer's uniform, it was at this stage that details which may otherwise have been overlooked – such as that the sporran belt was always made of whitened leather – were found. After this initial research phase, the uniform was then constructed. In the case of The Black Watch officer uniform I used completely original buttons, badges and insignia, as reproductions are often not available or simply do not meet the standards of accuracy required. However, it must also be considered that a modern reproduction item is sometimes preferable as original items which should be new often show 100 years of wear and tear. There are many companies which specifically make reproduction clothing and equipment. As a general rule, however, some considerable adaptation or tailoring is required to improve accuracy, complicating the process even further. As an example, we could consider 'Gaiters, Highland, Drab', worn by Highland regiments until 1915. A cursory glance at any photograph of a Black Watch soldier in 1914 shows us that these must have eight white buttons and be cut straight across the toe. This pattern is simply not available as a reproduction, but modern uniform can be altered to fit the bill, which illustrates the lengths to which some re-enactors will go to ensure accuracy.

BLACK WATCH OFFICER IN FULL KIT
(Re-enactment)
(Ruadhán Scrivener-Anderson)

Living history has also proved to be a very useful tool in the academic world. Experiments, such as the BBC's 'The Trench' documentary of 2002 have seen conditions during the First World War recreated on a large scale, in order to learn more about soldiers' lives, with a platoon of men living in trenches and rest camps for several weeks, while being constantly filmed. Even veterans of the Great War who were brought in to see the reconstructed trenches, such as Arthur Barraclough and Harry Patch, agreed that it was as close to the real thing as physically possible, although Patch did comment that it is impossible to recreate the fear men felt at the time.[2] Furthermore, private tactical events, such as the annual Second World War 'Monty's Men Trip' are frequently used to examine the tactics used during the period, although this is far harder to control and maintain authenticity, and smaller-scale events examining the everyday lives of soldiers are, as a rule, more successful. Recently, I attended a re-enactment where all involved slept in trenches, lived on period rations and undertook the duties of the soldiers of the time as closely as we thought possible. From exercises like this we have learned a great deal about the everyday hardships faced by our forebears in wartime. For example, we found that the chicken wire often used to give extra grip on duckboards has the adverse effect of ripping the hobnails out of soldiers' boots, and that wet carbolic soap stains everything else in a haversack bright pink.

While historical re-enactment can be a very useful tool for research, its primary form is as a means of bringing history to life for the general public. In some ways this could even have been considered to have an advantage over the academic text or even the static museum display, as it allows people to engage with historical ideas on a very personal level. However, there are significant issues to consider. The topic of historical accuracy has already been broached in reference to how one re-enactor, amongst many, researches and creates an impression, but this is not the same for all, and there is no authority to police historical accuracy. Cultural anthropologists Richard Handler and William Saxton rather boldly asserted that living historians define historical accuracy as isomorphism between a re-enactment and the event it is supposed to represent, however there is so much variation in the standards of individual living historians that many so called 're-enactments' are far from isomorphic.[3] Inevitably, this lessens the usefulness of living history as a tool for education, as the audience cannot always tell the difference between a well-researched and presented impression, and what may amount simply to a fancy-dress costume. They are after all generally there to learn rather than to judge. When it comes to portraying a well-known and interesting military unit such as The Black Watch, this problem can be increased, as there are a large number of re-enactors who attempt to portray members of the regiment during the First World War, some of whom may not be as well researched as others. This creates a serious issue for living historians. They have a responsibility to their audience to create an impression that is as historically accurate as possible, but unfortunately this is frequently not the case, and can lead to misinterpretations of history on the part of the audience.

As a small aside to this, it is interesting to consider another class of re-enactor, the soldier turned amateur historian. While many re-enactors are academic historians, with a thorough knowledge of their subject and techniques required to carry out effective research, and perhaps even with an increased consideration for the responsibility of conveying and teaching history, on the other end of the spectrum we see the military re-enactor whose relatively modern service becomes the main resource for their historical knowledge. This may seem all well and good. However, as soon as we begin to dig into the fine historical details it becomes clear that this argument is far from watertight, and that experience must be supplemented by research. For instance, someone who has served in a relatively recent conflict still cannot have had the experience of fighting in a kilt. Therefore, we see that although living historians, morally, should present an accurate impression of history, this is sadly not always the case, even though it is rarely deliberate.

Therein lies the necessity for the re-enactor to become an expert in their field. Research to a microscopic level, scrutiny of every account, examination of every photograph is required to fulfil the duty living historians have to their audience and the people they represent, or to create an accurate enough experience that we may learn something from it. Nonetheless, even when the re-enactor themselves go to the utmost effort to attain historical accuracy it can never be perfect. We cannot escape the fact that we live in the twenty-first century, and that a world war does not rage around us. As Harry Patch observed, we will never feel the fear of the men of over a century ago. In short, it would be remiss to assume that historical re-enactment is a perfect representation of the past, however it brings the history of The Black Watch, as well as all regiments and periods, to life in a unique and interesting way.

1   *Dress Regulations for the Army 1911* (Norwich: Tharston Press, 1986); *Clothing of the Army* (London: War Office, 1914).

2   R Van Emden, *The Trench* (Bantam Press, 2002), pp4-5.

3   Richard Handler and William Saxton, 'Dyssimulation: Reflexivity, Narrative, and the Quest for Authenticity in "Living History"', *Cultural Anthropology* (Volume 3, Number 3, August 1988), p242.

The Regimental Collect

The Reverend Professor
Norman Drummond

"There is not a man in all bonnie Scotland
whose heart does not beat more proudly at the
mention of The Black Watch."

WHETHER SAID together at The Black Watch Memorial Cairn in Aberfeldy, Black Watch Corner at Polygon Wood in Belgium or at so many memorials across the world, in Section or Platoon or Company Services in the field or at the conclusion of Battalion Church Parades, the Prayer of The Black Watch rarely fails to stir the heart, and often unexpectedly so.

As a young Black Watch Padre I remember being counselled by Padre Tom Nicol, Adjutant in The Black Watch during the Second World War and ultimately Assistant Chaplain General and thence Domestic Chaplain to The Queen in Scotland, with these words, *'remember to be there for the Black Watch and their families, particularly for the men on exercise and in action, and turn up when they least expect you!'*.

Perhaps that is what unexpectedly happens to us when we hear for the first time or pick up anew the words of the Prayer of The Black Watch.

It reminds us all that we are part of something really special for all those who have served and who do serve and who will continue to do so in years to come.

If ever evidence were need that The Black Watch is a family, then rarely more so when the Black Watch is at prayer.

THE REGIMENTAL COLLECT

O God, whose strength setteth fast the mountains,
Lord of the hills to whom we lift our eyes:
grant us grace that we, of The Black Watch,
once chosen to watch the mountains of an earthly kingdom,
may stand fast in the faith and be strong,
until we come to the heavenly Kingdom of Him,
who has bidden us watch and pray.
Thy son, our saviour and Lord.
Amen

APPENDIX

ASPECTS OF THE INDIAN
EXPEDITIONARY FORCE

T HE LAHORE AND MEERUT Divisions of the Indian Expeditionary Force each comprised three brigades of four infantry
battalions – one battalion of Regular British troops and three battalions
of Indian soldiers. The British component of the Bareilly Brigade of the
Meerut Division was the 2nd Battalion, The Black Watch, to which on
mobilisation were assigned the Indian 41st Dogras, 58th Vaughan's Rifles
(FF) and the 2/8th Gurkha Rifles.

Indian regiments were either 'Class Regiments' where all the men
were of one class such as the 2/8th Gurkhas, or 'Class Company
Regiments' where different ethnic classes each had their own company
such as the 58th Rifles, which comprised two double companies of
Sikhs, two of Pathans, and one each of Dogras and Punjabi Mussulmans.

The Indian soldiers, or sepoys, were long service professional soldiers,
generally experienced in frontier and open warfare, trained and led by
12 British officers and 18 Indian Viceroy Commissioned Officers (VCOs)
– per battalion – drawn by merit and seniority from the ranks of their
battalions. The VCOs had no power of command over British troops,
and a British officer, no matter how junior or inexperienced, always had
power of command over Indian officers. In general terms as described by
Corrigan, the British officer was 'the instigator and promulgator of policy,
while the Indian officer executed it' – a system which he claimed produced
excellent Indian officer platoon and company commanders.[1]

In the Indian Army, the British officer had to speak not only
Hindustani or Urdu, but also the language of his men which might be
Gurkhali or Pushto. This made British Indian Army officer casualties
extremely hard to replace given there was no regimental reserve of British
officers worthy of the name. Unfortunately, too, British officers not only
looked different from the sepoys and made a target for snipers, but in the

Indian Army they were expected to literally lead from the front, so their casualties tended to be excessively high. Casualties diminished somewhat when British officers were ordered to wear the same headdress as the sepoys and judging by pictures of groups of British and Indian officers taken after 1914 many had also taken to wearing a kurta tunic rather than conventional British officers service dress.

As in every war, the composition of divisions and brigades changed, but throughout the Great War the 2nd Black Watch remained as the permanent British Regular battalion of the Bareilly Brigade. It was joined by the Territorials of the 4th Black Watch in February 1915 and that unit remained part of the brigade until November 1915. The Indian battalions also changed: the 33rd and 69th Punjabis for example fought with The Black Watch at Loos while the 41st Dogras and 2/8th Gurkhas were reorganised after heavy losses – a situation made worse by the poor state of the Indian Corps reserves at that point in the war.

On the eve of the Partition of India in 1947, each regiment was allocated to either Pakistan or India. The 69th Punjabis, raised in 1759, became the senior regiment of the Indian Army, and in 1951 was styled 1st Battalion, Brigade of Guards. The 57th Wilde's Rifles (FF) and the 58th Vaughan's Rifles (FF) were allocated to Pakistan and continue to exist styled as the 10th and 11th Battalions, Frontier Force Regiment.

---

[1] Gordon Corrigan, *Sepoys in the Trenches:*
    The Indian Corps on the Western Front 1914-15 (Stroud: The History Press, 2006), p11.

AUTHOR BIOGRAPHIES

NORMAN FRASER BROWN

Dr Norman Fraser Brown MLitt (Dundee), BA Hons (Stirling) FSA Scot, joined The Black Watch in 1962 as a Junior Soldier and served for six years. He graduated from Stirling in 1975 and taught in secondary and special education in Stirling where he was both head teacher and education officer, and was involved in training probationer teachers in Scotland, as well as EFL teacher training in Pakistan and post-communist Romania. On retiral, he and Ronnie Proctor delivered *Your School, The Black Watch and the Great War* outreach programme to schools in the regimental area. He has contributed several chapters to Great War publications, and current research interests include the impact of the Great War on the Scottish communities of Latin America.

EARL JOHN CHAPMAN

Earl John Chapman is a native of Montreal and an avid military historian. Among other publications, his writings have appeared in *JSAHR, The Military Collector & Historian, Canada's Red Hackle, The Red Hackle*, and *The Canadian Military Journal*. He was the first recipient of the prestigious Gordon Atkinson Memorial Prize in Highland Military History, awarded annually by the Quebec Thistle Council. His latest book, *A Dangerous Service: Memoirs of a Black Watch Officer in the French & Indian War – John Grant, 1741-1828*, was co-edited with Ian M McCulloch in 2010.

STEWART COUPAR

Stewart Coupar was brought up in the village of Fowlis Wester and was educated in Crieff. He joined the Army in 1992 and served with The King's Troop, Royal Horse Artillery. He now works in the Local and Family History Department in the A K Bell Library, Perth. He is married and has three children. He had a number of relatives who served with The Black Watch during the Great War, including his great uncle Jim, from Lour near Forfar, who was a sergeant in the 5th Battalion and who went to France with them in 1914.

JOHN C DUNCAN

Reverend John C Duncan, MBE, BD (Aberdeen), M Phil (Trinity Dublin), a native of Dundee, was Assistant Minister at Knightswood St Margaret's Parish Church in Glasgow before being inducted and ordained Minister at Burntisland in Fife in 1987. In 2001, he joined the Army Chaplain's Department and served in Kosovo, Iraq, Afghanistan and with the UN in Cyprus. His final posting before retiral in 2016 as chaplain was as Padre to The Black Watch Battalion at Fort George. He was inducted as Minister of St Athernase Parish Church, Leuchars, in 2016 and is Chaplain to The Black Watch Association and to the RAF Leuchars Squadron of the Air Cadets.

ALISTAIR DUTHIE

Pipe Major Alistair Duthie was born in Pleasant Point, South Canterbury, New Zealand of Highland Scots ancestry. He enlisted in The Black Watch in 1998 and served for 20 years, including operational tours in Northern Ireland, Kosovo and Iraq and ultimately Pipe Major of the 1st Battalion. He was joint contributor, compiler and editor of *A Collection of Pipe Music of The Black Watch (Royal Highland Regiment)* and is currently writing a history of the pipers of The Black Watch, 1725-2006. He is also Pipe Major of the Perth and District Pipe Band and Piper to the City of Perth.

NEIL N GARDNER

The Reverend Neil N Gardner MA, BD, joined The Royal Army Chaplains' Department in 1991 and went on to serve as Padre to 1st Black Watch in Hong Kong, Pirbright and Belfast. He became Parish Minister of Alyth, Perthshire in 1998 and since 2006 has served as Minister of Canongate Kirk, the Kirk of Holyroodhouse and Edinburgh Castle. He is a domestic chaplain to HM The Queen.

NEIL HOBSON

Neil Hobson joined The Black Watch in 1965 on his seventeenth birthday and served in the regiment for 22 years in Britain, Canada, Malaya, New Zealand and on ceremonial duties in Korea and a number of tours on

Operation Banner. At one point he was part of the Scottish Infantry Depot Training Team and Army Careers and Information Team. On demobilisation, he settled in Perth and joined the Prison Service. Now retired, he takes great pleasure in working as a volunteer at The Black Watch Museum, where he enjoys taking guided tours and other front of house work.

ALISTAIR IRWIN

Born in Dundee in 1948 and a graduate of St Andrews University, Lieutenant-General Sir Alistair Irwin, KCB, CBE, was commissioned into The Black Watch in 1970. With the 1st Battalion he served in Hong Kong, West Germany and West Berlin and took part in several operational tours in Northern Ireland. His last two Army appointments were General Officer Commanding Northern Ireland and then Adjutant General (the Army Board member responsible for personnel matters) and he retired in 2005. He was the last Colonel of The Black Watch (Royal Highland Regiment) and the first Representative Colonel of The Black Watch, 3rd Battalion, Royal Regiment of Scotland. He was later Vice-Chairman of the Commonwealth War Graves Commission 2011-13, having served as a Commissioner since 2005. He has been President of the Royal British Legion Scotland and Poppy Scotland since 2006.

FIONA KANTZIDIS (NÉE PROCTOR)

Fiona Kantzidis BA Hons (Robert Gordon) PG Dip (Dundee), is a daughter of the regiment and has always shown a keen interest in the history of The Black Watch. Born in BMH, Colchester, she accompanied her parents on postings in the UK and Germany where she presented a bouquet to the Queen Mother, Colonel-in-Chief of The Black Watch. She graduated BA Hons from Robert Gordon University in Hospitality Management and PG Dip European Urban Conservation from Dundee. She works for Historic Environment Scotland as District Visitor Operation Manager managing historic sites.

ANNE McCLUSKEY

After marriage to Tom, Anne McCluskey MA (Joint Hons) Dundee, 'followed the drum' as an army wife for the 22 years of his career in The

Black Watch. Once back in civilian life, attendance at Dundee College of Commerce led to a recommendation to apply for entry to a degree course at Dundee University where she gained an MA with Joint Honours in History and American Studies. Her main area of historical interest is in local aspects of the social history of the Great War and how the service of individuals was reported on in local and national press. She is also the main contributor to Facebook page *'Black Watch Corner 3 May 2014'*.

TOM McCLUSKEY

Tom McCluskey retired from the Army in 1983 after 22 years and 100 days service as WO2, mostly with the 1st Battalion, The Black Watch, including postings to Cyprus, North Africa, BAOR, Belize and Northern Ireland and was founder member and previous office holder of the Angus Branch of The Black Watch Association. After civil employment with Ferranti Laser department, visits to the battlefields of France and Flanders reawakened his interest in Black Watch history and he was deeply involved in the establishment of the memorial at Black Watch Corner, Zonnebeke (south western corner of Polygon Wood, near Ypres), Belgium, unveiled in May 2014. His book *Black Watch Corner* appeared in 2016.

SANDY MacDUFF

Sandy MacDuff joined The Black Watch as a junior piper in August 1974 and was discharged in 1979 following service in the UK, Northern Ireland and Italy. However, when he joined the 1st Battalion, he served in B Company as a rifleman and later with the Mortar Platoon. On demobilisation, he returned to Perth where he worked for a well-known local firm as an ironmonger. He maintains close contact with The Black Watch through his membership of the Perth Branch of The Black Watch (Royal Highland Regiment) Association and has acted as Branch Standard Bearer on a number of important regimental occasions.

DAVID McMICKING

Major (Retired) David McMicking, LVO, was commissioned into The Black Watch in 1959, joined the regiment in Cyprus and later served in

Warminster, when in 1963 he was appointed Equerry to Her Majesty Queen Elizabeth the Queen Mother. In 1966, he returned to the regiment, first as Signals Officer, then as Adjutant at Kirknewton in 1967. He retired from the Army in 1973 having passed for, but declined Staff College entrance, finishing his service at Glencorse when he was also ADC to Lord Ballantrae at the General Assembly. On retiral, he joined John Menzies the booksellers. He has retained close contact with The Black Watch Association serving as Vice-Chairman and as Trustee of The Black Watch Castle and Museum.

GORDON MILLAR

Gordon Millar was a member of the Royal Observer Corps from 1981 until disbandment in 1995. He maintains a strong general interest in the history of the Great War through membership of the Western Front Association, and a research interest through study of the lives of Angus men who served. He has visited the Great War battlefields and Commonwealth War Graves Commission sites in France and Belgium and has taken part in a number of memorial ceremonies there. He also supports Commonwealth War Graves Commission grave recognition and wreath laying at a local level. He is an honorary member and current Treasurer of the Angus Branch of The Black Watch (Royal Highland Regiment) Association.

JULIE M ORR

Dr Julie M Orr MLitt (Dundee), MS (New Mexico State), BS (Utah State), Commander (Retired) US Public Health Service was born in Oakland, California, and currently resides in Montezuma County, Colorado. Prior to obtaining her doctorate in history at the University of Dundee she completed a career with tribal, state and federal environmental agencies in the US. In addition to her work in the US, she is a frequent visitor to Scotland. Her book, *Scotland, Darien and the Atlantic World,* was published in 2018.

DEREK J PATRICK

Dr Derek J Patrick is an Associate Lecturer in History at the University of St Andrews where in 2002 he gained a PhD for his thesis on the Scottish Parliament 1689-1702. He has published several articles on early modern Scotland but has a keen interest in the First World War. With Dr William Kenefick he was a founding member of the Great War Dundee Commemorative Project, is part of the Gateways to the First World War research network, and a former academic adviser to the BBC's *World War One at Home* project. He has a longstanding interest in The Black Watch and is an associate member of The Black Watch (Royal Highland Regiment) Association. His great grandfather, S-9242 Private John Patrick, 9th Black Watch, was killed in action on the Somme on 9 September 1916.

ROLAND PROCTOR

Major (Retired) Roland (Ronnie) Proctor, MBE, O St J, FSA Scot, current Provost of Angus, was born and educated in Kirriemuir, Angus. He joined The Black Watch as an Infantry Junior Leader in 1960 and served for almost 40 years both in the regiment and elsewhere including as instructor at Sandhurst, RSM Scottish Infantry Depot and 1BW in Werl, Germany. Commissioned in 1984, he was MTO, Air Operations Officer in South Armagh and on Staff at HQNI. On leaving the Army he was Assistant Regimental Secretary and Curator of The Black Watch Museum until retirement in 2011. He is the Secretary of The Black Watch Association, Honorary Curator of The Black Watch Museum and deeply involved in local and national veterans' organisations.

RODDY RIDDELL

Lieutenant-Colonel (Retired) Roddy Riddell, OBE, was commissioned into The Black Watch in June 1973 aged 19. He served in Germany, Hong Kong and Northern Ireland. He commanded the 3rd (Volunteer) Battalion, The Black Watch, from 1996-9 and retired in 2005, becoming the last Regimental Secretary. He was also President of the Perth Branch of The Black Watch Association for many years and is Vice-Chairman of the Association and current compiler and editor of the *Red Hackle*.

VICTORIA SCHOFIELD

Victoria Schofield is a journalist, historian and independent commentator. She is the author of the two-volume official history of The Black Watch (*The Highland Furies: The Black Watch 1739-1899* (2012) & *The Black Watch: Fighting in the Front Line 1899-2006* (2017)). She has also written a biography of Field Marshal Earl Wavell (*Wavell: Soldier and Statesman* (2006 and 2012)). Schofield read Modern History at the University of Oxford and was President of the Oxford Union. In 2004/5, she was the Visiting Alistair Horne Fellow at St Antony's College, Oxford.

ROBERT (BOB) MICHIE SCOTT JP

Robert Michie Scott, better known within the regimental family as 'Bob', is one of five generations of his family to have served in The Black Watch in a line of descent stretching from his grandfather and continuing through to his grandson. On demobilisation, he held the Queen's Warrant and with it the rank of sergeant major. In civilian life, he was a manager in industry, elected as a local councillor and served as a Justice of the Peace for nearly 30 years. He maintains his service to the regiment by running the Fife Branch of The Black Watch (Royal Highland Regiment) Association and serving on both the Association Welfare and Executive Committees.

RON J SCRIMGEOUR

Ron J Scrimgeour MA Hons (St Andrews), DipEd & Dip Psych (Dundee), was born in Dundee in 1947 in the jute mill tenements of the Burn – Brook Street, the proud son of a jute weaver and ship's rigger. His final appointment in a teaching career spanning 30 years was as Deputy Head of Carnoustie High School. He also served two terms as an elected member of Angus Council. He is an honorary member and strong supporter of the Angus Branch of The Black Watch (Royal Highland Regiment) Association and is in demand as a speaker on the history of Dundee and Angus jute mills.

RUADHÁN SCRIVENER-ANDERSON

Ruadhán Scrivener-Anderson is a final year history student at the University of Dundee. He is a member of Scots at War Living History Society, an organisation which conducts historical experiments, as well as working in public history. He has been an historical advisor to the BBC on several First World War documentaries. His main area of interest is the role of the junior officer during the Great War, and The Black Watch. He has numerous family links to The Black Watch, including to Alfred Anderson, the last Scottish veteran of the Great War.

ROBERT SIMPSON

Robert Simpson, better known as Rab, was born in Glasgow in 1936 and brought up in Arbroath. He completed his National Service in the Royal Army Ordnance Corps and re-enlisted in The Black Watch in 1962, serving in Germany, Libya and Cyprus. He was a drummer with the Pipes and Drums and played at the White House during their American tour in 1963. After demobilisation, he graduated from Duncan of Jordanstone College before beginning a career as a graphic artist. Rab was involved in the creation of the Great War Room in the old Black Watch Museum and was a founder member and stalwart of the Angus Branch of The Black Watch (Royal Highland Regiment) Association.

BRIAN SMITH

Brian Smith was born in Dundee in 1958 and is the grandson of Sergeant William Stewart Swan, DCM. He joined the 1st Battalion, The Black Watch, as a junior soldier at 16 and served for 14 years from 1974 to 1988. After demob, he worked on Balmoral Estate for over 20 years before taking early retirement and now lives in Forfar, working as a courier driver. He is also the Standard Bearer for the Angus Branch of The Black Watch (Royal Highland Regiment) Association.

ALISTAIR AND ERIC STEWART

Alistair and Eric Stewart are the grandsons of Private James Purgavie, author of the Purgavie Diary and the most recent in a line of family custodians of the violin and diary which featured in the vignette about the

Purgavie family souvenirs of the Great War. The brothers are approaching retirement and Alistair is particularly interested in family history and is heavily involved in researching other members of their extended family who also served in The Black Watch during both World Wars.

WILLIAM DONALD WHYTOCK

William Donald Whytock attended Blairgowrie High School before joining the Infantry Junior Leaders Battalion in 1974 at the age of 16. Following operational tours of duty in Northern Ireland and other service in the United Kingdom, Guyana, Canada, Belize and Rhodesia where he took part in Operation Agila in 1979-80, he was RSM of the Royal Tournament and of 1/51st Highland Volunteers in Perth from 1993 until retiral in 1998 after 24 years' service. He is third generation Black Watch and is a member of the Welfare Committee and an Executive Member of The Black Watch Association.

NORMAN DRUMMOND

Norman Drummond served as Chaplain to Depot The Parachute Regiment and thence The Black Watch (Royal Highland Regiment). He is Chaplain to The Queen in Scotland and Honorary Colonel of The Black Watch Battalion of the Army Cadet Force. Norman was appointed by the Scottish Government to chair WW100 Scotland and the Scottish Commemorations Panel and was the Special Representative for Scotland on the UK WW100 Advisory Group.

INDEX

After the numbers, 'i' indicates illustration; 'e' indicates endnote.

THE PUBLISHER

Tippermuir Books Ltd (est. 2009) is an independent publishing company based in Perth, Scotland.

OTHER TITLES FROM TIPPERMUIR BOOKS

Spanish Thermopylae (2009)

Battleground Perthshire (2009)

Perth: Street by Street (2012)

Born in Perthshire (2012)

In Spain with Orwell (2013)

Trust (2014)

Perth: As Others Saw Us (2014)

Love All (2015)

A Chocolate Soldier (2016)

The Early Photographers of Perthshire (2016)

**Taking Detective Novels Seriously:
The Collected Crime Reviews of Dorothy L Sayers** (2017)

Walking with Ghosts (2017)

No Fair City: Dark Tales from Perth's Past (2017)

**The Tale o the Wee Mowdie that wantit tae ken
wha keeched on his heid** (2017)

**Hunters: Wee Stories from the Crescent:
A Reminiscence of Perth's Hunter Crescent** (2017)

Flipstones (2018)

**Perth: Scott's Fair City: The Fair Maid of Perth & Sir Walter Scott –
A Celebration & Guided Tour** (2018)

**God, Hitler, and Lord Peter Wimsey: Selected Essays,
Speeches and Articles by Dorothy L Sayers** (2019)

Perth & Kinross: A Pocket Miscellany:
A Companion for Visitors and Residents (2019)

The Piper of Tobruk: Pipe Major Robert Roy, MBE, DCM (2019)

The 'Gig Docter o Athole':
Dr William Irvine & The Irvine Memorial Hospital (2019)

Afore the Highlands: The Jacobites in Perth, 1715-16 (2019)

'Where Sky and Summit Meet': Flight Over Perthshire – A History:
Tales of Pilots, Airfields, Aeronautical Feats, & War (2019)

Authentic Democracy: An Ethical Justification of Anarchism (2020)

'If Rivers Could Sing': A Scottish River Wildlife Journey.
A Year in the Life of the River Devon as it flows through the
Counties of Perthshire, Kinross-shire & Clackmannanshire (2020)

A Squatter o Bairnrhymes (Stuart Paterson, 2020)

In a Sma Room Songbook: From the Poems by William Soutar
(Debra Salem (ed.), 2020)

The Nicht Afore Christmas:
the much-loved yuletide tale in Scots (2020)

FORTHCOMING

The Perth Riverside Nursery & Beyond: A Spirit of Enterprise
and Improvement (Elspeth Bruce and Pat Kerr, 2021)

William Soutar: Collected Poetry
(Kirsteen McCue and Paul S Philippou (eds), 2021)

Fatal Duty: Police Killers and Killer Cops:
the Scottish Police Force 1812-1952
(Gary Knight, 2021)

Blood in the Snow (David W Millar, 2021)

A Scottish Wildlife Voyage (Keith Broomfield, 2021)

BY LULLABY PRESS
(an imprint of Tippermuir Books)

A Little Book of Carol's (2018)

Diverted Traffic (2020)

All Tippermuir Books titles are available from bookshops and online booksellers. They can also be purchased directly (with free postage & packing (UK only) – minimum charges for overseas delivery) from **www.tippermuirbooks.co.uk**

Tippermuir Books Ltd can be contacted at **mail@tippermuirbooks.co.uk**

Lullaby Press